Represent Yourself in Court

HOW TO PREPARE AND TRY A WINNING CASE

BY ATTORNEYS PAUL BERGMAN
& SARA J. BERMAN-BARRETT

EDITED BY ATTORNEYS MARY RANDOLPH
& RALPH WARNER

COVER ILLUSTRATION BY BUD PEEN

CARTOONS BY MIKE TWOHY

NOLO PRESS BERKELEY

YOUR RESPONSIBILITY WHEN USING A SELF-HELP LAW BOOK

We've done our best to give you useful and accurate information in this book. But this book does not take the place of a lawyer licensed to practice law in your state. If you want legal advice, see a lawyer. If you use any information contained in this book, it's your personal responsibility to make sure that the facts and general information contained in it are applicable to your situation.

KEEPING UP-TO-DATE

To keep its books up-to-date, Nolo Press issues new printings and new editions periodically. New printings reflect minor legal changes and technical corrections. New editions contain major legal changes, major text additions or major reorganizations. To find out if a later printing or edition of any Nolo book is available, call Nolo Press at (510) 549-1976 or check the catalog in the *Nolo News*, our quarterly publication.

To stay current, follow the "Update" service in the *Nolo News*. You can get a free two-year subscription by sending us the registration card in the back of the book. In another effort to help you use Nolo's latest materials, we offer a 25% discount off the purchase of any new Nolo book if you turn in any earlier printing or edition. (See the "Recycle Offer" in the back of the book.)

First Edition	December 1993
Second Printing	January 1995
Cover Illustration	Bud Peen
Cartoons	Mike Twohy
Book Design	Terri Hearsh
Production	Stephanie Harolde
Proofreading	Ely Newman
Index	Susan Cornell
Printing	Delta Lithograph

Bergman, Paul, 1943—
    Represent yourself in court : how to prepare and try a winning case / by Paul Bergman & Sara J. Berman-Barrett.
      p.   cm.
    Includes index.
    ISBN 0-87337-222-0
    1. Civil procedure--United States--Popular works. 2. Pro se representation--United States--Popular works.   I. Berman-Barrett, Sara J. 1964-   II. Title.
KF8841.B47   1993
347.73'5--dc20
[347.3075]
                        93-40929
                        CIP

DEDICATIONS

To Andrea and David,
and to all our readers whose active and knowledgeable participation in courtrooms across the country will improve the American system of justice.

ACKNOWLEDGMENTS

Our thanks to Jake Warner, Mary Randolph and Steve Elias. Your tireless and talented editorial work contributed immensely to the book, and your enthusiasm, vision and senses of humor inspired us to make the book the best it could be.

Thank you too to all the other members of the fabulous Nolo crew, for your hard work and dedication.

You have all been wonderful to work with.

—*PB, SBB*

TABLE OF CONTENTS

8 OPENING STATEMENT

9 DIRECT EXAMINATION

10 CROSS-EXAMINATION

11 CLOSING ARGUMENT

12 EXHIBITS

13 BASIC RULES OF EVIDENCE

ICONS USED IN THIS BOOK

Look for these icons to alert you to certain kinds of information.

 Warning. This icon alerts you to pitfalls you may encounter when preparing and presenting your case.

 Tip. This icon gives practical suggestions on handling a legal issue that may come up.

 Notebook. This icon reminds you to include a document in your "trial notebook," which you will put together to use in court.

 Resources. This icon highlights lists of books and other resources you may want to consult.

1

GOING IT ALONE IN COURT

This book provides the information you need to prepare for trial and represent yourself in court.

Whether you are a plaintiff (meaning that you have filed a lawsuit yourself) or a defendant (meaning that you have been sued), or whether you find yourself in state or federal court, understanding the procedures and techniques described in the book will help you present a persuasive, legally proper case.

If you had your "druthers," you might prefer to turn your case over to a trial attorney, who is trained to gather and present evidence in court. But a modern-day reality is that in many common situations it doesn't make economic sense to hire a lawyer. Perhaps you find yourself in a situation like one of these:

- You injured your back when you slipped on loose carpeting in an office building.

- You own a small manufacturing business and have sued a supplier for delivering faulty raw material.

- Your landlord has sued to evict you from your apartment, and you claim that the eviction is unlawful.

- You have filed a claim against your ex-spouse seeking increased child support.

- You are a building contractor who has been sued by a homeowner for using building materials other than those specified in a remodeling contract, and you claim that at the request of the homeowner you agreed to modify the contract after work was begun.

- Money that was left to you in trust by your parents has been depleted by improper investments made by the trust company having control of the trust assets.

In any of these instances (and many more), if you can't resolve your dispute in a friendly way you may have to go to court to protect your rights.

Unfortunately, with fees charged by lawyers commonly running in excess of $150 an hour, it may not make economic sense for you to hire one. Even if you win and are able to collect what the other side owes you, the lawyer's fees may devour much of your gain. As a result, representing yourself in court or dropping your claim or defense altogether may be your only realistic alternatives.

A.   THE SCOPE OF THIS BOOK

This book concentrates on what happens inside a courtroom in civil cases. You will learn how to figure out what evidence you need to gather to present a legally solid case whether you are a plaintiff or a defendant. Among other things, you will also learn:

- how to select a jury, if you are involved in a jury trial

- how to present your own testimony and conduct "direct examination" of your witnesses and "cross-examination" of your adversary's witnesses

- how to apply rules of evidence so that a judge will accept your admissible evidence and exclude your adversary's improper evidence

- how to locate, hire and effectively use expert witnesses

- how to present a persuasive opening statement and closing argument, and

- how to comply with courtroom procedural rules, such as those governing where and when to sit and stand, how to handle "exhibits" (tangible objects like photographs and receipts), and how to address the judge and opposing counsel.

The book guides you step by step through every phase of a civil trial, and each step is illustrated with sample dialogues.

CIVIL VS. CRIMINAL CASES

This book covers only civil cases, which arise when private citizens (including corporations and other associations) sue each other. Criminal trials, by contrast, occur when a state or the federal government seeks to punish someone for violating a criminal law. The major differences are:

- **The Result:** Civil cases typically involve money paid by one party to the other; criminal cases may result in fines paid to the government and imprisonment.

- **The Burden of Proof:** In most civil cases, a plaintiff wins by convincing a judge or jury by a "preponderance of evidence" that her claim is true. In criminal cases the prosecution must prove a defendant's guilt "beyond a reasonable doubt."

- **The Right to a Jury Trial:** You are entitled to a jury in all criminal cases, but not in all civil cases. For example, you are entitled to a jury trial in personal injury cases, but not in child custody and spousal support cases. Also, most states require unanimous jury verdicts in criminal trials, but agreement by only three-fourths of the jurors in a civil case.

Unless you are in court regularly, you may be uncertain about how a case proceeds from initial filing through trial. Therefore, this book also provides you with background information about what you can expect to see and what you need to do when you enter a courthouse and the courtroom in which your case will be heard. You will learn about where to file your court papers, how to subpoena witnesses (order witnesses to come to court and testify), the functions of a Clerk's Office and of a courtroom clerk, and the powers and duties of all the personnel who typically carry out courthouse business, including bailiffs, court reporters, interpreters, attorneys, jurors and, of course, judges.

This book concentrates on what goes on inside the courtroom. It does not provide detailed advice on how to decide whether to file or defend a lawsuit in the first place, or about the form and content of initial "pleadings" (a plaintiff's "complaint" or "petition" and a defendant's "answer" or "response"). We assume that you have already filed the initial documents setting forth your legal claims or defenses. Because, however, the pleadings typically determine the witnesses you call to testify and the evidence you present to a judge or jury, we do briefly discuss initial pleadings, so you'll understand how they affect what happens at trial.

The focus on courtroom activities also precludes the book from providing a comprehensive guide to the use of formal pre-trial "discovery devices" such as depositions and interrogatories, which a party can use to force reluctant witnesses to disclose what they know before trial. However, this probably will not put you at any disadvantage. Because of the expense and cumbersome nature of formal discovery, attorneys usually do not use it in smaller cases, and you probably won't either. Like you, attorneys are likely to gather evidence through informal questioning of potential witnesses. Nevertheless, either you or your adversary may decide to take a deposition or send out interrogatories. So the book does briefly discuss the most frequently used discovery devices, and explains how to use them as sources of evidence at trial.

B. CAN YOU REALLY REPRESENT YOURSELF?

Unless your case is unusually complex, the answer is yes—a resounding yes. You may not have all the legal training of a lawyer, but you do not need to go to law school to have common sense, to learn how to ask intelligible questions or to recognize what makes people and information believable. In the words of Oliver Wendell Holmes, one of the country's most revered United States Supreme Court justices, "The life of the law has not been logic, it has been experience." As these words suggest, your everyday life experience is the foundation of most of what you need to know to present a coherent, convincing case. Besides, as former Supreme Court Chief Justice Warren Burger was fond of pointing out, many lawyers are not such hotshots; they often come to court ill-prepared and lacking professional skills.

Nor need you be intimidated by the difficulty of the law or legal reasoning. Your trial will probably be concerned with facts, not abstract legal issues. For the most part, you can look up the law you need to know. (See Chapter 19, Legal Research.) It turns out that legal reasoning is no different from everyday rational thinking. Forget the silly notion that you have to act or sound like an experienced lawyer to be successful in court.

Both lawyers and non-lawyers with extremely varied personal styles can succeed in court. The admonition to "be yourself" is as appropriate inside the courtroom as out.

Finally, no matter how many times you read this book and how carefully you prepare, you will probably feel anxious when you represent yourself in court, especially if your opponent has a lawyer. Perhaps it will help you to realize that you aren't alone. Many professionals feel anxiety—particularly before a first performance—whether they are lawyers about to begin a trial, teachers about to teach a class or actors about to perform on stage. So take a deep breath and gather up your courage. As long as you combine your common sense with the principles and techniques described in this book, and are not afraid to ask a court clerk, a law librarian, an attorney or even the judge for help if you become confused, you should be able to represent yourself competently and effectively.

C. COPING WITH BEING A "STRANGER IN A STRANGE LAND"

Courts are public institutions belonging to the people, and you have the right to represent yourself. However, courts are also bureaucratic institutions with very heavy caseloads. Historically, filing clerks, courtroom clerks, court reporters and even judges have usually preferred to deal with lawyers rather than with people who represent themselves. (When you represent yourself, you may find yourself referred to as a "pro per" or "pro se" litigant—Latin abbreviations favored by judges and lawyers.) Although the increasing number of people representing themselves is beginning to change these attitudes in some places, many court personnel believe (often mistakenly) that because

FREE LEGAL HELP

Before deciding to represent yourself, you may want to explore the possibility of getting an attorney to help you for free. Here are several situations in which free help may be available:

- **If you're charged with a crime.** If you face criminal charges and cannot afford to hire your own lawyer, you have a constitutional right to an attorney at government expense. At your request, an attorney, often from a public defender's office, can be appointed to represent you when you are formally charged in court with a criminal offense.

- **If you've been injured.** If you have been injured and wish to sue if your injuries are severe enough, a lawyer may represent you on a "contingency fee" basis. This means that you pay attorney's fees only when and if the attorney recovers money for you; the attorney takes an agreed-upon percentage of that money as fees. The attorney's percentage varies from one part of the country to another, but it's common for a lawyer to collect 25% of the money if your case settles before trial and 35% if your case goes to trial.

⚠️ **You may have to pay for "costs of suit" in addition to attorney's fees.** Even if a lawyer takes your case on a contingency fee basis, you still have to pay "costs," which in a complex case can run into several thousand dollars. Costs include court filing fees, court reporters' fees for taking down what is said at depositions, expert witness fees and jury fees. However, if you win your case the judge will usually order your adversary to pay you back for these costs.

- **If you qualify for legal aid.** If you are without funds to hire an attorney, you may qualify for "legal aid." Legal aid lawyers are government lawyers who represent low-income persons in a variety of legal situations, including eviction defense, denial of unemployment compensation or other benefits, and consumer credit problems. If you think you might qualify, look in your telephone directory or ask a local attorney, lawyer referral service or elected representative for the nearest legal aid office. However, due to government funding cutbacks, in recent years legal aid offices have had to reduce the services they offer.

- **If your claim involves an issue of social justice.** If your dispute involves a social justice issue, an attorney with an interest in that issue may represent you on a "pro bono" (no fee or reduced fee) basis. For example, if your claim involves sexual harassment by an employer, abuse by a spouse or living companion, discrimination in housing or employment, freedom of speech or religion, or environmental pollution, you may find an attorney or organization who will represent you pro bono. Call a local bar association or a private organization that concerns itself with the kind of problem you face, such as the American Civil Liberties Union, the NAACP Legal Defense Fund, the Natural Resources Defense Council, the National Women's Law Center, or the Lambda Legal Defense and Education Fund (gay and lesbian rights).

lawyers know how the system works, the court personnel can do their work quicker and easier when they work with lawyers than when they work with pro pers.

So even if it is highly unfair, do not be surprised if you encounter initial hostility from court personnel. In your eyes, you are an individual seeking justice and doing what you have a right to do. But to the people who work in courthouses every day, you may be perceived as someone who will make their jobs more difficult. Instead of helping you, they may even attempt to throw obstacles at you in the hope that you will get discouraged and go away.

Knowing ahead of time that you may encounter a hostile attitude is the best weapon against it. Read and study this book and other legal resources, many of them available for free in your local library. Learn how to prepare and present a persuasive case, and follow correct clerk's office and courtroom procedures. If you believe that court personnel at any level are being rude to you, be courteous and professional in return, even as you insist upon fair treatment. By knowing and following court rules and courtroom techniques you can often earn the respect of the judge and the others who work in the courtroom, and as a result you may well find that they will go out of their way to help you.

D. USING A LAWYER AS A "SELF-HELP LAW COACH"

Even if it does not make economic sense for you to turn your entire case over to an attorney, you may want to hire one on an hourly basis as a legal coach, to give you occasional advice. Your legal coach may simplify your legal research, suggest evidence you should look for to prove your legal claims, explain a confusing rule of evidence, inform you of time deadlines, provide help with courtroom procedures that are peculiar to your local court system and not covered in this book, or suggest ways of making your arguments more persuasive.

Attorneys have traditionally either assumed overall responsibility for a client's case or declined representation. However, due to a combination of the economics and time demands of a modern law practice and increased competition from paralegals (trained attorney assistants), accountants and other professionals, it is likely that many attorneys will agree to act as a legal coach.

Throughout the book, as we explain the process of preparing for and conducting a trial, we suggest situations in which you may want to look to a legal coach for assistance. But don't consult a coach until you read through the entire book. You may find that this book either answers many of the questions you would pay a lawyer to answer or points you in the direction in which you will be able to easily find the answer on your own. (For detailed advice about hiring and working with a legal coach, see Chapter 18, Getting Help from Attorneys: Hiring a Legal Coach.)

WORKING WITH AN ATTORNEY WHO IS REPRESENTING YOU

This book can be of assistance to you even if you are represented by an attorney in the traditional fashion. Your case belongs to you, not to your lawyer. A good lawyer will be able to do a better job of representing you if you are informed and knowledgeable about the trial process and can participate in making critical decisions.

E. HOW TO USE THIS BOOK

This book is very different from other books written for non-lawyers. It does not focus on any single area of the law or type of legal problem, but serves as a guide to courtroom self-representation in any kind of case. Because of the book's unique nature, you may find the following comments and suggestions helpful.

1. If Time Permits, Read Through the Book in Its Entirety

This book is designed both to increase your overall understanding of the litigation process and to provide detailed advice about each stage of trial. So, unless you are already in the midst of trial and need to refer to a particular chapter immediately, begin preparing to represent yourself by reading through the book as a whole. As you become familiar with the litigation process, you will understand the significance of procedures and techniques that may initially seem peculiar or unnecessary.

LEARNING THE LINGO

There's no way to avoid it: If you represent yourself in court, you're going to run into a lot of unfamiliar legal terminology. This book tries to explain the most common jargon in plain English. For quick reference, check the Glossary at the back of the book.

2. Use This Book in Conjunction with Your Court System's Rules

This book can guide you through nearly every kind of trial in every court system (state or federal), because the litigation process is remarkably uniform throughout all of them. In part, this is because federal courts and most state courts share a "common law" heritage—a way of trying cases that came over from England and developed along with the country. And in part, it is because many local procedures are consistent with national legal codes (sets of rules and regulations). For example, the Federal Rules of Evidence govern the introduction of evidence in federal court trials. But around 40 states also use the Federal Rules in their trials. And even those states that have not formally adopted the Federal Rules have evidence rules that are remarkably similar to them. This means that for the most part, trials are conducted in the same way nationwide. Because of this basic uniformity, the book frequently refers you to specific rules which, even if they differ somewhat from your state's rule, should help you understand the procedures that will be followed in your case.

However, this book cannot serve as a complete guide to all the rules you need to know. For one thing, the exact rule in your court system may be somewhat different from the example we give. In that event, knowing of a specific federal or another state's rule can help you locate the rule in your state. (Chapter 19, Legal Research, will help you do this.) For another, each court system has procedural rules which, though important, cannot be covered in this book. For example, local court rules set time limits for filing various kinds of documents and page limits on the length of those documents. You will have to learn and comply with these local requirements.

That means that whenever you are concerned about a specific rule of evidence or procedure, you should always read your court system's specific provision. In general, the rule books you will need to have handy are these:

- **Your state's "Rules of Evidence."** These rules define the evidence you and your adversary are allowed to introduce for the consideration of a judge or jury. Evidence rules may be collected in an "Evidence Code" or a particular "chapter" or "title" of your state's laws, or they may be included in a larger collection of laws called "Rules of Civil Procedure."

- **Your state's "Rules of Court."** These are rules that set the procedures and deadlines that the courts in a state must follow. Generally, states have separate sets of rules for different kinds of courts. For example, a state may have one set of rules for its "Municipal Courts" (courts that try cases involving limited amounts of money), another for its "Superior Courts" (courts that try cases involving higher amounts of money) and still others for its "Appellate Courts" (courts that review the decisions of Municipal and Superior courts). (All the rules may, however, be published in a single book.) Some states also have separate sets of rules for specialized courts, such as Family Law Courts, which hear cases involving divorce, child custody and child support, and Probate Courts, which hear cases involving wills and trusts.

- **Your specific court's "Local Court Rules."** These rules define the rules for a specific courthouse, and generally allocate business between different courtrooms, specify where to file documents, set rules of courtroom behavior and the like.

STATES ORGANIZE THEIR TRIAL COURTS DIFFERENTLY

Some states have just one kind of trial court, which hears all sorts of cases. In Illinois, for example, "circuit courts" hear all kinds of disputes. But in California, cases that involve less than a certain dollar amount must be tried in Municipal Court, while larger cases go to "Superior Courts."

Books containing all of these rules should be available in a public law library. You may also want to purchase these books separately from the Clerk's Office (in the courthouse) or from a legal bookstore, so that you can have them close at hand to refer to as you read through this book and go to court.

⚠️ **You must learn the court rules.** Even though you are not a lawyer, judges will expect you to know and follow all court rules. If you miss a deadline, use the wrong kind of paper or violate some other rule, you will suffer the consequences even though you are a pro per litigant.

For instance, assume that you want to ask for a jury trial and that your local rule requires that a jury trial request must be made 30 days after the initial pleadings are filed. If you miss that deadline, you will not have a jury trial unless you go through a laborious process to request an extension of time to file your demand and the judge is willing to make an exception (don't count on it!).

3. Make a Trial Notebook

We strongly recommend that you prepare a "trial notebook." A trial notebook is a series of outlines covering such matters as what you must prove (or, if you are a defendant, disprove), the evidence you have available to prove (or disprove) those things, the topics you intend to cover on direct and cross-examination, a list of the names, addresses and telephone numbers of your witnesses, and the exhibits you plan to introduce into evidence. The notebook serves as your courtroom manager, because you can refer to it to make sure that you do not overlook evidence you planned to offer or an argument you intended to make.

As you read through the chapters describing the various stages of trial, you will find specific sections indicating how to prepare an outline for inclusion in your trial notebook. A separate chapter (Chapter 15, Organizing a Trial Notebook) pulls together suggestions from earlier chapters and describes how to organize a trial notebook.

F. USING THIS BOOK IF YOU DON'T GO TO TRIAL

Over 90% of all lawsuits filed are resolved without trial. If you can arrive at a fair resolution with your adversary without going to trial, you can save yourself time and money. By showing you how to prove and disprove legal claims, this book can help you arrive at a fair resolution of your dispute.

There are also many alternatives to trials that are gaining in popularity. If you become involved in one or more of them, you can still use this book to understand and prepare your arguments.

Here are the typical non-trial situations you may find yourself in.

1. Hearings

Depending on what kind of dispute you're involved in, you may find yourself in a hearing rather than a trial. For example, you'll probably have a hearing if you are seeking an increase or a decrease in spousal or child support following your divorce, or you need to prove how much money you are entitled to after a defendant has failed to answer your complaint. A court hearing is usually a short and narrowly defined proceeding in which you are not entitled to a jury. A judge conducts the hearing and makes a ruling. The other party to the dispute may not even be present in court. However, this book's advice is as pertinent to hearings as to trials. Many of the courtroom procedures and rules of evidence are exactly the same in a hearing as in a trial. And you still must offer evidence in a way that persuades the judge or hearing officer to rule in your favor.

2.   Arbitration

Arbitration is an alternative to trial that is often perceived of as quicker and less costly than trial. In arbitration, a privately agreed-to arbitrator, not a judge, rules on the case. There is no jury, pre-hearing procedures are more informal and the arbitrator is not strictly bound by rules of evidence. Arbitrators generally charge by either the full or half day; you and your adversary split the arbitrator's fee.

If you have a legal dispute, you may well find yourself involved in an arbitration rather than a trial. One reason is that in many states, judges have the power in certain kinds of cases to order you and your adversary to arbitrate a dispute. A second reason is that even though you didn't realize it, you may have signed an agreement that provides for binding arbitration of all disputes arising under the agreement. For example, if you are an investor who believes a brokerage house violated securities laws while handling your account, a condominium owner who has made a complaint against your condominium association for unreasonably restricting your right to remodel your unit, or a businessperson who wants to sue for breach of a written contract, you may have agreed in writing (in the broker's agreement, the condominium association's set of rules or the business contract) to arbitrate all disputes.

Though arbitration proceedings are generally more informal than trials, most of the principles described in this book also apply to arbitration. As in a trial, you and your adversary present evidence to the arbitrator through your own testimony and the testimony of witnesses. Like a judge, an arbitrator evaluates the credibility and legal significance of evidence in order to decide whether you win or lose.

Also, because most arbitrators are lawyers, their actions tend to be strongly influenced by their legal training. The rules and procedures they follow generally closely resemble those used by judges in trials.

 RESOURCES ON ARBITRATION

Without the Punches: Resolving Disputes Without Litigation, by Doyle & Haydock (Equilaw), a handbook prepared on behalf of a private organization that provides arbitration services.

Alternative Dispute Resolution: Panacea or Anathema, by Harry T. Edwards, 99 Harvard Law Review 668 (1986), an analysis of the advantages and disadvantages of arbitration and other dispute resolution procedures.

Dispute Resolution, by Goldberg, Sander & Rogers (Little Brown & Co.), a textbook setting forth arbitration principles and methods.

3.   Mediation

Another popular method of resolving disputes outside of court is mediation, which is generally more informal and less costly than arbitration. Mediation is a voluntary process in which you meet with your adversary in the company of a third person, the mediator. The mediator, who has no power to impose a solution, usually tries to facilitate settlement by clarifying each party's position, encouraging cooperation and suggesting possible solutions. Professional mediators charge for their services, typically by the hour. Normally, the parties split the mediator's fee.

Even though mediation may be informal, to use it to arrive at an acceptable solution you will probably need to demonstrate both to your adversary and to yourself that you have strong evidence to support your legal position, and that the evidence is admissible in court should mediation fail. Otherwise, you may make an unwise and unfair settlement just because you are afraid to go to trial. And just as in a trial, this book will help you represent your position effectively during mediation.

 RESOURCES ON MEDIATION

Mediation: A Comprehensive Guide to Resolving Conflicts Without Litigation, by Folberg & Taylor (Jossey-Bass).

Mediation Processes: Practical Strategies for Resolving Conflict, by Christopher Moore (Jossey-Bass).

A Student's Guide to Mediation, by Rogers & Salem (Matthew Bender).

A Guide to Divorce Mediation, by Gary J. Friedman (Workman).

4. Negotiation

The most ancient way to settle a dispute is negotiation, in which you sit down with your adversary and try to resolve your differences. Whether or not your case goes to trial, you will almost certainly find yourself negotiating some or all of the issues that are important to you.

Against this background, it doesn't normally make sense to interpret your adversary's offer to "talk settlement" as a sign of weakness. Nor should you be reluctant to be the one to suggest a negotiated settlement. In fact, judges, arbitrators and mediators routinely urge adversaries to explore settlement even if previous attempts have failed. It's a wise person who never closes the door to a reasonable settlement.

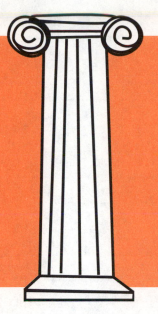

2

THE COURTHOUSE AND THE COURTROOM

Representing yourself in court can be like traveling to a different country. Courtrooms, like nations, have unique rules and customs and even a somewhat different language. Just as with traveling, a successful courtroom experience depends on knowing where you want to go, what the rules are during your journey and what to expect when you get to your destination.

If you think of this book as your access guide to trial, this chapter is the part that explains the duties and functions of various people you are likely to encounter, the "lay of the land," customs and etiquette of the natives and tips for dealing with them.

A. AN OVERVIEW OF DIFFERENT COURTS

Federal courts decide cases involving federal laws or the U.S. Constitution, and cases where the parties are from different states and the amount of money in dispute is more than $50,000. In the federal system, there are three levels of courts:

- District courts, where most trials occur

- Courts of Appeal, which hear appeals from the district courts

- The United States Supreme Court (the highest of the federal courts), which hears appeals in a few cases of its choosing.

There are also some specialized courts within the federal court system, such as tax and bankruptcy courts.

State courts decide all the matters that are not covered in federal courts. State courts handle disputes involving state constitutions and state laws covering a wide variety of subjects, such as contracts, personal injuries and family law. In some situations, either a state or a federal court can hear a case.

State court systems have a variety of different names for their courts. Many (but not all) states have two or more kinds of trial courts. The lowest level courts are often called small claims, municipal, city, justice or traffic court—all of which have fairly tight limits on the types of cases they can hear. The next level of trial courts typically handle larger civil cases, serious criminal cases and most divorce and other domestic cases. In addition, some states have specialized courts that handle only very limited types of cases, such as juvenile or probate; these may be divisions of the general trial court.

The next level of court, in most states, is courts of appeal, which can review trial court decisions. And last is the highest state court, often called the

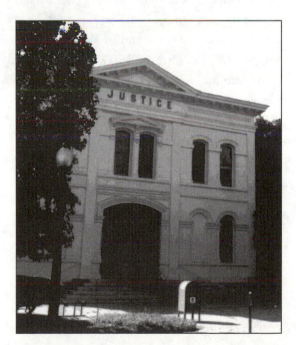

supreme court (in New York, called the Appellate Division). State supreme courts, like the U.S. Supreme Court, generally choose what cases they will hear from among the many requests they receive. They choose cases that deal with important legal issues, such as those affecting the legal weight and significance of future cases and the constitutionality of laws.

![warning triangle icon] **Make sure you're in the right court.** To conduct your own trial successfully, you first need to file the right documents in the right courthouse. (The documents and actions required to kick off a lawsuit are discussed in Chapter 3, Starting and Investigating Your Case.) And this chapter provides some basics on different kinds of courts, such as federal and state courts, and trial and appeals courts. It is crucial, however, as early on in the process as possible, that you verify that you are in the right court for your legal claims. You may have a choice of courts to bring your lawsuit in, but if you try to sue in the wrong court, your case may be kicked out. If you are a defendant and the plaintiff has filed the lawsuit in the wrong court, you may well be able to have the case dismissed.

Verify with the Clerk's Office, your legal coach (see Chapter 18, Getting Help From Attorneys: Hiring a Legal Coach) or your own research (see Chapter 19, Legal Research) to make certain what court you should be in. You must bring your case not only in the proper court, but also in the proper location. There are many trial courts; the rules of "venue" determine which location is proper for a particular lawsuit. Usually, it depends on where the defendant lives, works or does business.

To appeal a case means to go to an appellate court and ask that it review and overturn the lower court's decision. Usually, you can appeal only if you think the trial court made a mistake about the law that affected the outcome of your case. You cannot appeal just because you don't think a judge or a jury made the correct decision. A trial court is often called the "finder of fact," and its factual conclusions are almost always binding on an appellate court. (See Chapter 17, When Your Trial Ends: Judgments and Appeals.)

RESOURCES ON COURTS

For more information, you may want to look at a book on the United States legal system, such as *Law and the Courts: A Handbook about United States Law and Procedures*, by the American Bar Association Public Education Division (ABA).

B. A TYPICAL COURTHOUSE

Before looking inside a courtroom, let's first consider the courthouse as a whole. A courthouse is, in essence, a public office building for judges and their support personnel. Different courts are often located in different buildings; for example, the criminal court may be in a different building from the civil court.

Inside the main entrance to a courthouse, you will often find a directory, which lists particular courtrooms or offices. To locate the room you need, however, you may have to ask a guard, since courthouse directories tend not to be user-friendly. They may, for example, refer to courtrooms as "departments." They usually don't list helpful information such as where you must go to file legal papers or get information, and they often don't say where places like the cafeteria or law library are located. This is because it is assumed that lawyers—the courthouse's main clientele—know such things already.

BEEFED-UP SECURITY

As you enter some courthouses or courtrooms, especially in larger metropolitan communities, you may have to pass through a metal detector. Like airports, courthouses are now concerned about people bringing weapons in the building. There may also be a guard on duty.

You may feel a little lost or intimidated, especially on your first trip to court. The corridors—full of busy lawyers dragging huge briefcases, jurors roaming in bunches and the occasional armed guard standing by—can be rather imposing. It may help to know that you are not the only one who feels out of place. Since little effort is expended to orient the newcomer, new lawyers often get lost too. Of course, this lack of even minimal hospitality tends to hit pro pers like yourself the hardest.

It may help to remember the foreign country analogy; think of this as a very strange land where the people have a different culture and language. Learn their ways by putting aside any shyness you feel and asking for help as soon as you need it. If you don't get understandable answers, just keep asking. The courthouse is a public building, supported by your tax dollars; you not only have the right to be there but also to ask as many questions as you want.

Try not to get frustrated or angry. At times, court personnel can appear hostile even when they don't mean to be, simply because they are busy and usually overworked. Also, too often they assume that everyone who appears in court is experienced, and they don't take the little bit of extra time necessary to orient pro pers. With some patience, you will learn your way around the courthouse, and soon enough you may look so much like you know where you are going that people start asking you for help!

1. The Clerk's Office

One of the most important offices in the courthouse is the Clerk's Office. It's often located on the first or main floor. Typically, the Clerk's Office is where documents relating to all the cases pending or decided in a courthouse are filed and stored. If one building houses two or more courts, such as small claims court and civil court or federal district court and bankruptcy court, each court will have its own Clerk's Office. That's because each court has its own filing and record keeping procedure. You'll have to locate the Clerk's Office for the court hearing your case.

Don't confuse the Clerk's Office and a judge's clerk. Each judge (or courtroom) usually has an assistant called a "clerk." And that clerk may even have an office. But that is not the same as the central Clerk's Office in the courthouse, where documents are filed and stored. You will likely have to consult both the general Clerk's Office and your judge's clerk, as your case progresses. The duties of a judge's courtroom clerk are discussed in Section C, below.

You will need to go to the Clerk's Office when you file legal papers in your case. You may also deal with the Clerk's Office to check court rules and procedures throughout your case. For example, you will go to the Clerk's Office if you need to file documents such as a pre-trial motion (a request for a court order, discussed in Chapter 4, Pre-Trial Hearings and Motions) or to get a subpoena (court order to appear in court). You can also review documents in the court file, a master file that typically includes all documents filed by you, your opponent or issued by the judge.

WAITING ON LINE AT THE CLERK'S OFFICE

At many Clerk's Offices, like at the Post Office or bank, you'll probably file papers and talk to clerks over a counter or through a window. And, also like the Post Office, there may be bureaucratic details like rigid hours and different windows for different services. For example, even if you've been waiting patiently in line, the Clerk's Office may close at lunch time, or you may belatedly learn you waited in the criminal instead of the civil clerk's line. To avoid such problems, call ahead for information about hours and the specific procedures you must follow to file papers for your civil case.

Once you get to the front of the line, rule one is to be polite. The Clerk's Office personnel can help or hinder you, so it pays to try to get them on your side. Understand, however, that some clerks are prejudiced against pro pers. (A few even post signs warning you not to ask questions because they don't practice law.) So if you run into someone who is hostile, you must remain firm and not get intimidated. You are entitled to the procedural information you need, provided in language that you can understand. If you don't get it, ask to see the supervising clerk.

2.   The Law Library

Many courthouses contain law libraries that are open to the public. The first day you go to the courthouse, it may be a good idea to locate the law library, find out its hours and walk through to take a look. You will learn more about using the law library in Chapter 19, Legal Research, but the more comfortable you are there, the more user-friendly it will be.

Often, several courthouses rely on one central library, and a few states don't provide courthouse libraries at all. If you need to consult some legal research materials and your courthouse doesn't have a public law library, ask someone at the Clerk's Office or an attorney you pass in the hallway where the nearest public law library is located. It may, for example, be at a nearby law school.

3.   Courtrooms

The most important part of the courthouse is its courtrooms. We'll explore the inside of a typical courtroom in detail in Section D, below, but first a few words about the outside. Judges usually have their own regular courtrooms where they hold trials and other public hearings, and the judge's name and a number are usually posted on or next to the courtroom door.

Most courts prepare a calendar each day, listing the scheduled court hearings, and post it on or near the front door of the courtroom. And calendars for all courtrooms are usually posted in the Clerk's Office. Since a judge may be assigned to different courtrooms on different days or other calendaring changes may occur, it is good practice to verify the time and place of your court hearing both at the Clerk's Office and the courtroom.

A courtroom by another name is still a courtroom. The word "courtroom" may not appear on either posted calendars or the courtroom doors. Some courts use other words, such as "department." For example, you may see a sign like this outside a courtroom: DEPARTMENT 1 - JUDGE SUZANNE KAY.

Almost all trials are public, so unless there is a sign to the contrary, it's fine to walk into a courtroom, sit in the spectator section and observe. Always enter quietly so as not to disturb ongoing court proceedings.

4.   Other Offices

Courthouses contain offices for court personnel, from judges to secretaries. They may also house the offices of local officials, such as the city or county attorney and public defender, and law enforcement officers, such as the sheriff or marshal. Courthouses sometimes contain office space for legal newspapers (newspapers that feature articles about current cases and advertisements for lawyers, legal secretaries, court reporters and other legal services). You may not need to deal with any of these offices personally.

Don't forget to eat. It's hard to function on an empty stomach, so you may want to ask if the courthouse has a snack bar or cafeteria. Many do, but the location is often so obscure you wouldn't find it on your own.

C.   THE COURTROOM PLAYERS

Who will you find in a typical courtroom? What are their roles? You need to understand, if only to know who to approach for advice when you have questions.

1.   The Judge

The judge is the man or woman, usually wearing a black robe, who sits on a raised platform at the front of the courtroom and presides over pre-trial hearings and trials. As their principal duties, judges:

- conduct hearings for and make rulings on pre-trial motions and discovery disputes

- preside over pre-trial conferences and facilitate settlement conferences

- control the trial of your case, subject to legal rules of evidence and procedure

- make legal rulings, such as deciding whether a particular piece of evidence can be presented in court or whether it must be excluded (not considered in evaluating the case)

- decide who wins and loses, and how much the loser must pay in damages, when there is no jury, and

- instruct the jury as to the law they must follow in rendering their verdict, in jury trials.

A judge by any other name is still a judge. The words "court," "bench," "magistrate," "commissioner" and "justice" are sometimes interchanged with the word "judge." ("Justice" typically refers to a judge on the highest appeals court in a state or in the United States Supreme Court.) So if the judge asks you to "approach the bench," that means the judge wants you to step up close so she can talk to you and your opponent privately. You'll refer to the judge as "Your Honor" or "the court." For example, you might say, "I ask that the court [meaning the judge] instruct Ms. Loretta Charles, a witness the defendant intends to have testify later on today, to leave the courtroom immediately."

Some judges hear criminal matters, others conduct only civil (non-criminal) proceedings, still others hear only cases involving juveniles. Judges' powers depend on the courts in which they preside. For instance, judges in small claims courts usually have power only to grant a limited sum of money damages, often between $2,500 and $5,000.

Judges in appeals courts do not conduct trials at all, but review decisions of trial courts. (See Chapter 17, When Your Trial Ends: Judgments and Appeals.) In large communities, where there are many judges, some judges may conduct hearings on pre-trial concerns but not the trials themselves. (See Chapter 4, Pre-Trial Hearings and Motions.)

It follows that a different judge may be assigned to your case during different parts of the litigation process. For example, one judge may rule on your opponent's pre-trial motion to dismiss the case, another may conduct settlement negotiations, and still another may preside over the trial. (For information on how to challenge a judge (have the judge removed from your case), see Chapter 7, Selecting the Decision-Maker.)

Cases are also sometimes decided by someone known as a "judge pro tem" (short for the Latin, "judge pro tempore"). Generally, a judge pro tem is a practicing lawyer who is appointed to serve as a temporary judge. You almost always have a right not to accept a judge pro tem and to insist on a regular judge. However, if you exercise this right, your case may be delayed. If you agree to have your case heard by a judge pro tem, the pro tem has all the powers of a regularly appointed judge.

In some courtrooms, the judge is called a commissioner or magistrate. A commissioner or magistrate, typically an employee of the court system, is appointed to act as a judge and hear cases relating to a particular subject matter or in a particular court, such as city, municipal, small claims or traffic court. U.S. Magistrates are appointed by judges of federal district courts (federal trial courts); they hear pre-trial matters in civil and criminal cases and conduct some trials. Sometimes, the magistrate will hear a case (if the parties agree), and make a recommendation to the district court for a particular ruling; the district court judge signs the actual court order.

2. The Judge's Court Clerk

The judge's clerk (also called the court clerk or the judge's court clerk) is a member of the court clerk's staff who works for a particular judge. The judge's clerk has many duties, including preparing and maintaining the judge's calendar (often called the "docket"), which like an appointment calendar lists the dates and times for trials and other matters. The judge's clerk normally sits at a desk in front of the judge's bench. Either the clerk or the bailiff (see Section 4, below) will check you in when you arrive in the courtroom.

The judge's clerk also retrieves case files, which are maintained and stored in the main Clerk's Office. Your case file consists of the papers, briefs, pleadings and other documents having to do with your case that have been filed—that is, delivered to the court's custody to be stored as permanent public records.

During trial, the judge's clerk keeps custody of exhibits, administers oaths to witnesses, jurors and interpreters, and generally helps the judge move cases along. If there are papers you must present to the judge during a court proceeding, you may be directed to hand them to the court clerk (or sometimes the bailiff), who will then pass them on to the judge or file them in the court file. For example, you may need to show the clerk a copy of a subpoena you served on a witness who did not appear.

When a judge makes a final decision or issues an interim order (decision on an issue that arises before the close of the case), the judge's clerk typically prepares the order for the judge to sign, although some judges request attorneys or pro pers to prepare the orders.

3. Law Clerks

Many judges, especially in federal and higher level state courts, have law clerks. Law clerks are often recent law school graduates. To assist their judge, law clerks:

- research the legal issues presented by the parties

- assist the judge with legal questions that arise before and sometimes during trials, and

- help draft the written orders or opinions judges sometimes produce to explain their rulings.

GETTING ADVICE FROM CLERKS

Generally, you are not supposed to discuss the merits of your case with any court personnel without the other side present (called an "ex parte" contact). And clerks cannot give legal advice. However, you may ask commonplace procedural questions of the judge's clerk or law clerk, such as how you might get an extension ("continuance") for a court deadline you will not be able to meet. The judge's clerks (both the court clerk and law clerk) can also be a very valuable resource for routine questions about local court rules and special procedures unique to your judge. For example, a judge may want an extra copy (called a "courtesy copy") of pleadings you file with the main Clerk's Office to be sent directly to her courtroom.

If you are concerned that your question may be improper, try explaining the general idea of what you want to ask before you proceed with the full question. The most important thing to remember is to be especially nice to the judge's clerk and law clerk. They work with the judge on a daily basis, and they will not hesitate to tell the judge when someone has been rude to them.

---

4. The Bailiff

The bailiff, often classified as a peace officer and commonly dressed in uniform and armed, is an official of the court. As part of a wide range of duties, the bailiff:

- maintains order and decorum in the courtroom—for example, by removing disruptive spectators from the courtroom

- takes charge of juries

- escorts witnesses into and out of the courtroom, and

- hands exhibits to witnesses who are testifying, unless the court clerk does this.

5. The Court Reporter

In most courts, a person called a court reporter records every word that is said during any official ("on the record") proceeding in the courtroom. During the proceeding, the reporter will read back testimony of a witness or a statement of a lawyer or pro per, upon request of the judge. If you want something read back for your own or the jury's benefit, you must ask the judge for permission to have the court reporter read it back.

In a few courts, such as small claims and some lower level state trial courts, a court reporter is used only if the parties request one. And some courts now record proceedings with tape recorders. Someone (often a clerk) still runs the tape recorder, so that statements can be played back at the judge's request.

Speak clearly for court reporters and tape recorders. When you're in court, stand tall and speak up so that a tape recorder or court reporter can correctly record your statements. Speak directly into the microphone if one is provided. Have your witnesses speak up too. And avoid interrupting, except when it is essential, such as in order to make objections. (See Chapter 14, Making and Responding to Objections.) It's difficult for a court reporter, and sometimes for a judge or jury, to sort out what's said when two or more people talk at once.

Court reporters will prepare a transcript booklet of what was said at a particular court session, upon the request of a party or the judge. It is often necessary to get a transcript if you plan to appeal. (See Chapter 17, When Your Trial Ends: Judgments and Appeals.) Court reporters typically charge by the page to prepare transcripts. Depending on the length of the hearing, they can be costly—several hundred dollars for just a few hours of court time.

6. Interpreters

Interpreters translate for witnesses and parties who have difficulty speaking or understanding English. Interpreters are sworn to interpret accurately. Parties typically pay for interpreters in civil cases—a one-day trial may cost between $150 and $300 for a common language such as Spanish, and as much as three or four times that for a less common language. In most cases you cannot bring in just anyone (such as a friend or relative), even if that person would be well qualified to interpret.

So, if you or a witness need an interpreter, ask the Clerk's Office, your judge's court clerk or your legal coach how to arrange for a court-certified interpreter.

7. Jurors

Jurors are people drawn from the area in which the court is located, to evaluate evidence and render verdicts in both criminal and civil cases. Typically called to be available for a couple of weeks at a time, potential jurors may never actually serve on a trial either because they are never needed or because the judge or a party dismisses them.

When jurors do serve on civil trials, their job is to decide whether claims are factually valid, and, if money is awarded, how much the winning party should receive. In limited situations, judges can overturn a jury's verdict or modify the amount of damages the jury awarded. (See Chapter 17, When Your Trial Ends: Judgments and Appeals.)

In typical civil jury trials, there are between six and 12 jurors and a few alternates, in case a juror gets sick or is unable to finish the trial. In contrast to criminal cases, which often require a unanimous jury, most states allow civil cases to be decided when three-fourths of the jurors agree.

Many cases do not come before juries; they are handled by judges alone. In a few situations, you are not allowed a jury; for example, judges alone handle many family law, bankruptcy and pre-trial matters. For some types of cases, where a jury trial is an option, neither you nor your adversary will want a jury. (See Chapter 7, Selecting the Decision-Maker.)

8.   Parties

Parties are the people or organizations (such as businesses or nonprofit groups) in whose names a case is brought (usually called "plaintiffs") or defended (usually called "defendants"). Cases can involve multiple defendants and sometimes multiple plaintiffs. As a pro per (sometimes called "pro se") you are a party who is representing yourself.

9.   Witnesses

Two kinds of witnesses may appear at a trial: ordinary witnesses and expert witnesses.

a.   Ordinary Witnesses

Witnesses testify under oath to information they know through personal knowledge. In the language of the courtroom, they may testify only to things they have perceived with their own senses, meaning what they have personally seen, heard, smelled, tasted or touched. For example, a bystander at a car accident may come into court and, when asked what she saw, say, "I saw the red car go through the stop sign and hit the blue car." However, if the owner of the blue car went home after the accident and told his neighbor (who did not witness the accident) all about it, the neighbor could not testify about how the accident actually occurred. The reason is that the neighbor did not perceive the accident.

Except for reimbursement of the costs of coming to court (a limited allowance for things like mileage to and from the courthouse), ordinary witnesses cannot be paid to testify. You can obtain a subpoena (court order) to compel a witness to come to court and testify, but typically only if the witness lives or works relatively near the court-

house—in some courts, within 100 miles. (For more details on subpoenas, see Chapter 9, Direct Examination.)

b.   Expert Witnesses

After a judge rules that a witness is qualified as an expert, that person can testify based on her special knowledge or training. Experts are not just medical doctors or rocket scientists, but also people such as auto mechanics, building contractors and computer programmers.

Experts testify under oath either about what they have personally seen or heard (like ordinary witnesses) or, more commonly, give their opinions about what conclusions should be drawn from testimony given by non-expert witnesses.

Unlike other witnesses, experts can be and almost always are paid for their time in preparing for and giving testimony, in addition to reimbursement for costs of coming to court. (See Chapter 16, Expert Witnesses.)

10.   Attorneys

Attorneys—also called counsel, counselors or lawyers—speak and act on behalf of parties. Attorneys generally handle most aspects of a case for the parties they represent. For example, during trial an attorney may:

- question witnesses to bring out testimony that helps the client's case or refutes the opposing party's evidence (see Chapters 9 and 10 on Direct and Cross-Examination)

- object to improper testimony, exhibits or arguments of the opposing party (see Chapter 14, Making and Responding to Objections), and

- argue to the judge or jury how the facts and law show that her client should win the case (see Chapter 11, Closing Argument).

Attorneys also perform many out-of-court functions, such as conducting legal research, advising clients on strategy, drafting legal documents and negotiating settlements on behalf of their clients. Attorneys also sign and arrange for documents to be filed with the court and served (delivered) to the other party and witnesses on behalf of their clients.

In some courts, attorneys may be asked to draft court orders after a judge has made a ruling. This may be the judge's final decision or an interim decision, such as a ruling to exclude a certain document from being admitted into evidence.

As a party representing yourself, you will perform many of the functions that a lawyer does for a client. If your opponent is represented by a lawyer, you are expected to deal with the lawyer and not directly with your adversary. This means you should make phone calls to the attorney, not your opponent, and when you serve legal papers on your opponent, you should deliver them to the attorney. However, since you aren't a lawyer (who is forbidden from directly contacting someone rep-

resented by an attorney), there may be an exceptional situation where, if the opportunity arises, you will want to bypass the lawyer and talk to your opponent directly, perhaps in an effort to settle the case.

You should be aware too, in case you are concerned that your opponent is not getting information from his lawyer, that another rule of professional conduct requires lawyers to communicate certain important information to their clients. For example, if you make an offer of settlement to the attorney, she must communicate it to her client, even if she thinks it's a bad proposal.

Even when you represent yourself in court, you may want to hire a lawyer as a "coach" to help you find the applicable law and advise you on particular questions as your case progresses. (See Chapter 18, Getting Help from Attorneys: Hiring a Legal Coach, for more on self-help law coaches.)

11. Spectators

Most court proceedings are open to the public, so family members, friends and even total strangers may watch hearings and trials. You may find it helpful to enlist supportive friends to come to court with you and perhaps assist by carrying things and taking notes for you.

Spectators must usually sit in the back of the courtroom behind what is called "the bar"—actually a small fence or gate—that divides the area immediately surrounding the judge and jury from the rest of the room. In some courts, and especially in cases of spousal battering or sexual harassment, judges may grant permission for non-lawyer supporters to sit next to you at counsel table (place at the front of the courtroom where lawyers and pro pers sit while presenting their cases, discussed in Section D, below), to provide moral (though usually not verbal) support. If this is something you feel will help you present your case more effectively, ask the judge for permission.

D. THE COURTROOM AND ITS PHYSICAL LAYOUT

Even though as a pro per you are not expected to perfectly understand court rules and legal principles, you'll want to know where you should sit and stand and where everyone else belongs when you go to court. The more familiar you are with the lay of the land, the more easily you will find your way around—and look and feel confident doing so. Here are those parts of courtroom found in most state and federal courthouses.

1. Spectator Area

The spectator area is usually in the back of the courtroom, often separated from the rest of the courtroom by a bar or low partition. Members of the public sit in this area, as will you if you go to visit a courtroom. After checking in with the clerk, attorneys, parties and witnesses usually stay in this area until the name of their case is called (announced) by the judge or clerk.

2. Jury Box

The jury box is where jurors sit during the jury selection and throughout trial. Traditionally it seats 12 jurors, although many states now use smaller juries in civil actions. The jury box area remains empty when there is no jury or the jury is out of the courtroom.

3. Jury Room

The jury room is separate from and often behind or adjacent to the courtroom itself. During jury trials, this is where jurors go to evaluate the evidence, deliberate and decide what their verdict will be.

4. Witness Box

This box-like area, also called the witness stand or just the stand, is located to the left or the right of the judge's bench, on the same side of the courtroom as the jury box. It is where witnesses sit when they testify. Before they are asked to testify, witnesses either sit in the spectator area or in the corridor outside the courtroom (if the judge has excluded them until they are called to the stand).

It is fairly routine for witnesses to be excluded (kept out of the courtroom until it is their turn to testify) so that their testimony is not influenced by what other witnesses say, but you may have to ask the judge to direct the witness to wait outside. Let your witnesses know ahead of time that they may be excluded so that they won't feel the judge is biased against them if he asks them to leave. You might suggest that they bring a book to read while they wait.

5. Judge's Bench

The judge's bench is the raised wooden desk or podium at the front of the courtroom where the judge sits. No attorneys or parties may go near the bench except upon the judge's request or by asking

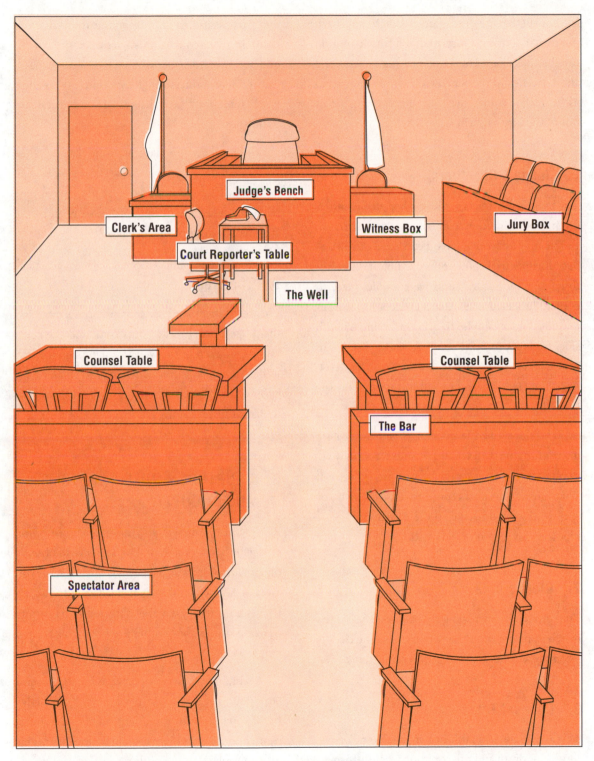

A TYPICAL COURTROOM

the court (the judge) for permission to approach the bench. During a jury trial, it's fairly common for the judge or a lawyer or pro per to request a short meeting at the bench (sometimes referred to as "a sidebar conference"), to discuss some point out of the jury's hearing.

6.   Judge's Chambers

The judge's chambers are his or her private office, often a room adjacent to or behind the courtroom. Judges may ask you to have a conference in chambers during a trial or other proceeding, if they want to go "off the record" and have a quiet place to confer. Judges use such conferences for various reasons—for example, to admonish one or both sides for inappropriate conduct in a jury trial or to urge one or both sides to settle. (See Chapter 4, Pre-Trial Hearings and Motions, for more on settlement conferences.)

If you are asked to go into chambers and are uncomfortable with whatever is said, you may request that the conference be put on the record. That means the court reporter would come in, or you would all go back into the courtroom so the reporter can record what is said.

7.   Clerk's Area

The court clerk usually sits on the side of the judge's bench opposite from the witness box. The clerk is often present during the court's proceedings.

8.   Counsel Table

This area includes a table or two, chairs and sometimes a podium and microphone where attorneys and parties sit during trials and hearings on their cases. In most courtrooms, you make arguments and question witnesses while standing at the podium or microphone, though some judges may allow you to remain at the counsel table or stand closer to the witnesses.

You'll take your place at counsel table when your case is called. If the counsel tables are labeled for plaintiff or defendant, sit at the appropriate table. If they are not, the plaintiff usually sits on the side that is closer to the jury box.

9.   The Well

The well is the space between the counsel table and the judge's bench. The court clerk and the court reporter may sit in the well area. Don't go into the well area, unless the courtroom is so small or the architecture is such that you must pass through it to take your seat at the counsel table.

E.   COURTROOM RULES, CUSTOMS AND ETIQUETTE

Representing yourself, you may feel a bit insecure, especially before you have had a chance to observe other courtroom sessions. This is normal since you are not trained and experienced in conducting trials, and you may have been treated with hostility or heard stories about other pro pers being treated that way.

Again, just as if you were traveling to a distant land, you will have a more pleasant and productive trip if you follow local customs (in this case courtroom etiquette) and are as polite as possible. This section explains some of those customs.

1. Dress in a Business-like Manner

Generally, in court you should dress like you are going to a job interview or a professional job—suits for men and suits or dresses for women. Better to overdress than to underdress. Federal courts tend to be more formal than state courts.

In lower courts, such as traffic, municipal or justice courts, however, it's appropriate to dress as you normally dress for your work—particularly if you come to court directly from your job. For example, if you are a contractor, dancer or security guard, and are coming from work, you don't need to change into lawyers' clothes, a suit and tie.

2. Be Courteous to Everyone, Especially Court Personnel

Not only is this a good way to treat everyone, it's particularly important in court, where you are likely to need a bit of helpful advice from time to time. You may also need small favors, such as a five-minute recess or for the clerk to notify you if your case is called and you need to be out of the courtroom for a minute to use the rest room or make a phone call. And you will have questions—even the most experienced attorneys do—such as how to label exhibits or file legal papers. Court personnel are much more apt to grant your requests and help you out if you are polite. It's as simple as that.

3. Check in When You Enter the Courtroom

When you enter the courtroom, check in with the court clerk. Give your name and case number, and ask if the court's schedule is on time and when the clerk believes your case will be called (heard by the judge). If court is in session when you enter the room, wait until the judge takes a break or pauses long enough after a proceeding is finished that you can discreetly hand the clerk a note with your name and case number saying you want to check in.

4. Stay Close Until Your Case Is Called

Clerks usually have a good handle on the judge's schedule, but sometimes things go faster than anticipated because other parties aren't ready or a case is settled at the last minute. Or the judge may call cases out of order. Also, some courts schedule hearings in blocks, so that several matters are all set for the same time. In these courts, judges often take the routine or quick matters first and the cases or hearings they feel will take up more time after all the routine items are finished. Sometimes, judges put cases on "first call" or "second call," meaning earlier or later in the time block, and the lawyers or pro pers can request that their case be heard earlier or later depending on their schedules.

For all these reasons, if you need to leave the courtroom, even for a minute, it's best to let the clerk know where you are in case the judge is ready for your case sooner than expected. Just like the train, sometimes the judge won't wait.

When the judge is ready to hear your case, the clerk or the judge will call out your name and the names of the other parties in your case. You will stand and say that you are present and ready to proceed. When the judge or clerk motions for you or tells you to come forward, you will take your seat at the counsel table.

MASTER CALENDAR SYSTEMS

In some courts, the first judge you are assigned to go see is not the judge who will be presiding over your trial, but what is called the "master calendar judge." The master calendar judge is a bit like a tour organizer who takes bunch of tourists into one central office first and then assigns them to particular tour guides according to what sights they will see, what language they speak or how big the group is. The master calendar judge evaluates a whole slew of cases as to how long they will take and what's likely to be involved in trying them. She sometimes tries to help the parties with settlement negotiations. Then, based on the cases and on availability of particular courtrooms, the master calendar judge assigns those cases that are ready for trial out to other courtrooms.

In assigning the case, the judge might say something like, *"Nolo v. Klotchman* to Department 2, trailing." This means your case will be heard by the judge in courtroom 2, but that it will trail (follow) one or more other cases. The Clerk's Office should be able to tell you if your court uses a master calendar system and, if so, how it works.

5.   Talk Respectfully to the Judge

As a general rule, you should always stand when addressing the judge. Only if you see that attorneys routinely talk to the judge while seated at the counsel table, as is the practice in some state courts, should you sit while you speak to the judge. Even then, it might be worth showing the courtesy of standing until the judge says you may be seated. If you are unable to stand for medical reasons, tell the judge that at the outset of the proceedings.

Always call the judge "Your Honor" when you speak to him or her. Do not say "Sir" and especially not "Ma'am." In court, by long-running tradition, "Your Honor" is the neutral, respectful term used by all. You are not giving up your democratic dignity by using it.

6.   Don't Speak Directly to Opposing Counsel

When your case is being heard, always address the opposing attorney or pro per through the judge, not directly. For example, say, "Your Honor, this morning Ms. Ellis stated here in court that she would not be calling any other witnesses. Now she has stated that she intends to call two additional witnesses. I ask that they not be allowed to testify." Do not turn to Ms. Ellis directly and say, "You said you wouldn't call any other witnesses."

Always address or refer to attorneys, parties and witnesses by last names—for example, Mr. Neustadt or Ms. Doherty. Even if you have talked a lot on the phone and the person has told you to call him by his first name, use last names in court. This is to maintain the formal, respectful courtroom tone.

7.   Find Out About Special Procedures

All judges follow the same broad procedural rules discussed in this book. Nevertheless, some judges have their own preferences as to detail, and if you can learn these, you will be well served. One good way to start is by watching your judge in action before your day in court; another is by talking with the clerk or a lawyer who has appeared before your judge. (For more information on researching your judge's background and style, see Chapter 7, Selecting the Decision-Maker.)

8. Don't Talk to the Judge About the Case Without Opposing Counsel Present

Legal rules prevent ex parte (one sided) contacts with the judge. You wouldn't want the other lawyer to talk to the judge out of your presence; you should follow the same rules. Normally, if a judge or one party suggests a meeting either at the judge's bench (sometimes called a sidebar conference) or in the judge's chambers (office), both sides must be represented. Sometimes it will be up to you to help arrange a mutually convenient time for such a meeting.

9. Never Talk to Jurors About the Case Before the Verdict

If you are conducting a jury trial and happen to pass one of the jurors in your case in the hallway, a nod, smile or "hello" is permissible. But do not enter into any discussion with a juror or make any remarks or comments about your case that a juror could possibly overhear.

10. Be Discreet

Do not discuss your case with witnesses, family members or anyone else in any public place where you can be overheard, such as the elevators, bathrooms or cafeteria. The lawyer for your opponent is likely to know many people in the courthouse, and your words may quickly be passed along.

11. Ask for Help If You Are Treated Badly

Once a trial starts, it is normally too late to request a different judge. (See Chapter 7, Selecting the Decision-Maker, for how to challenge a judge before trial.) This does not mean, however, that you are helpless if you are treated in a demeaning or hostile way. For example, if you ask a simple question and are given a stern lecture that only idiots appear in court as pro pers and that you should immediately hire a lawyer, it's pretty clear that you are facing a steep uphill battle. However, you can:

- Ask to speak to the judge privately. If the judge agrees, tell her that you are doing your best to follow the rules, and point out politely that you have the right to represent yourself and be treated respectfully.

- Write a letter to the presiding judge (head or chief judge) of the court. The Clerk's Office can tell you who this is. Describe the specific instances in which you were treated unfairly and ask that another judge be assigned to your case.

- If all else fails, consider filing a written motion with the court requesting a mistrial, disqualifying the judge on the grounds that the judge's bias (prejudice) against pro pers is making it impossible for you to have a full and fair trial.

If the judge's clerks or law clerks treat you unfairly or rudely, follow similar guidelines. First try speaking with them in a polite but firm way. If they do not improve, write a note to the judge (or presiding judge if you don't get anywhere with your judge) about the problems.

3

STARTING AND INVESTIGATING YOUR CASE

Almost nobody wants to go to court. So people usually attempt to resolve disputes out of court, informally, before filing a lawsuit. For example, if someone owes you money from a contract you both agreed to, you will most likely ask the person for the money before suing. If your request is denied, you may try another phone call, a written request for payment (demand letter) or perhaps a face-to-face negotiation session. Assuming enough money is at stake, your next step might be to show you mean business by hiring a lawyer to call or to write on your behalf. If you still haven't gotten paid, you might suggest a formal mediation or arbitration proceeding. (See Chapter 1, Going It Alone in Court, for more on these out-of-court processes, called "alternative dispute resolution" or ADR).

Eventually, however, if the person who owes you money continues to refuse to pay, you have a choice to make: you can either bring a lawsuit or write off the money.

⚠ Can You Sue? These days, many companies, such as banks, realtors and insurance companies, include mandatory arbitration or mediation clauses in the contracts you sign to do business with them. These provisions mean you must resolve any dispute you have with the company through one of these out-of-court dispute resolution methods; you cannot bring a lawsuit in court.

If you decide to file a lawsuit, what you do before your case gets to trial—including the documents you write and investigations you conduct—can often have a big impact on the trial itself. For that reason, this chapter gives you an overview of how people start and investigate lawsuits. But the main focus of this book is to explain the in-court process of trying a civil case. Each state's courts and the federal courts follow different pre-trial procedures, and this book does not attempt to comprehensively cover the myriad of procedural details you may encounter getting your lawsuit into court and wending your way through the litigation process. Instead, as we recommended in Chapter 1, as soon as possible you should obtain information on the specific rules followed by your court system (your state or the federal courts). (See Chapter 1, Going It Alone in Court, Section E.)

RESOURCES ON PROCEDURAL RULES

To locate resources that can help you learn the necessary procedural rules involved in civil lawsuits, see Chapter 19, Legal Research. For a quick summary, try West's *Civil Procedure in a Nutshell,* by Mary Kay Kane (West Publishing Co.). For more detailed information, we recommend the following:

Civil Procedure, by Friedenthal, Kane and Miller (2nd Ed., West Publishing Co.)

Civil Procedure, by James and Hazard (4th Ed., Little, Brown & Co.)

Moore's Federal Practice, by James W. Moore (Matthew Bender)

Federal Procedure Forms, Lawyer's Edition (Lawyer's Coop/Bancroft Whitney)

Fundamentals of Litigation for Paralegals, by T. Mauet and M. Maerowitz (Little Brown & Co.).

A.   DO YOU HAVE A GOOD CASE?

Before you decide to file a lawsuit, you should do at least enough research and investigation to be sure that the facts and law support a legally valid claim. For example, the fact that your adversary gave you a menacing look is not a legally valid claim, unless the look was accompanied by some threatening action. Or, if a car lightly touched your fender but did not damage your car or hurt you in any way, you don't have a solid legal claim.

But many of the disputes and injuries that occur in our daily lives do give rise to legally valid claims. A typical problem for which you may want to sue to recover damages (money) is the auto accident in which you suffered broken bones, pain and a damaged car, or a contract you made to have a new roof built, which the roofer breached by using inferior quality materials, causing the new roof to leak.

But even if your claim is valid, it won't be worth your while to bring a lawsuit if your adversary has no money or assets, since you will not be able to collect any money if you win. So before you go to court, be sure to read about collecting judgments.

(See Chapter 17, When Your Trial Ends: Judgments and Appeals.)

HOW TO SETTLE A PERSONAL INJURY CASE

If you are injured by someone else's intentional or negligent (careless) acts, chances are good you will be dealing with that person's insurance company. For the uninitiated, this isn't easy since the insurance company's personnel are experienced in dealing with personal injury ("P.I.") cases and you probably aren't. To help you close this information gap, take a look at *How to Win Your Personal Injury Claim,* by Joseph Matthews (Nolo Press). It takes you step-by-step through the insurance claims system, explaining how to determine what your claim is worth and how to negotiate a fair settlement.

RESOURCES ON EVALUATING YOUR CASE

Shepard's/McGraw Hill publishes a 15 volume series called *Preparing for Settlement and Trial* by the Shepard's Editorial Staff. It's compilation of articles on current legal topics such as age discrimination, construction site accidents, securities fraud and products liability. Each article has information to help a lawyer assess the strengths and weaknesses of a case, including checklists that point out what to ask for in discovery and citations to relevant legal authorities.

B.   HOW A LAWSUIT BEGINS

In the beginning of a lawsuit, the parties must file several documents with the court.

1.   Plaintiff's Complaint

The complaint is the document that starts a lawsuit. It sets forth the legal claims and what action the plaintiff (person bringing the lawsuit) wants the court to take.

> **The names may change, but pleadings are essentially the same.** A complaint or initial pleading is called a "petition" in some courts or for some types of cases. When the term "petition" is used, the person suing is called the "petitioner," and the person responding is called the "respondent."

For example, someone hurt in a car accident may sue the other driver. In the complaint, the plaintiff may ask the court to order the other side, usually called the defendant, to pay monetary damages to compensate the plaintiff for bodily injuries and damage to his car from the accident. Translated into everyday language, that complaint may say something like:

"The defendant hit my car. He hit my car because he carelessly ran a red light, which is against the law. I suffered damages in the amount of $100,000 because of his carelessness—$10,000 for the car repairs, $50,000 for medical bills, $20,000 in wages I lost since I couldn't work because of the injuries and $20,000 for the tremendous pain suffered. Therefore, I want the court to order the defendant to pay me $100,000."

To draft (write up) your complaint in the proper format, you should first determine if your court requires you to use a court-approved form. Ask at the Clerk's Office and read the court rules. If you don't have to use a specific court-approved form, follow the example of many lawyers and consult a legal form book in the law library. As the name implies, form books are collections of legal documents written in a fill-in-the-blank style. (See Chapter 19, Legal Research, for more on legal form books.)

> **Check your local court rules before you try to file anything.** In many courts, it is customary, and may be required by court rule, to submit papers on "pleading paper," which is just 8½" by 11" paper with line numbers running down the left side of each page. You can get a supply of this paper at a stationery store. Or, if you use a computer to type your documents, check to see if your word processing program offers it as a built-in option.

Some courts impose other rules on how papers must be presented. They may, for example, require two holes to be punched at the top of the page, so papers can be inserted directly into the court's file folder. They may require you to attach what's sometimes called a "blue-back"—a stiff piece of blue paper—to the back of your papers.

> **Sample forms are illustrations, not models.** Throughout this book, you will find examples of legal documents that you are likely to encounter. We include these samples only to give you an idea of what the documents may look like. Because rules differ in different court systems, the actual documents used in your case may vary greatly from the samples. (See Chapter 19, Legal Research, for how you can find forms that meet specific requirements in your court.)

SAMPLE COMPLAINT

1 Nolo Pedestrian
   [Street Address]
2 [City, State, Zip Code]
   [Phone number]
3
   Plaintiff in Pro Per
4

5

6

7

8   THE _____ COURT OF _____ COUNTY

9   STATE OF _____

10

11 Nolo Pedestrian,   )
)
12   Plaintiff,   )
)
13   v.   )   Case No. _____
)
14 Sarah Adams,   )   COMPLAINT
)
15   Defendant.   )
)
16 _____)

17

18   1. On approximately January 1, 19XX, at 3 p.m., while plaintiff was crossing Main Street at Elm

19 Street in the City of _____, defendant Sarah Adams drove her truck through the

20 crosswalk, negligently failing to stop for plaintiff, and thereby injuring plaintiff.

21   2. As a result of defendant's negligent driving, plaintiff's leg was broken, causing substantial pain

22 and suffering, medical expenses, and lost income.

23   WHEREFORE, plaintiff prays for judgment against defendant in the sum of $100,000 plus costs and

24 interest.

25

26   *Nolo Pedestrian*
                                          _____
27   Nolo Pedestrian, Plaintiff in Pro Per

28

💡 **You can amend your complaint.** Pleadings such as the complaint can normally be amended (changed) after they are filed. For example, assume you are Nolo Pedestrian, the plaintiff suing Ms. Adams in her car accident example just above. After you have already filed a complaint against her, you determine that the companies that manufactured the car and the brakes may also be legally liable, and you want to add these companies as defendants.

Typically, if the defendant has not yet responded by filing an answer, you do not need permission from the court to amend. But you do need permission from the judge if the defendant has already answered your complaint. In that case you will have to file another paper with the court, a request for "leave" (permission) to amend your complaint, in which you state the reasons for the changes.

2. Summons

After a complaint is filed with the Clerk's Office (along with the required filing fee), the court issues a paper called a "summons." The purpose of a summons is to let the defendant know she is being sued and to tell her a number of important facts about the case, including the names of the plaintiff and defendant (called the parties), the name, address and phone number of the plaintiff's lawyer (if she has one), the case number (assigned by the Clerk's Office) and the dates the next pleading (normally, the defendant's answer) must be filed.

Generally, the plaintiff then arranges for the summons and complaint to be served on (physically delivered to) the defendant. Rules about how a summons and other legal documents must be served (called "service of process") must be strictly followed. If they are not, sometimes the lawsuit cannot go forward. Service of process is governed by Federal Rule of Civil Procedure 4 in federal courts, and you can usually find local service rules in your state's Civil Procedure statutes. (See Chapter 19, Legal Research, for more on finding legal rules and reference books.) Here are some rules about service of process that apply in many court systems:

- Normally, as a party to the lawsuit, you may not personally serve your own complaint and summons (if you are the plaintiff), or your own answer (if you are the defendant). You also cannot serve your own motions (requests for a court order) or subpoenas (court orders compelling someone to come to court). Another person must serve these pleadings for you. In some states, legal documents must be served by a law enforcement officer (sheriff, marshal or constable) or a licensed, private process server; in other states, any adult not connected with the lawsuit can serve legal papers.

- A complaint must be served on the defendant within a certain time after it is filed. For example, in federal courts a complaint and summons must be served within 120 days after filing (Federal Rule of Civil Procedure 4(j)) and within 60 days under certain state rules.

- To serve legal documents on a business—for example, when your adversary is a company rather than an individual—you usually don't have to serve them personally. In most cases, it's enough to have the document dropped off at the business place and have a copy of the document mailed to the business address where it was left.

- Some courts don't require personal delivery at all in certain circumstances; they allow service by regular U.S. mail.

- Courts require proof of service, usually in the form of a signed document that states when, how and on whom the complaint and summons were served. Often, you must file a proof of service whenever you file any type of pleading with the court. (See Federal Rule of Civil Procedure 4(g).) There's usually a deadline for filing. For example, a proof of service must be filed within 90 days of filing the complaint in some court systems.

You can be reimbursed for filing fees. The filing fee that the plaintiff pays when the complaint is filed with the Clerk's Office is considered one of the "fees and costs of suit." That means if the plaintiff wins the lawsuit, the court may order the defendant to reimburse the plaintiff for the filing fee. American courts typically do not, however, order the losing party to pay the winner's attorney fees.

3. The Defendant's Response

A defendant must answer within a short period of time (often 30 or fewer days) after being properly served with a complaint and summons. For example, under Federal Rule of Civil Procedure 12(a), the defendant has to serve an answer within 20 days after the complaint and summons is served.

If a defendant fails to respond in time, the plaintiff can apply for what's known as a "default judgment." (A default judgment is a court order granting a judgment against the defendant to pay the amount requested in the complaint, based on the defendant's failure to answer or defend against the lawsuit after having been given proper notice.) In some courts, the plaintiff simply files a Request for Default Judgment with the Clerk's Office. In other courts, the plaintiff must appear in court to show the judge that the threshold requirements for a valid claim have been met (this is sometimes called a "prove up" hearing).

Once a default judgment is "entered" (filed and written into the official court records), it has the status of any other judgment. It is as if the plaintiff had conducted and won a full trial. A defendant may, however, move very quickly to have it set aside (undone and taken off the record). A judge will usually set aside a default judgment only if the defendant was not served properly, or if the defendant's failure to answer the complaint or show up in court is excusable. For instance, if the defendant was in the hospital at the time the papers were served, or the defendant's attorney neglected to respond on behalf of the defendant, the judge might set aside a default judgment. (For reference, default judgments in federal courts are governed by Federal Rule of Civil Procedure 55, reasons for setting them aside by Rule 60(b).)

If you are a defendant and you have not defaulted, there is more than one way in which you can respond to a complaint. You can file a document called a "demurrer" or a "motion to dismiss complaint for failure to state a claim," which are documents stating that the complaint does not state a legally valid claim (governed in federal court by Federal Rule of Civil Procedure 12(b)). Or, more typically, you file an "answer"—a document that denies the allegations in the complaint. For

SAMPLE PROOF OF SERVICE

1   Nolo Pedestrian
     [Street Address]
2   [City, State, Zip Code]
     [Phone Number]
3

     Plaintiff in Pro Per
4

5

6

7

8   THE _____ COURT OF _____ COUNTY

9   STATE OF _____

10

11   Nolo Pedestrian,   )
)
12   Plaintiff,   ) Case No. 12345
)
13   v.   ) DECLARATION OF SERVICE BY MAIL
)
14   Sarah Adams,   )
)
15   Defendant.)
)
16   _____

17   Ms. Dana Lauren, the undersigned, hereby declares:

18   I am a citizen of the United States. I am over the age of 18 years and not a party to the within

19   action. On February 28, 19XX, at the direction of Nolo Pedestrian, Plaintiff in Pro Per, I served the

20   within COMPLAINT FOR NEGLIGENCE AND SUMMONS on the following interested party by mailing,

21   with postage thereon fully prepaid, a true copy thereof to:

22   Greta Charles, Esq., Attorney for Sarah Adams, Defendant

23   [Street Address]

24   [City, State, Zip Code]

25   I declare under penalty of perjury that the foregoing is true and correct.

26   Executed at [City, State] on February 28, 19XX.

27

28   *Dana Lauren*
                    Dana Lauren

example, the answer filed by Ms. Adams, defendant in the car accident case, will in essence state, "I wasn't careless, so I don't owe the plaintiff any money at all."

A defendant may also admit some of the plaintiff's allegations, deny others or state that he doesn't have the information necessary to know whether an allegation is true or false. (See Federal Rule of Civil Procedure 8(b).) For example, if the first allegation of the complaint simply stated that you were driving on Elm Street on the date of the accident and you (Sarah Adams) were in fact driving there, then you would probably admit that allegation, and then go on to deny the other allegations that you contend are not true.

In addition to admitting or denying the charges in a complaint, a defendant's answer may also con-

tain "affirmative defenses." These are reasons why the defendant should not be held liable for the acts in question. (Affirmative defenses are governed in federal court by Federal Rule of Civil Procedure 8(c).) You can see in the sample answer that in addition to denying she was careless, Adams stated an affirmative defense: because the accident occurred more than two years ago and the two-year statute of limitations (deadline) to file a personal injury case has expired, it is too late now for the plaintiff to sue.

4. Counterclaim

Counterclaims are often part of a defendant's answer. They seek to turn the lawsuit around by stating that the plaintiff committed legal wrongs against the defendant and that it's the defendant

"We'll see your hundred thou and countersue you a million."

SAMPLE ANSWER

1	Sarah Adams, Defendant
	[Street address]
2	[City, State, Zip Code]
	[Phone number]
3	
	Defendant in Pro Per
4	
5	
6	
7	
8	THE _____ COURT OF _____ COUNTY
9	STATE OF _____
10	

11	Nolo Pedestrian,	)
12	Plaintiff,	) Case No. 12345
		)
13	v.	) DEFENDANTS ANSWER TO
		) PLAINTIFFS CIVIL ACTION
		) FOR NEGLIGENCE
14	Sarah Adams,	)
		)
15	Defendant.	)
16	_____	)

17

18   Defendant Adams answers the complaint as follows:

19   1.   Defendant admits that on January 1, 19XX she was driving in the vicinity of Elm and Main

20   Streets, but Defendant denies each and every other allegation in paragraph 1.

21   2.   Defendant denies each and every allegation in paragraph 2.

22   Defendant asserts the following affirmative defense:

23   Plaintiff is barred from pursuing the cause of action stated in Plaintiff's Complaint under the

24   State of _____'s applicable statute of limitations for negligence actions as it occurred

25   more than two years before the Complaint was filed.

26   WHEREFORE Defendant prays that Plaintiff take nothing and that Defendant be awarded all

27   fees and costs of suit.

28   *Sarah Adams*
                                          Sarah Adams, Defendant in Pro Per

who is entitled to money damages or other relief from the plaintiff. As far as the counterclaim is concerned, the original defendant takes on the role of plaintiff. For example, defendant Adams' counterclaim may allege, "I was not careless, and besides, if the plaintiff hadn't run out into the street between two parked cars, then he would have seen me and I wouldn't have had to jam on my brakes to stop for him. That caused the $2,000 kitchen cabinets I was transporting to break. It took weeks to get them replaced, so I was late on a important construction job, which cost me $6,000. Between that and the two broken cabinets, the plaintiff owes me $10,000."

5. Cross-Complaint (or Cross-Claim)

Another pleading that may be filed early in a case is a cross-complaint. This document, filed by a defendant, brings a third party into the lawsuit. The defendant claims that the third party is really responsible for whatever harm the plaintiff suffered. For example, the substance of a cross-complaint Adams might file would be, "Yes I hit the plaintiff, but the accident happened because my defective brakes failed. Therefore, the plaintiff should be suing the manufacturer of the car; I don't owe the plaintiff anything."

C. INVESTIGATING YOUR CASE INFORMALLY

As discussed above, before you file or respond to a lawsuit you should research enough of the facts and law to at least be clear that you do have a legally valid claim or defense. But you will almost certainly need to do more research once your initial pleadings have been filed. You have to determine what facts you need to prove to support your legal claims or disprove the plaintiff's claims and, given the rules of evidence and procedure, how best to prove them. You'll want to talk to witnesses and locate key documents, some of which you may be able to use during your trial. (See Chapter 12, Exhibits.) You will also use what you learn in pre-trial investigation to help analyze the strengths and weaknesses of your case and that of your adversary.

For instance, assume you are the plaintiff in a car accident case. You probably want to talk informally with any witnesses to the accident and read (or re-read) the police report (if the police came to the scene and wrote up a report). You may also want to go back to where the accident occurred and map out or photograph where you, your adversary, witnesses and other vehicles were at the time of the crash.

Evidence can disappear or fade. If you intend to photograph a scene or interview witnesses, try to do so as soon as possible after the situation that caused your dispute occurred. Any substantial delay may cause locations to change in appearance and memories to fade.

You can often gather a lot of information informally from all sorts of sources (often for little or no money) by just asking for it. For example, you can:

• Ask for copies of all sorts of government and business records that affect your claim, such as bank records, medical charts, police reports and insurance claims forms. (Chapter 12, Exhibits, explains how to use such documents in court.) You may have to pay for photocopying, but that probably won't cost too much.

- Search public records for information about your opponent. This information can often be valuable in deciding whether the defendant has sufficient assets to allow you to collect your judgment if you win your lawsuit. For example, if your adversary owns real estate, that will show up in the files of the county land records office where the property is located.

- Get information that a private company maintains on file, such as financial documents or complaints it has received.

- Ask your opponent for copies of any documents you feel may help you. For example, assume you are suing the roofer who put up a new roof that collapsed during a rainstorm. To determine whether inferior supplies were used, you may ask the roofer for copies of invoices for the materials and supplies purchased before and during the time she repaired your roof.

Some people and companies will let you look through documents without putting up a fight at all; others will do so only after you negotiate with them a bit. If your opponent refuses to give you information, you can try a little persuasion. Call or write and say something like, "I can, as you know, get a subpoena (court order) requiring you to deliver this information, but it would be less costly and simpler for everyone if you just give me the documents I have requested."

You can use more formal, court-authorized methods of gathering information from your adversary, called "discovery," which are discussed in Section D, below.

 It doesn't hurt to ask. With informal investigations, the bottom line (to quote the Rolling Stones) is, "You can't always get what you want, but if you try sometimes you get what you need." And sometimes what you need may come from the least likely places. For instance, if you are suing:

- your landlord for failure to keep the apartment livable, your apartment manager or a long-time tenant may have a great deal of information about the landlord's history of maintaining the building

- your former employer for age discrimination in firing you, company employees may talk to you about company policies having to do with hiring and firing older workers, or

- the driver of the car that side-swiped you, surprisingly even the defendant's friends or family may talk to you about the facts of your dispute, the defendant's injuries or her drinking problem.

You never know until you ask.

RESOURCES ON INVESTIGATING CASES

One book that develops comprehensive theories, guidance and sample dialogues for investigating cases is *Fact Investigation: From Hypothesis to Proof*, by David Binder and Paul Bergman (West Publishing Co.)

A fairly long series called *Modern Trials*, by Melvin M. Belli, Sr. (2nd Ed., West Publishing Co.) includes a significant amount of material on researching and preparing, as well as presenting, many types of complex personal injury cases. It is geared toward trial lawyers.

D. DISCOVERY

Discovery is the name for formal investigation about the facts of a case. Parties conduct discovery in order to prepare for trial. Mostly it consists of one party asking the other party or a witness written or oral questions or requesting the admission of certain facts. A party may also ask to see documents and records that are in the exclusive control of the other party. Some kinds of discovery, such as interrogatories (written questions), can usually only be directed to parties to the lawsuit. Others—depositions (oral questioning), for example—can be used to gather valuable information from witnesses and other people not named in the lawsuit. The most common forms of discovery—interrogatories, depositions, requests for production of documents and requests for admission—are explained in this chapter.

The scope of discovery inquiries is fairly broad. Under Federal Rule of Civil Procedure 26 and many similar state rules, a party can ask for any information that is likely to lead to admissible evidence, even if the information itself is not admissible. (Chapter 13, Basic Rules of Evidence, discusses admissibility of evidence.)

Usually, discovery cannot begin until a complaint has been filed. Generally, it is conducted by the parties, following court rules without direct court supervision, unless a problem develops. Parties can, however, ask the court to order (compel) answers when someone refuses to answer legitimate discovery requests or gives insufficient, evasive or argumentative answers.

In the past 20 years, the discovery process has become riddled with abuses. Some lawyers ask for piles of information about every possible aspect of a case, to which the other side responds with a discovery blitz of their own. Too often the result is an out-and-out discovery war. Such wars sometimes take place to pressure opponents into settling—for example, when a deep-pocketed defendant (such as a big corporation) inundates a small business or individual plaintiff with so much discovery the plaintiff is forced to settle because it costs too much money and time to respond. Other times, excessive discovery is used by lawyers to generate big fees.

To combat such abuses, many courts have adopted streamlined discovery rules. Typically, they require each side to simply and quickly disclose all key facts about their cases to each other at the outset. Also, some judges set discovery time limits at the first pre-trial hearing (often called a "status conference" or "pre-trial conference") so that all discovery is completed promptly. Many judges now handle certain routine discovery disputes by phone to speed up the process and are quick to sanction (fine) lawyers and pro pers who deliberately abuse discovery. Check with the judge's law clerk or court clerk to see if the court or your judge follows special discovery dispute resolution procedures.

RESOURCES ON DISCOVERY FORMS

For sample forms and further information, consult a book on discovery practice in your court, or a lawyer's continuing education or law practice guide book on the specific kind of discovery you want to conduct. Two books you may use are:

Bender's Forms of Discovery (Matthew Bender)

Mastering Written Discovery: Interrogatories, Documents, and Admissions, by John Hardin Young (Butterworth Legal Publishers).

Discovery must usually be completed within fairly tight deadlines. Mark them on your calendar and plan to abide by them. If you absolutely cannot complete all your discovery in time, try to get your opponent to agree (stipulate) to an extension. Sometimes the court must sign off on any such extensions, especially if they excessively delay the litigation process.

Because discovery is largely handled by the parties without court intervention, you and your adversary can resolve many issues that arise. For example, you can agree:

- to extend the time you have to answer interrogatories or requests for admission

- to produce a copy of a document at the next court hearing you both are scheduled to attend rather than send it (if it's in storage), or

- to have the other party come to your office to inspect documents, so you don't have to box and deliver them.

Keep written records of everything you and the other side agree to, in case there is a problem later on. Send a letter confirming whatever the other side tells you they will do, noting too whatever you say you will or won't do and the date your agreement took place. Keep copies of such letters and of all the discovery requests you send or respond to.

1. Interrogatories

Interrogatories are written questions that your adversary must answer under oath. This means the person answering is subject to the laws against perjury for responding falsely to questions. Interrogatories are governed by Federal Rule of Civil

Procedure 33 and similar state rules, but these rules may be modified by local rules. For example, local rules may limit the number of questions you can ask.

Interrogatories may pertain to any subject that is likely to lead to evidence you can eventually use in your case. That means you (and your opponent) can ask a fairly wide variety of questions. For example, if you are the plaintiff in a car accident case and you want to determine whether the defendant's judgment was impaired by alcohol or drugs, you can send the defendant interrogatories asking, "What, if any, chemical substances did you ingest on the day of the accident?" Or to see if the person was on the way to or from an important meeting or was nervous or distracted because of some other event that day, ask, "Describe all your activities during the few hours before the accident."

Interrogatories are generally an inexpensive method of obtaining useful information. However, they are far from perfect. Since you are not present when your adversary answers, he can give vague or evasive answers and you can't easily pin down a more exact response. For example, answering the question above about the defendant's activities before the accident, she might simply say she "worked all day." That doesn't tell you specifics about whether she worked at her office, went to an important meeting or made job site inspections. Remember this when writing interrogatories and try to make your questions narrow enough to get the information you need.

2. Depositions

Depositions are oral questions answered under oath. (Federal Rules of Civil Procedure 27-32 focus on depositions.) Depositions usually take place out of court, often in law offices. At a pre-arranged time, the person who will answer questions (the deponent) comes to the office of the person taking the deposition, or any other agreed-upon location. A court reporter takes down everything that is said and later produces a written transcript.

You can obtain very useful information from taking the deposition of your opponent (and if your adversary is a business, someone who represents the business, such as the owner or manager), a witness, an expert or someone else who has information about your case. But depositions are costly, since you must pay a court reporter to attend and transcribe the session. And they are time-consuming to schedule, prepare and conduct.

Since you can often get enough information about the facts in your case through informal investigation and written discovery (such as interrogatories and requests for admission, that are less expensive than depositions), you may not need to conduct any depositions at all. You'll probably want to wait until you have tried to obtain the information you need informally and inexpensively before scheduling a deposition.

SCHEDULING A DEPOSITION

For the most part, you can schedule a deposition where and when it is convenient to you. Lawyers often schedule depositions in their own offices. If you have an office, you may want the deposition to be on your home turf. If you do not have access to an office, you may schedule the deposition at your home, a hotel or your opponent's or her lawyer's office.

You must give reasonable written notice (often at least ten days, but check your rules) of the scheduled date and time to your adversary and the deponent. You can obtain a sample notice of deposition from the court clerk or a form book.

You also will need to serve the deponent with a subpoena (the legal document that compels the person to appear at the deposition), along with notice of the deposition. (More on subpoenas in Chapter 9, Direct Examination.) And if you want the deponent to bring along copies of documents you want to see or use in questioning the person, you must also serve him with a special type of subpoena called a "subpoena duces tecum" (also explained in Chapter 9).

Next, arrange for a court reporter to record the deposition. Ask your legal coach or someone in the Clerk's Office to recommend a good court reporter, or check a legal newspaper or the phone book. For a 2- to 3-hour deposition, court reporter rates may range from $200 to $450, so it pays to shop around.

Lastly, it is good practice to confirm the date, time and place with your adversary, the deponent and the court reporter before the deposition.

Deposition questions can cover most any aspect of your case, and things people say on the record in a deposition can and often will be used in trial. (Chapter 10, Cross-Examination, discusses how to use information obtained in discovery to impeach (discredit) witnesses' credibility at trial.) For example, assume Sarah Adams (the defendant from the car accident case above) said in deposition that at the time of the accident she was on the way to the hospital to pick up her daughter, who had just been injured at school. But later, at trial, she says she was just out for a drive at the time of the accident—not headed anywhere in particular. As plaintiff, you may ask permission to read from the deposition transcript in order to show the judge or jury Ms. Adams's inconsistent statements. You may even ask her to read from the transcript, then ask her a question like, "In your deposition you said you were on the way to the hospital, but a few moments ago you told this court you were out for a drive. Where were you going?" Such a question may well damage her believability, unless she has some way of reconciling the conflicting statements.

While the scope of proper discovery is generally broad (anything likely to lead to admissible evidence), certain questions are improper. And, just as you can object during trial when your adversary asks an improper question, so too can the deponent during a deposition. It's improper to ask someone to divulge information told to a lawyer or doctor in confidence. Questions that are totally irrelevant to the case are also improper. For example, if you are the defendant in a car accident case, it is improper for the plaintiff to ask if you've ever had any extramarital affairs. (How to deal with objectionable questions is discussed in Chapter 4, Pre-Trial Hearings and Motions.)

If you or one of your witnesses is asked an improper question, you can object to the question and refuse to answer. If a dispute about objections cannot be resolved between the parties (by re-phrasing or withdrawing the question), you may need a judge to resolve it. Often this can be done by phone or fax, but it may require a formal court hearing.

IF YOU ARE DEPOSED

- Listen carefully to the questions.

- Tell the truth.

- Don't volunteer information. Answer only the question asked—no more, no less.

- If you are asked more than one question at a time, ask the questioner to break them up.

- If you are confused, tired or uncomfortable, ask for a break. (You might confess your weak bladder at the outset of the deposition so you don't feel awkward taking frequent bathroom breaks.)

- If you don't hear or understand a question, ask that it be repeated—as many times as is necessary for you to understand it.

- If you believe a question is objectionable, state your objection clearly, on the record. If a question really seems out of line, request that your adversary ask all her other questions and let the judge decide if you have to answer this one. Otherwise, answer the question after objecting, so that you can at least preserve your right to later argue that the information be kept out at trial.

RESOURCES ON DEPOSITIONS

The Deposition Handbook: A Guide to Help You Give a Winning Deposition, by Virginia A. Lathan (Curry-Co Publications) is a clearly written, short and simple guide for taking depositions or being deposed.

3. Requests for Production of Documents

Requests for production of documents are written requests for the opposing party to locate and deliver (or send) specific documents that they possess that relate to your case. (See Federal Rule of Civil Procedure 34 and similar state rules.) Like interrogatories, requests for production of documents are generally an inexpensive method of obtaining useful information.

It is important, if you make this type of request, to describe specifically the documents you want your adversary to produce. For example, you cannot simply say something as vague as, "Give me every document you have relating to our lawsuit."

What types of documents do you want to review? If you are the plaintiff in a car accident case, you might send a document production request to the defendant for:

- a copy of the pink slip, to help you prove the defendant owned the car

- the defendant's proof of insurance, to help determine whether you will ever be able to collect the money if you win the case

- receipts from any recent repairs or servicing of the car, to help you prove the car was in working order—which in turn can help refute defendant's claims that it was the brakes, not her carelessness that caused the accident

- the defendant's business appointment book, to learn if and when the defendant had scheduled appointments on the day of the accident—if she were going to an important meeting at the time she hit you, she may have been distracted.

Request documents early on in the case. For documents that you know you need to see from the beginning of your case, it's best to send your requests for production early on, along with interrogatories. Often, however, it is only through ongoing informal investigation, interrogatories or depositions that you learn what documents to request. If so, you will need to send a document production request later or send more than one request. And you may need to request extra time if you don't receive your opponent's answers to interrogatories until just before the discovery deadline and don't have time to request documents.

Reading through and analyzing documents received from your adversary may help you understand the facts of your case, prepare to examine witnesses and plan other aspects of handling your case up to and during trial. For example, while he is testifying on the stand, you may want to show the witness notes from his business appointment book and ask him to tell you about the various appointments he had that day.

You may also introduce into evidence (have considered by the judge or jury) some of the documents you receive from the other side. (Chapter 12, Exhibits, explains how to introduce exhibits into evidence.)

4. Requests for Admissions

Requests for admissions are true-false questions that ask a party to admit, under oath, the truth of particular facts. (For reference, see Federal Rule of Civil Procedure 36 and similar state rules.) You can

SAMPLE REQUEST FOR PRODUCTION OF DOCUMENTS

```
 1    Nolo Pedestrian
      [Street Address]
 2    [City, State, Zip Code]
      [Phone Number]
 3
      Plaintiff in Pro Per
 4

 5

 6

 7

 8              THE _____ COURT OF _____ COUNTY

 9                        STATE OF _____

10

11    Nolo Pedestrian,                        )
                                              )   Case No. 12345
12                      Plaintiff,            )
                                              )   PLAINTIFF PEDESTRIAN'S FIRST
13    v.                                      )   REQUEST TO DEFENDANT ADAMS FOR
                                              )   PRODUCTION OF DOCUMENTS
14    Sarah Adams,                            )
                                              )
15                      Defendant.            )
                                              )
16    _____

17

18        Plaintiff Nolo Pedestrian requests, pursuant to Federal Rule of Civil Procedure 34 which our state has

19    adopted, that Defendant Sarah Adams produce the following documents by delivering them to the

20    office of Nolo Pedestrian located at [Address] within 30 days from the date of service of this Request:

21        1.  Registration and proof of ownership of the truck driven by Defendant Adams which struck Nolo

22    Pedestrian on  January 1, 19XX.

23        2.  Receipts and records showing all maintenance and repairs to the truck referred to in Request 1

24    above, during the one-year period before January 1, 19XX.

25        3.  Copies of Defendant Adams' business records reflecting Adams' appointments on January 1,

26    19XX, the day of the accident in question in this lawsuit.

27
                                              Nolo Pedestrian
28                                            _____
                                              Nolo Pedestrian, Plaintiff in Pro Per
```

use them to find out what your opponent will admit in court and what will be contested. You can send requests for admission only to your named adversaries, not to witnesses or others who aren't parties to the lawsuit.

The big advantage to this type of discovery is that if your opponent admits something, he or she is bound by that admission at trial. The judge will accept (or in a jury trial, the judge will instruct jurors to accept) already admitted facts as true. So it is crucial to be careful about what facts you admit and to keep close track of the facts your opponent admits.

> ⚠️ **Answer admissions requests on time.** Usually, if a party does not admit or deny each request for admission within 30 days after being served, the statements are deemed admitted, meaning they will be treated as true at trial. In other words, the judge or jury will accept the fact and consider it as evidence in your case. It is therefore critical to answer admissions requests by the deadline. And if you make any agreement with the other side to extend the time to answer a request for admissions, put it in writing and keep a copy.

Often, admissions requests are used after other discovery has taken place to narrow down the remaining issues for trial. For example, you can ask your adversary to admit the following: "I, Sarah Adams, consumed at least one alcoholic beverage within the hour before the accident occurred during the day of March 31." If she doesn't answer your requests for admission on time and they are deemed admitted, it will be an uncontested fact

that she consumed some alcohol. If she admits she drank some alcohol, you will still probably want to develop evidence regarding when and how much she drank (for example, by talking to potential witnesses and maybe deposing the defendant herself), but this admission would clarify your task. And if she denies she did, you know you must take another tack or continue looking for evidence from other sources.

Another possible request for admission is, "At the time of the accident, I was en route to an important business meeting." If the defendant admits this or fails to respond (and the fact is deemed admitted), it will help prove your theory that she was careless because she was thinking about her business meeting instead of concentrating on the road.

If you are served with a request for admissions from your opponent, you have several choices. Whichever you choose, however, remember to respond within the allotted time or you will have admitted all the facts as true. You can:

- Admit a fact as true. If you know something is true, admit it. If you don't, and your opponent later proves the fact at trial, even if you win the case, your opponent can request the court to sanction you (punish you, usually with a fine) for failure to admit something you knew was true.

- Deny the statement, if it is untrue.

- Object to the question, if objectionable.

- State that you neither admit nor deny the fact because it is disputed or because you do not have enough information to admit or deny it.

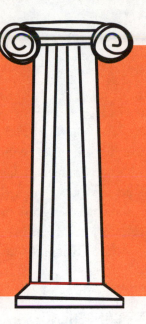

4

PRE-TRIAL HEARINGS AND MOTIONS

You will likely have to appear in court at least once, and maybe several times, before your trial occurs. The most common reasons are to attend pre-trial conferences and hearings on motions. These proceedings, and the legal documents filed in conjunction with them, are the focus of this chapter.

A. PRE-TRIAL CONFERENCES

At some point before your case goes to trial, the court may require one or more pre-trial conferences. (For reference, in federal courts, pre-trial conferences are governed by Federal Rule of Civil Procedure 16.) The main purpose of a pre-trial conference (sometimes called a status conference) is to identify the issues remaining to be resolved and focus the evidence that will be presented at trial. But judges can also use them to set discovery deadlines, and a trial date and ensure that your case is moving along. Some courts will resolve these issues by telephone so the parties do not have to go to court. Check with the Clerk's Office in your court.

Often, you and your adversary must prepare and bring to this conference a document called a "pre-trial memorandum." This specifies the uncontested and contested legal and factual issues, the exhibits that will be introduced and witnesses who will testify at trial, and the jury instructions (rules the judge will read to the jurors before they go off to reach a verdict).

Your court may have special forms; ask at the Clerk's Office. If it doesn't, you can find forms for pre-trial memoranda in the law library, in form books on civil litigation. (See Chapter 19, Legal Research.)

Sometimes a pre-trial memorandum must be prepared jointly—that is, you must meet with your adversary (by phone, by mail or in person) to coordinate and provide the information requested by the court. This process (sometimes called a "meet and confer") encourages parties to settle the case before it goes to trial or at least agree on certain issues so as to narrow the scope of the dispute.

B. SETTLEMENT CONFERENCES

Some settlement conferences take place between the parties, out of the judge's presence altogether—for example, at your office or that of your adversary's lawyer. But the judge may also conduct a settlement conference, either as part of a pre-trial conference or separately. Over 90% of lawsuits settle (end in an agreement between the parties before a judgment is rendered), so most courts require or at least encourage settlement conferences in order to push the process along.

If a judge conducts a settlement conference, it will typically take place in the judge's chambers (office) with all parties present. Some judges vigorously push the parties to settle, even suggesting a dollar amount; others just let each side describe the strengths and weakness of their case and ask a few questions to encourage dialogue between them. Some judges have individual conferences with each party too. If your judge does this, be sure to ask that anything you say remain confidential.

Regardless of where and how it takes place, a settlement conference can be a good opportunity to resolve issues without the cost and delay of trial. If you either choose to or are required to attend a settlement conference (sometimes abbreviated as

"MSC" for mandatory settlement conference), know the strengths and weaknesses of your own case. Be prepared to:

- Try to figure out where the judge stands with respect to your case. Often the judge will signal fairly clearly how she views the case. For example, if she strongly encourages you or your adversary to settle, ask yourself why. Does she think one side's case is weak?

- Try to learn more about your adversary's case. What are they going to contest? What will they admit? Are they willing to settle? Don't be afraid to ask pointed questions. The judge's approach may be to get all the cards out on the table, and the judge may have the same questions you do.

- Try to negotiate a compromise with the other side. It doesn't have to be a winner-take-all deal. You can agree to accept part of what your adversary wants from you (if you are the defendant), or part of what you want from your adversary (if you are the plaintiff). Or you can strike a new bargain. For example, if you are suing a building contractor, your settlement could include partial payment in cash and the rest in remodeling your home.

"Why don't you fellows just go outside and settle this in the parking lot?"

SHOULD YOU SETTLE?

To negotiate effectively, try to put aside your emotional involvement in the dispute and make a businesslike analysis of whether it makes sense to settle. Look at:

- How much time and money are involved. For example, if you estimate that preparing and trying your case might involve 150 hours of your time, and you value your time at $30 per hour, it's obvious that it would make sense to settle now for at least $4,500 less than you might expect to get at trial.

- How good a chance you have of winning at trial. Analyze the strengths and weaknesses of your case and your adversary's.

- How time-consuming or costly it will be to collect the judgment if you do win.

- How tired you are of fighting with your adversary. Psychologically, is it taking a toll on you or your family? Are you missing a great deal of work (or play) preparing for and dealing with the case?

C.   PRE-TRIAL MOTIONS

A motion is a request, usually in writing, for a judge to make an order (decision or ruling) with regard to a legal issue that arises in the course of a lawsuit.

The issue may simply be a scheduling matter, such as in a motion to request a continuance (extension of time). For example, you may want to request that the trial itself be postponed from May 1 to June 1. Or, the issues may be complex and cut to the very heart of the case, such as a motion for summary judgment (a request for the judge to make a final judgment without going to trial because affidavits establish that the facts are not in dispute).

Making and responding to motions (called motion practice) can be confusing, but do not let it daunt you. If you believe there are issues you can or should resolve before trial, you may benefit from filing a motion. If your adversary files a motion, review and analyze the facts and legal issues in the motion and any documents attached to it. Go over them with your legal coach, if you have one. Then, carefully provide enough factual and legal analysis (described below) to formulate reasoned responses, and present your position to the court in a written response and orally at the court hearing, if one occurs.

1. Motions: An Overview

Since this book's main focus is trial, the information on motions is meant as background. This chapter highlights some of the important rules and procedures involved in pre-trial motion practice, but it is not a comprehensive guide. Courts have rules you should consult governing how and when motions can be filed.

a. When Motions Are Made

Depending on what you're asking the court to do, a motion can be made before, during or after trial. Some motions are made orally and others in writ-ing, depending on the rules of court and the type of decision you are requesting that the judge make. For example, during trial, parties make oral motions to strike (delete improper testimony from the record). This chapter focuses mainly on motions that arise before trial, most of which must be made in writing. Check the rules in your court to be sure.

MOTIONS MADE DURING AND AFTER TRIAL

The following motions can be made during and after trial:

- **Motion in Limine.** A request for a court order excluding irrelevant or prejudicial evidence, typically made at the outset of a jury trial. (See Chapter 14, Making and Responding to Objections.)

- **Motion to Strike.** A request that the judge delete improper testimony from the trial record. It's usually made after the judge has ruled that particular testimony is not admissible. (See Chapter 14.)

- **Motion for a Directed Verdict.** Typically made in a jury trial after the plaintiff has presented evidence, this motion is a request that the judge rule against the plaintiff without letting the matter go to the jury. The usual reason is that the plaintiff has not established the legal claims as a matter of law. (See Chapter 17, When Your Trial Ends: Judgments and Appeals.)

- **Motion for Judgment Notwithstanding the Verdict ("JNOV").** Also in jury trials, this is a request by one party for the judge to rule against the other party, after the jury has already decided in the other party's favor. This motion effectively asks the judge to overrule the jury (See Chapter 17, When Your Trial Ends: Judgments and Appeals.)

b.   Who Can Make a Motion

Only a named party to the case, such as you or your adversary, may file a motion. Witnesses, for example, may not make motions.

c.   The Basic Motion Process

The party bringing a motion usually must write several documents (discussed below, in Section 3). Then, the opposing party has a chance to oppose the motion. Unopposed motions are often granted by the judge without a hearing. If the motion is opposed, frequently the judge will decide, based on the parties' papers alone without scheduling a hearing in court, whether to grant or deny the motion. If a hearing is scheduled, it will be before a judge (no jury) and will likely be relatively short—often much less than 30 minutes. A hearing gives the parties a chance to answer questions from the judge and argue the motion.

Some judges do not even preside over trials, only motions (called "law and motion" courts or divisions in courthouse lingo). Because these courts are busy, the judge has probably considered similar motions countless times before and likely has many other motions on calendar the same day as yours; you may have only a few minutes to state your reasons for wanting or objecting to the motion. The judge's ruling on a motion may be made at or after the hearing. If it's made later, you will be notified about the judge's decision by mail.

d.   Frivolous Motions

A party must have a valid legal basis for filing a motion.

Some people use motions for reasons other than what they state in their papers—for example, to delay proceedings or to increase their adversary's costs, perhaps in an effort to force their adversary to drop the case or settle cheaply and quickly. Do not do this. Make sure any motion you bring is truthful and that what you request is legitimate.

Judges have begun to crack down on frivolous (without a valid legal basis) motions. A party who can show that the other side has filed a frivolous motion may request sanctions (punishment—usually a fine) against both that party and her attorney. If one side files a series of frivolous motions, the judge may even rule that the other side wins the case.

If your adversary has acted outrageously, in a way that prejudices your case, you can make a motion for sanctions. For example, you may ask for sanctions if your adversary has asked for repeated continuances seemingly for the purposes of delay or harassment. Or, ask for sanctions if your adversary refused to stipulate and forced you to go to court for a continuance even though you gave an excellent reason (such as your being in the hospital) why the earlier date was not suitable.

Like other motions, a motion for sanctions should state what you want and why, and should include supporting documentation describing what happened, such as a declaration or affidavit, discussed in Section 3, below. For example, if your adversary repeatedly forces you to come to court on frivolous motions, you may ask the court to order him to pay your expenses in preparing for and attending those hearings.

Don't ask for sanctions unless your adversary's conduct is outrageous. Sanctions are serious business, and most judges do not impose sanctions unless a party's conduct is fairly outrageous. It makes sense to ask for sanctions only in extreme cases, and to be sure of the facts before you make accusations.

2. Is a Motion Necessary?

Before making a written motion or responding to one made by your adversary, try to informally reach an agreement. For example, if you need to postpone a deadline, you might ask your adversary to agree to a "continuance." If the other side agrees, you can prepare a document called a "Stipulation to Continue [insert name of what's been continued]." Ask the court clerk and check the rules in your court for any special procedures for preparing and filing one. Typically, both you and your adversary must sign the stipulation and file it with the court. If both sides agree, the court will probably grant the continuance without requiring either you or your adversary to appear in court. The clerk will then schedule the matter for a later date, as agreed, and notify the parties of the new date and time.

A sample of a stipulation for a continuance of the hearing date on a motion for summary judgment is shown below.

3. What Goes into a Motion

Your motion must tell the court exactly what you want and why you want it. Unfortunately, legal proceedings are rarely that simple; you must put your request and reasoning in the form the court requires and expects. (For reference, Federal Rule of Civil Procedure 7(b) governs the form of motions in federal courts.) This section discusses documents you typically must prepare in order to make a motion.

a. Notice of Motion

A legal document called a "Notice of Motion" gives notice to (informs) your adversary that you are bringing the motion, so that she has time to prepare for the court hearing and possibly respond in writing. Your Notice of Motion should tell the other party:

1. When the motion will be heard. This means the court hearing date, time and place.

2. The grounds (reasons) for your motion.

3. What supporting documents you will be referring to in your request to the judge, such as "points and authorities" (written legal arguments which support the reasons for your motion with citations to relevant laws) or declarations or affidavits (sworn factual statements).

b. The Motion

The motion is your request to the judge for a specific court order. It states what you want and why you are entitled to that particular order. To justify your request, sometimes it's enough to include a short reference to the rule of law that entitles you to the order, especially for routine matters. (See sample motion for continuance in Section 7, below.) Other times, however, especially in more complex motions, you may need to list (cite to) other relevant legal authorities, such as court cases, and explain how those authorities support your position. This type of explanation and citation is

SAMPLE STIPULATION TO CONTINUE

```
1   SARAH ADAMS
    [Street address]
2   [City, State, Zip Code]
    [Phone number]
3
    Defendant in Pro Per
4

5

6

7

8          THE _____ COURT OF _____ COUNTY

9                      STATE OF _____

10
                                      )   CASE NO. 12345
11  Nolo Pedestrian,                  )
                                      )
12                    Plaintiff,      )
                                      )   STIPULATION TO CONTINUE HEARING ON
13      v.                            )   PLAINTIFFS SUMMARY JUDGMENT MOTION
                                      )
14  Sarah Adams,                      )
                                      )   Date:   April 15, 19XX
15                    Defendant.      )   Time:   10:00 a.m.
                                      )   Place:  [Court Address]
16                                    )           [City, State, Zip Code]
                                      )           Courtroom 10
17  _____)

18

19

20  Defendant Sarah Adams and Plaintiff Nolo Pedestrian agree to the following:

21     The parties jointly request that Plaintiff's Motion for Summary Judgment, set for hearing before this

22  Court on April 15, 19XX, be continued to a date and time convenient to the Court, on or after June 15,

23  19XX.

24

25  _Sarah Adams_____          _March 8, 19XX_____
    Sarah Adams, Defendant  in Pro Per       Date
26

27  _Nolo Pedestrian_____          _March 1, 19xx_____
    Nolo Pedestrian, Plaintiff in Pro Per     Date
28
```

called a Memorandum of Points and Authorities. (Consult a legal form book or your self-help law coach for more on how to prepare this type of document. See Chapter 19, Legal Research.)

c.   Supporting Documentation

As supporting documentation, you may need to include statements of facts in the form of a declaration or affidavit (see sample, below, in Section 7). You may also include copies of other relevant documents as exhibits (attachments).

4.   Scheduling a Court Hearing on a Pre-Trial Motion

Some motions are made, responded to and ruled on by the judge in writing—all without a court hearing. In some courts, motions can be argued on telephone conference calls. But many times, a party bringing a motion must obtain a court hearing date for the judge to consider and rule on a motion. The court clerk can tell you how to obtain a hearing date in your court. In many places, you schedule a date by phoning the court. The clerk will assign you a hearing time and enter your case on the court docket (calendar) for that day.

When you phone the clerk, be prepared to give your case name and number, the type of motion and an approximate time you want to schedule the hearing (if you have a choice). For example, you might say: "Yes, this is Sarah Adams, the defendant in *Pedestrian v. Adams*, Case No. 12345. I would like a court date, if possible in about six weeks, for a summary judgment motion."

Sometimes, courts have a particular time or day of the week devoted solely to hearing motions ("law and motion" day) or special law and motion judges

(different from the judge who will conduct your trial). When you call, ask the clerk when motions are heard.

> 💡 **Double-check the judge's calendar.** Court schedules sometimes change at the last minute. For example, judges sometimes try to clear their calendars (hear routine or uncontested matters first, then move on to disputed and or complex proceedings) or otherwise change their calendars around. It is good practice to check with the judge's clerk the day before just to verify the time of your hearing and how early you should be there. This may have an extra advantage, too, of showing the clerk that you respect the courtroom routine and appreciate the clerk's help.

5.   Serving and Filing Your Documents

To give your adversary adequate notice, you must often have the papers served at least ten to 15 days before the motion is due to be heard in court. Federal Rule of Civil Procedure 6 (d) requires notice of at least five days for most types of motions; local rules often extend that time period.

Ask the court for time to respond to a motion. If your adversary schedules a motion and gives you less than one week's notice of the hearing date and time, you may want to let the judge know. The judge may reschedule the hearing or reprimand your adversary—especially if you have not had time to respond or prepare. To protect yourself, always note the date you receive documents from your adversary or the court.

Most courts allow you to serve (deliver) your Notice of Motion, Motion, Reply and related documents by mail. (Federal Rule of Civil Procedure 5, Sections (a), (b) and (c), and your state's equivalents govern how service must be made.) The papers you serve should include a copy of your proof of service, a signed document stating when, how and on whom the Notice was served. Keep a second copy of the proof of service for your records and file the original with the court, as required by your court's rules.

Typically, you are not allowed to serve your own documents; check the rules in your court. Often you must have an adult who is not a party to the lawsuit mail or deliver your documents. The person who actually serves your motion for you is the one who should sign the proof of service.

In addition, you must typically file originals with the court. (See Federal Rule of Civil Procedure 5 (d) and (e) or the rules in your state which govern filing papers with the court.) You can file legal papers in person at the courthouse Clerk's Office (where you filed your complaint or answer), or you may be able to file documents by mail. Check your local rules and talk to a clerk (or your legal coach), for other rules, such as the number of copies you must file. You may want to take an extra copy to the court to "conform" (stamp the document as filed on the date received) and give back to you for your files. If you file your documents in person, you can wait for your conformed copy. If you mail the documents, you may need to send an extra copy clearly marked "Please Conform and Return to [your name and address]" with a self-addressed, stamped envelope.

6. Court Hearings on Motions

Before a judge grants or denies a written motion, the judge may hold a brief court hearing. There are no jurors and normally no witnesses, although sometimes a judge will want to hear testimony in connection with a complex motion. But, typically, any factual information from you, your adversary or a witness is presented in the form of a declaration or affidavit—a statement of facts personally observed, which is dated and signed under penalty of perjury.

Some judges issue a tentative ruling, based on the papers you and your adversary have filed, a day or two before the hearing. It states which way the judge is inclined to rule (for or against the motion) and sometimes the reasons for the judge's decision. Ask the court clerk if your judge makes tentative rulings and when you can call to find out a particular ruling. It may help to know in advance what the judge thinks so that you can use the hearing to respond to the judge's particular concerns.

On the day of your hearing, the clerk will call out the name of your case when it's your turn. You and your adversary will go to counsel table to argue the motion. Whoever brought the motion (called the movant or moving party) will usually argue first.

After the movant, the respondent (party responding to the motion) argues. Both sides make points based on the law and the facts, showing why the judge should or should not grant the request. Since the judge already has documents setting out the parties' positions, it is usually unwise to repeat exactly what is in the papers. The whole hearing typically lasts no more than ten to 15 minutes.

Watch a motion hearing before arguing one. A good way to get a feel for how argue a motion is to go sit in on a motion in the court where you will argue before your hearing. Note where people sit and stand, where the microphones are, how much time the judge seems to spend with people and what types of questions she is asking. Also, use any time you have before your hearing begins to review your own notes and observe carefully what the judge seems to expect from others arguing before you.

Though a hearing is not a trial, you should observe the same formalities when arguing a motion. Stand when you make your presentation, and address the judge as "Your Honor." Don't talk directly to or argue with your adversary (or her lawyer). (See Chapter 2, The Courthouse and the Courtroom.)

At the end of the hearing, the judge will often make a final decision, either orally or in writing. Other times, the judge may decide to take the matter "under submission." That means the judge will think about it and let you know the ruling later, in writing.

If the judge makes an oral ruling, take detailed notes to be sure you know its exact terms. Also make sure you know who is in charge of writing up the order and notifying all interested parties (people who are affected by the ruling). Sometimes the clerk prepares the order for the judge to sign; other times the judge asks one party (most often the winning party) to draft the order for the judge to sign, and give notice of the court's order. If you are asked to draft an order, refer to your notes and check with the clerk as to exactly what form the notice should take. One good approach is to ask the clerk for a sample and a list of everyone who must be notified.

WHO MUST BE NOTIFIED

In many cases, the notice list (names and addresses of the interested parties who should be notified about court decisions in the case) is relatively short: your adversary and the court. However, a notice list can be quite long. For example, even in the most routine bankruptcy matters, notice of motions must often be given to all creditors (people owed money).

Because notice can be defective (invalid) if necessary people are not included, find out who must be "noticed" (notified) of specific decisions that arise in your case. Do this by checking your state and local rules about notice (or federal and local rules if you are in federal court). Also, if the judge asks you to draft an order, ask the judge directly who must be given notice.

---

7.   Common Pre-Trial Motions

This section focuses on common pre-trial motions: those relating to continuances, discovery issues, summary judgment and dismissing a complaint. It contains sample motion papers and dialogues from court hearings to give you an idea of what may come up when you bring or respond to a motion.

> ⚠️ **Don't rely on these sample motions.** The sample motions in this chapter are only illustrations. To draft (write) a motion in your case and be certain you are using the format and language required by your court, refer to your local court rules and a legal form book. Form books, often used by lawyers to prepare motions, also contain helpful explanations about the relevant legal references and factual information (called "Points and Authorities") you may need to include to support the position you are taking in your motion. (Chapter 19, Legal Research, discusses form books.)

a. Motion to Dismiss

If a defendant thinks the plaintiff's claims are not legally valid, the defendant can ask the judge to dismiss the complaint before trial. Essentially, the defendant is saying, "Even if everything the plaintiff says in the complaint is true, the plaintiff isn't entitled to anything from me." The defendant makes this request by filing a motion to dismiss a complaint for failure to state a claim (in some courts this is called a demurrer, pronounced "de murr er").

For example, say the plaintiff's complaint asserts a legal claim of assault, alleging that you gave the plaintiff a menacing look. A look, though perhaps frightening and even rude, does not by itself amount to an act for which the plaintiff can bring a valid lawsuit. Only if you had also taken some threatening action, such as swinging your fist, would the plaintiff have a legally valid claim of assault.

If the motion is denied, and the complaint is held to be valid, the defendant will have a short time (often another 30 days) to answer the complaint. If the motion is granted and the complaint dismissed, the judge may allow the plaintiff a chance to amend (fix), refile and reserve the complaint and summons on the defendant.

b. Motion for a Continuance

The purpose of a motion for a continuance is to delay the date of a hearing, settlement conference, deposition or even the trial itself. For example, if you will be hospitalized for surgery when a motion is supposed to be heard, or if a witness will be out of the country on the date set for trial, ask for a continuance.

Some courts routinely grant one continuance, especially if the other side does not object; others want to see a good reason for the delay before they grant a continuance. This may be especially true in courts that have adopted "fast track" or expedited procedures—streamlined systems to move cases along at a faster pace than in traditional systems. You may be granted a continuance if a scheduled surgery causes you to be hospitalized but denied a continuance if you are simply going on vacation.

If you are the moving party, and you cannot reach an agreement with your adversary about a postponement, you will need to tell the judge, in your papers, why the current date is bad. Next, point out that you and the other side have discussed the problem. The judge will likely appreciate your efforts to handle the matter in a friendly way.

If you oppose a continuance, emphasize in your reply papers why a delay would prejudice (hurt) you. For example, you may point out that an important witness will not be available if trial is delayed. Or you may argue that the other side appears to be requesting repeated continuances in an effort to stall or force you to settle.

For example, assume you are Sarah Adams, a building contractor whose truck struck a pedestrian (named Nolo) as he crossed Elm and Main Streets. Mr. Nolo has sued you; you are the defendant and you are representing yourself. You had barely sent your answer (reply to the plaintiff's complaint) when the plaintiff's attorney sent you a Notice of Motion for Summary Judgment (request for the judge to resolve the case without going to trial because the facts are not in dispute).

You believe the plaintiff's attorney is bringing the motion because he thinks you will be easily intimidated as a pro per, and won't know how to respond. You think he's hoping to get a quick court judgment or advantageous settlement if he moves fast, before you get a chance to prepare. All you know for sure is that you were not driving carelessly, and that you dispute the plaintiff's claim that you were negligent. In addition, you believe that investigation may reveal that the plaintiff's injuries did not come from your truck, but from some pre-existing injury. To oppose the motion, you will need to show that there is a factual dispute that should go to trial. But you need additional time to gather evidence about what really happened. So far, you have not had a chance to conduct any discovery or other investigation.

You should first contact the other side and ask them to agree to continue the hearing to a later date. You do, and they refuse. (Keep records of your request and their refusal.) You are left with two choices:

1. Oppose the summary judgment at its scheduled date and time, with little evidence to back up your legal position.

2. File a motion for a continuance of the summary judgment motion hearing, so you have time to find at least enough evidence to show that there is a genuine dispute of facts.

You decide to bring the continuance motion. After calling (or writing, if your rules require it) the clerk to get a hearing date for your continuance motion (see Section 4, above), you draft a Notice of Motion, Motion and Declaration, which might look something like the ones shown below. A sample reply, which your adversary might file to oppose you motion, is also shown below.

SAMPLE NOTICE OF MOTION AND MOTION REQUESTING CONTINUANCE

1   SARAH ADAMS
[Street Address]
2   [City, State, Zip Code]
[Phone Number]
3

Defendant in Pro Per
4

5

6

7

8   THE _____ COURT OF _____ COUNTY

9   STATE OF _____

10

11   Nolo Pedestrian,   )   CASE NO. 12345
)
12   Plaintiff,   )   NOTICE OF DEFENDANT'S MOTION AND
)   MOTION REQUESTING CONTINUANCE OF
13   v.   )   PLANTIFF'S SUMMARY JUDGMENT MOTION;
)   DECLARATION OF SARAH ADAMS
14   Sarah Adams,   )
)   Date: March 17, 19XX
15   Defendant.   )   Time: 10:00 a.m.
)   Place: [Court Address]
16   )   [City, State, Zip Code]
)   Courtroom 10
17   )

18

19   TO PLAINTIFF AND HIS ATTORNEY(S) OF RECORD:

20   You are notified that on March 17 at 10 a.m. in Courtroom 10, Defendant Adams will bring a

21   motion to continue the Plaintiff's Summary Judgment Motion. The Plaintiff's Summary Judgment

22   Motion was originally scheduled for April 15,19XX. The Defendant will move the court to continue that

23   date for at least 60 days so that Defendant has adequate time to conduct discovery and respond to

24   the Plaintiff's Motion.

25   This Motion is based on the Notice of Motion, the Motion itself and the attached Declaration of

26   Defendant Adams. Any responses to this Motion must be served not later than March 12, 19XX.

27   Date: March 6, 19XX   *Sarah Adams*
                                         _____
28   Sarah Adams, Defendant in Pro Per

SAMPLE MOTION

<u>MOTION REQUESTING CONTINUANCE OF</u>

<u>PLAINTIFF'S SUMMARY JUDGMENT MOTION</u>

Defendant Adams moves this Court for an order continuing the hearing on Plaintiff's Summary Judgment Motion, presently scheduled for April 15, 19XX, to a date not less than 60 days after April 15, 19XX. In support of this motion, Defendant asserts:

1. Defendant was served on February 28, 19XX, with the Plaintiff's Summons and Complaint.

2. Defendant was served on March 5, 19XX, with the Plaintiff's Notice of Hearing on Summary Judgment Motion scheduled for April 15, 19XX.

3. Because Defendant has not had adequate time to conduct discovery, Defendant cannot adequately respond at this time to the Plaintiff's Motion.

4. Under Federal Rule of Civil Procedure 6(b), this Court has discretion to extend the time period in which Defendant must respond to the Motion and continue the date at which Plaintiff's Motion will be heard.

WHEREFORE, Defendant requests that this Court continue the hearing date of Plaintiff's Motion to a date not earlier than 60 days after April 15, 19XX, and extend the amount of time within which Defendant must respond to that Motion accordingly.

Date: March 6, 19XX

Sarah Adams
———————————————————
Sarah Adams, Defendant in Pro Per

-2-

SAMPLE DECLARATION

<u>DECLARATION OF SARAH ADAMS</u>

I, Sarah Adams, declare under penalty of perjury:

1. I am the Defendant Sarah Adams, and I am acting as my own attorney in the case of Pedestrian v. Adams (Case No. 12345) currently pending in the _____Court of _____ County in the State of _____.

2. On February 28, 19XX, I received the Plaintiff's Summons and Complaint.

3. On March 5, 19XX, I received notice of the Plaintiff's Summary Judgment Motion originally scheduled for April 15, 19XX.

4. As of March 5, 19XX, when I received the notice, I had not yet had time to take any discovery to obtain information I need to adequately defend myself in the pending case.

5. I intend to send at least one set of interrogatories to the Plaintiff. I also plan to depose Cynthia White, a witness at the scene of the accident.

6. On March 5, I phoned Plaintiff's lawyer and explained to her that I need additional time in order to conduct and complete this discovery so that I can adequately respond to the Plaintiff's Summary Judgment Motion. But she refused to agree to a continuance.

7. After the Plaintiff refused my request to continue the Summary Judgment Motion, I prepared this Motion for Continuance and had it set for the earliest available court date, March 17, 19XX.

I declare under penalty of perjury that the foregoing is true and correct.

Date: March 6, 19XX   Signed: *Sarah Adams* _____
                                         Sarah Adams, Defendant in Pro Per

-3-

SAMPLE DECLARATION OF SERVICE BY MAIL

1	SARAH ADAMS
	[Street Address]
2	[City, State, Zip Code]
	[Phone Number]
3	
	Defendant in Pro Per
4	

THE _____ COURT OF _____ COUNTY

STATE OF _____

Nolo Pedestrian,	)	CASE NO. 12345
	)	
Plaintiff,	)	DECLARATION OF SERVICE BY MAIL
	)	
v.	)	
	)	
Sarah Adams,	)	
	)	
Defendant.	)	
	)	

Ms. Dana Lauren, the undersigned, declares:

I am a citizen of the United States. I am over the age of 18 years and not a party to this action. On of March 6, 19XX, at the direction of Sarah Adams, Defendant in Pro Per, I served the within NOTICE OF DEFENDANT'S MOTION AND MOTION REQUESTING CONTINUANCE OF PLAINTIFF'S SUMMARY JUDGMENT MOTION; DECLARATION OF SARAH ADAMS on the following interested party by mailing, with postage thereon fully prepaid, a true copy thereof to:

Loretta Charles, Esq.
Attorney for Nolo Pedestrian
[Street Address]
[City, State, Zip Code]

I declare under penalty of perjury that the foregoing is true and correct.

Executed at [City, State] on the 6th day of March 19XX.

Dana Lauren
Dana Lauren

SAMPLE REPLY OPPOSING MOTION

1 LORETTA CHARLES, Esq.
   [Street Address]
2 [City, State, Zip Code]
   [Telephone]
3
   Attorney for Nolo Pedestrian, Plaintiff
4

5

6

7

8   THE _____ COURT OF _____ COUNTY

9   STATE OF _____

10

11   ) CASE NO. 12345
    Nolo Pedestrian,   )
12   )
                            Plaintiff.   ) NOTICE OF OPPOSITION TO DEFENDANTS
13   ) MOTION REQUESTING CONTINUANCE OF
       v.   ) PLANTIFFS SUMMARY JUDGMENT MOTION
14   )
    Sarah Adams,   )
15   ) Date: March 17, 19XX
                            Defendant.   ) Time: 10:00 a.m.
16   ) Place: [Court Address]
)   [City, State, Zip Code]
17 _____)   Courtroom 10 _____

18

19 TO DEFENDANT ADAMS, IN PRO PRO:

20   Plaintiff objects to Defendant's Motion to Continue Plaintiff's Summary Judgment Motion originally

21 scheduled for April 15, 19XX. Defendant has had ample time to investigate. The facts are clear and

22 not in dispute, and the Court's and parties' time would be greatly economized by going forward with

23 the Motion on the date and time scheduled. This Notice of Opposition to Defendant's Motion is based

24 on the Notice itself and the attached Declaration of Plaintiff Pedestrian.

25

26 Date: March 9, 19XX   *Loretta Charles*
                                                 _____
27   Loretta Charles, Esq.
                                                 Attorney for Plaintiff Nolo Pedestrian
28

SAMPLE DECLARATION

<u>DECLARATION OF NOLO PEDESTRIAN</u>

I, Nolo Pedestrian, declare under penalty of perjury that:

1. I am the Plaintiff, Nolo Pedestrian, in the case of <u>Pedestrian v. Adams</u> (Case No. 12345) currently pending in the _____ Court of _____ County in the State of _____ .

2. On or about February 28, 19XX, I caused Defendant Sarah Adams to be served with a Complaint and Summons.

3. On or about March 5, 19XX, I caused Defendant Sarah Adams to be served with a Notice of Motion and Motion for Summary Judgment.

4. The defendant has had approximately 10 days from the date she received the Complaint, and nearly two years since the accident occurred, to investigate this case.

5. The facts are clear and undisputed in this simple negligence action. They are set out in the Summary Judgment Motion and Declarations supporting that motion, which was filed with this Court on or about March 5, 19XX.

The above is true and correct to the best of my personal knowledge.

Date: March 8, 19XX   Signed: *Nolo Pedestrian*
                                                 _____
                                                 Nolo Pedestrian, Plaintiff

The date for the hearing on the continuance motion arrives. You arrive in court, a few minutes early, dressed in a businesslike manner, and check in with the clerk, giving your name and the case name and number. You then wait until your case is called. Finally you hear the clerk or judge say "*Nolo Pedestrian v. Sarah Adams. Are the parties present?*" If you and your adversary have both checked in, the clerk may tell the judge that you are here. You both stand to signify your presence. When the judge calls or motions for you to approach, you take your places at counsel table.

In this instance, you are the moving party (the one making the motion), so you will likely be called on first. Typically the judge will ask what you have to say. Here's what might follow:

1 **You:**

Good morning, Your Honor. I am Sarah Adams, the defendant in this matter. I am a building contractor here in [city], and I am representing myself. The reason I am requesting a continuance is simple. The plaintiff scheduled a summary judgment motion two weeks after my answer was filed. I have not had time to thoroughly investigate the case. I plan to serve interrogatories on the plaintiff. I will also probably take one or more depositions. I feel strongly that once I have investigated more thoroughly, I will be able to demonstrate that I was not careless.

2 **Judge:**

This is not trial, and I don't want to hear arguments or testimony.

3 **You:**

Your Honor, I was merely trying to say that I think I will be able to show very soon that there are significant factual disputes, but I need more time. This summary judgment motion is premature. And, having to go forward with one now would unfairly prejudice my right to a fair hearing in this case.

As you see by the judge's comment, the judge may interrupt to ask questions or steer you toward the proper issues. Here the judge may continue with questions about the discovery you plan to take, the facts as you know them right now or whether you have tried to get the opposing party to stipulate to a continuance. The judge may also turn to your adversary.

4 **Judge:**

What are your objections to such a continuance?

5 **Your adversary (Responding Party):**

Your Honor, as stated in our papers, we feel the defendant has had ample time to conduct discovery. We have not been served with any interrogatories or received notice about any depositions. We don't believe the defendant really intends to conduct any discovery. The defendant just wants to try to keep this matter pending as long as possible to force a settlement. My client is injured....

6 **Judge:**

Do you have any response?

7 **You:**

Well, yes, Your Honor. That is simply not true.

I have no hidden agenda of forcing a settlement. I just want to be treated fairly and to have sufficient time to prepare. My adversary is represented by counsel, but I am not a lawyer and I am not as familiar with all of the legal proceedings. I have been working on interrogatory questions and will get them out as soon as I possibly can. Just 60 more days, which can't possibly hurt them, would be most helpful for me to get the facts straight and know how to respond to the summary judgment motion.

8   Judge:

Motion granted. Defendant will have an additional 60 days to respond to plaintiff's summary judgment motion.

If the judge rules your way, don't allow your elation to get in the way of your need to clarify some key information. You need to record the exact date and time the case is continued to and find out whether, as the victorious party, you will be responsible for preparing the court order (the document, signed by the judge, that officially changes the date of the hearing).

c.   Discovery Motions

If problems arise during discovery, you or your adversary may need to go to the judge with a motion asking the court to order the other side to comply with discovery requests. If you send interrogatories, for example, and your adversary refuses to answer one or more of them, you can file a motion asking that the judge compel an answer. If a person who is ordered to answer still refuses to do so, the judge can sanction (fine) or hold him in contempt of court. Contempt of court usually means imposing a fine or even a short jail sentence if he continues to refuse to comply with a court order.

The flip side of a motion to compel a response to discovery is called a motion for a protective order —an order allowing you not to answer certain questions. (In federal courts, these orders are allowed under Federal Rules of Civil Procedure 26(c) and 30 (d).) A party can seek a protective order if the other side's discovery request causes undue annoyance, embarrassment, oppression or expense.

Try to get your adversary to agree before you file a motion. Before filing a motion to compel a response to discovery or for a protective order (to avoid having to respond to discovery), try to get your adversary to give you some or all of the information voluntarily. For example, if your adversary doesn't respond adequately to your interrogatories, don't rush into court. Instead, try to work out the problem— perhaps by rephrasing the questions. You might even write a formal letter setting forth why you believe you have a right to the information (if they are objecting) or why you feel you should not have to reveal the information (if you are objecting to your adversary's discovery requests).

A persuasive letter indicates that you mean business and are not willing to drop the issue, and it may resolve the dispute. And if your negotiations ultimately fail and you eventually bring a motion, the letter (which you can attach as an exhibit) shows the judge that you attempted to resolve the matter without costing the court time and money, but that the other side simply refused to cooperate.

You may want to consult your legal coach before answering questions to see if they are improper. But it is generally improper to ask questions that:

- Force someone to reveal a confidential, privileged communication, such as a statement made to a lawyer during a lawyer-client consultation, to a doctor during a medical examination or to a spouse.

- Require an enormous amount of time, money or other resources to comply with. For example, if you are a small business owner and you are asked to produce every piece of paper you signed having to do with your employees for the last three years, you may ask that the request be confined to a shorter, more relevant time period or otherwise narrowed.

- Are asked to harass rather than to discover some admissible evidence—for example, a question about sexual history or a possible past criminal record.

- Are in no way relevant to the case. Although the standard for relevance in discovery is much looser than in the trial itself, neither you nor your adversary can seek information about matters that are totally unrelated to the case.

(Federal Rule of Civil Procedure 37 and your state's equivalents govern discovery disputes.)

If the court finds you have shown good cause for a protective order, the judge can help you out in a variety of ways, from blocking your adversary's entire discovery request to limiting the people who must attend a deposition, sealing (keeping confidential, out of the public record) the discovery or otherwise regulating the request.

Resolve discovery disputes with a phone call if you can. Since discovery problems are frequent, and going to court to resolve them is expensive and wasteful, many courts have established a phone conference procedure so that a judge can quickly resolve such disputes. Check with the court clerk or your judge's clerk to see if such a procedure is available.

Obviously, if you are initiating a motion to compel, it is because you need the information and believe your request is reasonable. Your papers must tell the judge why this is true. Usually this means saying how it will be helpful to lead you to relevant evidence in your case, and that it will not hurt or unfairly prejudice your adversary to reveal it.

If you are opposing your adversary's motion, you need to give the judge a good reason why you should not have to turn over the information requested. The grounds listed above are some of the reasons you may assert.

For example, say a request asks you to describe each and every conversation you've had with your business partner, Edwin, during the last ten years. Especially if you and Edwin do business on a daily basis, putting together the description requested would be a full-time job for many months, if not impossible. In this case, you will at least want to have the request narrowed down.

To illustrate this motion, turn again to the case about the auto accident at Elm and Main, *Nolo Pedestrian v. Sarah Adams.* This time, assume that you are the plaintiff. You were crossing the street when the defendant's truck hit you. You are trying to prove that the defendant, a building contractor, had gotten a phone call reporting a missed job site inspection just before the accident occurred. You will try to show at trial that the call caused her to be distracted and drive carelessly. As part of your discovery, you have requested these documents:

- records pertaining to all other traffic accidents in which Defendant has been involved, to see if she has had other similar accidents

- business books and records from her business, to determine how common missed inspections are, and how much money is at stake because of a missed inspection

- her phone bill for that month, to verify the exact time the inspection phone call was received.

You served the defendant with a request for production of documents asking for driving and business records. She refused to produce these documents because she is represented by a lawyer who is trying to bully you. You get the feeling they think that if they refuse your discovery requests, you won't know what to do and may just give up without fighting. But you have confidence in yourself (and you have this book), so you fight back. You bring a motion to compel the production of the requested documents.

Before you can go to court, of course, you have to get a hearing date, and draft, file and serve your motion to compel. (See Sections 4 and 5, above.) When your hearing date arrives, after you check in and wait for your case, your hearing may proceed as follows.

1 **Judge:**

Mr. Pedestrian, I have read your papers, and you have undoubtedly seen my tentative rul-

ing. I am inclined to grant your request as to the business records and phone bill, and order Ms. Adams to produce them immediately. But I am going to deny the driving record request. Do you wish to add to your written arguments?

2 **You (Plaintiff Pedestrian):**

Yes, Your Honor. I would ask that the court also order the respondent to produce the driving records. It is essential to my case to see how many other people have suffered from her negligence in the past.

3 **Judge (turning to the respondent/defendant):**

Do you have any response?

4 **Ms. Miller, Defendant's attorney (Respondent):**

Yes. As Your Honor knows, such evidence, even if it existed, would be inadmissible evidence of prior acts —not to mention irrelevant to what happened on the day of the accident in question. We should not be required to produce that driving record now or ever, and strongly urge that your tentative ruling be made final as to that issue.

[For more on why such evidence would not be admissible in court, See Chapter 13, Basic Rules of Evidence.]

5 **Judge:**

So ordered. Ms. Adams does not have to produce her driving records. Now, as to the business records and phone bill. Respondent, do you have any good reason why the movant should not be allowed to inspect these?

6   **Ms. Miller:**

Again Your Honor, these records are irrelevant to the case. My client's business had nothing to do with the accident. Plaintiff ran in front of my client's truck, she tried to swerve, but….

7   **Judge:**

This is not the trial. I am not going to hear evidence today. Your client has her version, and the plaintiff has his. Unless you can tell me why he should not be allowed to fully investigate his theory, which includes reviewing your business records, I will order you to produce them.

8   **Ms. Miller:**

Your Honor, even if you were to believe my client's business records are relevant, which we contend they are not, the plaintiff's request is too broad. He has asked for all my client's business records from the past five years. If he is really just concerned about the cost of missed inspections, then at least we would ask that you limit the request to those inspections we missed during the month of the accident only. Otherwise, their request will put my client out of business. She'll have to spend all her time going through back records, and will lose many new projects because of it.

9   **Judge (turning to you):**

Any response?

10   **You:**

Nothing I haven't written in my papers, Your Honor. The defendant's business records are

essential for me to prove how much the fact that she missed an inspection that day distracted her and caused her to be careless. We must look at one year's worth of figures, at the very least, to make an accurate….

11   **Judge:**

O.K. I will allow the request but limit it to the six months before the accident and to only those documents directly related to missed site inspections. Movant, will you draft the order and give notice?

12   **You:**

Yes, Your Honor, I will prepare the order.

To follow up on exactly how the order should read, you might say something like this:

13   *Your Honor, could you please review your exact order and possibly have your clerk give me a sample? I have never prepared an order and I want to be sure it is correct.*

14   **Judge:**

The clerk can assist you as to the format and, again, my order was that your request for the driving records is denied. The request for the phone bill was granted and the request for the business records was granted in part. Defendant is ordered to produce all business records pertaining to missed inspections in the past six months and the phone bill in questions. Next matter on calendar, Jack v. Jill.

d.   Summary Judgment Motion

Trials often occur for one of two reasons: either people don't agree about what happened (the facts) in a given situation, or they don't agree on the correct legal consequences of certain facts they all admit happened. If you and your adversary agree on the important facts, but do not agree on what law should be applied, you don't need to go to trial. The judge can take your agreed-on version of the facts, determine how the law should apply to the situation and issue a ruling—all without a trial.

To ask a judge to rule on a case in this way, either side makes what's called a motion for summary judgment. This can save you and your adversary a tremendous amount of money, since it cuts down or eliminates costs such as subpoenaing and preparing witnesses, preparing arguments and taking time off work for trial.

Try to settle the case before bringing a summary judgment motion. Before going to court on a summary judgment motion, you will likely want to enter into some settlement negotiations with your adversary, to try to resolve the case without the costs to either of you of paying for the court hearing.

When you bring a summary judgment motion, you are asking the judge (there is no jury) to base her ruling on the undisputed facts, which you and your adversary have presented in documents. These may include documents called affidavits or declarations (sworn statements of parties or witnesses), contracts or other evidence. If you don't want the judge to decide the case based on your adversary's summary judgment motion, you need to show, in your reply and at the court hearing if one is scheduled, that some facts are disputed. And you must say why a trial is needed—for example, that it is crucial you have the opportunity to cross-examine your adversary's witnesses. Stress the legal policy favoring a party's right to go to trial.

Don't be scared by a summary judgment motion. Summary judgment motions are sometimes used by lawyers to try to intimidate pro pers, claiming that no facts are in dispute when plenty really are. Don't fall for this. Assess the facts on both sides, and if you continue to believe you have a genuine dispute, fight the motion by filing an Objection to Summary Judgment Motion. Include in your Objection a written statement of the factual questions you believe exist, supported by affidavits or declarations.

If a summary judgment motion is denied, then you will proceed with the trial. But if the motion is granted, the judge will make a final decision for or against you by applying the law to the agreed-upon facts. In making that decision, the judge will not have any live witnesses, just the written evidence you and your adversary have submitted and the legal arguments you each have made in your papers. You will not have a chance put witnesses on the stand to testify or cross-examine the other side's witnesses, as you would in trial. But the judge's summary judgment will be binding just like the judgment or verdict rendered in a completed trial.

Summary judgments are final. You cannot have a trial after the summary judgment if you don't like the court's decision. For this reason, it's wise to prepare thoroughly if you are bringing or defending against a summary judgment motion. (For reference, see Federal Rule of Civil Procedure 56 and your state equivalents.)

Just as with the other motions, remember to properly schedule and notice your court hearing, and file and serve the necessary documents. (See Section 3, 4 and 5, above.)

Here's how a summary judgment hearing might proceed. Assume that the defendant contractor, Sarah Adams, from the car accident example above, is responding to the plaintiff's summary judgment motion. The plaintiff is represented by a lawyer but Adams is not. Arguments at the hearing may proceed as follows:

1 Judge:

I have Plaintiff's summary judgment motion and Defendant's opposition to that motion here. Unless you, Ms. Adams, can tell me why I should not, I intend to grant plaintiff's motion, and decide this case as a matter of law based on the facts presented to me. It seems to me that the facts are not disputed, and that it is in the interests of efficiency and all parties involved for me to decide the legal questions now, without proceeding to trial.

2 Adams:

Your Honor, it is true there is some evidence we both agree to. We both agree that my truck hit the plaintiff at Elm and Main. But there are several other very important facts about which we don't agree.

First, the plaintiff was injured only slightly by my truck. According to Dr. Even's affidavit, which I've included in my opposition papers, the plaintiff's serious injury, the one he really wants money for, was a pre-existing injury. The plaintiff's declaration states that injury was caused by my truck hitting him. We clear-

ly have a fact dispute and Your Honor [or the jury, if you will have one] must listen to all the evidence and decide who is right.

Second, the plaintiff contends that I was distracted and not paying attention to the road at the time of the accident. But, as I submitted in my sworn declaration, this is not true. I was driving especially carefully at the time, because I had expensive kitchen cabinets in my truck. My statement shows that I was only going 15 m.p.h. Then, without warning, the plaintiff dashed out from between two parked cars. These are crucial questions of fact, and they need to be decided in trial.

3 Plaintiff's attorney, Ms. Charles:

By way of response, Your Honor, you have all the facts necessary to make a fair, full and final determination of law in this case. The plaintiff's declaration states he was crossing the street at Elm and Main. No one disagrees. It further states that as he entered the street, the defendant's truck hit him. No one disagrees. The facts are clear. The only thing left to do is determine whether or not the defendant was negligent—an issue of law, Your Honor. Both sides have put forth detailed evidence in the declarations attached to our motions, the arguments have been set forth, and it would be a clear waste of time and money for the court and everyone involved to start dragging witnesses into court for each and every point in the case.

4   **Adams:**

Your Honor, I should not be deprived of the right to cross-examine the plaintiff and his witnesses. My affidavit indicates that he ran out in front of my truck, and that I was watching the road carefully. The plaintiff wants you to decide the matter on the papers so his story will not be exposed to cross-examination. But my right to a fair trial will be denied if you grant this motion, Your Honor. I renew my request that you deny the motion and that a trial date be selected.

5   **Judge:**

In light of Ms. Adams' arguments this morning, and given that it appears there are significant issues of fact and credibility, I have decided to deny the plaintiff's motion, and the matter of Pedestrian v. Adams *will proceed to trial. The clerk will notify you when a trial date has been selected.*

5

WHAT YOU NEED TO PROVE AT TRIAL:
THE PLAINTIFF'S PERSPECTIVE

Once your case gets to trial, you must prove that the claim (or claims, if you have more than one) you made in your complaint are accurate. To do this you'll have to prove specific facts. This chapter explains how to figure out exactly what facts you have to prove to win your claim, and how to organize a Legal Claim Outline which identifies the elements you have to prove, the facts with which you will prove them and the evidence you will offer at trial to prove these facts.

A. THE ELEMENTS OF A LEGAL CLAIM

It is essential that you understand that any legal claim you make almost certainly consists of separate elements. It's a little like a beam of light passed through a glass prism; what at first looks like a unitary beam of light in fact consists of separately colored bands. In the same manner, what looks like a unitary legal claim based on negligence, breach of contract, breach of warranty or almost any other type of claim in fact consists of separate legal elements. To win a claim, you must prove each and every one of its elements at trial.

To demonstrate how claims are made up of separate elements, let's examine three common legal claims.

1. Claim for Negligence

Negligence occurs when one person's carelessness causes harm to another. How does the law define how careful we must be? Lawyers often describe it this way: we must all exercise "ordinary and reasonable care." If we don't, we are negligent, and if our negligence causes harm we are legally responsible to pay for it. Here are some common examples of negligence:

- a traffic accident is caused by careless driving

- a store employee neglects to mop up a wet spot on the floor, causing a customer to fall

- a road is poorly designed, resulting in a car sailing over an embankment

- a bank fails to provide adequate safety for an Automated Teller Machine, resulting in robbery of a customer.

Here's where the concept of legal elements comes in. Start by understanding that you cannot win at trial just by showing that a defendant behaved carelessly. You have to prove each of the legally required elements of a claim for negligence, which (in most states) are:

1. **Duty:** The defendant owed you a legal duty of care.

2. **Breach of Duty (Carelessness):** The defendant acted unreasonably.

3. **Causation:** The defendant's carelessness directly caused you harm.

4. **Damages:** You suffered economic losses, property damage, personal injuries or psychological distress.

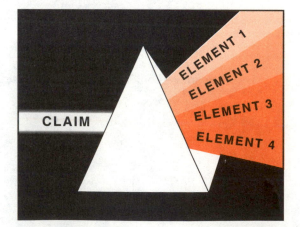

UNDERSTANDING CAUSATION

In some books describing negligence, as well as in some standard (form) complaints for negligence, you may see a reference to an element called "proximate cause" or "legal cause." These terms are just another way of saying that a defendant is liable for negligence only if the negligence directly causes the harm.

For example, assume that a defendant carelessly hits you with a car and breaks your right leg. Recovering from surgery to your right leg and walking with the aid of a cane, you slip on ice and break your left leg. You sue the defendant for both injuries. The defendant will probably be liable (legally responsible) for damages attributable to the injury to your right leg because she directly caused the injury. But probably, the defendant would not be liable for your broken left leg; a judge would not regard the defendant's negligence as a direct (proximate) cause of that injury.

Difficult issues can arise over whether a defendant's negligence is the direct cause of your injuries. If you are in doubt about whether you can prove causation, contact a legal coach with experience in personal injury cases as long before trial as possible.

2. Breach of Contract Claim

A breach of contract occurs when a person violates the terms of a legally valid contract. Here are some typical breach of contract situations:

- A seller refuses to honor an oral agreement to sell a consumer a car at the agreed-upon price.

- A manufacturer ships defective products to a retailer.

- A borrower fails to repay a loan.

- A company refuses to pay agreed-upon compensation to an independent contractor.

Like a negligence claim, a claim for breach of contract consists of individual elements, and to win at trial you must prove all of them. The elements you have to prove are:

1. **Formation:** You and the defendant had a legally binding contract.

2. **Performance:** You did everything you were required to do under the contract.

3. **Breach:** The defendant failed to perform as required by the contract.

4. **Damages:** The defendant's breach produced actual economic losses.

Oral contracts are often valid. Many people think that a court will enforce contracts only if they are in writing. However, oral agreements are often enforceable, though you may have more difficulty proving their terms. A law known as the "Statute of Frauds" (so named by the English in 1677, which gives you some idea of the pace of change in legal terminology) will tell you whether yours is one of the relatively few types of contracts that must be in writing to be enforced. To find your state's Statute of Frauds, look in an index to your state's civil laws or ask a law librarian for help.

3. Legal Malpractice Claims

Legal malpractice occurs when an attorney fails to use at least ordinary legal skills when representing a client. Generally, the elements necessary to establish a legal malpractice claim are:

1. **Duty:** The defendant attorney owed you a duty to use at least ordinary legal skills.

2. **Carelessness:** The defendant attorney failed to use at least ordinary legal skills in carrying out a task.

3. **Causation:** The defendant attorney's carelessness directly caused harm to you.

4. **Damages:** The harm you suffered resulted in actual economic loss to you.

There is a higher standard of care for professionals. If you compare the elements of an ordinary negligence claim with the elements of a legal malpractice claim, you will see that they are largely identical. The difference is that a professional (for example, an attorney, doctor or architect) cannot avoid liability by showing that she simply acted reasonably. An attorney, for example, must act with the care and knowledge of a competent attorney. For further information on professional malpractice, consult a torts (civil wrongs) treatise in your law library. (Chapter 19, Legal Research, discusses how to use treatises.)

B. HOW TO FIND THE ELEMENTS OF YOUR CLAIM

You may have to do a bit of legal research to track down the elements of your claim. The complaint that you used to initiate your lawsuit may not identify your claim's elements, because many court systems do not insist that complaints do so. If your claim is based on your adversary's violation of a statute, the text of the statute may not identify the separate elements that you have to prove. In fact, the elements of a claim may be buried in appellate court opinions which you may have difficulty finding.

Here are some places to look for the elements of your claim:

• Your state's book of standard jury instructions. Jury instructions identify the elements of claims, which you must prove whether your case will be tried with or without a jury.

• Books called legal outlines, written as quick refreshers for law students on subjects such as torts and contracts, typically list the elements of common claims. They are generally available in law bookstores near law schools.

If you need more help, consult your self-help legal coach or a law librarian. (See Chapter 19, Legal Research, for additional suggestions on doing your own legal research.)

Once you identify the elements of your claim, list them in the Legal Elements section of your trial notebook. (See Chapter 15, Organizing a Trial Notebook.)

C. PROVING EACH ELEMENT

As the plaintiff, you must prove each element of a claim or lose the case. To illustrate this critical point, let's focus briefly on a typical attorney malpractice claim. Assume that you wish to file a lawsuit against your former attorney, Jean Blue. About two years earlier, you went to see Blue after you were injured on your neighbor's property.

LEGAL CLAIMS

Most small lawsuits involve breach of contract or negligence claims, which are discussed above. But there are hundreds of other legal claims. A few of the more common ones are defined below.

⚠ **This list is for general background information only.** Each state has its own rules on the specific elements required to prove these legal claims, and you must know those elements before trying to bring or defend against a lawsuit. Chapter 19, Legal Research, explains how to find your state's list of the elements of a legal claim.

Assault. The plaintiff has a reasonable fear or concern that the defendant is about to commit an immediate battery. (Assault can also be a criminal offense.)

Example: Someone threatens you with a knife.

Battery. The defendant deliberately and offensively (that is, in a way the plaintiff would not permit) touches the plaintiff. (Battery can also be a criminal offense.)

Example: Someone hits you.

Breach of fiduciary duty. A fiduciary (someone who occupies a position of trust) fails to live up to that duty of trust, and as a result the person to whom the fiduciary owes the duty of trust suffers loss.

Example: A trustee (someone who is in charge of the property in a trust) spends trust money for her own use instead of using it for the trust's beneficiary.

Conversion. The defendant intentionally converts to his own use some property of the plaintiff.

Example: You lend your stereo to a friend, who later sells it without your permission and keeps the money.

Defamation (libel and slander). The defendant makes to third persons (or causes to be made to third persons) a statement about the plaintiff, and the statement harms the plaintiff's reputation.

Example: A newspaper prints statements that falsely claim a teacher had been convicted of a crime.

False imprisonment. The defendant intentionally and unlawfully restrains the plaintiff's freedom of movement.

Example: A salesperson refuses to let a shopper leave a store when there's no legitimate reason to think the shopper was trying to steal anything.

Fraud (intentional misrepresentation). The defendant knowingly makes a statement that misrepresents a fact, with the intention of inducing the plaintiff to rely on that statement, and the plaintiff justifiably relies on that statement and suffers loss.

Example: A salesperson tells a prospective buyer that a water purification system will make water safe, when the salesperson knows that it won't. The buyer, relying on the statement, buys the system and as a result loses the money spent on it.

Private Nuisance. The defendant prevents or disrupts the plaintiff's use and enjoyment of his property.

Example: Your neighbor lets his dogs bark at all hours of the day and night, making it impossible for you to use your back yard.

Public Nuisance. The defendant causes a health or safety hazard to the residents of a particular area.

Example: A chemical plant lets toxic fumes drift onto neighboring property, posing a health threat to the residents.

Trespass. The defendant goes onto someone else's property without permission.

Example: Your neighbor parks her car in your front yard.

Blue agreed to handle your case but neglected to pursue it. When she finally filed a lawsuit on your behalf against your neighbor, the legal time limit in which the suit could have been filed (the statute of limitations) had expired, and your suit was thrown out of court.

In assessing whether you can win a malpractice suit against Blue, start with two obvious points: Blue had a duty to represent you competently, and her failure to file suit before the statute of limitations expired is carelessness that constitutes a breach of that duty. So the first two elements (listed in Section A, above) are satisfied.

But as you can see from the list of elements, you must also show that as a result of the breach you suffered actual economic loss. Logically, to do this you must be able to convince the judge or jury that you would have won the suit against your neighbor

had Blue filed it on time. Put another way, if the judge or jury decides that you would have lost the case against your neighbor, Blue's breach of duty didn't actually harm you, and you would lose the malpractice case.

D. YOUR BURDEN OF PROOF

As the plaintiff, you carry the "burden of proof." This means that in order to win at trial, you must convince a judge or jury that *each element* of your legal claim is true or you lose.

But how convincing does your proof have to be? In most civil cases, your burden of proof is "a preponderance of the evidence." In other words, even if a judge or jury thinks that the probability that you have proved the truth of an element is

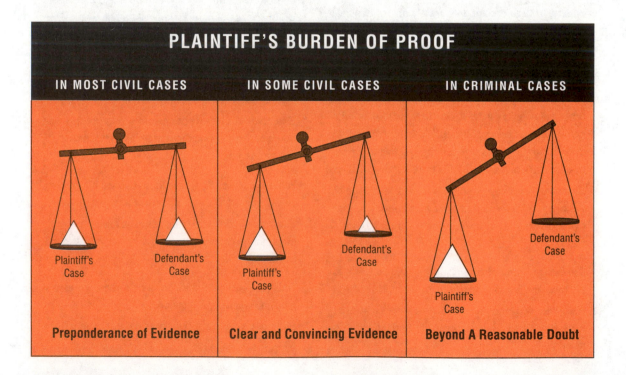

PLAINTIFF'S BURDEN OF PROOF

IN MOST CIVIL CASES	IN SOME CIVIL CASES	IN CRIMINAL CASES
Plaintiff's Case Defendant's Case	Plaintiff's Case Defendant's Case	Plaintiff's Case Defendant's Case
Preponderance of Evidence	**Clear and Convincing Evidence**	**Beyond A Reasonable Doubt**

only slightly better than 50%, you have successfully carried your burden of proof as to that element.

A higher burden of proof is, however, occasionally required. In a few types of civil cases, such as those involving claims for fraud and breach of an oral agreement to make a will, you may have to prove the truth of each element by clear and convincing evidence. While no precise mathematical difference separates "clear and convincing evidence" from "a preponderance of the evidence," your evidence generally has to be stronger to win a claim requiring this higher burden of proof.

When preparing for trial, be sure you know what burden of proof you have to meet. The best sources of this information are jury instructions for your type of claim, a legal treatise that discusses the elements of your type of claim or your self-help law coach. (See Chapter 19, Legal Research.)

Explain the burden of proof to a jury. To illustrate the civil burden of proof during closing argument, many plaintiff's attorneys like to hold their arms out to either side in imitation of a scales of justice. They then tilt very slightly to one side to indicate that if the plaintiff's evidence has moved the judge or jury even slightly in the plaintiff's direction, the plaintiff has met the burden of proof.

You may not want to be so theatrical at trial. But you will want to let the jury know that you don't need to prove any element of your legal claim beyond a reasonable doubt, as a prosecutor must do in criminal cases; convincing the jury by 50.01% is good enough. (See Chapter 11, Closing Argument.)

E. HOW TO IDENTIFY FACTS PROVING THE ELEMENTS OF YOUR CLAIM

You might reasonably think that once you've identified the elements of your claim, you can tell exactly what facts you have to prove to win at trial.

Unfortunately, it's not so simple. As you can see from reading the lists of elements (Section A above), legal elements are abstract concepts. The abstract language of legal elements is no accident; elements have to be stated in broad terms if they are to apply to a wide variety of possible conduct.

For example, let's look more closely at the second element of a negligence claim: that the "defendant breached the duty of care." This language doesn't refer to any specific, provable conduct. For example, in an auto accident case it doesn't tell you whether you should prove that a defendant driver breached the duty of care by speeding, driving under the influence of alcohol or driving carelessly in some other manner.

Similarly, in a claim for breach of contract, one element you have to prove is that you and the defendant had a "legally binding contract." This language doesn't tell you what exactly makes a contract legally binding.

The abstract language of legal elements would not be a problem if you or a witness could go into court and simply testify that, "While driving on June 3, the defendant breached the duty of care," or that "The contract was legally binding." But testimony must refer to what witnesses actually saw and heard—what was said in conversations, what people did, how events unfolded. You and your witnesses must testify about happenings *in your specific case* that satisfy the legal elements. After hearing about the competing versions of what actually took place, it is up to a judge or jury to decide whether a duty of care was breached, whether a contract was legally binding or whether any other legal element has been satisfied.

There is no magic way to identify the facts that will satisfy each element in your case. For the most part, it works just fine to rely on your everyday experience and common sense. For example, assume that you are suing a door-to-door seller of a water purifying system for fraud. You claim that the salesperson induced (tricked) you to purchase the system by making false claims about it. After doing some research, you find that one of the elements of a fraud claim is that the defendant made a false statement "with knowledge of its falsity." You know that neighbors who previously bought the same system from the same seller had complained to the seller that the system did not improve their drinking water. Your common sense should tell you that this is a fact you can prove to satisfy the "knowledge of falsity" element. You can then line up your neighbors to testify and provide evidence of this fact.

Common sense won't always suffice, however. For example, in a breach of contract case, you may find that in order to prove the element, "legally binding contract," you must prove "consideration." But "consideration" is another abstract term, and you may not know its meaning in a legal context. In such

situations, an easy method of making sure you know what you have to prove is to consult a law dictionary. (By the way, "consideration" refers to the profit or other benefit that each party to the contract was to receive.)

LAW DICTIONARIES

Two excellent law dictionaries, which should be readily available in any public or law library, are:

Law Dictionary, by Stephen Gifis (Barron's Educational Series).

Dictionary of American Legal Usage, by David Mellinkoff (West Publishing Co.).

A reference book that may help you identify facts that satisfy legal elements is *American Jurisprudence Proof of Facts* (Lawyers' Cooperative Publishing Co.). This is a multi-volume treatise that discusses how to prove hundreds of legal claims. While the facts you will have to prove in your case will undoubtedly be different from the facts discussed in the treatise, the treatise may assist your understanding of what you have to prove.

To illustrate how to identify facts that satisfy abstract elements, this section provides examples for three kinds of lawsuits: negligence, breach of contract and attorney malpractice, the three legal claims described in Section A above. Even if your claim is one of these, the facts you will have to prove in your case will of course be different. But the process you will go through to identify facts will be very similar.

Identifying facts is crucial. We cannot overstate the importance of making sure that you know before trial what facts you will try to prove to satisfy each element of your claim. Otherwise, you may lose at trial not because your witnesses were not credible or because your claim was an improper one, but because you neglected to prove facts to satisfy each element of your claim.

A good way to organize your thoughts as you go through this process is to make an outline of each element, the facts you will need to prove it, and the evidence you will use to prove the facts. (Samples are shown below.) It will let you know, at a glance, if you have identified facts to prove each element, and it will also be a good reference for you during your trial. Depending on the type of claim you have made, your outline may have as many as four, five or six elements. Devote a separate page to each grouping of element, fact and evidence to organize your case as clearly as possible. (If the same item of evidence is relevant to more than one fact, simply include it on more than one page. Section F, below, discusses evidence.)

A fact by any other name is still a fact. In the course of your legal research, you may run across the terms "material facts" or "ultimate facts." This is simply more legal jargon, which refers to facts that satisfy legal elements. All the facts set forth below are material facts or ultimate facts.

1. Claim for Negligence

Your story: About 3 p.m. on March 31, you were standing on the corner of Elm and Main Streets, waiting to cross the street. When the light in your direction turned green, you stepped off the curb into the crosswalk. You had gotten about one-third of the way across the street when you suddenly saw a truck driven by the defendant, Sarah Adams, bearing down on you. You tried to get out of the way, but the truck struck you. You suffered a broken leg, which took four months to heal, and were left with a permanent limp. An eyewitness will testify that you were in the crosswalk when the truck made a left turn and struck you.

Adams is a building contractor. During her deposition, she admitted that her truck struck you and that just moments before the accident she had gotten a call on her car phone telling her about a missed inspection on a big job she was working on, and that she turned left to visit that job site. Adams denies that she drove carelessly.

You file a complaint against Adams for negligence and find the list of elements you must prove. (See Section A, above.) Now you're ready to write down a specific fact that satisfies each element. Do not worry about your exact words—this process is only for your benefit. Neither the judge nor the defendant will ever see your list.

Element 1:

The defendant owed me a legal duty of care.

Fact:

At the time of the accident, Adams was driving a truck in the immediate vicinity of where I was a pedestrian crossing the street.

You may not need to prove the duty of care. As a general rule, a defendant has a duty of care towards anyone who is likely to be harmed by the defendant's careless conduct. Because Adams admits striking you, you would probably not need evidence to prove this fact.

Element 2:

The defendant acted unreasonably.

Fact:

Adams made a left turn when she was thinking about a job problem and not paying attention to pedestrians in the road.

Element 3:

The defendant's carelessness directly harmed me.

Fact:

Being hit by Adams' truck broke my leg and left me with a limp.

Watch out for the "preexisting injury" defense. In many personal injury cases, a defendant will try to deny causing your injuries by offering evidence that an injury you say resulted from the defendant's conduct actually existed before that conduct took place.

Element 4:

I suffered economic losses, personal injuries and psychological distress.

Fact:

My broken leg had to be operated on. I lost two weeks of work, was on crutches for four months, was in constant pain during that period and had medical expenses of $50,000. Also, I was left with an embarrassing permanent limp, soreness and stiffness.

2. Claim for Breach of Contract

Your story: On February 14, you hired the defendant, Von Jarrett, a contractor, to build an addition of 600 square feet onto your house. The price was $75,000. The written contract called for a down payment of $5,000, and then for periodic payments, tied to defined completion stages, until the job was finished. The contract called for the addition to be completed by June 14.

Jarrett stopped working around the beginning of April and demanded an additional $20,000 over and above the $75,000 to finish the job. Because you had properly made all due interim payments and because by refusing to continue working Jarrett breached the contract, you refused to pay the additional money and hired another contractor to complete the work. After you hired the new contractor, you learned that Jarrett had used substandard materials, which had to be replaced. Your total cost for the addition (including replacing the substandard materials) ended up being $110,000. You also had to pay $3,000 extra to stay in a hotel two months longer than you anticipated.

Element 1:

We had a legally binding contract.

Fact:

On Feb. 14, Jarrett made a written promise to build a 600-square-foot addition onto my house, and I promised in writing to pay a total of $75,000 by the time the job was complete.

💡 **Exchange of promises is sufficient.** In a contract case, one party's promise is adequate "consideration" for another party's promise. Stripped of legal jargon, this means that if each party receives a benefit from the other's promise (which is almost always true in a business transaction), a contract is formed unless the judge regards the transaction as a gift from one party to the other.

Element 2:

I did everything I was required to do under the contract.

Facts:

I paid Jarrett a down payment of $5,000 and when the first and only stage of the work was completed by Jarrett an additional $15,000. In addition, I provided Jarrett with complete access to my property to do the work. That's all the contract required me to do.

Element 3:

Jarrett failed to fulfill his side of the contract.

Facts:

Jarrett stopped working on the addition in early April, when the addition was only partially complete. Jarrett also refused to complete the addition unless I promised to increase the total contract by $20,000 even though I had made all payments due under the contract. Also, Jarrett did not use the quality of materials called for by the contract.

Element 4:

Jarrett's breach produced actual economic losses.

Facts:

Because of Jarrett's refusal to complete the job for the contract price and his substandard work, I had to hire another contractor to complete the addition according to plan, for a total cost of $110,000. My damages include the $35,000 that I had to pay in excess of the $75,000 contract price for the addition, as well as $3,000 in additional living expenses because I couldn't live in the house for two extra months while the addition was completed.

3.   Claim for Legal Malpractice

Your story: A number of years ago your stepmother hired an attorney to draft a will leaving her entire estate to you. After she signed the will, your stepmother gave birth to a son. Sometime later, she wanted to make sure that the son would get no part of her property. Your stepmother called the same attorney, who assured her that no change in the will was necessary—all of the stepmother's property would still go to you under the will. After your stepmother's death you discovered that under your state's law, which was in effect when your stepmother called the attorney, the son was automatically entitled to half ($60,000) of your stepmother's estate despite the terms of the will. Your state's law, known as a "pretermitted heir statute," states that a child born after a will is made takes half of the estate no matter what the will says, unless the child is specifically disinherited.

Element 1:

The lawyer owed me a duty of professional care.

Fact:

Defendant is a licensed attorney who was hired by my stepmother to prepare a will leaving all her property to me.

Element 2:

The lawyer failed to use at least ordinary legal skills.

Fact:

After the lawyer drafted a will for my stepmother which made no reference to a child, my stepmother told the lawyer that she had given birth to a son and asked if she had to change her will to make sure all her estate went to me. The lawyer mistakenly told her that she did not have to change her will to disinherit the son.

Element 3:

The lawyer's carelessness was the direct cause of harm to me.

Fact:

Because of the lawyer's advice, my stepmother failed to change her will to disinherit her son.

Element 4:

I suffered actual economic losses.

Fact:

I lost $60,000 that I would have received had the will been changed to disinherit the son.

⚠️ **State laws vary as to a lawyer's duty to a will beneficiary.** Your claim against the lawyer can succeed only if the lawyer's duty of professional care extends to you, the beneficiary under the will. In some states, a lawyer has no duty towards will beneficiaries, but only to a client (here, your stepmother). If your case arises in one of these states, the claim would not succeed even though the lawyer was careless.

⚠️ **Disinheritance laws in your state may be different.** If you are involved in a dispute involving children omitted from a will, check your state's "probate" or "wills" laws very carefully. In most states, a child omitted from a will is entitled to a share of a parent's estate only if the child was born after the will was signed. But in a few states, a child omitted from a will may receive a share of a parent's estate even if the child was already alive when the will was signed.

F. LOOKING AHEAD TO TRIAL: ORGANIZING YOUR EVIDENCE

Once you have an outline of the facts satisfying each element of your claim, you can add greatly to its usefulness by taking the next step: listing under each fact the most important evidence you will introduce to prove it.

If your opponent agrees, you don't have to prove everything. A stipulation is an agreement between you and your adversary. You can stipulate to many things, including the truth of a fact. To arrange for a stipulation, before trial simply ask your adversary to agree to certain facts. For example, you might say, "Are you willing to stipulate that you are a licensed attorney and that my stepmother hired you to prepare her will?" If necessary, support your request for a stipulation with reasons, saying something like, "The stipulation will save us both time, because I won't have to present evidence. And you don't really dispute this fact anyway." Once you and your adversary reach an agreement, write out its terms, sign it and ask your adversary to sign it as well. That way you will prevent your adversary from suddenly denying the existence of a stipulation at trial and leaving you unprepared to offer evidence. (For a sample stipulation, see Chapter 12, Exhibits.)

For example, look back at Element 1 in the legal malpractice case. The fact that satisfies the element of duty is that the defendant was a licensed attorney who was hired by your stepmother to prepare a will leaving all her estate to you. Under this fact, list the evidence you will offer to prove it. For example, the will may be bound in a cover that has the defendant's name and address on it, and you may have a canceled check showing payment by the stepmother to the defendant for the will. You could also produce evidence by demanding that the defendant bring to court the file showing that your stepmother had been a client. Finally, the defendant may stipulate (agree) that he is an attorney and that your stepmother hired him to prepare her will. If the attorney stipulates to this fact, you needn't prove it at trial. In that event, your outline of facts and evidence for Element 1 will look like the one shown below.

Claim: Legal Malpractice

Element 1:

The lawyer owed me a duty of professional care.

Fact satisfying Element 1:

Defendant is a licensed attorney who was hired by my stepmother to prepare a will leaving all her estate to me.

Evidence to prove fact:

a. Defendant has agreed to stipulate that he is a licensed attorney who prepared my stepmother's will.

b. The will names me as sole beneficiary.

You can use this same procedure for each element that you have to prove. For a somewhat more complex example, look back at Element 2 in the same legal malpractice case. To satisfy this element you have to introduce evidence that after the lawyer drafted the will, your stepmother told the lawyer that she had given birth to a son and asked if she had to change her will to make sure all of her estate went to you, and that the lawyer told her that she did not have to change her will to disinherit the son.

As you can see, one thing you have to prove is that the will that the attorney drafted made no reference to a son. The will itself is evidence of this fact, and you should include a reminder in your Legal Element Outline to introduce the will into evidence. (See Chapter 12, Exhibits.)

Offering evidence of what your stepmother told the attorney, and what she was told in return, may be more difficult. Your stepmother, your most obvious source of evidence, is deceased.

Of course, the defendant may admit the conversation—but you would hardly be going to trial if the defendant admitted this fact. Perhaps you or another relative or friend heard your stepmother talking to the defendant, or at least heard her say that she was going to find out from the attorney if she needed to change her will. In addition, you may have to call another estate planning attorney as an "expert witness" to testify that the defendant's failure to advise your stepmother to change her will was legal malpractice. An expert's testimony may be necessary because the average judge or jury is unlikely to know what "competent legal skills" are in this context. (See Chapter 16, Expert Witnesses.)

Let's briefly look at Elements 3 and 4. To prove that the lawyer's advice was the direct cause of your stepmother's failure to change her will, you may offer evidence (from you, a relative or a friend) that your stepmother said that she was not going to change her will because her lawyer said that she didn't have to. And to prove that you lost $60,000, you may offer evidence of the will itself (which demonstrates that your stepmother wanted you to inherit her entire estate), testimony from the son that he received $60,000 of your stepmother's estate, or receipts and records from your stepmother's estate proving that $60,000 of the estate was paid to the son.

Claim: Legal Malpractice

Element 2:
The lawyer failed to use at least ordinary legal skills.

Facts satisfying Element 2:
After the lawyer drafted a will for my stepmother which made no reference to a child, my stepmother told the lawyer that she had given birth to a son and asked if she had to change her will to make sure all her estate went to me. The lawyer mistakenly told her that she did not need to change her will.

Evidence to prove fact:
a. My stepmother's good friend James went with her to the attorney's office and heard the lawyer tell my stepmother she didn't need to change her will to leave me everything.
b. Expert witness will testify that the lawyer's mistaken advice was legal malpractice.

After you complete the outline of the facts and evidence necessary to prove each element of your claim, put it in your trial notebook. The outline will be a big help in guiding your presentation of evidence at trial. (See Chapter 15, Organizing a Trial Notebook.)

G. LEARNING ABOUT YOUR ADVERSARY'S CASE

Even though you're a plaintiff, you should read Chapter 6, which discusses trial preparation from the defendant's perspective. Understanding how the defendant is likely to attack your case at trial gives you a chance to prepare a response.

6

WHAT YOU NEED TO PROVE AT TRIAL:
THE DEFENDANT'S PERSPECTIVE

As a defendant, you prepare your case in much the same way as a plaintiff does: figuring out exactly what you want to prove at trial and deciding what evidence you'll present to prove it. Begin by following these three steps:

1. List each legal claim (for example, breach of contract, fraud or both) that the plaintiff made in the complaint.

2. List the elements of each claim—that is, what the plaintiff must prove to win on the claim. (See Chapter 5, What You Need to Prove at Trial: The Plaintiff's Perspective.)

3. Identify the facts with which the plaintiff is likely to try to satisfy each element.

    Once you have finished Step 3, you then do one or both of the following:

    a. Identify evidence you can offer to disprove the facts you listed in Step 3.

    b. Identify your own facts that contradict the facts that you listed in Step 3, and identify evidence you can offer to prove your own facts.

    You'll end up with an outline that looks like the one shown below.

    Depending on the type of claim the plaintiff has made, your outline may have as many as four, five or six elements.

Legal Claim:

Element 1:

Plaintiff's fact for Element 1:

Evidence disproving this fact:
a.
b.
c. (etc.)
My contradictory fact:

Evidence proving my fact:
a.
b.
c. (etc.)

Element 2:

Plaintiff's fact for Element 2:

Evidence disproving this fact:
a.
b.
c. (etc.)
My contradictory fact:

Evidence proving my fact:
a.
b.
c. (etc.)

Now let's go through these steps and see how following them can help you to win at trial.

A. IDENTIFYING THE ELEMENTS OF THE PLAINTIFF'S LEGAL CLAIM

Legal claims consist of discrete elements, and a plaintiff must prove every element to win on that claim. Chapter 5, What You Need to Prove at Trial: The Plaintiff's Perspective, explains how to identify the elements of common claims, such as negligence or breach of contract. It is imperative that you read this material, because you need to build your defense around those same elements. Using the instructions in that chapter, list the elements of each claim the plaintiff made in the complaint.

Don't rely on the plaintiff's complaint. The plaintiff's complaint will state whether you have been sued for negligence, breach of contract, fraud or some other legal claim. However, the complaint probably will not list the elements of the legal claim, because court rules in most states do not require it.

B. IDENTIFYING THE PLAINTIFF'S FACTS

As Chapter 5 also explains, all legal elements are abstractions. Knowing what legal elements the plaintiff must prove doesn't tell you the specific facts the plaintiff will try to prove at trial. For example, knowing that one element of a plaintiff's negligence claim is that you acted carelessly doesn't tell you specifically what the plaintiff will try to

prove you did that was careless. The plaintiff must try to prove specific facts at trial for each of a claim's elements, and you must try to anticipate what those facts are.

Fortunately, figuring out the facts a plaintiff will try to prove to satisfy each legal element usually does not require technical legal knowledge on your part. Using common sense, you can usually identify the plaintiff's facts by matching what you know about the plaintiff's case to the elements the plaintiff has to prove.

For example, from Chapter 5, you know that there are four elements of a negligence claim:

1. **Duty of care:** You owed the plaintiff a legal duty of care.

2. **Breach of duty:** You acted unreasonably.

3. **Causation:** Your carelessness caused the plaintiff harm.

4. **Damages:** The plaintiff suffered economic or other loss.

Now assume that you are a defendant in a negligence case based on an automobile accident. You know from your settlement discussions with the plaintiff's lawyer that the plaintiff's position is that you were exceeding the speed limit, and that the plaintiff suffered a broken arm, incurred medical bills of $10,000 and lost a week's wages at work. Common sense tells you that the fact that the plaintiff will try to prove to satisfy the element of "breach of duty of care" is that you were speeding, and that to prove "damages" the plaintiff will try to prove that his arm was broken, he had medical expenses of $10,000 and he lost a week's wages. You can begin organizing this information in outline form, like the one shown below.

> ### Legal Claim: Negligence
>
> Element 1:
>
> Duty of Care
>
> Fact Plaintiff will try to prove:
>
> The plaintiff was in an area where he was likely to be harmed if I drove carelessly.
>
> Element 2:
>
> Breach of Duty
>
> Fact Plaintiff will try to prove:
>
> I was speeding when the accident occurred.
>
> Element 3:
>
> Causation
>
> Fact Plaintiff will try to prove:
>
> My speeding caused the plaintiff to suffer a broken arm.
>
> Element 4:
>
> Damages
>
> Fact Plaintiff will try to prove:
>
> As a result of his broken arm, plaintiff had medical bills of $10,000 and lost a week's wages.

Usually, you can find out all you need to know about the plaintiff's case through informal discussions and standard pre-trial contacts. Some of these opportunities include:

- **Your personal dealings with the plaintiff and the plaintiff's associates.** You almost certainly will have had a variety of contacts with the plaintiff, employees or other business associates of the plaintiff and with the plaintiff's lawyer leading up to the filing of the lawsuit. Most lawsuits are preceded by oral discussions and written demands that provide information about the plaintiff's legal position.

- **Negotiation and settlement discussions.** Even after the lawsuit is filed, you and the plaintiff (or the plaintiff's lawyer) will probably discuss possible settlement of your dispute, either informally or in a pre-trial conference conducted by a judge. (See Chapter 4, Pre-Trial Hearings and Motions.) During these discussions, you should be able to find out most of what you need to know about the plaintiff's case. In trying to convince you to agree to a certain settlement figure, the plaintiff will probably refer to the facts he is prepared to prove at trial and much of the evidence he will rely on to prove them.

Settlement offers and statements can't be admitted at trial. The law's policy is to encourage litigants to settle disputes before trial. To encourage litigants to speak openly during settlement discussions (whether conducted by a judge or between the parties informally), no court system allows dollar offers to settle or statements made during settlement discussions to be admitted as evidence. (See for example Federal Rule of Evidence 408.) So while you will learn information about the plaintiff's case during settlement discussions, you cannot offer evidence that the plaintiff offered to settle the case or of any statements made by the plaintiff during those discussions.

- **Direct inquiry.** Don't overlook that favorite information-seeking device of generations of parents and teachers: ask! Most people are socialized to respond to direct questions, and they are likely to follow that habit during pre-trial discussions. For example, you know that in a negligence case the plaintiff has to prove that you behaved carelessly. If you are unsure about what the plaintiff claims you did that was negligent, you may ask, "In what way do you claim that I was careless?"

- **Formal discovery.** As a non-lawyer, you may be reluctant to initiate formal discovery, such as depositions, interrogatories and requests for admissions. But if informal methods of finding out about what facts the plaintiff will try to prove have not worked, discovery may be worth a try. For instance, in a negligence case you can send an interrogatory to the plaintiff asking, "Please state each and every fact you rely on that demonstrates that I was careless." Similarly, to find out about the plaintiff's claimed damages, during a deposition you can ask the plaintiff, "Please tell me all the personal injuries you claim you suffered as a result of the accident." In both instances, the plaintiff must respond to your questions under oath.

Formal discovery, although it's more expensive than informal methods of learning about facts, does have a big advantage: the way you use it at trial. For example, an admission made in response to your request for admission is binding on the plaintiff if you present it at trial. That means, for example, that if the plaintiff admits in response to your request for admission that "the car was blue," the plaintiff can't argue the point at trial.

Similarly, if the plaintiff (or a witness for the plaintiff) gives a different answer while testifying at trial than she gave at her earlier deposition, you can impeach (attack the credibility of) the witness by bringing up the inconsistent deposition answer. For instance, assume that at trial the plaintiff testi-

fies that "the light turned green when ___ feet away from the intersection." During her pretrial deposition, however, she testified that "the light turned green when I was about 10 feet from the intersection." You can impeach the plaintiff's testimony at trial by introducing the conflicting deposition testimony to show that her story has changed. If you can successfully impeach the plaintiff or the plaintiff's witnesses on one or two important points, the judge or jury may doubt the credibility of her entire case. (Impeachment techniques are discussed in Section D, below, and in Chapter 10, Cross-Examination.)

C. DEFEATING ANY ONE ELEMENT OF A CLAIM

To win at trial, the plaintiff must prove facts for each and every element of a claim. In most civil cases the plaintiff's burden is to convince a judge or jury that facts are true by a "preponderance of the evidence," which is the same thing as saying that the plaintiff must establish that the chances are at least slightly better than 50% that the plaintiff's facts are true.

But as the defendant, you have one big advantage over the plaintiff. To win on a claim, you need only prevent the plaintiff from proving the truth of at least one fact for that claim. Because the plaintiff and not you has the burden of proof, you do not have to prove that the plaintiff's evidence is untrue. You only have to raise enough doubt in the judge's or jury's mind about any one element to prevent the plaintiff from winning.

For example, assume that you are sued for negligence. At trial, the plaintiff succeeds in proving three of the four elements of negligence by a preponderance of the evidence. That is, the plaintiff persuades a judge or jury that (1) you acted carelessly; (2) your careless actions were the direct cause of the plaintiff's loss; and (3) your careless actions produced actual damages. However, the plaintiff is unable to convince the judge or jury by a preponderance of the evidence as to the remaining element, that you had a duty towards the plaintiff to act carefully. You win! The plaintiff met the burden of proof for three of the four elements of negligence, but not for the fourth.

This kind of scenario is very plausible. For example, in one recent case a number of investors sued an accounting firm for conducting an audit negligently. Relying on the audit, the investors had invested money in a company, and lost money when the company turned out to be in far worse financial condition than the audit suggested. The court decided that the accounting firm was negligent and that its negligence directly caused economic damages to the investors. However, the court also decided that the accounting firm had no duty towards the investors because the firm had no idea who the investors might be. The result: the accounting firm won the case.

D.   DISPROVING THE PLAINTIFF'S FACTS BY IMPEACHING WITNESSES

Once you have a good idea of the facts the plaintiff will offer to satisfy each element of a claim, you should next identify any evidence you can offer to disprove them. Remember, if you can prevent the plaintiff from proving any one element,

you win. One way to disprove the plaintiff's facts is to come up with evidence that casts doubt on the credibility of your adversary's evidence. If the judge or jury simply doesn't believe the plaintiff's key testimony on some fact, chances are the judge or jury will conclude that the plaintiff has not met the burden of proving that fact. Damaging a witness's credibility is called "impeaching" the witness.

If you are going to impeach an adverse witness during trial, normally you have to identify evidence casting doubt on credibility before trial. To help you look for such evidence when you are talking informally to potential witnesses or perhaps even taking a deposition, here is an overview of the common ways to attack a witness's credibility. Most of them should be familiar to you from everyday life.

1.   Bias

If you have evidence suggesting that a witness has a financial or emotional interest in the outcome of a case, you can offer it at trial to show that the witnesses is biased. For example, assume that the lawsuit against you is based on negligence, and the fact the plaintiff is trying to prove is that you were driving too fast. (This fact satisfies one of the elements of negligence, "breach of duty of care.") To support this claim, the plaintiff plans to call a witness to testify that you were driving 50 m.p.h. in a residential area. If you can get the witness to admit that she has made disparaging remarks against the social group to which you belong or that she is a close friend or relative of the plaintiff, or stands to gain financially if the plaintiff wins, the judge or jury may conclude that the witness has a bias that casts doubt on the believability of her testimony.

Similarly, you can argue that a doctor called as an expert witness by the plaintiff to testify to the severity of the plaintiff's injuries is biased if you can show that the doctor has received a large payment to examine and testify for the plaintiff.

2. Impaired Ability to Observe

Evidence indicating that a witness did not have a good opportunity to see what the witness claims to have seen can be very helpful to your case. For example, in the same negligence case, if you can show that the witness saw you driving for only a split second, had terrible eyesight, saw you from a long distance or had consumed three martinis a half hour before seeing the accident, you can attack the witness's believability based on her impaired ability to observe.

3. Prior Inconsistent Statements

Evidence that before trial a witness made statements that conflict with the witness's trial testimony can make for a devastating attack on credibility. For instance, if at trial a witness testifies that you were driving 50 m.p.h., and you then introduce a sworn deposition or even an oral statement by the same witness saying you were going 40 m.p.h., or saying that he couldn't tell how fast you were going, you can cast serious doubt on his credibility.

If you can offer evidence to impeach the plaintiff's version of events, include it in your Legal Claim Outline. For example, if you have evidence that a witness for the plaintiff, Johnson, made two oral statements that are inconsistent with his expected testimony, you would update Element 2 in your Legal Claim Outline as follows:

> **Legal Claim: Negligence**
>
> Element 2:
>
> Carelessness (Breach of Duty)
>
> Fact Plaintiff will try to prove:
>
> I was going about 50 m.p.h. when the accident occurred.
>
> Evidence disproving this fact:
>
> a. Johnson told a police officer after the accident that he didn't get a very good look at my car before the accident.
>
> b. Johnson told me on the telephone that he didn't think that I was going more than 40 m.p.h.

E. PROVING YOUR VERSION OF EVENTS

As a defendant, you are not limited to trying to disprove what the plaintiff claims are facts. You may also testify and call witnesses in support of your own version of events. And remember that to prevail, you needn't convince the judge or juror that your version is correct; you simply need to offer enough evidence to lead the judge or juror to doubt that the plaintiff has carried his burden of proof as to any single element. This second approach is the legal equivalent of the sports saying, "The best defense is a good offense."

To prepare to offer your own version of events, again simply use common sense and the information you gather before trial. Look at the list of elements and identify for any or all elements a contradictory fact for which you can offer credible evidence. For example, assume that you have been sued for breach of contract. The plaintiff, Andrea, claims that after a series of negotiations you orally agreed on September 22 to buy her stamp collection for $15,000. After checking the elements necessary to prove a breach of contract claim, you see that one of the elements that Andrea must try to prove is that a binding contract was formed. In this case, the fact that she will try to prove for that element is that on September 22 she agreed to sell and you agreed to buy her stamp collection.

But you deny agreeing to buy the stamp collection. Your version of the September 22 conversation is that you agreed to buy Andrea's stamp collection for $15,000, but only if she also threw in her coin collection. Andrea said that she would think about your proposal and get back to you. That's the last you heard from her until you were sued. So at trial you will try to prove a contradictory fact for the element of "binding agreement." To show that there was no binding agreement, you will try to prove that you offered to buy Andrea's stamp

and coin collection for $15,000 and that Andrea never accepted your offer. In your Legal Claim Outline, you will list this information as shown below.

Legal Claim: Breach of Contract

Element 1:
There was a legally binding contract.

Fact Plaintiff will try to prove:
On September 22, I agreed to buy her stamp collection for $15,000.

Evidence disproving this fact:

My contradictory fact:
On September 22, I offered to buy her stamp and coin collections for $15,000, but she never agreed to my proposal.

Evidence for my contradictory fact:
a. My testimony that this is what happened on September 22.
b. Testimony of dealer Jim Pelowski, who says that on September 24 plaintiff offered to sell her stamp collection to him for $15,000. This shows that she didn't reach an agreement with me.

F. PUTTING THE DEFENSE STRATEGIES TOGETHER

Let's put the two defense approaches you've just read about together in a single example to help you understand how you can use both to defend yourself at trial. We'll use the negligence claim introduced in Chapter 5; put yourself in the position of the defendant, Sarah Adams.

Here's the scenario: The plaintiff contends that at about 3 p.m. on March 31 he was standing on the corner of Elm and Main Streets, waiting to cross the street. When the light in his direction turned green, he stepped off the curb into the crosswalk. He had gotten about one-third of the way across the street when he saw your truck bearing down on him. He tried to get out of the way, but failed and your truck struck him. As a result he had to undergo an operation for a broken leg that took four months to heal, had medical expenses of $20,000 and was left with a permanent limp. The plaintiff will offer evidence that you are a building contractor, and that just before the accident you received a call on your car phone from your office informing you of a missed inspection on one of your big remodeling jobs. He will argue that the call distracted you, and that you carelessly neglected to see him in the crosswalk. He will produce a witness who claims to have seen you looking out the driver's side window of your truck instead of straight ahead.

You agree with the plaintiff that at about 3 p.m. you were driving a pickup truck approaching the intersection of Main and Elm, and that you had just gotten the call from your office about the missed inspection. But you will offer evidence that missed inspections are fairly common, and that the phone call in no way distracted you. Also, you were driving with expensive kitchen cabinets in the back of your truck, so you were driving especially carefully. After waiting for traffic coming the other way to clear, you made a left turn onto Elm. As you did so your eyes were on the road. You plan to offer evidence that the plaintiff's witness, who will say that she saw you looking out your driver's side window, is the plaintiff's fiancee, and so is biased. In addition, you will impeach her with her state-

ment to a police officer at the scene of the accident that she was not paying close attention to your truck before it struck the plaintiff.

Your version of what happened next is that as you straightened out and started driving at a normal rate of speed on Elm, the plaintiff suddenly ran out from between two parked cars directly into the path of your truck. You braked, but could not avoid hitting the plaintiff. Nevertheless you were not going much more than 5-10 m.p.h. when you struck the plaintiff, and do not believe that you broke his leg. Indeed, an orthopedic doctor who examined the plaintiff's X-rays and other medical records at your request is prepared to testify for you that the plaintiff's leg problem was an old injury that was not caused by your hitting him.

Based on the information above, at trial you can attack the credibility of at least one of the plaintiff's facts. That is, you can impeach the plaintiff's witness based on her possible bias and the inconsistent statement she made to a police officer. You can also try to prove two contradictory facts of your own based on your evidence: that you were driving carefully and that you did not cause the plaintiff to break his leg. Based on this information, your Legal Claim Outline will look like the one below.

Once you have completed it, place your Legal Claim Outline in your Trial Notebook. Devote a separate page of your notebook to each element you plan to contest. This way you will not get confused in the heat of trial as to what evidence pertains to which fact. If the same evidence pertains to more than one element, simply include it on more than one page.

Legal Claim: Negligence

Element 1:

I had a legal duty of care towards Plaintiff.

Fact Plaintiff will try to prove:

At the time of the accident, I was driving a truck in the immediate vicinity of where the plaintiff was a pedestrian crossing the street.

Evidence disproving this fact:

None. [You might as well stipulate (agree) to the truth of this fact. You will not contest this fact. As a matter of law, you had a duty to the plaintiff to drive safely. Whether the plaintiff was in the crosswalk, running out from between two cars or standing on his head and barking for a fish, the plaintiff was in the vicinity of your truck.]

Element 2:

I breached the duty by acting carelessly.

Fact Plaintiff will try to prove:

I drove carelessly by making a left turn while not paying attention to pedestrians in the road.

Evidence disproving this fact:

The plaintiff's witness is not credible—as his fiancee, she is biased. Also, she has made inconsistent statements about her ability to observe. She now says that she saw me looking out the driver's side window, but right after the accident she told a police officer that she wasn't paying close attention to my truck before the accident.

My contradictory fact:

I was driving carefully with my eyes on the road.

Evidence proving my fact:

Nothing was distracting me; phone calls about missed inspections are routine. Also, I was driving especially carefully because I had expensive kitchen cabinets in the back of my truck that I was going to deliver to another job.

Element 3:

My careless driving directly caused harm to the plaintiff.

Fact Plaintiff will try to prove:

Being hit by my truck directly caused the plaintiff's leg to be broken.

Evidence disproving this fact:

I have no information to impeach the plaintiff.

My contradictory fact:

I did not break the plaintiff's leg; any leg problem that he had was due to an old injury not caused by my truck.

Evidence proving my fact:

Dr. Even will testify based on examining the plaintiff's medical records that the plaintiff's leg problem was caused by an old injury.

Element 4:

Plaintiff suffered economic losses and personal injuries.

Fact Plaintiff will try to prove:

Plaintiff's broken leg had to be operated on. He was on crutches for four months, was in pain during that period, and he has a permanent limp. His medical expenses were $20,000.

Evidence disproving this fact:

None. All these things may be true, but I wasn't the cause of them and I wasn't careless.

7

SELECTING THE DECISION-MAKER

Trial by jury is one of the traditions of the Anglo-American legal system. But many cases, especially civil cases, are decided by a judge sitting without a jury. Some kinds of cases never have a jury; only a judge is allowed to decide them. Usually, however, the parties themselves decide whether a case is tried to a jury. In most court systems, judges decide cases unless one of the litigants makes a timely pre-trial request for a jury trial and posts jury fees.

This chapter discusses your role in choosing who will decide your case. You'll learn how to find out if you are entitled to a jury trial. And you'll see that even if you are, as a pro per litigant you are almost always better off choosing a judge trial. However, yours may be the unusual case that should be tried to a jury, or your adversary may put in a jury trial request. Therefore, this chapter also takes you through the entire jury selection process.

A.   ARE YOU ELIGIBLE FOR A JURY TRIAL?

Whatever your personal preference between judge and jury, a jury trial may not be available for your case. For example, you are not entitled to a jury trial if you are seeking not money but an order that your adversary do something (injunctive relief), such as tear down a building that encroaches on your property. Also, in most states you cannot have a jury trial in cases involving child support and child custody. In most other cases, such as those involving personal injury, breach of contract, professional malpractice, libel or slander, you are entitled to a jury trial.

AND YOU THOUGHT WE WON OUR INDEPENDENCE

The reason that jury trials are not available in all kinds of cases is that many of our legal procedures trace their roots to England, where in centuries past there were two kinds of courts, law courts and equity courts. Each handled different matters. Jury trials were available in courts of law but not in courts of equity. Today, even though these ancient distinctions between courts have largely disappeared, your right to a jury trial often depends on whether English courts would have dealt with your case in the law or equity courts. Ironically, England, which started the whole mess in the first place, has nearly eliminated jury trials in civil cases altogether.

Check out your options. If you are considering requesting a jury trial, first check with the court clerk to make sure that you are entitled to one. If the clerk cannot tell you, seek the advice of an experienced trial lawyer.

B.   ARE YOU BETTER OFF WITH A JUDGE TRIAL OR A JURY TRIAL?

As a pro per, you are generally better off trying your case to a judge than to a jury. By not going before a jury, you eliminate a number of procedural hassles. For example, you do not have to worry about:

- how long before trial you have to make a jury request

- depositing jury fees with the court

- preparing jury instructions. (Chapter 11, Closing Argument, discusses jury instructions.)

In addition, a judge trial is likely to be more informal and easier for you to conduct than a jury trial. For example, in the absence of a jury your judge may not insist on strict adherence to courtroom procedural rules and rules of evidence. And, of great importance, you can reasonably expect a judge to ignore inflammatory, irrelevant or other inadmissible evidence from your adversary that slips by you because of your unfamiliarity with evidence rules. Jurors, however, may well be influenced by the evidence even if the judge tells them to disregard it. (See Chapters 13, Basic Rules of Evidence, and 14, Making and Responding to Objections.)

Despite the additional complexities a jury trial brings, you may prefer one because you think that a jury will be more sympathetic to your case than a judge. But whether a judge or a jury trial is more likely to produce a favorable result is a complicated question, one that many experienced lawyers readily acknowledge rarely has an easy answer. Lawyer "folk wisdom" often points to choosing a jury if a case has emotional appeal, and choosing a judge if a case is complex and based on technical legal questions. However, even lawyers are wary of such broad stereotypes. Your knowledge of the attitudes and values of the people in your community is probably more relevant than general folk wisdom.

For example, assume that you have sued two police officers for using excessive force when mistakenly arresting you. If the trial will take place in a conservative law-and-order community where likely jurors regularly back "the boys (or girls) in blue," but several local judges have a reputation for being highly independent of local politics, you may want to choose a judge trial. By contrast, if many of the people in the community have themselves been victimized by overzealous police officers, and local judges have close ties with police officer associations, you may be better off with a jury trial.

As a rough guide to juror attitudes, talk to acquaintances who seem representative of the people who are likely to become jurors. How do they react to your case? Even allowing for feelings of personal friendship, do they seem sympathetic to your position? Or do they have a negative reaction, perhaps because your case seems to depend on legal technicalities? Such discussions can help you decide whether to opt for a jury trial.

C. YOUR OPPONENT'S RIGHT TO CHOOSE A JURY

Be aware that you may end up with a jury trial even if you prefer a judge trial. This is because your adversary has an independent right to request a jury trial. If your adversary requests a jury trial, you will have one whether or not you want one.

D. DISQUALIFYING A JUDGE

Judges wield much power, even in jury trials. A judge, not a jury, decides what evidence may be admitted and (subject to broad guidelines) how other important procedural rules will be applied. A judge even has the power to overturn a jury verdict and either enter a different verdict or order a new trial. (See Chapter 17, When Your Trial Ends: Judgments and Appeals.)

If you are unhappy with the background or the attitudes of the judge who has been assigned to preside over your case, consider disqualifying the judge, whether or not you plan to have a jury trial.

1. Automatic Disqualification

Under federal law and the laws of many states, you have the right to disqualify your assigned judge even when a jury will decide your case. For example, in California and in federal court, you have the right to file an affidavit (your sworn statement) to disqualify a judge on the ground that the judge is biased. (Cal. Code of Civil Procedure § 170.6; 28 United States Code § 144.) You needn't prove that the judge is prejudiced. Once you file the affidavit, another judge is automatically assigned to preside over the trial. However, this free disqualification is almost always a one-shot opportunity. You must accept the next judge who is assigned unless you can prove that the new judge is actually biased against you or has an obvious conflict of interest.

Watch your deadlines. Your right to disqualify a judge is likely to be subject to strict time deadlines. You may have as little as ten days after a judge has been assigned to preside over your trial to disqualify the judge. Check your local rules carefully for deadlines for disqualifying a judge.

2. Who Will Be Your Judge?

Some court systems use "all-purpose judges," meaning that the judge assigned to your case the moment it is filed will preside over all court proceedings, from pre-trial motions to trial. If your case is assigned to an all-purpose judge, you may

have plenty of time to check out and consider disqualifying her.

But in other court systems, you may not learn who will preside over your case until the day it is set for trial. If you find yourself in this kind of court system (and you can easily find out by asking the court clerk when you file a complaint or answer), you will have to check into the backgrounds of the various judges to whom your case may be assigned. Armed with that knowledge, you can disqualify a judge within the time allowed if you decide to do so.

Beware of pro tem judges. Because judges pro tem don't have independent status (they serve at the pleasure of the court) they can be less likely to make a controversial ruling than a regular judge for fear of not being rehired. Even more important, since many pro tems do not conduct trials as frequently as judges and do not attend judges' training and continuing education sessions, they may not be as familiar with the law that affects your case. Nolo Press (the publisher of this book) regularly receives complaints about inadequate pro tem judges.

3. Investigating a Judge

Your right to disqualify a judge is of little use unless you know enough about the judge's background and attitudes to make an informed judgment about how fair your judge is likely to be. Here are some of the ways to investigate a judge:

• **Check with lawyers, especially your self-help law coach if you have one, about the judge's reputation.** Ask what kinds of cases the judge handled before going on the bench, about whether the judge is generally plaintiff-oriented or defendant-oriented, how the judge might react to your type of case, and what the judge's attitude towards a pro per litigant is likely to be.

- **If you live in an area that has a newspaper directed towards lawyers, find out if it publishes biographies of judges.** Many legal newspapers publish judicial profiles that describe judges' law practice backgrounds, their attitudes towards litigation and the community organizations to which they belong. Often, judicial profiles also contain capsule "reviews" by attorneys who have appeared in a judge's court. (In California, these biographies are compiled in a regularly updated book called "Judicial Profiles," which is available to the public in law libraries.)

- **If you have time, sit in the courtroom while the judge who is assigned to your case presides over a different trial.** Observe the judge's attitude, listen to the rulings the judge makes and watch how the judge works with parties, lawyers and witnesses. Though you cannot make definitive judgments based on a short observation, you may gain some insight as to whether the judge will be fair-minded in your case.

E. MAKING A TIMELY JURY TRIAL REQUEST

Even if your case is eligible for trial by jury, in most court systems it will be tried by a judge alone unless you or your adversary makes a jury trial request.

Jury requests must usually be made in writing well in advance of trial and even before a trial date is set. For example, if your case is in federal court, your "demand" for a jury trial must be served on your adversary not later than ten days after service of the last pleading, often the defendant's answer. (Federal Rule of Civil Procedure 38.) And in California, a party wanting a jury trial must make a written Notice of Motion for a jury trial within five days after an "at issue memorandum" has been filed. (Rule 377 of the California Pre-trial and Trial Rules.) (An "at issue memorandum" is simply a document indicating that all parties have been served and estimating the likely amount of time required for trial. Your court system may well require the filing of a similar document, though it may not go by the same name.) If you miss the request deadline, you waive (give up) the right to a jury trial.

If you want a jury trial, carefully check your court's rules for the deadline for making the request. Rules about deadlines for jury trial requests are often found in a book of civil procedure rules or local court rules. If you have difficulty finding the rule for your court system, ask a court clerk or a law librarian or check with your legal coach.

Pay jury fees on time. People selected as jurors receive a small amount of money for each day they serve, and in civil cases the parties themselves pay this money. In most court systems, whoever requests a jury usually has to pay a deposit of one day's jury fees (often $50-150) before trial. You can lose your right to a jury trial if you fail to post jury fees on time.

You can recover jury fees from your adversary if you win. Jury fees are a "cost of trial," which ordinarily the loser of a trial must pay to the winner. If the jury decides the case in your favor, be sure to ask the judge to order your adversary to reimburse you for any jury fees you paid.

F. HOW THE JURY SELECTION PROCESS WORKS

The exact procedures for selecting a jury vary from one court system to another, but they are in general the same in all courts. On the day your case goes to trial, when your case is called, a group of prospective jurors is selected at random from a large pool of prospective jurors. If the jury will consist of the traditional 12 jurors, about 30 prospective jurors will be called. But because in many court systems civil juries consist of only six or eight jurors, the jury pool is likely to be correspondingly smaller.

The pool of prospective jurors is bought into the courtroom, and a smaller group of 12 (or fewer) jurors is chosen at random and seated in the jury box. After they are seated jurors are often referred to by number, with "Juror No. 1" typically occupying the seat in the upper left hand corner of the jury box. This group is the initial jury panel. The other prospective jurors remain in the courtroom, ready to replace any prospective jurors who are excused (dismissed) from serving on the jury.

Once the prospective jurors are seated in the jury box, the judge (or the judge and the parties) ask them questions. The goal of this questioning process, which goes by the old French term, "voir dire," is to select a fair and impartial jury. (By the way, don't worry about the exact pronunciation of voir dire. Like recipes for Caesar salad dressing, everyone's is different. For what it's worth, we pronounce it "VWAR-DEER.")

Initially, jurors are usually questioned by the judge about their general personal backgrounds, such as their marital status, occupations and previous jury service. Then either the judge or you and your adversary will question them further, searching for biases that might prevent them from being fair and impartial. These questions typically relate directly to the evidence that will be offered in the upcoming trial. For example, say you're suing an attorney for legal malpractice for giving erroneous advice about a will, as a result of which you didn't get an inheritance. It makes sense for you (or the judge) to question the prospective jurors both as to their experiences with or biases for or against attorneys. In addition, you may ask them if they have ever received property through a will or failed to receive property when they expected to.

Similarly, if you are involved in a negligence case and there is a claim that you or your adversary had been drinking before an accident, you (or the judge) will probably question the prospective jurors about their attitudes towards and experiences with alcohol. For instance, they will probably be asked whether or not they drink, what they think about people who drink and whether they think it possible for a person to drink alcohol without becoming drunk.

Many voir dire questions are asked of the jury panel as a whole. For example, you may ask, "Have any of you personally hired an attorney in connection with a will?" Other questions are put to individual prospective jurors. For instance, assume that a prospective juror named Mike Asimow raised his hand in response to your question about having hired an attorney in connection with a will. You may then ask a question such as, "Mr. Asimow [or "Juror No. 3"], please tell me about your experience with the attorney."

WHO QUESTIONS THE PROSPECTIVE JURORS?

Traditionally, lawyers did almost all of the voir dire questioning. However, over the years many judges have come to believe that allowing lawyers to question prospective jurors takes up too much time and is used by lawyers to try to persuade jurors of the merits of their case rather than to simply select a group of impartial jurors. For example, a defense lawyer in a negligence case may ask, "Ms. Johnson, just because Ms. Nolo happened to get hurt when she came uninvited to my client's house, you don't think that she should automatically recover any damages, do you?" By asking dozens of questions such as these, some lawyers have managed to make jury selection take longer than the trial itself! As a result, today many judges conduct most or all voir dire questioning.

If your case will be tried to a jury, find out ahead of time how the judge who will preside over your trial handles voir dire. You will probably have to ask the judge's court clerk, because local court rules may leave the procedure up to the judge. Here are the likely alternatives:

- Your judge may ask only a few background questions and leave most of the questioning to you and your adversary.

- The judge may conduct most of the voir dire but allow you and your adversary a limited amount of time to ask questions afterwards.

- The judge may conduct all of the voir dire, but invite you and your adversary to submit written questions that the judge may choose to ask.

After the panel of jurors has been questioned, you and your adversary are allowed to excuse prospective jurors in a process called "challenging jurors." (See Section G. 2, below, for more on this process.) Prospective jurors are challenged and excused one at a time, with the plaintiff usually getting to exercise the first challenge. For example, a plaintiff may say, "I wish to excuse Juror No. 5." (In some courts, the parties send notes to the judge indicating which prospective jurors they want to excuse. The judge then does the actual excusing, so that the remaining jurors cannot blame a friend's dismissal from the panel on either party.)

If the judge allows the challenge, the challenged juror will be sent back to the jury room, and a new prospective juror will be selected at random from the original jury pool. The new Juror No. 5 is then questioned, and then the defendant has a turn to challenge a juror. The defendant can then challenge any one of the original prospective jurors or the new No. 5. Or the defendant can temporarily pass, meaning that the right to challenge goes back to the plaintiff.

The question-and-challenge process continues until both sides accept the same group of jurors, or until both sides have challenged as many prospective jurors as they are allowed by local court rules. At that point the court clerk officially swears in the jury and trial—mercifully—begins.

G. YOUR RIGHT TO CHALLENGE JURORS

Since part of the jury selection process entails challenging and excusing prospective jurors, you need to understand the two kinds of juror challenges and the important distinctions between them.

Keep track of jurors. If you will have a jury trial, devote a section of your trial notebook to jury selection. You can include in that section a box chart which, for a 12-person jury, looks like this:

Juror 1	Juror 2	Juror 3	Juror 4	Juror 5	Juror 6

Juror 7	Juror 8	Juror 9	Juror 10	Juror 11	Juror 12

As each potential juror takes a seat, write the juror's name in the numbered space corresponding to her seat in the jury box. If that juror is removed, cross out the name and write in the new one. In the remaining space, take notes on the jurors' answers during voir dire questioning so that you can ask follow-up questions (if you are able to) and exercise challenges.

1.   Challenges for Cause

A challenge "for cause" asks a judge to excuse a person as a prospective juror on the ground that a legal impediment to that person's service as a juror exists. Normally, the impediment is something in a person's background or answers to questions indicating that the person is not fair and impartial. You and your adversary are allowed an unlimited number of challenges for cause, because you are both entitled to jurors who are fair.

Sometimes, the basis of a challenge for cause is so obvious that a judge herself will excuse a juror as soon as it becomes apparent. For example, assume that in response to a judge's initial background questioning, a prospective juror states that she is personally acquainted with you or your opponent. That juror will probably be excused by the judge at once on the ground that it is almost impossible for a person who knows one of the parties to judge a case fairly on the evidence presented in court. Likewise, a judge will immediately excuse a prospective juror who has a job that will inevitably bias the juror's attitudes towards you or your adversary. For example, assume that you are suing a lawyer for legal malpractice. The judge will probably excuse for cause any prospective jurors who are lawyers or who work for insurance companies that write legal malpractice insurance. Finally, the judge will probably excuse for cause any prospective jurors who appear to be ill or infirm or unable to serve for the length of time your trial is likely to last.

Usually, however, judges do not excuse jurors on their own. It is up to you to ask the judge to excuse a juror for cause on the ground that the juror's personal background or voir dire answers demonstrate bias against you. The judge will grant your request if she agrees that a prospective juror is biased.

To persuade a judge to grant your challenge for cause, you may have to convince the judge that a prospective juror is biased. Your adversary can also get into the act and may well try to persuade the judge that the juror has not demonstrated bias. After all, the same answers that prompt you to think that a prospective juror may be biased against you will probably lead your adversary to want that person to serve on the jury.

Let's illustrate briefly how an argument over a challenge for cause might proceed. Assume that you are the plaintiff in a negligence lawsuit. You know that there will be evidence that you drank a beer one hour before the accident, and that the defendant will argue that because you had been drinking the accident was your fault. During voir dire, Juror No. 3, Ms. Morrow, said that she does not drink, that she does not serve liquor of any type in her house and that in her opinion, people would be far better off if they never drank alcohol. At the same time, she said that she could be fair to you, and would not decide the case against you simply because you had taken a drink. However, you do not trust Juror No. 3 to decide the case fairly; based on what she said and how she said it, you think she is likely to be biased against you because you had a drink. Here is how you might try to persuade the judge to excuse Juror No. 3 for cause:

1 **Judge:**

Ms. Nolo, it is your turn to challenge.

2 **You:**

Your Honor, I challenge Juror No. 3 for cause.

3 **Judge:**

What is the basis of your challenge?

4 **You:**

Your Honor, she said that she is a lifelong teetotaler. She never drinks, she does not associate with people who drink, and she thinks that nobody should drink. She is entitled to that belief, but I don't think that someone who has those beliefs can give me a fair trial. There will be some evidence that I had a beer, and from what she said, it's clear that she'd be biased against me because of that.

5 **Judge:**

Mr. Scott [opposing counsel], *any response?*

6 **Mr. Scott:**

Yes, Your Honor. We oppose the request and ask that you deny the challenge for cause. Ms. Morrow described her beliefs, which many people share, but she said that she will be fair, that she will listen to the evidence for both sides, and that she will base her decision strictly on the evidence and not on her personal beliefs. I see no basis for a challenge for cause.

7 **Judge:**

Well, based on what I heard, she said she could be fair and has in no way prejudged the case. If we kicked everybody off the jury who doesn't drink or thinks drinking is a social problem, we'd have trouble putting juries together. I don't think there's enough here to sustain a challenge for cause. I'm going to deny the request.

Losing a request to dismiss a juror for cause is not uncommon. As long as a prospective juror claims to have an open mind and promises to base a decision strictly on the evidence, many judges feel that a challenge for cause should not be granted. But having lost the argument, you may still be able to remove Juror No. 3 by exercising a peremptory challenge, discussed in Section 2, below.

2.   Peremptory Challenges

A peremptory challenge is one that you can exercise for any reason whatsoever. Unlike a challenge for cause, you don't have to explain or justify your challenge to the judge. For example, perhaps you want to excuse Juror No. 8 because she has an occupation that suggests to you that she will not give you a fair shot, because she smiled at your adversary but not at you or because she dresses in a way that you do not like. Or maybe your intuition tells you, "This is not a person who I want making a very important decision that affects my future." The point is that you have a right to excuse any prospective juror with a peremptory challenge by simply telling the judge that you wish to "thank and excuse Juror No. 8."

If all this sounds too good to be true, be aware of a major restriction on peremptory challenges: you get only a few. This makes sense—if the number of peremptory challenges were unlimited, you or your adversary could excuse all the jurors in the pool. The exact number of allowed peremptory challenges varies from one court system to another. For example, in federal civil trials, each party gets only three peremptory challenges. (28 United States Code § 1870.) In California, each party gets six peremptory challenges, while Arizona allows four peremptories each. (Cal. Code of Civil Procedure § 231; Ariz. Rule of Civil Procedure 47(e).)

Before trial, read your state statutes and court rules very carefully and talk to the court clerk so that you know how many peremptory challenges you will be allowed. You do not want to use up your last peremptory challenge on a whim, only to have the next prospective juror be someone you really do not like. Remember, your adversary has the same number of peremptory challenges as you, and may excuse jurors who you really want to have on the jury.

💡 **Make a challenge for cause rather than a peremptory challenge whenever possible.** If you think that a prospective juror's background or responses to voir dire questioning demonstrate bias against you, always try to convince a judge to excuse a juror for cause before you exercise a peremptory challenge (assuming that you have a peremptory left). Since excusing a juror for cause does not cost you one of your precious, limited number of peremptory challenges, you are much better off convincing a judge to grant your challenge for cause than exercising a peremptory challenge.

But if you have no peremptory challenges left, do not challenge a juror for cause unless you are confident your challenge will be granted. It's almost always a bad idea to have a juror on the panel who you have unsuccessfully challenged for cause. If the juror you tried to dismiss for cause did not think ill of you before you argued that she was biased, think of how she is likely to feel towards you after you have pointed out in public why she is likely to be unfair! (For example, return to the example of your challenge to Ms. Morrow in Section 1, above.)

H. WHAT JURORS SHOULD YOU CHALLENGE?

Just reading about the jury voir dire process may convince you that you are generally better off with a judge than a jury trial. Deciding who is likely to be fair-minded and who may be biased can be a difficult task. However, the fact that you are not an attorney does not put you at a big disadvantage. For example, in a recent nationally reported case, a judge granted a defense attorney's request to excuse a juror in the middle of a trial, on the ground that the juror appeared to be biased against the attorney's client. After he was excused, the juror told reporters he was in fact very sympathetic towards the lawyer's client! Most trial attorneys admit that selecting jurors is based as much on intuition and common sense as on anything else, and that your most crucial tasks are to listen and observe carefully. If you pay close attention to what prospective jurors say and how they say it, there is no reason why you cannot do as good a job of selecting jurors as an attorney.

Perhaps no area of the law has been as dominated by lawyer folk wisdom as selection of jurors. Traditionally, lawyers have drawn upon broad stereotypes when deciding whether to exercise peremptory challenges. For example, people who belonged to certain groups were said to be more emotional, and therefore good plaintiffs' jurors. People with other backgrounds were thought to be careful with money and therefore good defense jurors. Today, in our multicultural and complex society, broad stereotypes tend to be of little value. You are probably better off learning as much as you can out about each prospective juror's personal background and evaluating how someone with that background is likely to react to your evidence.

For example, if you are 25 years old and were injured in a traffic accident when going from one party to another at 2 a.m., you may not want a 74-year-old person who never goes out at night to sit on your jury. If you claim that you were illegally fired from your position as an executive earning over $100,000 a year, you may not want a person who works for the minimum wage sitting on your jury. And if you are a tenant seeking the right to remain in your apartment by fighting what you claim is an unlawful eviction notice, you may not want a landlord on your jury. Admittedly, such decisions also rest on stereotypes: that a 74-year-old shut-in might resent a young "party animal," that a person who works for minimum wages might be unable to identify with a corporate executive and that one landlord will sympathize with another. But at least these assumptions rest on specific factors rather than broad categories.

I.   WHAT TO ASK PROSPECTIVE JURORS

Whether or not you are allowed to question jurors yourself (remember, some judges only let you submit questions for the judge to ask), think carefully about what information will help you decide whether a person can be fair and impartial in your case.

Word your questions in a way that encourages prospective jurors to talk about their experiences and attitudes, rather than give yes or no answers. For example, compare these questions:

a. Will you be biased against me just because I had one beer to drink an hour before the accident?

b. How do you feel about someone who drinks one beer and then drives a car an hour later?

You don't have to play the voir dire game. As an alternative to the approach of questioning and challenging prospective jurors, at least one authority, California Superior Court Judge Rod Duncan, suggests that a pro per litigant may be better off simply standing up and saying something like, "These look like good and honest people to me. I'm not a lawyer and neither are they, and I trust them to apply the law fairly. No questions." Or, you might make the same type of statement and ask only, "Will any of you hold it against me because I'm not a lawyer and I may make a few mistakes trying to represent myself?"

An advantage of this approach is that you show from the outset that you are not going to try to pretend you are a lawyer. Particularly if your adversary is represented by counsel, the jurors may empathize with your "little guy vs. big guy" approach. On the other hand, to fully carry out this alternative approach you have to be willing to forgo all challenges. You should, however, be able to rely on your judge to excuse on his or her own any prospective juror who demonstrates an obvious bias against you.

A prospective juror can answer the first question yes or no. But even a juror who says no may harbor attitudes that would prevent the juror from being fair and impartial towards you. The second question, by contrast, encourages the juror to talk. The answer may give you a better gauge for deciding whether to exercise a challenge. Remember that a prospective juror's "body language" and how you and a juror relate to each other as people is probably at least as important as any specific response the juror gives.

List the topics you plan to cover during voir dire. In the jury selection section of your trial notebook, write down the topics you plan to ask about during voir dire. You won't need to ask general background questions; the judge will ask those. Instead, focus on the facts of your case.

Unless your judge allows you only to submit written questions, do not write out specific questions. If you do, you may keep your face buried in your notes rather than maintaining eye contact with the juror you are questioning and talking as one person to another.

Here's an example of how to prepare for and conduct voir dire questioning. Say you're the plaintiff in a breach of contract case, suing a building contractor for doing shoddy work and then stopping work on a 600-square-foot room addition to your home. Before trial, you made a note in your trial notebook to ask prospective jurors about their previous contacts with building contractors, whether they had any problems and if so how the contractor handled them and whether they were especially sympathetic towards contractors.

1 You:

Ms. Sossin, I believe you said that you had some work done by a building contractor, is that right?

2 Juror:

Yes, we did.

3 You:

When was that?

4 Juror:

Let's see, I guess a little over four years ago.

5 You:

What did the work involve?

6 Juror:

It was just after my husband and I moved into our house. We loved it, but the den was very small. I have a large collection of Beatles albums, posters and other memorabilia, and I wanted a larger den to display them in. So we knocked out the back wall and extended the den by about 10 feet. Altogether, we added about 150 square feet to the room.

7 You:

Did you hire a contractor to do the work?

8 Juror:

Yes.

9 You:

How did you go about finding a contractor?

10 Juror:

Well, we called on a couple of ads, and asked friends for some recommendations. I think we got about three or four estimates, and went with one that was not the cheapest, but that seemed like he'd do a good job.

11 You:

How did the job turn out?

12 Juror:

Very well. No major problems, maybe a couple of the usual little ones.

13   You:

What do you mean by "little ones?"

14   Juror:

I remember one problem was the ceiling. I know I asked for a smooth ceiling, but he sprayed that cheaper stuff that looks like cottage cheese up there. When I said that wasn't what we wanted, he said there must have been a misunderstanding, that the price he had quoted was for the ceiling he had sprayed. It turned out that's what the contract said; we knew we had asked for a smooth ceiling and didn't notice that the contract said something different. We worked it out; we paid a little more and got our smooth ceiling.

15   You:

Were you happy with how the contractor worked that problem out?

16   Juror:

Yes, I'd say so. The remodel cost a little more than we thought it would, but he said that he charged us less for a smooth ceiling than he would have if it had been in the contract in the first place.

17   You:

Any other problems that you remember?

18   Juror:

No.

19   You:

As you know, in this case I'm suing a building contractor for doing substandard work and refusing to finish my job. Is there anything about the experience you had with your contractor that might make you lean towards one side or the other in this case?

20   Juror:

Not at all.

21   You:

As you sit there now, what is your attitude about building contractors, based on your own personal experience and any other things you've heard about?

22   Juror:

I'd say that the person we dealt with was very professional, but I've heard that not all contractors are that way. I guess they're like people in any other line of work—some good ones, some not so good.

23   You:

Do you think you can give both sides a fair trial in this case?

24   Juror:

Oh, yes.

25   You:

You wouldn't pay more attention to what the defendant says just because you were satisfied with the contractor you worked with?

26   Juror:

Not at all.

27 You:

Would you have any special sympathy for the defendant just because he's a building contractor?

28 Juror:

No.

29 You:

All right, thank you Ms. Sossin; I appreciate your candor. Now, Mr. McCalla, I believe that you also raised your hand….

Transcript Analysis: These questions do a good job of getting the prospective juror to discuss her experiences with a building contractor. Although you ask directly whether she has any special sympathy towards contractors (No. 27), you mostly ask her to talk about those experiences. No matter how she answers No. 27, you may decide to exercise a peremptory challenge if you think that her other answers and manner of speaking suggest that she is likely to feel favoritism towards your adversary.

Your entry for this juror in the jury selection box chart of your trial notebook might look like the following:

Juror 3

- Hilary Sossin
- Mid-20s
- Graphic artist
- Married - no kids
- Never served on jury
- Had work done by contractor
  Satisfied, only "little problems"
  Doesn't seem particularly pro or
  anti building contractors

Ask voir dire questions in a conversational manner. Studies suggest that many prospective jurors resent attorneys' voir dire questioning, feeling that they have somehow been placed on trial. They may be even more resentful of questions coming from a pro per, especially if you try to come off sounding like Perry Mason. So when you ask voir dire questions always be polite, avoid lawyer imitations and err on the side of brevity. Try to ask questions "person-to-person," apologize if you ask a question that even you cannot understand, and even try to smile when appropriate.

Keep this respectful attitude even if you plan to exercise a peremptory challenge against a juror. Jurors often empathize with each other, and you don't want a juror on the panel who is angry at you for excusing a fellow juror in an unkind way.

J. ALTERNATE JURORS

If the judge thinks that your trial will last more than a few days, the judge may seat (impanel) a regular jury panel of 12 (or fewer) jurors as well as one or two alternates. The alternate jurors sit next to the regular jurors and listen to all of the testimony, but do not take part in the deliberations or the decision unless one of the regular jurors drops out. That way, the trial doesn't have to start all over again if a juror becomes ill or for some other reason must cease acting as a juror.

If no alternates have been selected, and a juror drops out before the conclusion of your trial, or more jurors drop out than there are alternates to replace them, one possibility is to start the trial all over again. That may involve relocating witnesses, missing additional days of work and incurring additional expenses. Another possibility is to ask your adversary to stipulate (agree) to proceeding with the remaining jurors. If you both agree, a judge will almost always allow you to proceed with fewer than the regular number of jurors. Obviously, you are more likely to prefer this latter possibility if you think the trial has gone well. If the trial has not gone well, the former possibility gives you a chance to present a stronger case to a new jury. And don't overlook the possibility that your threat to insist on a whole new trial may strengthen your bargaining position if you and your adversary decide to reopen settlement discussions.

RESOURCES ON JURY SELECTION

Jury Selection in Civil and Criminal Trials, by Ann Fagan Ginger (Lawpress Corp.). A two-volume treatise on analyzing and selecting jurors, with particular emphasis on civil rights and law reform types of cases.

Jury Selection, by Judge Walter Jordan (Shepard's/McGraw-Hill). A single-volume treatise that describes common legal grounds for exercising challenges for cause and provides sample voir dire questions for both plaintiffs and defendants in a variety of kinds of civil cases. An appendix lists how many peremptory challenges are allowed in each state.

Fundamentals of Trial Techniques, by Thomas Mauet (Little, Brown & Co.). Chapter 2 contains a short overview of jury selection procedures and sample questions.

Jury Selection, by V. Hale Starr and Mark McCormick (Little, Brown & Co.). This book provides sample voir dire questions for a variety of cases and reviews some of the psychological literature on non-verbal communication. It also has a lengthy review of a simulated voir dire exercise, complete with pictures and backgrounds of prospective jurors.

8

OPENING STATEMENT

Opening statement is your first opportunity to outline the evidence you plan to offer the judge or jury. Like a good map, your opening statement should guide the judge or jury through the testimony they are about to hear and documents they will see.

Giving an overview—the big picture of your case—is important. Oral testimony is normally presented during trial by a number of different witnesses in a question-and-answer format, and it can be difficult for the judge or jury to follow. They can easily get lost in the details and miss your overall story. Also, if a particular part of your witnesses' testimony is crucial to your case, you can flag it in your opening statement, so the judge or jury will pay special attention to it during the trial.

It's important to keep in mind, though, that your opening statement should provide only a preview of your case. It is not the time to argue how the evidence proves you should win—that comes much later, at closing argument. (See Chapter 11, Closing Argument.)

A. SHOULD YOU MAKE AN OPENING STATEMENT?

Opening statements are optional, and lawyers sometimes choose not to make them. (In legal jargon, this is called "waiving" opening statement.) Sometimes, in relatively uncomplicated cases, they figure the judge will pick up all the necessary information soon enough. Or, the judge may already have a good idea what the case is about from the pre-trial conference. (See Chapter 4, Pre-Trial Hearings and Motions.) In fact, it is for this rea-

son—to avoid repetition—that many lawyers waive their opening statements when trying a case to a judge alone.

You may not even be given the chance to make an opening statement. Your judge may consider an

---

HOW A TRIAL PROCEEDS

1. *Jury Selection**

2. Opening Statements
   - Plaintiff's Opening Statement
   - Defendant's Opening Statement**

3. Plaintiff's Case
   - Plaintiff's Direct Examination of Plaintiff's Witnesses
   - Defendant's Cross-Examination of Plaintiff's Witnesses

4. Defendant's Case
   - Defendant's Direct Examination of Defendant's Witnesses
   - Plaintiff's Cross-Examination of Defendant's Witnesses

5. Closing Arguments
   - Plaintiff's Closing Argument
   - Defendant's Closing Argument

6. *Jury Instructions*

7. *Jury Deliberation*

8. Verdict/Judgment

*   Italicized stages occur only in jury trials.

**   Defendant may choose to postpone making an opening statement until just before she presents her case (see Section B, below).

opening statement a waste of time, especially if there is no jury, and may not let you make an opening statement. If this happens, you may have to just proceed with the case. But you can try to assure the judge, diplomatically, that your statement will be brief. Also, you can tell the judge that you believe an opening statement will clarify an important point.

If you are the plaintiff, you should rarely if ever voluntarily forgo your opening statement. You want to make the most of this opportunity to tell the judge or jury about your case. After all, the burden of proof is on you, so it is an excellent idea to get the first words in.

If you are the defendant, you likely will want to give an opening statement on the theory that the best defense is a good offense. But you may decide not to make an opening statement or to make a very brief one, if your defense rests primarily on undermining the plaintiff's evidence.

For example, if your strongest theory is that the plaintiff has insufficient evidence to prove one of the elements of her claims, you may not need to outline your own evidence. Your opening statement may be quite effective if it merely states that, as the defendant, you are not obligated to prove anything, that the burden of proof requires the plaintiff to prove every element of her claims by a preponderance of the evidence and that the evidence will clearly be insufficient for the plaintiff to meet that burden. (See Chapter 5, What You Need to Prove at Trial: The Plaintiff's Perspective, and Chapter 6, What You Need to Prove at Trial: The Defendant's Perspective.)

Don't dwell on the burden of proof in opening statement. You may not argue during opening statement. (See Section D, below.) Since the judge may regard comments about the burden of proof and the insufficiency of the evidence as argument, keep them brief.

B. WHEN TO MAKE YOUR OPENING STATEMENT

As the term suggests, opening statements are made at the very start of a case. In a jury trial, opening statements are made after the jury has been selected and sworn in. In a judge trial, the time for opening statements occurs right after the court clerk or judge calls (announces) the case for trial.

The judge will probably ask you, if you're the plaintiff, whether you want to make an opening statement. But because some plaintiffs trying a case before a judge alone choose not to make an opening statement, the judge may assume you wish to skip your statement and start the trial by asking you to call your first witness. If this occurs, ask the judge for permission to make your opening statement.

Defendants have a choice about when to make an opening statement. The defendant who wants to make one can either:

- Make an opening statement immediately after the plaintiff's opening statement; or

- Wait until after the plaintiff has presented all her evidence and the defendant has cross-examined all the plaintiff's witnesses, before the defendant calls her own witnesses. This is called "reserving" opening statement.

If you are the defendant, there are at least a couple of advantages to making your opening statement right after the plaintiff's. Perhaps the most important is that you immediately show the judge or jury that there are two sides to the story. If you don't deliver your opening then, you take a risk that the plaintiff's story will become fixed in the jurors' or judge's mind before you get to present your evidence.

However, there also can be advantages to reserving your opening statement until after the plaintiff has testified, presented all her witnesses and you have had a chance to cross-examine those witnesses. You not only may avoid revealing evidence the plaintiff doesn't know about, but you also have a chance to tailor your statement to the plaintiff's evidence. Finally, your opening will be fresh in the minds of jurors or the judge when you present your evidence. This allows your statement to serve as a more effective road map through your evidence.

Pick whichever order seems best in your case, but don't be overly concerned about your decision. There is no one right way.

© 1979 M. Twohy

"Mornin' folks."

C. HOW TO PUT TOGETHER YOUR OPENING STATEMENT

In some cases, opening statements include explanations of legal principles, trial procedures and other information, but the main objective is to preview or outline the evidence. When representing yourself, your best bet is almost always to make a brief opening statement, probably no more than five minutes, and stick to the essentials discussed below. It is even more important to avoid giving a long opening statement in a judge trial than in a jury trial. Judges, unlike jurors, are used to following along with testimony and figuring out what is essential to a case.

1. Introduce Yourself and Your Main Witnesses

If the judge who presides over your trial is new to you, introduce yourself. As a short and sweet introduction, you may say:

Good morning, Your Honor. I am David Martinez. I am a homeowner and I am representing myself today in this case for breach of contract against the defendant, Ira Isaacs, the building contractor who repaired my roof.

During a jury trial you may omit this if you already introduced yourself during jury selection. If, however, the judge conducted all the jury questioning and you never got to mention your name, go ahead and introduce yourself to the jury now.

You can also introduce the various witnesses—perhaps previewing a bit of what they will testify about during trial. As the defendant in a negligence case, for instance, you can say:

Good afternoon, Your Honor. I am the defendant in this case, Sarah Adams. I am a building contractor here in town, and I am representing myself in this case brought by the plaintiff, Mr. Pedestrian. Both Mr. Pedestrian and myself will testify, as will three other main witnesses. Ms. Cynthia White will be testifying about how Mr. Pedestrian crossed in the middle of the street, darting out between several parked cars, and about how difficult it was to see him. And Kevin Reback, a college student and part-time salesperson will testify that I was driving at a safe, normal speed. And, Dr. Even will testify about Mr. Pedestrian's pre-existing injury to the leg he claims was hurt by the accident.

2. Explain the Purpose of Your Opening Statement

After you introduce yourself, briefly tell the judge or jury what's coming in your opening statement. For example, in a jury trial you might say:

Ladies and gentlemen, I will briefly tell you about the testimony you will hear and the documents I am going to introduce into evidence in this case. Since you will hear detailed accounts from witnesses later, for now I will just summarize the main points.

If your case is before a judge alone, you might say,

Your Honor, as you know I am representing myself today. I will do my best to present all of my evidence as clearly as I can and follow the court's rules to the best of my ability. So, very briefly, I will go over the witnesses you will hear from and documents I plan on introducing into evidence to give you an idea of what this case is about in a nutshell.

Don't be surprised if the judge cuts you off at this point, especially if this same judge handled your pre-trial conference. If you feel strongly that your opening statement will be helpful, ask the court to allow you just one minute to make a certain point. Otherwise, proceed, as the judge will likely direct you, to call your first witness.

3.   Summarize Your Evidence

If you are the plaintiff, during trial you must prove facts supporting each element of your legal claims. (See Chapter 5, What You Need to Prove at Trial: The Plaintiff's Perspective.) Accordingly, in your opening statement, you will want to mention at least some of the evidence that you will offer to provide that proof.

Let's look at an example based on a legal malpractice case. You are suing your deceased stepmother's attorney for legal malpractice because the attorney failed to advise your stepmother, in response to her request, that she needed to change her will to disinherit a child born after the will was signed. Even though the will says you are to receive everything, because of the attorney's neglect you are now being forced to share your stepmother's estate with the child. You may say:

The evidence will show that my stepmother called the defendant and asked whether it was necessary to change her will after having a new child who she did not want to take any of her property. The defendant admits he is a licensed attorney in this state. You will hear from my stepmother's best friend that she heard my stepmother say she wanted all her property to go to me and not to her son. My stepmother did not want him to have her money because she knew he had problems, and she believed he would waste the mon-

ey. She also knew I had two children to support. You will also see proof in letters she wrote me through the years saying that she wanted me to have all her property. But because the defendant negligently advised her, the son she wanted to disinherit will get half her property, and some $60,000 that my family and I need desperately will now go to him—just what my stepmother wanted to prevent.

Although it's unlikely, a case can be dismissed if the plaintiff's opening statement is deficient. A defendant can ask the judge to dismiss the lawsuit (this is called declaring a nonsuit) if the plaintiff's opening statement shows that the plaintiff does not have evidence to prove each of the required elements of her legal claims. So, if you are the plaintiff, when summarizing the evidence, be sure to at least touch on some facts which help prove each element of your legal claims. (See Chapter 5, What You Need to Prove at Trial: The Plaintiff's Perspective.)

If you are the defendant, however, it's best not to ask the judge to dismiss the lawsuit for this reason. Judges usually allow plaintiffs some, and often a great deal of, leeway. And by saying what evidence the plaintiff has failed to prove so early in the case, you may end up helping the plaintiff fix the defects and present sufficient evidence on all the right points during the trial.

4.   Tell the Judge or Jury What You Want

Ask explicitly, at the outset, for the ultimate result you want. This sometimes gets lost in the many details presented during trial. Make it easy for the judge or jury to know what you want from them. For example:

Your Honor, after hearing all the evidence, I hope you will rule that the defendant breached our contract to repair my roof, and order that he pay me the $20,000 I had to pay to get it repaired properly.

D.   WHAT NOT TO SAY DURING OPENING STATEMENT

There are two important pitfalls to avoid when you make your opening statement: Do not discuss evidence that may not become part of the court record, and do not argue.

1.   Don't Refer to Evidence That May Not Be Presented

If you are not sure what a witness will say, don't tell the judge or jury what you think the witness will testify to. There are two good reasons for this. First, if your speculation turns out to be wrong, your opponent (or even the judge) may point out your misrepresentation during closing arguments. This can make you look bad. Second, if you distort key testimony or misrepresent a crucial fact, and it becomes clear that your opening prejudiced your opponent's case, your adversary can ask the judge for a mistrial.

If the judge declares a mistrial, he or she will stop the trial and set a new one. A mistrial is granted when something jeopardizes a party's right to a fair trial. For example, assume you hope the defendant will testify that she had three martinis before she got in her truck and that she was not watching the road when she hit you, but you are not sure exactly what she will say. If you tell the jury that the defendant consumed the three drinks before the accident, and it turns out that no evidence is admitted to support your assertions, you may have seriously damaged the defendant's chances of getting a fair trial. And you'll raise the chances of the judge declaring a mistrial.

> **Use "The evidence will show" in your statement.** It can be helpful to introduce some of your comments with the phrase, "The evidence will show…." This forces you to stick to evidence you can and will prove during trial and not shift into argument. Even if you omit the phrase when you actually speak in court, writing it in a draft statement before trial may serve as a reminder to summarize only evidence you know will be presented.

Similarly, do not refer to documents or other exhibits that you are not certain will be admitted into evidence. For example, do not refer to a business record you hope to introduce unless you are certain you can lay a foundation showing it is trustworthy. (See Chapter 12, Exhibits.)

How do you know what evidence you can refer to so that you can make a legally bulletproof opening statement? There are a number of ways to be sure you are on safe ground. It's safe to mention evidence if:

- You can testify about that evidence from your own personal knowledge.

- It involves a fact that was referred to in a letter, business or government record, or other admissible exhibit that you will present in evidence. (See Chapter 12, Exhibits.)

- Your opponent or a witnesses corroborated the information in pre-trial discovery. For example, your adversary made the statement in interrogatories or requests for admission, or a witness or your opponent said so in deposition.

- One of your witnesses, whom you have interviewed many times, has stated this information very clearly each time you interviewed her. While there is always some risk that even one of your own witnesses may change a story on the stand, if you have interviewed the person thoroughly before trial, and you trust her, you can probably feel comfortable that the evidence will not suddenly change at trial.

2. Do Not Argue

You are not allowed to argue during your opening statement. In addition to the usual meaning of "argument"—raising your voice or demeaning your adversary—in this context, argument also means going beyond just stating what you will prove and how you will prove it. Demonstrating why the facts and law compel the judge or jury to arrive at a particular result is considered argument. You can think of it this way: your opening statement should be a preview, not an analysis.

Unfortunately, the line between merely presenting evidence and arguing about or analyzing that evidence is not always clear. To help you stay on proper footing, let's look at some of the verbal techniques that are generally considered argument, so that you can avoid them in your opening statement.

a. Don't Discuss Credibility

The credibility (believability) of each witness is important—often critical—to the resolution of a case. The judge or jury will likely accept evidence from someone they believe but discredit what they have difficulty believing. You will strive to bring out both positive and negative credibility issues in your direct and cross-examinations, as well as in your closing argument. But during opening statement, you are not allowed to say why the judge or jury should believe you or your witnesses or why they should discount the testimony of your opponent's witnesses.

Let's look again at an example using the attorney malpractice case about the will dispute (Section C.3, above). Your stepmother's best friend, Lori Van Lowe, a clinical psychologist by profession, will testify on your behalf. She is not to receive anything under the will and doesn't stand to gain anything from the case. The only reason she is testifying is that, as a close friend and confidante of your stepmother, she likely knew better than anyone else what your stepmother wanted.

This background may show that Ms. Van Lowe is a credible witness. And in your closing argument, you will be allowed to tell the judge or jury exactly how the information demonstrates her credibility. (See Chapter 11, Closing Argument.) During your opening statement, however, you must confine yourself to simply stating the evidence, or else you may slide over the line into impermissible argument. For example, it is acceptable to say:

Ladies and gentlemen, a woman named Lori Van Lowe will be one of the chief witnesses in this trial. She was a close friend and confidante of my stepmother, so she knew better than anyone else what my stepmother wanted. Ms. Van Lowe, a clinical psychologist by profession, will not receive anything under my stepmother's will—no matter who wins this case.

By contrast, it is *impermissible* argument to say:

Ms. Van Lowe is believable. She has nothing to gain from saying I was to take under the will. She knows about human nature because she's a psychologist. And, she is far more believable than the lawyer, whose professional reputation is at stake.

b.   Don't Draw Inferences from Evidence

Another no-no during opening statement (though an essential part of your closing argument), is drawing inferences from evidence. By drawing an inference, we mean linking the evidence to the facts you are trying to prove or disprove.

For example, let's look at an item of evidence in a breach of contract case. Assume you are the plaintiff who hired a builder to put a new roof on your home. After the roof was completed, a storm hit, and the neighbor's tree fell onto your home. The roof caved in immediately. An inspection showed the builder used ultra-thin plywood instead of the stronger product you contracted for.

In your opening, you can properly say:

As the contract which will be put into evidence in this case shows, on January 4, I hired the builder Corrie Kaufman to put a new roof on my house. After the roof was completed, a storm hit and the neighbor's tree fell on our home. The roof caved in immediately. We then hired Danica Bradley, a building inspector who will be testifying about the report she made, which showed that the builder used ¼" plywood instead of the ½" plywood we contracted for.

But you cannot ask the jury to make an inference about the facts. For instance you may *not* say:

After the roof was completed, a storm hit, and the neighbor's tree fell on our home. The roof caved in immediately. It's obvious that the builder used inferior quality wood because he was trying to earn extra profits at my expense.

In the first (proper) example, you have evidence from the inspector that the builder actually used ¼" plywood, a breach of the contract term that required using a thicker grade of wood. But in the second (improper) example, you are asking the jury to make an inference that the roofer used thin plywood to make extra profits. Without specific evidence to support this assertion, you must wait until closing argument to ask the judge or jury to draw this inference.

Let's take a look at another example. Assume you are the plaintiff in a car accident case. You sued the defendant, Sarah Adams, for negligence because her truck hit you at Elm and Main Streets. To help prove that the defendant was speeding, you will offer evidence that just before the accident she got a call on her car phone telling her about a problem on one of her jobs, and she changed course to drive to the job site.

It would be proper to say:

Ladies and Gentlemen, you will hear evidence that just before the accident, Ms. Adams got a call on her car phone telling her about a problem on one of her job sites, and she changed direction to go at once to that job site.

It would be improper to add to the above remarks:

Ms. Adams must have been very upset by the phone call, and in a hurry to get to the job site. That's why she was speeding.

In the proper example, you refer only to the evidence that will be testified to. In the second example, you improperly tell the jury what inference to draw from the evidence. The second example is, however, perfectly proper for your closing argument.

c.   Don't Personally Attack Your Adversary

It is clearly inappropriate to attack your opponent personally. Don't, for instance, add to your comments above by saying:

And besides, it's clear that this slimy builder [pointing and making a face at the defendant] was trying to make a quick buck. He screwed me because he knew I didn't have the time to stand there and watch every minute of work he did.

The judge may sharply reprimand you for such attacks, and if you are trying your case to a jury, you will not impress and may greatly offend them. In rare instances, a judge may feel you so violated the rules and prejudiced your opponent as to merit a mistrial. So stick to the evidence and be respectful, even if your adversary *is* slimy.

If your adversary personally attacks you, take the high road. Don't fall into the trap and argue back. The judge or jury may find your opponent's comments just as distasteful as you do, causing them to lean in your favor. If the comments get too offensive, either object (that the comments are not within the proper scope of opening statement) or ask to speak to the judge at the bench. Then tell the judge that you feel your opponent's comments are inappropriate and prejudicial. Request that the judge admonish (reprimand and warn) your opponent to stop making them.

E.   TIPS FOR REHEARSING AND PRESENTING YOUR OPENING STATEMENT

Most of these suggestions apply any time you speak in court, and they are especially helpful for a strong opening statement.

1.   Use an Outline, but Don't Read a Speech

After deciding what you want to say, write out your opening statement. Then, practice saying it, both alone in front of a mirror and with a trusted friend, to hear how it flows and to get comfortable with it. Also, you may ask your legal coach to briefly review it and make suggestions for improvement or warn of any impermissible material you have inadvertently included.

In court, however, do not read the full opening statement. Reading word-for-word makes you sound stilted and boring, and it keeps you from making important eye contact with the judge or jurors. Instead, outline your key points on a sheet of paper. Keep the outline in your trial notebook, which you will take to court with you. (See Chapter 15, Organizing a Trial Notebook.) Take a quick look at your outline before you go up to speak, and then refer to it as needed during your opening statement. You can look down briefly and verify that you are on track as you pause between sentences or thoughts. Remember, the outline is just a guide. You can still do a fine job if your actual statement varies from it.

A completed sample outline is included in Section F, below. The general format for your outline may look like the one shown below.

> **Opening Statement Outline**
>
> 1. Introduce Yourself and Your Main Witnesses
> Me: I'm not an attorney, but I'll try my best
> Witness #1:
> Witness #2:
> 2. Roadmap (what you plan to cover in your statement and what they can expect in trial)
> Summary now; details about testimony and exhibits later, during trial.
> First you will hear evidence then you will decide case. Judge will instruct you on law.
> 3. Summarize Evidence
>   (element-by-element for your claims)
>   a. Element 1:
>   (evidence supporting element 1)
>   b. Element 2:
>   (evidence supporting element 2)
>   c. Element 3:
>   (evidence supporting element 3)
>   d. Element 4:
>   (evidence supporting element 4)
> 4. Bottom Line:
> Rule in my favor; Order

Remember, this is your case. You know the facts. You don't have to memorize details, just say what happened. And if you go to court with a good outline, you can use it as a checklist of points. That way you can relax and be assured you won't forget important items.

2. Speak Slowly and Strongly

Speak a bit more slowly than you do in normal conversation. This allows you to think clearly as you talk and helps the judge or jury follow your points. Also, speaking slowly makes it less obvious when you pause to find something in your notes or to think about how to phrase a particular point. (Use this same technique later in the trial, when you are asking questions of witnesses or making arguments to the judge or jury.)

Practice speaking slowly. Many people speed up without even realizing it because they are nervous in court. You may find it rather difficult to slow down if you are used to speaking rapidly.

Also, you must speak up. The judge or court reporter will likely tell you if you can't be heard, but jurors may not feel comfortable doing this. You don't want jurors deciding against you because they didn't hear something you said.

3. Stand at the Lectern

Standing is proper whenever you speak in court. It is a sign of respect. Standing gives you an air of authority and control. It also helps you project your voice. In most courtrooms, there will be a lectern for you to use, but if one isn't available stand behind counsel table.

F. SAMPLE OPENING STATEMENT

Let's look at a completed opening statement in a case where you are a pedestrian suing a building contractor named Sarah Adams for negligence. Adams' truck hit you as you walked across Elm Street, at the corner of Elm and Main streets. In your jury trial, your opening statement may proceed as follows:

1 *Good morning. My name is Nolo Pedestrian. I am representing myself in this action against the defendant, Ms. Adams. I am not an attor-*

ney, and I don't know all the technical rules of trial, but I will do my best.

2 The evidence you will hear today will show that at about 3:00 on the afternoon of March 31, I was crossing the street at Elm and Main. I was in the crosswalk when the defendant's truck hit me.

3 You will hear me and others testify under oath about the details of the accident. So for now, let me just give you an overview, to help you follow along.

4 First, I will testify. I will tell you when I saw her truck coming at me. Then I'll explain how I tried to get out of the way. I'll tell you how she hit me and broke my leg. I'll explain how it took four full months for my leg to heal, and I'll show you the doctor bills that back it up.

5 Then you will hear from a witness, Cynthia White, a stranger to me at the time, who saw the whole accident. She will confirm just how the defendant hit me.

6 Then evidence will be presented showing that just moments before she struck me, the defendant got a call on her car phone telling her about a missed job inspection.

7 You will hear all this testimony. And I'll show you some photos and doctor bills.

8 Then, after the judge gives some important instructions on how you should weigh the evidence, it will be up to you to deliberate earnestly and make the right decision. I hope that decision will be to hold the defendant responsible for the pain and loss of income she caused, and to award me the $100,000 I need and deserve to recover from this injury. Thank you."

Transcript Analysis: In No. 1, you set the tone as a respectful person representing yourself and trying your best. And in No. 2, you properly use "the evidence will show" technique to give a nice preview of the facts of the case, being sure to stay on the right side of the line between reviewing evidence and impermissibly arguing your case. Next, in No. 3 you signal that you are just giving the judge and jury a road map and not every detail.

In No. 4, you preview your own testimony and the exhibits you will introduce. You are properly careful not to present too much detail in your opening statement lest you bore the judge or jury and risk their not listening carefully during trial. You appropriately avoid saying why they should believe you over the defendant.

No. 5 illustrates the dangers of stating what you expect another witness will say. If Cynthia White doesn't testify as you promised, your opponent may point the contradiction out to the judge or jury, making you look foolish. And if the misrepresentation is severe, your adversary can ask for a mistrial.

What you have promised here is that Ms. White will "confirm just how the defendant hit" you. So long as you are reasonably certain she will confirm this (you have interviewed her many times and know that she saw things the same way you did), you are probably fairly safe with this statement, especially since you did not put specific words in her mouth.

In No. 6, you refer to evidence from the defendant. You normally should not discuss the defendant's testimony or evidence you think the defendant will present. There is too much risk of getting it wrong. But in this example you are on fairly safe ground mentioning the defendant's phone call, especially if you have other evidence of the call, such as her phone bill (if she called out), a note on an inspection form that she had the conversation, her own admission that she got the call, or a witness who saw her holding the phone to her ear. That way, if she denies being on the car phone before the accident, you can introduce your other evidence.

You properly do not ask the jury to draw the inference that the reason the defendant hit you was because the call distracted her and she wasn't paying attention to the road. That would be impermissible argument, well beyond the scope of previewing the facts. You will have a chance to tie the evidence to the facts you need to prove and convince the judge or jury they stack up in your favor during your closing argument. (See Chapter 11, Closing Argument.)

Last, in No. 8, you properly ask for a ruling in your favor. That alone is not considered argument. It can be helpful to let the jury or judge know from the outset what you want, and may bring you one step closer to winning.

G. SAMPLE OUTLINE FOR YOUR TRIAL NOTEBOOK

Though it may be helpful for you to write out your full opening statement in order to practice it, you will want to summarize it in an outline form to actually use as you speak. That way, you will not read word for word but you also won't forget important points. An outline for the sample opening statement above is as follows. Yours may look different, but so long as you hit the main points it should be helpful for you.

Introduction

I'm not an attorney, but I'll try my best.

The Evidence Will Show… (basic facts, e.g., Adams driving on public streets, Elm and Main—hit me in crosswalk.)

(This covers element 1, Duty to drive with care)

Roadmap

- This opening statement is a "roadmap"
- I will summarize testimony and exhibits now, give details later, and tell you a little bit about the order in which things will proceed.

Summary of Evidence

I will testify, White will testify and Adams' records show:

- She was distracted when driving, she was looking down and talking on the car phone rather than paying attention to the road. Adams' business records show this

  (This covers element 2, Breach of Duty, Adams driving carelessly)

- White will testify: she saw Adams' truck hit me.

  (This covers element 3, Causation, her carelessness caused my injury)

I will testify:

- I paid money in doctor bills, lost money from being out of work for four months; and have suffered tremendous pain.

  (This covers element 4, Damages)

Bottom Line

- After you hear all the evidence, the judge will instruct you and you will decide.
- Rule in my favor; Order that the defendant pay $100,000 for my pain, doctor bills and lost wages.

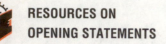

RESOURCES ON
OPENING STATEMENTS

For more detail on preparing effective opening statements, you may look for a continuing education or lawyer practice guide in your state on "Opening Statement." You can also consult:

Trial Advocacy in a Nutshell, by Paul Bergman (2nd Ed., West Publishing Co.), an easy-to-read, helpful and inexpensive paperback about effective and persuasive trial techniques. Chapter 5 covers both opening statements and closing arguements.

The Trial Process: Law, Tactics and Ethics, by J. Alexander Tanford (The Michie Co.), a textbook on trial practice which includes excerpts from many other leading books and dialogues of trial scenarios.

Fundamentals of Trial Techniques, by Thomas Mauet (Little, Brown & Co.).

9

DIRECT EXAMINATION

Direct examination is your primary chance to explain your version of events to the judge or jury and to undercut your adversary's version. It consists of your own testimony and the testimony of your witnesses in response to your questions.

Despite the dramatic images presented in movies and television, you are unlikely to either uncover significant helpful information when you cross-examine your adversary's witnesses or to change a judge's or jury's mind with a stirring closing argument. Direct examination is your best chance to tell your side of the story to the judge or jury, and well-organized and credible direct examinations are the key to success at trial. This chapter will help you plan and carry out persuasive direct examinations.

![warning] **Know exactly what you need to prove or disprove.** Direct examination testimony should be built around the legal claim or claims set out in the plaintiff's complaint. If you are the plaintiff, you must prove facts that satisfy each element of a claim. If you are the defendant, it is your job to disprove one or more of your adversary's facts. If you are uncertain of a claim's elements and the facts you are trying to prove or disprove, reread Chapters 5 and 6.

A. DIRECT EXAMINATION AS STORYTELLING

This chapter will help you with many of the technical aspects of direct examination, including the kinds of questions you are allowed to ask and how to comply with the requirement that a witness's testimony be based on personal knowledge.

But leaving aside the mechanics for a moment, it's important that you understand that presenting an effective direct examination is very similar to telling an absorbing story in an ordinary social situation. You'll want to focus a judge's or juror's attention on the events that are the most important to your claim or defense by spending time on the details of those events. You'll move more quickly through less important events. And you'll want to make sure each of your witnesses tells a clear, easy-to-follow story that dramatically builds to the main events by drawing out evidence in chronological order. Have your witnesses testify as much as possible in their own words, so a story sounds like it is coming from them and not from you. And, if you have photographs or any other records to back up your witnesses' stories, introduce them into evidence as testimony unfolds to convince your key listeners (judge or jury) that the stories are accurate. (Chapter 12, Exhibits, explains how.)

B. OVERVIEW OF DIRECT EXAMINATION PROCEDURES

Direct examination begins after opening statements. The plaintiff begins by conducting direct examination of her first witness, who may be the plaintiff herself. The defendant then has a chance to cross-examine that witness. The plaintiff then puts on her next witness, and again the defendant has the opportunity to cross-examine. Only after the plaintiff finishes presenting witnesses ("rests her case") does the defendant conduct direct examination of his witnesses. After each one of the defendant's witnesses testifies, the plaintiff similarly has an opportunity to cross-examine.

Direct examination controls the scope of cross-examination. When it's your turn or that of your adversary's to cross-examine, questions must relate to the topics covered during direct examination. For example, if you call a witness only to testify to your whereabouts at 8 a.m., your adversary cannot cross-examine that witness about a series of events having nothing to do with where you were at 8 a.m.

After the direct and cross-examination of each witness, the judge normally excuses the witness from further testimony. This means that neither you nor your adversary can ask any more questions of the witness unless you get the judge's permission to question the witness further. This questioning is called "redirect examination." If you want to ask your witness more questions following your adversary's cross-examination, say something like, "Your Honor, before you excuse the witness I'd like to ask a few more questions on redirect examination." Redirect is limited to the scope of cross-examination, meaning that you may only ask questions pertaining to the subjects that your adversary went into on cross-examination. You cannot rehash all of a witness's direct examination testimony on redirect; the purpose of redirect is to offer evidence in response to testimony your adversary brought out during cross-examination.

After your redirect, a judge may also allow your adversary to conduct brief "recross," limited to the scope of your redirect. After that, the witness will definitely be excused, and your next witness will be called. Then the cycle of direct, cross and perhaps redirect and recross repeats itself until you have called all of your witnesses.

As you can see, at each successive stage of testimony, the scope of questions is limited to what was covered during the preceding stage. This means that each phase of testimony is narrower than the one that came before. This funnel effect can be a problem if you conclude a witness's direct examination without asking about an important subject, since the scope rule would seem to forbid you from going back and opening up a new subject after your adversary cross-examines. Happily, a possible solution exists as long as a witness has not been excused. You can ask the judge for permission to "reopen" the witness's direct examination when it is your turn to conduct redirect. Say something like, "Your Honor, I know that this is redirect, but I ask permission to reopen the direct examination to ask just a few questions." Your request to reopen tells the judge, "Oops, I forgot something. As long as the witness is still right here, it's only fair to give me a chance to ask about it now." Usually, the judge will (especially in non-jury trials) grant your request, so you aren't unfairly punished for forgetting to ask some questions.

C. PREPARING FOR DIRECT EXAMINATION

Just like a play in a theater, an effective direct examination is usually the result of careful planning. Here are the important steps you should take before trial to present your strongest possible case.

DIRECT EXAMINATION

1. Subpoena Your Witnesses

A subpoena (sometimes spelled "subpena") is a court order to a witness to come to court. A properly subpoenaed witness who fails to show up at the time and date specified is subject to arrest.

Once you are assigned a trial date, ask the court clerk to issue a subpoena for each of your witnesses. Subpoenas are free, and are usually issued in blank. You can easily fill in the name of the case, the witness's name, the time and date the witness must appear and other necessary information. In some court systems you can personally serve a subpoena on a witness, but in many others you must get the marshal, licensed process server or an adult friend to serve your subpoenas.

You should subpoena all of your witnesses, even friendly ones who are anxious to testify for you. This is not a sign of distrust. Unless you have subpoenaed a witness, your judge may deny your request for a continuance (postponement) of the trial if an emergency or illness prevents the witness from coming to court on the day of trial. The witness can also show the subpoena to his supervisor at work to be excused to attend the trial.

All court systems impose limits on who you can subpoena, when the subpoena must be served and how much you must pay witnesses for their attendance at trial. (See for example Federal Rule of Civil Procedure 45.) While these rules vary somewhat from one court to another, here is an overview of typical requirements.

- **Territorial limits.** Most courts' subpoenas are legally valid only if served on a witness who lives or works within certain territorial limits, often around 100-150 miles from the courthouse. A subpoena served on a person who is outside these limits is ineffective, and the person does not have to obey it.

- **Witness fees.** In most court systems, you must tender (offer) to the witness, in advance, the court attendance and mileage fees set by your local statute—typically about $30-$60 per day.

> **You can recover witness fees if you win.** After trial, the judge has the power to award "costs of suit," including witness fees, to the winning party. So if you win the trial, ask the judge to order your adversary to pay your witness fees.

- **Time limits.** Your subpoena must be served on a witness long enough before trial to give the witness reasonable notice of when she is to come to court. For a witness whom you have already informed of the trial date and who has no conflicting demands, serving a subpoena the day before trial may be reasonable. For other witnesses, reasonableness may require service of a subpoena weeks in advance of trial.

> **Find out about "on call" procedures.** Ask the court clerk if the court rules in your state have an "on call" procedure. With an on call procedure, a subpoenaed witness does not have to report to the courtroom until you need the witness's testimony. The witness agrees to come to court when you telephone and ask her, but need not waste hours sitting idly in the courthouse corridor.

- **Subpoena duces tecum.** If you want a witness to bring receipts, records, notices or other documents and articles to court, ask the clerk to issue a "subpoena duces tecum." A subpoena duces tecum has space for describing the documents you want a witness to bring to court. Fill it out, identifying exactly what documents the witness is to bring. Then have the subpoena duces tecum served on the witness.

2.   Outline Your Direct Examination

You must know what you're going to ask before you're standing in the courtroom and the judge tells you to call your first witness. To organize your questioning, it's helpful to make an outline for each direct examination you plan to conduct. A sample is shown below.

> In the direct examination section of your trial notebook, include an outline of your testimony and one for each witness whose direct examination you plan to conduct. (See Chapter 15, Organizing a Trial Notebook.)

Some attorneys like to include in their outlines both all the evidence they plan to elicit during a witness's direct examination, and also the questions they plan to ask. While writing out a few important questions and answers makes sense, don't write down too much detail. Direct examinations rarely proceed exactly according to plan, and a pre-determined list of dozens of questions may end up confusing you more than it helps.

An outline is usually adequate if it refers to the main points in a witness's story and includes a few questions you want to be sure to ask. If you plan to offer any exhibits such as business records or photographs into evidence during a witness's testimony, your outline should refer to those exhibits and the "foundational" evidence you have to introduce to make the exhibits admissible. (See Chapter 12, Exhibits.)

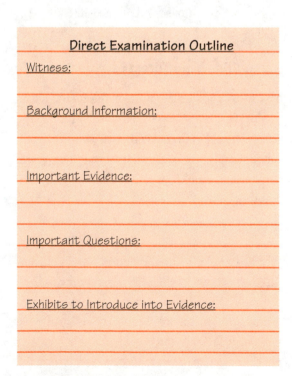

Direct Examination Outline

Witness:

Background Information:

Important Evidence:

Important Questions:

Exhibits to Introduce into Evidence:

Make sure your outline is user-friendly. You'll want to use your direct examination outline for each witness when you ask questions. So as you make it, think of the little details that can affect your questioning. For example, if you have sight problems, write extra big or copy your typed outline on a photocopy machine that enlarges. You may also find it useful to use a fluorescent marker to highlight the most important testimony.

3. Rehearse Each Witness's Testimony

Even though you may have talked to a witness often, always have a final meeting with the witness to rehearse your questions and the witness's answers. You want the witness to know what evidence you are after and the kinds of questions you will ask. You don't need to script every word of your direct examination, but the rehearsal will help your witnesses testify completely and confidently. You may wish to follow the lead of many attorneys and actually run through a practice direct examination. And if you know or strongly suspect the types of questions your adversary is likely to ask on cross-examination, it is a good idea to ask them yourself during rehearsal to give your witness practice in coping with them.

Before rehearsing testimony, consider returning with the witness to the scene of important events, assuming that its appearance has not changed radically. The visit may lead the witness to remember details that add credibility to the witness's testimony.

Some witnesses think that it is improper to rehearse testimony before trial. But it's both proper and routine, and your witness should know that. Also, remind your witness that the purpose of the rehearsal is not to influence the witness's testimony; all you want is the truth. That way, if your adversary asks on cross-examination whether you coached your witness to make up a story, your witness can answer honestly, "No. Ms. Nolo and I talked about what she was going to ask me, but she just told me to tell the truth."

If you are going to ask a witness to identify a document or a photograph or to draw a diagram as part of direct examination, make sure you rehearse this. You don't want a somewhat nervous witness suddenly becoming unable to identify an impor-

tant exhibit in the middle of trial! (See Chapter 12, Exhibits, for information on how to admit exhibits into evidence.)

For example, say your case involves an auto accident in an intersection. During the rehearsal, you and the witness can draw the intersection, including fixed landmarks such as traffic signals and crosswalks. At trial, you may begin the witness's testimony about the diagram by asking the witness what has already been drawn and then asking the witness to make further markings—for example, paths of cars—as the direct testimony unfolds. (See Chapter 12, Exhibits, for an example of how to do this.)

"Eileen Willis, come on down!"

Practice your questioning. An unexpected answer or objection may throw you off stride and cause you to ask leading or other improper questions. The best way to prevent this is to practice your questioning, both during rehearsal with each witness, perhaps with a friend, and in your own mind.

Mentally formulate different questions for eliciting the same evidence in response to different answers a witness may give and then think about which of the possible questions will be proper and which improper. If necessary, write out specific questions that you have difficulty phrasing properly and include them in your outline to give you the comfort of a written backup. This pre-trial practice will prepare you for the unexpected developments that almost always occur during trial.

When you rehearse with your witnesses, you can also offer a few suggestions that may enhance the credibility of their testimony:

- Remind a witness to make occasional eye contact with the judge or jury while testifying. People often come across as more credible when they look listeners right in the eye. Tell the witness something like, "I'll ask you, 'Please tell the jury what happened after the chicken crossed the road.' Then you should look at the jury when you answer."

- Ask a witness to dress in conservative business attire. A witness need not wear a suit or expensive clothes, but should dress in a manner that indicates respect for the court.

Familiarize yourself with your judge's direct examination procedures. Before trial, visit the courtroom where your trial will take place. Ask the clerk whether your judge has any general rules about direct examination. For example, one judge may insist that you stand at a podium when asking questions; another may allow you to sit at counsel table. Most judges, however, will not let you stand next to the witness or wander about the courtroom when asking questions. Also, if you plan on showing an exhibit to a witness, find out whether your judge will allow you to personally hand the exhibit to the witness or whether you should give it to the bailiff to hand to the witness.

Violating such rules will not make or break your trial. But knowing how a judge expects you to question witnesses lets your judge know that you have prepared thoroughly and seriously, frees you to concentrate on your witness's testimony and allows your witnesses to relax and present convincing testimony.

D. PRESENTING YOUR OWN TESTIMONY ON DIRECT EXAMINATION

As you undoubtedly know from watching movies and TV, direct examination usually unfolds in a question-and-answer format: an attorney asks questions, and a witness answers them. But what happens when you are a pro per litigant serving both as attorney and witness?

A humorous answer was provided by the movie *Bananas.* In one of the well-loved courtroom scenes,

Woody Allen is representing himself in a trial. When it comes time for him to testify, he asks a question from counsel table, runs up to the witness stand to answer it, runs back to counsel table to ask another question, and so forth.

Luckily, the procedure in real courtrooms is not nearly so strenuous. Normally, when it is your turn to testify, tell the judge something like, "Your Honor, I'm now going to testify in my own behalf." Then walk to the witness box, remain standing and swear or affirm to tell the truth. Then sit in the witness chair and give your evidence as you would tell a story. Because most judges are used to the question-and-answer procedure, however, you may find that the judge occasionally stops your narrative and asks questions.

You can look at notes to refresh your recollection. If you think you have forgotten to say something while testifying, ask the judge for permission to review your notes. Say something like, "Your Honor, I think I've forgotten something here. May I have permission to return to the counsel table for a moment to review my notes?" Just like any other witness, you may review any document to refresh your recollection. (See Section E, below.) Once your memory is refreshed, return to the witness box and carry on with your testimony.

For example, assume that you are a tenant, and the landlord is suing you for not paying your rent. You are testifying on your own behalf, trying to prove that you legally refused to pay because the landlord failed to maintain your apartment in a habitable condition. (Many states have a law re-quiring landlords to keep rental units livable.) Your testimony about the leaky ceiling problem in your apartment might look like this:

1 **You:**

The worst time I remember was on March 12. I came home from work and saw about five separate leaks in the living room. There were more in the bedroom and the kitchen. A couple of leaks I couldn't even put a bucket under, because the water was just dripping down the walls.

2 **Judge:**

Excuse me, Mr. Nolo. The water dripping down the walls, are you referring to leaks in the living room?

3 **You:**

Yes, Your Honor.

4 **Judge:**

So three of the leaks were away from the walls and you put buckets under those, but the other two you couldn't?

5 **You:**

That's right.

6 **Judge:**

All right, please continue.

7 **You:**

Well, I got right on the phone and called the landlord and told him about the leaks. He said that he'd get around to it when he had a chance, but that a lot of his tenants were complaining so I'd just have to wait my turn. Well, two weeks went by ….

Transcript Analysis: Here, you present your testimony largely in story form. As is common, however, the judge interrupts to ask questions. When she does, you stop your narrative to answer the questions, and then continue telling your story.

Testify first or last. Whether you are the plaintiff or the defendant, you may call your witnesses and testify personally in whatever order you choose. However, you are generally better off testifying either first or last.

The usual advantage of testifying first is that you give an overview of your whole case and have a chance to capture a judge's or jury's immediate attention. By testifying last you lose this chance to frame your case but gain the opportunity to address problems that arose during the testimony of your other witnesses and make a strong final impression. If you or your adversary request it, the judge is likely to order all witnesses to remain out of the courtroom until after they testify. But as a party to the case you can be present throughout the trial. Thus, you may be the only witness for your side who is personally aware of problems that arise during other witnesses' direct examinations.

E. HOW TO QUESTION WITNESSES

When it's your turn to question a witness, you may not know where to start. This section gives you a structure that will let you plan an effective direct examination.

Do not make speeches. A frequent complaint of judges is that pro per litigants often violate the orderly process of trial by making argumentative speeches during direct examination instead of presenting evidence through testimony and questions. The time to make a speech summing up your case is closing argument, not direct examination.

For example, assume that your landlord is trying to evict you from your apartment for making excessive noise in violation of a lease provision requiring tenants not to disturb the neighbors. You call Bernie Rhodes as a witness to testify that there was no excessive noise on the two nights that, according to a landlord's witness, your stereo was blaring. Examine this sample testimony:

1 You:

Now Mr. Rhodes, tell us about June 3 and 4.

2 Your Witness:

Mr. Nolo, those were the nights that you and I were working on the Keck proposal. It was due on June 5, and we were working pretty much all night in your apartment on both those nights.

3 You:

Did we play the stereo in the apartment on those nights?

4 Your Witness:

I remember that we played it a little one of the nights when we stopped to have a pizza, but I know it wasn't real loud.

5 **You:**

Do you remember if anyone knocked at the door asking us to turn down the volume?

6 **Your Witness:**

No, I'm sure that didn't happen.

7 **You:**

Your Honor, this proves what I've been saying all along. Mr. Rhodes was inside the apartment with me on both nights and as he told you there was no loud music. We were working on a very important proposal that had to be finished, and there's no way we'd mess ourselves up by blasting a stereo.

Transcript Analysis: Your outburst in No. 7 is an improper speech. When conducting direct examination of a witness, you are limited to asking questions. It is improper for you to argue about the credibility and significance of evidence, until closing argument.

1. Begin With Background Questions

Direct examination begins when you call a witness (yourself or someone else) to the stand, and the witness takes an oath to tell the truth. At that point the judge will turn to you and say something like, "You may proceed."

After taking a deep breath, you may want to start right in on the witness's story. But before you do, ask a few questions about the witness's personal background. Witnesses who are not used to giving testimony or being in court often gain confidence (and therefore look more credible) when they can begin their testimony by talking about their own background. At the same time, the personal background testimony tends to humanize witnesses in the eyes of a judge or a jury.

For example, here is how you might begin the direct examination of your witness, Ilene Johnson:

1 **You:**

Ms. Johnson, are you employed?

2 **Your Witness:**

Yes. I'm the assistant manager of the Brentwood branch of First Savings and Loan.

3 **You:**

How long have you been employed at the bank?

4 **Your Witness:**

Just about eight years now. I started out as a teller and then went through a management training program. I became an assistant manager a little over three years ago.

5 **You:**

Could you briefly tell us what you do as an assistant manager?

6 **Your Witness:**

I'm basically responsible for hiring and training the teller staff.

7 **You:**

All right. Now, turning your attention to the afternoon of March 12....

If a witness is not employed, consider other possible background topics. For example, if a witness is in college, ask the name of the college and the witness's course of study. Or if a witness is a parent, ask the names and ages of the witness's children. Obviously, you want to emphasize information that makes the witness appear to be someone the judge or jury can rely on. So if your witness is serving a life sentence for murder, or if the witness's only interests are TV talk shows and soap operas, you may want to skip personal background questioning altogether!

No matter what theme you choose to pursue, your background questioning should not generally be much longer than the sample above, since technically the information is not relevant to the meatier testimony the witness will give. But if you are brief, judges normally allow background questions so that the witness can relax and the judge or jury can learn a little bit about the person.

BACKGROUND QUESTIONING OF EXPERT WITNESSES

Background questioning of witnesses must usually be brief because the information you elicit has nothing to do with whether a witness's testimony is accurate. Not so with an expert witness, who by definition is a person whose special skills or knowledge enables her to interpret evidence that is beyond the understanding of the average judge or juror. Before an expert witness testifies, you have to demonstrate to the judge that the witness has special knowledge, skill or experience. This ordinarily requires extensive background questioning about the witness's qualifications. (See Chapter 16, Expert Witnesses.)

💡 **Don't nominate your witness for the Nobel Prize.** Most judges will not allow you to ask about honors and achievements a witness may have received or good deeds a witness may have performed. For example, a witness may be the Employee of the Month, the Citizen of the Year, a volunteer in the pediatrics ward of a hospital or the Little League President. Judges typically think of this kind of information as going beyond personal background and into a witness's moral character, and evidence of moral character is rarely admitted in civil trials.

---

2. Ask Legally Permissible Questions

After you conclude background questioning, you are ready to ask questions to elicit a witness's story. All questions fall into one of four broad categories:

- narrative questions
- open questions
- closed questions
- leading questions.

Rigidly classifying a question in one category or another is unimportant. What is essential is that you become familiar enough with these different types of questions to know which types you are usually allowed to ask at different stages of a trial and which you are not. During direct and redirect examination you are primarily limited to asking open and closed questions.

In addition, familiarity with the different types of questions allows you to adjust your questioning technique according to whether you want a witness to tell a story in his or her own words (use open questions), or to testify to specific information (use closed questions).

a. Narrative Questions

Narrative questions are broad and open-ended. They ask a witness to describe an entire series of events. Here are some examples:

- "Please tell us everything that happened on February 14."

- "Describe the events leading up to the signing of the contract."

Because narrative questions allow witnesses to describe events in their own words, they have the advantage of avoiding any suggestion that you are telling a witness what to say. However, many judges believe that if questions are too open-ended, witnesses (especially non-expert witnesses) will refer to legally improper evidence and waste time with irrelevant digressions. Your judge may not allow you to ask narrative questions or may severely restrict your use of them.

b. Open Questions

Like narrative questions, open questions invite witnesses to testify in their own words. But typically an open question limits a witness to a description of a specific event or condition. Open questions are one of your principal direct examination tools, because most witnesses make their best impressions on a judge or jury when they are allowed to be themselves and tell a story in their own words.

Here are some open questions:

- "Can you describe the condition of the car after the accident?"

- "What happened when you entered the room?"

- "After you received the letter, then what happened?"

- "Please tell us what was said in this conversation."

- "How did he react when he found out that they would not extend the lease?"

- "Please describe the condition of my daughter when we picked her up from my ex-spouse."

Because open questions allow witnesses to respond in their own words but do not invite a long story (narrative) of an entire series of events, most judges allow them. In their view, open questions pose less of a risk that a witness will refer to improper evidence or digress into irrelevancies.

c. Closed Questions

Closed questions ask witnesses for specific pieces of information. They do not invite a witness to expand on an answer. Here are some examples:

- "What color was the car?"

- "On what day of the week did the meeting take place?"

- "After you told her that the tool sets were back-ordered, how did she reply?"

- "What time was it when my ex-spouse brought my son home?"

- "How long was it until I was returned to regular job duties?"

- "What's the last thing the manager said before closing the door?"

Just like open questions, closed questions are one of your principal direct examination tools. Sometimes you do not want witnesses to describe events in their own words. Instead, you want to focus the judge's or jury's attention on a specific piece of information. You may want to do so either because a witness has neglected to mention the information in response to an open question, or because you want to emphasize particular testimony that a witness has already given.

d.   Leading Questions

Leading questions suggest the answer you want a witness to give; they are basically statements in question form. Examples:

- "The car was red, wasn't it?"

- "Isn't it true that he never said anything about needing the manager's approval?"

Because they indicate your desired answers, leading questions violate the guiding principle of direct examination: that your job is to ask the questions, and your witnesses' job is to provide the information. If you ask leading questions of friendly witnesses, the witnesses are very likely to agree to whatever you say. So if your adversary objects, the judge will probably not allow you to ask leading questions during direct examination. (See Chapter 14, Making and Responding to Objections.)

Despite the general policy forbidding leading questions during direct examination, they are permitted in a variety of special circumstances. The two most common arise when you elicit evidence of a witness's personal background or evidence that is "preliminary." Preliminary evidence is undisputed evidence that you want to run through quickly, in order to get to important testimony. Examples:

- During personal background questioning you may ask, "You've been employed by the school district for over 15 years now?"

- Your adversary agrees that a meeting took place on August 31 but disputes what was said during the meeting. Before you ask your witness what was said during the meeting you may ask, "A meeting took place on August 31, correct?"

- Your ex-spouse admits that he has done carpentry work for a Mr. Edwards and a few others, but claims that he does not earn enough to pay court-ordered child support. Before going into how much Edwards paid your ex-spouse, you may ask Edwards, "My ex-husband did carpentry work for you during June and July of this year, is that correct?"

- Your adversary admits that Dr. Phibes, an expert on the valuation of coin collections, examined your coin collection but disagrees with Phibes' opinion as to its value. You may properly ask Dr. Phibes, "Now, you examined my coin collection, right?"

- You call an auto mechanic to testify to the extent of the necessary repairs to your car following an accident. Your adversary admits that the mechanic repaired your car on June 22-23, but disagrees that all of the problems were caused by the accident. You may properly ask the mechanic, "You are the Exoff mechanic who repaired my car on June 22 and 23, right?"

You can also ask a leading question when you want to help a witness find her place in the story if your direct examination has been disrupted by a somewhat lengthy court recess. For example, say that your witness testified that the traffic light in your direction was green when you entered the intersection. Following that answer, the court recesses for lunch. When you resume after lunch, you may begin by asking the witness, "Before lunch, you testified that the traffic light in my direction was green when I entered the intersection, correct?" Though the question is leading, you are not putting words in the witness's mouth. You are simply repeating evidence the witness has already given to get the witness (and the judge and jury) back on track following a break in the testimony.

You may also ask leading questions during your direct examination of a "hostile" witness. (See Section F, below.)

3. Establish a Witness's Personal Knowledge

When you're planning the testimony you want to elicit on direct examination, it's crucial to understand that you must show that a witness is testifying from personal knowledge. (This rule doesn't apply to expert witnesses; see Chapter 16, Expert Witnesses.) This means that you must show that a witness personally observed, heard, smelled, touched or tasted whatever the witness is testifying about. Second-hand information may be good enough for TV talk shows and supermarket tabloids, but it won't work in court—a judge or jury can't take it into account in arriving at a verdict.

> ⚠ **Make sure you understand other evidence rules.** In addition to the requirement that a witness have personal knowledge, a variety of other evidence rules affect the admissibility of evidence, such as the "relevance rule." The most important of these rules are discussed in Chapter 13, Basic Rules of Evidence. Please be sure to read and understand that material before planning your testimony.

Usually, you do not have to make any special effort to show that a witness has personal knowledge; the testimony itself demonstrates it. For example, assume that you have brought suit against the owner of a dog that bit you on October 3. You call Jordan Miller as a witness to testify to the dog's attack on you. After the personal background questions, your direct examination of Miller continues as follows:

1 You:

Mr. Miller, where were you about four o'clock on the afternoon of October 3?

2 Witness:

I was outside my house, watering my front lawn.

3 You:

Did you see me that afternoon?

4 Witness:

Yes, I saw you walking your dog about two houses down from mine.

5 You:

Did anything happen to me as I was walking

my dog?

6   **Witness:**

Yes. You were attacked by a German shepherd.

Transcript Analysis: With no need of complicated techniques, you have established that Miller has personal knowledge because he testified that he personally saw what happened to you.

Now let's see how the personal knowledge requirement works when you want a witness to testify to another person's statement. Jordan Miller is still testifying, and you want to ask him about what the dog owner said after his dog bit you. This portion of Miller's direct examination goes like this:

7   **You:**

Mr. Miller, what happened next?

8   **Witness:**

The German shepherd ran back across the street. Then a man came running over and said that he was very sorry for what his dog had done.

9   **You:**

How do you know this is what he said?

10   **Witness:**

I was standing only a few feet away from him; I could hear very clearly.

11   **You:**

Did he say anything else?

12   **Witness:**

Yes, he said that the dog got out of his yard through a hole in the fence that he hadn't had time to fix.

13   **You:**

Do you see the man who made those statements?

14   **Witness:**

Yes, he's sitting over there [indicating the defendant].

Transcript Analysis: Again, without any special effort you have shown that Miller has personal knowledge of what the defendant said after the attack.

HOW TO IDENTIFY PEOPLE IN THE COURTROOM

Pointing to a person in the courtroom while testifying is often the only way a witness can identify who made a statement or engaged in some other type of conduct. For example, in the dog bite case testimony above, a witness points out your adversary as the person who made a certain statement. But be careful how you ask a witness to identify a person in the courtroom. It is improper to ask a leading question such as, "Is the defendant sitting over there the person who made the statement?" Instead, as in the example, ask a non-leading question: "Do you see the man who made those statements?"

Pointing isn't always the only way to identify someone. If a witness personally knows the person whose conduct you want the witness to talk about, you can simply ask, "Who made the statement?" and expect the witness to say something like, "It was Doris Defendant who said that."

If a witness points to a person in the courtroom, the court reporter cannot record the silent gesture. To make sure the record reflects the identification, say something like, "May the record show that the witness pointed to Doris Defendant."

Now let's look at an example where a witness lacks personal knowledge. Assume that Miller's direct examination continues like this:

15   **You:**

Mr. Miller, do you know whether this dog has ever bitten other people?

16   **Witness:**

Yes, the dog bit three others before she bit you.

Transcript Analysis: In this example, you have not shown that Miller has personal knowledge of the dog's previous attacks. For all the judge can tell, Miller may know about three prior attacks only because other people have told him about them. Miller would then be testifying to second-hand information. So if your adversary objects, or perhaps even if he doesn't, the judge is likely to exclude the evidence in No. 16, meaning that the judge or jury could not consider that evidence in arriving at the verdict. (See Chapter 14, Making and Responding to Objections.)

If you forget to show that a witness has personal knowledge, normally you can readily fix the problem. Here is how you could do so in the Miller example:

17   **Judge:**

Ms. Nolo, that last answer [No. 16] is improper because you have not demonstrated that the witness has personal knowledge of previous attacks by the dog. I'm striking that answer from the record.

18   **You:**

Sorry, Your Honor. Mr. Miller, let me ask you this. Did you ever personally see the dog bite

other people?

19   **Witness:**

Yes. I've seen that same dog attack and bite three other people.

Here, with just one additional question you have shown that Miller has personal knowledge of the prior attacks, and the testimony in No. 19 will be admissible (assuming, of course, that it does not run afoul of other evidentiary rules; see Chapter 13).

Special Personal Knowledge Rules for Conversations: Many judges apply a special personal knowledge rule for conversations. Before asking about what people said to each other (either in person or on the telephone), they want the witness to testify to three things:

* when the conversation took place

* where the conversation took place

* who was present during the conversation.

For example, assume that you are the owner of an apartment building and that you have brought suit to evict a tenant, Denise Beilenson, for keeping dogs in her apartment in violation of her lease. You have called Shelly Resnik as a witness to testify that she was present when Beilenson admitted to you that she was keeping three golden retrievers in her apartment and that she had no intention of getting rid of them. Your direct examination of Resnik might go as follows:

1   **You:**

Ms. Resnik, do you remember a conversation between me and Ms. Beilenson about dogs?

2   **Witness:**

Yes, I do.

3   You:

When did this conversation take place?

4   Witness:

If I remember right it was on the 13th of April.

5   You:

And where did the conversation take place?

6   Witness:

Down by the apartment's swimming pool.

7   You:

Was anyone else present during this conversation?

8   Witness:

No, just the two of you were talking. I was sitting a few feet away but I didn't notice anyone else around.

9   You:

Now, please tell us what was said during this conversation.

Transcript Analysis: Having shown that the witness knows when the conversation took place (No. 4), where it took place (No. 6) and who was present (No. 8), you have satisfied the personal knowledge rule for conversations and in No. 9 properly proceed to elicit what was said. True, question No. 1 indicates to the witness that you want to hear testimony about a dog conversation, which to a stickler may seem leading and therefore improper. But few judges would deem it either leading or an improper question. The usual rule is that you can call a witness's attention to the subject matter of his or her testimony as long as you do not indicate your desired answer.

Don't worry if a witness doesn't remember exact details. The fact that a witness can't remember an exact date, time or other background fact about a conversation (or other event) rarely defeats personal knowledge so as to prevent admissibility of testimony concerning the conversation. If your witness cannot be specific, elicit her or his best estimate. Even testimony that "The conversation took place in early April," or that "It took place sometime in April," will usually be good enough to show personal knowledge.

---

4.   Refresh a Witness's Recollection If Necessary

You should almost always rehearse a witness's testimony before trial. (See Section C, above.) Nevertheless, even the best prepared witness may suffer a lapse of memory while testifying. For example, in response to a question you know a witness can answer, the witness might respond, "I don't remember." If this happens, do not panic. It's perfectly proper to attempt to "refresh the witness's recollection" with a document that refers to the information the witness has forgotten.

You can use any helpful document as a refresher, such as the forgetful witness's deposition or an informal written statement. The document needn't have been personally prepared by the forgetful witness; you may refresh one witness's recollection with the statement of a different witness, a receipt, a police report or any other document.

Assuming that you have handy a document that you think will refresh the flagging memory of your forgetful witness, here's a little ritual you should follow:

Step 1: Ask the witness whether looking at the document might help refresh his recollection.

Step 2: If the witness responds that looking at the document might help, mark it as an "exhibit," show it to your adversary and then ask the judge for permission to approach the witness. (See Chapter 12, Exhibits.) When permission is granted, walk to the witness box and show him the specific portion of the document that contains the information you hope will refresh his recollection.

Step 3: Take the document away from the witness and return to the place where you are asking questions.

Step 4: Ask the witness if his memory is refreshed.

Step 5: If the answer is yes, go on and ask the question necessary to produce the testimony.

⚠️ **Your adversary may introduce the "refreshing" document into evidence.** In federal court and most state courts, you cannot offer the document you use to refresh a witness's recollection into evidence, unless of course it's admissible for some other reason. (See Federal Rule of Evidence 612.) However, your adversary is allowed to offer the document into evidence if the adversary chooses to do so. Therefore, be careful about the document you use to refresh recollection. If it contains information that your adversary wants to get before the judge or jury, the document may prove more helpful to your adversary than to you.

Here is an example of how the process works. You are examining Mr. Houston. He has unexpectedly forgotten information a building contractor told him about the type of wood the contractor was to use on the front of his house. Luckily, you have a document referring to the forgotten information, and proceed as follows:

1 **You:**

Mr. Houston, did the contractor say anything about the kind of wood he would use for the front of the house?

2 **Witness:**

Hmmm— I'm pretty sure he did, but I just can't remember.

3 **You:**

Do you think it might refresh your recollection if you looked at the estimate the contractor prepared? [Step 1]

4 Witness:

It might.

5 You:

Your Honor, I'm holding a written estimate marked Exhibit A. Counsel for the plaintiff has seen it. May I approach the witness for the purpose of refreshing his recollection? [Step 2]

See Chapter 12 for a discussion of marking and using Exhibits.

6 The Judge:

Go ahead.

7 You:

Okay, Mr. Houston, please look Exhibit A over, especially this section right here [pointing].

After waiting a few moments, you pick up the document and take it back with you to where you are asking questions. [Step 3]

8 You:

Now do you remember what kind of wood the contractor said he would use on the front of the house? [Step 4]

9 Witness:

Yes, I do.

10 You:

And what did he say? [Step 5]

11 Witness:

He said he would use cedar siding.

 Remove the document before eliciting your desired testimony. When refreshing recollection, remember to remove whatever document you have shown the witness before asking if the witness's memory has been refreshed (see No. 7). The reason is that under the evidence rule barring "hearsay," the witness cannot testify to what the document says. (See Chapter 13, Basic Rules of Evidence.) But if the witness testifies to his or her present recollection as refreshed by the document, no hearsay is involved.

OFFERING DOCUMENTS AND OTHER OBJECTS DURING DIRECT EXAMINATION

Tangible objects such as receipts, letters, business records, photographs and computer printouts are often extremely important at trial. They convince a judge or jury of the accuracy of your testimony and that of your witnesses. They also add interest to your presentation of evidence (remember the old saying that "a picture is worth a thousand words") and provide hard evidence to support fallible human memory.

At trial, any tangible object that you want to introduce into evidence is called an "exhibit." While presenting exhibits is not usually difficult, you generally have to follow a number of preliminary steps (called "laying a foundation") before your exhibits can be received in evidence. Different types of exhibits require different steps. For example, the foundation necessary to introduce a photograph into evidence is very different from that required to introduce a business record into evidence. For this reason, we've given exhibits a chapter of their own. (Chapter 12, Exhibits.) Because you will typically offer exhibits into evidence during direct examination, make sure that you understand the material in Chapter 12 before you plan direct examination testimony.

F. HOSTILE WITNESSES

Subject to subpoena limitations, you can call and question any person who has information helpful to your case, even your adversary or someone else who is antagonistic to you. If you decide to call such a person as a witness, ask the judge for permission to treat the person as a "hostile witness." If a judge rules that a witness is hostile, you have the right to conduct direct examination of the witness with leading questions. (See for example Federal Rule of Evidence 611, Texas Civil Rule of Evidence 611 and similar rules in almost all other states.)

For example, assume that you are involved in a child custody dispute with Jan, your ex-spouse. You are pretty sure that a co-worker of Jan's has seen Jan drunk on at least two occasions in the presence of your young children. You want to call the co-worker as a witness to help prove that Jan should not be awarded custody of the children. On the other hand, you know that Jan and the co-worker are dating. The co-worker is unwilling to meet with you informally, and you cannot afford to take the co-worker's deposition. Moreover, according to Jan the co-worker supports Jan's request for custody.

In this situation, if you do subpoena the co-worker as a witness, at the trial ask the judge for permission to approach the bench before beginning the co-worker's direct examination. Tell the judge that the co-worker has been uncooperative, and ask for permission to treat the witness as a hostile witness. The judge may grant immediate

APPROACHING THE BENCH

permission or delay a ruling until after the co-worker begins testifying and the judge has a chance to evaluate if the witness is antagonistic to you. When and if the judge rules that the witness is hostile, you may ask leading questions.

The advantage of leading questions is that you can limit the witness's testimony to the specific topics that support your claims. They do not give an antagonistic witness an opportunity to launch into areas supporting your adversary that you don't want to cover. For example, here are some of the questions you might ask the co-worker in the child custody case:

- "You have been dating Jan for about three months, correct?"

- "You and Jan took my children to a football game last October 9, right?"

- "And Jan got drunk at the game, right?"

- "Jan had so much to drink that you had to help Jan to the car?"

- "And my children were with you the entire time?"

While of course you have no guarantee that a hostile witness like the co-worker will answer honestly, leading questions at least allow you to control the subject matter of the testimony.

⚠️ **Other evidence rules are important too.** A variety of other rules also affect whether direct examination questions are proper. For example, you should avoid questions that are "compound" or "vague," or call for "hearsay" or "character evidence." These additional rules are described in Chapter 13, Basic Rules of Evidence.

G. THE JUDGE'S ROLE

It is important to recognize that judges have a good deal of discretion over what questions they will allow you to ask. For example, federal judges may exercise "reasonable control over the mode and order of interrogating witnesses and presenting evidence." (Federal Rule of Evidence 611 (a).) No two judges interpret the term "reasonable" in exactly the same way. The same question that Judge A considers a proper "open" question, Judge B may consider an improper "narrative" question. Similarly, a judge will often allow much more deviation from strict rules of evidence in non-jury trials than in jury trials because the judge feels capable of ignoring any improper evidence you bring out by your questioning.

Pay attention to any instructions a judge gives you about how to question a witness. If you are uncertain about whether you can ask a certain kind of question, do not be afraid to ask your judge for permission to approach the bench and ask the judge how to elicit the information you want.

For example, let's examine how to ask a judge for help if your adversary makes an objection that confuses you. You have just concluded preliminary questioning and now want to ask your witness to testify to a conversation in which your adversary agreed to buy your car.

1 **You:**

Can you please tell the jury what was said during this conversation?

2 **Opponent:**

Objection, Your Honor. That calls for a narrative response.

3   **Judge:**

I'll sustain the objection.

4   **You:**

Your Honor, I'm a bit confused. May we approach the bench?

5   **Judge:**

Briefly. Both counsel please approach the bench.

6   **You (at the bench):**

Your Honor, I didn't think this question called for a narrative answer. I just want the witness to testify to what was said during this one conversation. I'm not quite sure what to do.

7   **Judge:**

Ms. Nolo, I sustained the objection because I think your question is too broad. Ask a narrower question; don't try to get the whole conversation with one question. Please resume your places and proceed.

8   **You (back at the podium):**

Let me ask you this. Tell us how the conversation got started.

9   **Witness:**

The first thing I remember is that you told the defendant that you were willing to reduce the price of the car by $500.

10   **You:**

And how did he reply?

Transcript Analysis: Here, the judge exercises discretion by sustaining a narrative objection to a question that many other judges would consider proper (No. 3). Rather than guess at the problem and getting yourself more confused, you ask for permission to approach the bench and then ask for help (No. 6). The judge makes a suggestion (No. 7) and you then begin to go step-by-step through the conversation (Nos. 8-10).

THE ROLE OF OBJECTIONS IN ENFORCING EVIDENCE RULES

A party to a lawsuit who believes that the other party has violated a rule of evidence or procedure during trial can object. For example, if your adversary asks an improper leading question during direct examination, violates the personal knowledge rule or commits some other evidentiary sin, or an adverse witness improperly rambles on in response to a proper question, you may say "Objection" and succinctly state the reason for your objection. If the judge deems the objection valid ("sustains" the objection), the information cannot be considered by the judge or jury in arriving at its verdict. A judge can also rule that evidence is inadmissible on her own, without waiting for a party to object. (See Chapter 14, Making and Responding to Objections.)

H.   A SAMPLE DIRECT EXAMINATION

Let's look at a sample direct examination transcript, followed by an analysis of the questioning techniques. This transcript has been shortened for illustrative purposes. A real direct examination is likely to be considerably longer.

This example is based on a negligence case (first described in Chapter 5, What You Need To Prove at Trial: The Plaintiff's Perspective) in which a building contractor named Sarah Adams allegedly made a careless left turn and as a result struck you while you were in a crosswalk. Adams admits striking you with her truck, but claims this occurred only because you suddenly ran out from between two parked cars a short distance north of the intersection.

After testifying yourself to what happened, you call Cynthia White as your next witness. Ms. White was at the intersection and saw the accident. In your direct examination of her you want to emphasize that you were in the crosswalk and that Adams made the left turn carelessly because she was not paying attention to the road. You subpoenaed Ms. White even though she was very willing to come to court and describe what she saw. Then, under your local court's on call procedure, you phoned her when the court broke for lunch and asked her to come to court at 1:30. Ms. White is escorted to the witness stand by the bailiff, placed under oath by the clerk and seated. You go to the podium and begin asking questions. The direct examination goes as follows:

1 You:

Ms. White, please state your full name for the record.

2 Witness:

Cynthia White.

3 You:

Ms. White, are you employed?

4 Witness:

Not at the moment. I'm going to college.

5 You:

Which college do you attend?

6 Witness:

Vernal College in Atlantic Highlands. I'm working on a Masters in psychology.

7 You:

So you've already completed your undergraduate work?

8 Witness:

Yes, about seven years ago. Then I went to work to earn some money so I could go back to school.

9 You:

Ms. White, were you at the intersection of Main and Elm at about 3 p.m. on the afternoon of March 31 of last year?

10 Witness:

Yes, I was.

11 You:

And did you see an automobile accident?

12 Witness:

Yes.

13 You:

Where were you when the accident occurred?

14 Witness:

I was in my car, stopped for a red light. I was heading south on Elm, and I was stopped just north of Main waiting for the light to change.

15 You:

Were any cars stopped in front of you?

16 **Witness:**

No, I was the first car in line. Actually, traffic was pretty light, and I don't know if anyone was behind me.

17 **You:**

Did you notice me at that intersection?

18 **Witness:**

Yes I did. I saw you step off the curb and begin to walk across Elm. The light was green for you.

19 **You:**

Is there any particular reason that you noticed me?

20 **Witness:**

I heard some young children shouting on the corner where you had been standing, so I looked over in your direction. That's when I saw you step off the curb.

21 **You:**

Did I walk into any particular area of the street?

22 **Witness:**

Yes, you were in the crosswalk.

23 **You:**

What happened after you saw me step off the curb into the crosswalk?

24 **Witness:**

I turned to look out my front window to see if the light had changed to green yet. That's

when I saw her [pointing to the defendant Adams] heading east on Main and begin to make a left turn to go north on Elm.

25 **You:**

Let the record reflect the witness is pointing to the defendant, Sarah Adams. Then what happened?

26 **Witness:**

She speeded up as she made the left turn. Then I suddenly realized that you were in the crosswalk, and I looked to see if you were in any danger. Just about then is when her truck ran into you.

27 **You:**

How long were you watching the truck before you saw it hit me?

28 **Witness:**

That's hard to say exactly. I'd say about five seconds.

29 **You:**

And can you estimate the truck's speed during the time it was making the left-hand turn?

30 **Witness:**

At least 30-35 m.p.h., much too fast.

31 **You:**

How long have you been driving?

32 **Witness:**

Over 15 years.

33   **You:**

Before her truck hit me, could you see where the defendant was looking while she made the left turn?

34   **Witness:**

Yes, I could see her. At least part of the time, she was looking back over her right shoulder out the back window of her pickup truck.

35   **You:**

Is there any reason you can remember that?

36   **Witness:**

Yes, seeing her look behind her like that is what made me think that you might be in danger, and that's why I turned back to see if you were still in the crosswalk.

37   **You:**

After the truck hit me, what happened?

38   **Witness:**

Well, I pulled over to the curb and ran into a store to call an ambulance. Then I went out and stayed with you until the ambulance came.

39   **You:**

And what was the defendant doing?

40   **Witness:**

She pulled over to the opposite curb, and just sat in the cab of her truck until the police came about ten minutes later.

41   **You:**

Thank you. No further questions at this time, Your Honor.

Transcript Analysis: You begin Cynthia White's testimony with a few personal background questions (Nos. 1-8). Since Ms. White is not employed, you quite properly ask a few questions about her college studies. These questions probably help her relax, and they tell the judge or jury a little bit about her.

Then you properly show that Ms. White is testifying from personal knowledge (Nos. 9-12). Note that No. 9 is a leading question because all the information is in the question, leaving the witness only to answer "yes." But a judge will probably allow you to ask this leading question, since it is preliminary: Adams does not dispute the fact that White was at Main and Elm and that an accident took place at that location.

Ms. White's testimony is in the form of a story. You begin by setting the scene before the accident (Nos. 13-17), and end by showing what happened immediately afterwards (Nos. 37-40). Within the story is certain crucial evidence that you want to emphasize. For example, you want the judge or jury to know that Ms. White had a particular reason to see you step into the crosswalk (No. 20) and to see the defendant looking back over her shoulder (No. 36). You also show that she observed the defendant's truck long enough to estimate its speed (Nos. 28-30). While there is no minimum amount of time a witness must observe a truck to have sufficient personal knowledge to be able to estimate its speed, a judge will probably think that under ordinary circumstances five seconds is more than adequate. Also, you suggest that because Ms. White is an experienced driver, her estimate of speed is likely to be reliable (No. 32).

In eliciting Ms. White's story, you use a variety of types of questions. For example, Nos. 19 and 23 are open questions. They allow Ms. White to testify in her own words, but since they do not invite her to narrate an entire series of events they are permissible.

By contrast, Nos. 27, 29 and 31 are closed questions; you ask for specific pieces of information. This is perfectly sensible; you need to have the witness testify to the speed of the truck (No. 30), and you have to show that she saw the truck long enough to be able to give an estimate (No. 28). Yet, neither question is leading; you do not suggest how long Ms. White saw the truck, or what its speed was.

Finally, look at Nos. 39 and 40. On the surface, you are just completing the story of what happened. But the fact that the defendant did not get out of her cab to check on your condition after the accident seems cold-hearted. That information may make a judge or jury feel sympathetic towards you and hostile towards the defendant. While you cannot offer evidence on the ground that "it paints me in a sympathetic light," or because "it shows that my adversary is really a jerk," often you can get in this kind of emotional evidence in the course of telling the story.

Look at the witness you're questioning. Whether you stand at a podium or sit at the counsel table when asking questions, lay your outline in front of you. As each witness testifies, check off information to make sure you do not overlook important evidence. However, look at the witness who is testifying as much as possible and not at your outline. A judge or jury may lose interest in a witness's testimony if your face is buried in an outline and you are not paying attention to the testimony.

10

CROSS-EXAMINATION

Cross-examination is your opportunity to question any witness who testifies against you, including your adversary. Among non-lawyers, cross-examination is surely the most misunderstood phase of trial. For starters, forget about all those TV and movie dramas where a snarling cross-examiner shouts angry questions at a beleaguered witness from a distance of two inches. In fact, nothing will bring the wrath of a judge down upon a pro per litigant (or a lawyer) quicker than overly argumentative cross-examination questions. Normally, you must cross-examine from a podium or counsel table, and the manner of questioning must show respect to the judge and the system of justice at all times. The fact that you believe a witness to be a damnable liar does not change this one bit.

A second popular misconception concerns how much helpful evidence you can realistically hope to elicit during cross-examination. Again, TV and movies create a false image, this time that lawyers routinely win cases during cross-examination by tricking witnesses into blurting out vital information. But in the real world, an adverse witness is unlikely to change major portions of his story just because you question his credibility. So while you'll want to do the best job you can on cross-examination, you'll probably win or lose on the strength and credibility of your testimony and that of your witnesses on direct examination. (See Chapter 9, Direct Examination.)

A. AN OVERVIEW OF CROSS-EXAMINATION

Your adversary will probably conclude a witness's direct examination by saying, "No further questions at this time." The judge will then turn to you and say something like, "Ms. Nolo, you may cross-examine."

If you are at all uncertain about what you will ask on cross-examination, ask the judge for a few minutes to think about your questions. Lawyers are often granted this courtesy, and you should be entitled to no less. Use the time to look over the cross-examination outline in your trial notebook (see section H below). In general, you are best off asking no more than a few questions. Otherwise you may end up rehashing the entire direct examination, pointlessly giving your adversary's witness a chance to repeat damaging information.

Once you begin to cross-examine, behave exactly as you did (or will do, if you are the defendant) during direct examination. As on direct, all you are permitted to do during cross-examination is ask questions. You may not make speeches commenting on an adverse witness's testimony, argue with a witness or approach the witness without the judge's permission.

💡 **It's okay to read prepared questions during cross-examination.** On cross-examination it is usually effective to read prepared questions to an adverse witness. Unlike with direct examination of a friendly witness, a judge or jury won't dismiss the testimony you elicit as scripted.

After you finish cross-examination, your adversary may ask the court to ask additional questions on redirect examination. This gives the adversary a chance to bring out additional testimony in response to testimony you elicited during cross-examination, but is not to be used to rehash a witness's entire direct testimony. Following redirect you will be allowed to ask questions on recross-examination, after which the judge will probably excuse the witness.

1. The Two Goals of Cross-Examination

You can pursue two goals during cross-examination. One line of questioning is affirmative: you seek to produce evidence from a witness called by your adversary that supports your version of events. This will be possible more often than you may think. Few witnesses are all good for one side and all bad for the other.

Repeat helpful evidence from direct examination. Do not be surprised if your adversary asks her witness to testify to some information during direct that is helpful to you. It is an oft-used tactic. Your adversary may hope that by "hiding" information that helps you in a long direct examination, the judge or jury will overlook it. But to counter this tactic, you have the right to elicit the same helpful evidence during your cross-examination, even if it involves asking a witness to repeat exactly the same testimony already given on direct. Doing so emphasizes it for the judge or jury.

The second goal is to impeach adverse witnesses; that is, to cast doubt on their credibility. Using

the impeachment techniques discussed later in the chapter (Section E below), you try to give a judge or jury a reason to distrust the accuracy of the adverse witness's testimony.

It's fine to pursue both goals. You do not have to choose between goals one and two. During cross-examination of a single witness, you may try both to elicit information supporting your version of events and to impeach harmful evidence. When you do pursue both goals, as a general rule seek the affirmative information first. An adverse witness may be far less cooperative after you have tried to impeach her!

2. The Permissible Scope of Cross-Examination

The questions you ask during cross-examination must pertain to (be "within the scope" of) the topics that were explored on direct examination. Impeachment of a witness is allowed because you are attempting to weaken the credibility of direct examination testimony. But if you try to ask about a topic not addressed in your adversary's direct examination that supports your version of events, your adversary may object that your questions are beyond the scope of direct. In response, you may point out to the judge that she has discretion under evidence rules (such as Federal Rule of Evidence 611) to interpret the scope of direct rule broadly. (And many judges do so.)

Even if the judge sustains (agrees with) your adversary's objection, all is not lost. You can recall the same witness to the stand yourself after your adversary finishes presenting all of his evidence (rests his case), and ask the same questions that you were not allowed to ask on cross-examination. When you do recall the witness, ask the judge to rule that the witness is a "hostile witness." A judge's ruling that a witness is hostile to you gives you the right to ask leading questions even though technically you are conducting the witness's direct examination. (Hostile witnesses are discussed further in Chapter 9, Direct Examination.) In fact, pointing out to the judge that it will be a waste of court (and witness) time for the same witness to return to court at a later time is often an effective argument for asking a judge to overrule (deny) your adversary's beyond the scope objection.

B.   SHOULD YOU CROSS-EXAMINE?

You have a right to cross-examine every witness who testifies against you, but you are by no means required to do so. Perhaps it makes sense to some people to climb a mountain just "because it is there," but cross-examining a witness just because she is sitting in the witness box is foolish.

If you don't reasonably expect to elicit information that helps prove your version of events, and you don't think that you can impeach the witness on an important point, don't cross-examine. When the judge invites you to cross-examine, just say, "No questions." That way the witness cannot take advantage of your cross-examination to retell his story. And if you do not cross-examine, your adversary cannot conduct redirect examination, eliminating yet another chance for the witness to repeat his version of events.

Because adverse witnesses' stories are likely to sound better to a judge or jury the second or third time around, one of the worst things you can do on cross-examination is to conduct an aimless "fishing trip." You "fish" when you ask a question in the hope that a witness will give a response that impeaches him, but without factual support for that hope. For example, assume that an adverse witness testifies that you ran a red light. You ask on cross-examination, "What were you doing when you saw me run the light?" You have no idea what the witness was doing, but hope that the witness will respond that he was memorizing the Gettysburg Address or was otherwise so preoccupied that he couldn't possibly know what color the light was. Unfortunately, in this situation a witness will almost invariably give an answer that solidifies his direct examination testimony. For example, he might answer, "Your question reminds me that I was studying the traffic at that intersection in meticulous detail as part of a government research safety project." If your only alternative is to fish, you are far better off saying, "No questions."

While setting out any general rules about cross-examination is risky, here are some types of witnesses that should cause you to think twice or thrice before cross-examining:

- Expert witnesses, who are likely to know much more about the subject of their testimony than you do and thus are especially likely to retell their story during cross-examination. (See Chapter 16, Expert Witnesses, for more on this issue.)

- Witnesses who you think have even more damaging information than your adversary elicited during direct examination. Don't give them a second chance to hurt you.

• Witnesses with whom a judge or jury is likely to sympathize, such as children or elderly or infirm witnesses.

Offering impeachment evidence during direct examination. As any devotee of Perry Mason reruns knows, because of its dramatic effect, impeachment often takes place during cross-examination. However, cross-examination is not the only time you can offer impeaching evidence. Though it may be less dramatic, usually you can also introduce impeachment evidence when it is your turn to conduct direct examination.

For example, instead of asking a plaintiff's witness during cross-examination whether he had consumed three martinis a half hour before he supposedly saw you driving too fast, you can impeach the witness by later calling your own witness to testify that the plaintiff's witness was seen drinking martinis. The advantage of this choice is that the plaintiff's witness cannot undercut the force of the impeachment by immediately offering an explanation such as, "Yes, I did have three martinis, but I take medication that renders them as harmless as lemonade." The disadvantage is that you may lose the impeachment evidence altogether if you cannot produce your impeachment witness at trial.

C. HOW TO ASK QUESTIONS ON CROSS-EXAMINATION

It's crucial not to allow an adverse witness to retell her entire story on cross-examination. Fine advice, you may say. But just like, "Buy low, sell high," the key is in figuring out how to do it.

1. Ask Leading Questions

During cross-examination, the key to eliciting evidence without giving a witness a chance to retell a story is to ask leading questions. (Leading questions are explained in Chapter 9, Direct Examination.) Because they call on witnesses to respond only by saying yes or no, leading questions do not give a witness a chance to rehash direct examination testimony.

Questions are leading when they suggest the desired answer. Leading questions are improper on direct examination, when you're questioning your own witnesses, on the theory that a friendly witness will give the suggested answer even if it's not completely accurate. But leading questions are proper on cross-examination, because there is little risk that an adverse witness will falsely agree with you. Here are some typical leading questions:

• "You never told me the date the inspector would come by to inspect the plumbing, did you?"

• "The first time that you saw the light it was already red, correct?"

• "Isn't it true that you couldn't actually tell which person said 'Stop'?"

Since each of these questions is nothing more than an assertion of the answer you want the witness to give asked in the form of a question, you can see why leading questions—especially short, unambiguous ones—typically limit the scope of a witness's answer. In each example, the only answer the witness is called on to give is yes or no.

Stay in control during cross-examination. Increase the power of leading questions on cross-examination by asking them in a firm (not nasty) voice that suggests that you expect nothing more than yes or no in response. And to further inhibit an adverse witness from straying from your script, keep your questions short.

For example, if you want an adverse witness to agree that "The wolf huffed and puffed until he blew the house down," break it up into two questions: "The wolf huffed and puffed, correct?" and "He continued to huff and puff until he blew the house down, isn't that right?"

2. Interrupt Non-Responsive Witnesses

Despite your best efforts, an adverse witness may attempt to give a narrative response to a leading question. For example, assume that the following dialogue takes place during your cross-examination:

You:

And then Jill came tumbling after, right?

Witness:

You could say that, but you've got to remember that Jill and her brother Jack had only one pail between them. I know for sure that Jack was carrying the pail….

Here, even though your question calls for a yes or no answer, the witness launches into a retelling of his story. Fortunately, you have the power to stop the witness from pontificating. Quickly hold up your hand and say, "Excuse me." When the witness pauses, ask your next question. If the witness continues to talk, ask the judge to intervene by saying something like, "Your Honor, I object; the witness is not answering my question." Assuming that the judge agrees with (sustains) your objection, ask the judge to delete the answer from the record ("strike the answer") and to tell the jury (if there is one) to disregard the testimony the witness gave before you could stop him from talking. If the witness launches into diatribes on more than one occasion, you may also ask the judge to instruct the witness to stop making speeches and to answer only what you have asked. Most witnesses will be very cowed by a judicial reprimand.

Remember, however, that judges have a good deal of discretion when it comes to the scope of witnesses' answers. Occasionally, even if you ask a question that calls for a yes or no answer, a judge may allow a brief explanation if the judge believes it is necessary to allow a witness to answer accurately.

3. Use Exhibits If They Are Helpful

If your adversary offered exhibits (such as reports, photographs or receipts) into evidence during direct examination, you may ask a witness to refer to those exhibits during your cross-examination. Once an exhibit is admitted into evidence it is the property of the court, not of the party who offered it. For example, assume that during an adverse witness's direct examination your adversary offers into evidence a photograph of his car to show the damage it sustained in an accident. You now want to use that photograph to call the judge's or jury's attention to the open bottle of beer shown on the front seat. On cross, you may show the photograph to the witness and ask about the object depicted on the front seat.

To do this, begin by retrieving the exhibit. Often, you will find it either in a shallow box on the counsel table or on the court clerk's desk. But it may be on the judge's bench, in which case you should ask the judge for "permission to have Exhibit 3." To show the exhibit to a witness, ask the judge for permission to approach the witness. (Check this procedure with the court clerk, or watch what the other attorney does. Some judges prefer for the bailiff to transport an exhibit from wherever it is to the witness while you remain at the podium or counsel table.) Then, ask the witness to refer to the exhibit and ask your question: "Ms. Spillenger, please look at Exhibit 3 and tell us if the object on the front seat depicted in that exhibit is an open bottle of beer."

Offering exhibits during cross-examination. Rules of evidence allow you to offer exhibits into evidence during cross-examination of adverse witnesses in the same way as you can during your testimony or direct examination of your witnesses. Whenever possible, however, offer exhibits into evidence only when you or your witnesses are testifying.

D. ELICITING HELPFUL EVIDENCE

Affirmative questioning (questioning to bring out evidence that supports your version of events) during cross-examination can be very effective. A witness called by your adversary may well have some information that helps you, and focusing on

that helpful information may lead a judge or jury to conclude that the witness hasn't hurt you.

For example, consider an incident from the well-publicized 1993 federal court criminal prosecution of the four Los Angeles police officers who were charged with using illegal force to arrest Rodney King. One of the defendants called a Highway Patrol Officer, Melanie Singer, to testify that she was an eyewitness to the arrest and that King was acting in an aggressive, threatening manner towards the arresting officers. But on cross-examination by the prosecutor, Officer Singer cried on the stand as she testified that the defendant officers had kicked and struck King far too long and that she felt helpless to stop it. Without in any way attacking Officer Singer's credibility, the prosecution turned a defense witness into a witness who did not damage its case.

How can you elicit evidence on cross-examination that supports your own case? As with direct examination, start by looking at the facts you're trying to prove. (Remember, even as a defendant you may have facts that you are trying to prove. See Chapter 6, What to Prove at Trial: The Defendant's Perspective.) Then review the information you gathered before trial, whether through informal discussions, negotiation discussions or formal discovery, to identify information a witness has that supports those facts.

Let's take as an example a legal malpractice claim. Say you're suing a lawyer for negligently failing to advise your stepmother that in order for you to inherit all of the stepmother's property in accord with a will the lawyer had previously drafted, she had to change the will to specifically disinherit a child she gave birth to after the will was executed. You have presented all of your evidence and rested your case, and the lawyer's direct examination has just concluded. He testified that he prepared a will for your stepmother, that she came into the office to talk to him a couple of years after the will was executed, and that while she did talk casually about her relatives he is sure that she never said anything about having given birth to a child since signing her will.

You now have an opportunity to cross-examine the lawyer. From what you found out from the lawyer's answers to a brief set of interrogatories that you sent to him before trial, you know that estate planning is not the lawyer's specialty, and that he does about a will or two per year. Also, the lawyer has a paralegal (an assistant) whom he relies on to take down most of the information from will clients. This information does not impeach any testimony the lawyer gave on direct examination, but you want to elicit it during cross-examination to support your fact that the lawyer was careless. Your cross may go like this:

1 **You:**

Mr. Lawyer, preparing wills is not your legal specialty, is it?

2 **Witness (Defendant):**

Not my specialty, no.

3 **You:**

You probably don't do more than a will or two a year, right?

4 **Witness:**

Well, that's probably about right. But let me add that….

5 **You:**

Excuse me. Your Honor, the witness has answered the question. I object to further testimony.

6 **Judge:**

Yes, that's right. Objection sustained.

7 You:

My stepmother came to see you a couple of years after she signed the will you prepared for her, right?

8 Witness:

Yes, I've testified that she did.

9 You:

And you didn't conduct her interview by yourself, did you?

10 Witness:

Not entirely, no.

11 You:

You asked your paralegal assistant to get most of the information from her, right?

12 Witness:

Most of it, but of course I talked to her too.

13 You:

And a paralegal is not an attorney, right?

14 Witness:

That's true.

Transcript Analysis: This cross-examination does not directly attack the lawyer's direct testimony that the stepmother said nothing to him about a child born after the will was made. Instead, you concentrate on information about the lawyer's experience and client interview procedures that support your factual contention that the lawyer was careless.

All of your questions are leading, which gives the witness no opportunity to retell his own story.

And when the witness tries to explain an answer (No. 4), you quite properly and courteously stop his explanation by objecting that the witness has already answered your question. When the judge sustains your objection (No. 5), you promptly ask your next question. Since you stopped the lawyer quickly, you needn't ask the judge to strike any testimony from the record. (If the lawyer's answer to your questions contradict his interrogatory answers, you could impeach him with his contradictory interrogatory answers.)

You may also be able to base affirmative cross-examination on a witness's oral statement. For example, assume that you are seeking to regain custody of your children from your ex-spouse. Your ex-spouse calls one of your neighbors, Linda, as a witness to testify that you often have strangers staying overnight in your apartment. Another neighbor, Dick, has told you that in talking to Linda one day recently, Linda said a number of nice things about you—including that your apartment is always neat and clean and that she always feels comfortable asking you to watch her children for a few hours. On cross-examination of Linda you want to have her testify to this information because it is affirmative evidence for your custody. To do so, you might ask a series of questions such as:

- "Linda, whenever you've seen my apartment it's always been neat and clean, right?"

- "In the last year you've often asked me to watch your children for a few hours, correct?"

- "And you always feel comfortable asking me to watch your children, don't you?"

Here you do not impeach Linda's testimony that strangers often stay overnight at your apartment. Rather, you use Linda's oral statements to Dick as the basis of an affirmative cross-examination of Linda. (If Linda gives testimony that conflicts with what she told Dick, you may impeach her by later calling Dick as a witness.)

Note that these questions are within the scope of Linda's direct examination because they pertain to your fitness as a parent, the topic that Linda was asked about on direct.

E. IMPEACHING ADVERSE WITNESSES

Your second cross-examination goal is to impeach an adverse witness and give a judge or jury some basis for doubting the witness's credibility. Despite the incredible variety of events that give rise to litigation, there are really only a few legally-accepted impeachment methods that arise regularly. Most of them, such as raising the possibility that a witness is biased or prejudiced, will be familiar to you, because they are based on the same logic you rely on in everyday life to evaluate what you hear and see.

1. Bias in Favor of Your Adversary

"Bias" refers to a witness's emotional or financial interest in favor of your opponent. If you can show bias, you hope the judge or jury will doubt the credibility of the witness's testimony.

An emotional interest can arise from such sources as family loyalty and friendship. For example, if you can use cross-examination to establish that Sarah is testifying on behalf of her childhood friend Hilary, or that Adam is testifying on behalf of his cousin Kevin, the judge or jury may not believe (or at least discount) Sarah's or Adam's testimony.

As you probably realize, a financial interest arises when a witness stands to gain financially if your adversary wins. For instance, one spouse or business partner may be testifying on behalf of the other in a situation where any financial gains resulting from the trial would be shared by both.

Whether the source of the bias is emotional or financial, the basis of impeachment is the same: the witness's interest in the outcome arguably casts doubt on the accuracy of the witness's testimony. Of course, the judge or jury may believe a witness despite his emotional or financial interest. But the possibility of bias will probably make the judge or jury more skeptical of the adverse witness's testimony.

Here's an example of how to impeach a witness on cross-examination based on bias. Assume that you are the homeowner in a breach of contract case, and have sued the building contractor you hired to do a remodeling job. You claim that he failed to complete the job and that he used substandard workmanship. On direct examination, Wilkins, one of the contractor's employees, testifies that you orally agreed to give the contractor two additional months to complete the work. Wilkins also testifies that a couple of weeks before this conversation you agreed to wait at home so a building inspector could sign off on the rough plumbing, and that when you failed to do so you caused a delay in the project. You dispute everything Wilkins says: you never agreed to a two-month extension, and the reason you did not wait for the building inspector is that neither Wilkins nor anyone else told you that the plumbing was supposed to be inspected. So in addition to testifying yourself on these points during your direct examination, you want to impeach Wilkins if you can.

When you took Wilkins' deposition before trial, you learned that he has had some discussions with the defendant about soon becoming a partner in the defendant's contracting business. Based on this information, you may cross-examine Wilkins in an effort to show that he has a potential financial interest in seeing the defendant win the case. You want the judge or jury to infer that since Wilkins has hopes of becoming the defendant's business partner, he both wants to remain on good terms with the defendant and to share ownership of a financially stable business. Here's how the cross-examination might go:

1 **You:**

Mr. Wilkins, you've worked for the defendant for about nine years, right?

2 **Witness:**

That's right.

3 **You:**

And you and the defendant have discussed your becoming a partner in the business, right?

4 **Witness:**

Well, there's nothing definite about that.

5 **You:**

But you hope to become a partner, don't you?

6 **Witness:**

We've talked about it, yes.

7 **You:**

That means you would put money into the business?

8 **Witness:**

Yes.

9 **You:**

So you want this business to be worth as much as possible in case you become a partner, right?

10 **Witness:**

I suppose so.

Transcript Analysis: In No. 4 Wilkins tries to downplay his potential interest in the business. However, in No. 5 you stick to your guns and ask if Wilkins has a long-term interest in the business. No. 5 is legally proper question; you have a right to press for an unequivocal answer. By contrast, you would be improperly argumentative if you asked this additional question: "And because you want the business to be worth as much as possible, you've lied on the stand, haven't you?" Such an attempt to put words in Wilkins' mouth is not a question, though if put in a less inflammatory way it is possibly material for your final argument. Note that your questions are leading and leave Wilkins no room to retell the story he told on direct examination.

Questioning to bring out bias can often be even shorter than this. Assume that instead of learning that Wilkins hopes to become a partner in the defendant's business, you've learned that Wilkins and the defendant are brothers. In that case, you might just use one question to show that Wilkins has an emotional stake in the outcome of the case:

1 You:

Mr. Wilkins, you're the defendant's brother, right?

2 Witness:

Yes.

💡 **Impeach using what you learned through discovery.** By working backwards, you can see that if you want to impeach a witness as biased at trial, you should always try to find evidence of bias before trial, either through informal discussions with people who know a witness or through formal discovery tools such as written interrogatories and depositions, though the latter may be costly. Discovery tools are discussed in Chapter 3, Starting and Investigating Your Case.

---

2. Prejudice Against You

In legal terms, prejudice is the flip side of bias. Instead of showing that a witness is biased in favor of your adversary, you show that a witness might be prejudiced against you.

For example, assume that one of the witnesses who testifies against you in a traffic accident case is your former spouse, with whom you have argued bitterly concerning the custody of your children. If you bring out your former spouse's bitterness towards you during cross-examination, the judge or jury might disbelieve or at least partially discredit the former spouse's testimony.

To illustrate how this works, let's put the contractor's employee, Wilkins, back in the witness box. Now assume that you noticed that on a couple

of occasions when he was working on your new addition, Wilkins appeared to have had too much to drink. You reported this fact to Wilkins' employer, the defendant. As a result of your complaint, Wilkins was suspended for two weeks without pay. In this situation, after Wilkins testifies, you may cross-examine to show that he is prejudiced against you:

1 You:

Mr. Wilkins, I made a complaint about you to your employer, didn't I?

2 Witness:

I remember that, yes.

3 You:

My complaint was that you had come to work having had too much to drink on a couple of occasions, right?

4 Witness:

That's what you said. But that's not the way it was.

5 You:

Your Honor, that last sentence is improper. I just asked him what my complaint was, I didn't ask him for his side of things.

6 Judge:

Yes, that's improper. I'll strike the second sentence.

If this is a jury trial, the judge might instruct the jury to disregard Wilkins' improper remark.

7 You:

So you know I made this complaint?

8 Witness:

Yes.

9 You:

And because of my complaint, you were suspended two weeks without pay?

10 Witness:

Yes, I was.

Transcript Analysis: Again, because all of your questions are leading, and because they all focus on the specific topic of prejudice, you give Wilkins no chance to retell his story. When Wilkins does try to throw in information not called for by your question (No. 4), you properly object. The judge strikes the improper testimony, meaning that the judge or jury must totally ignore that testimony when weighing the evidence and making a decision.

3.   Prior Inconsistent Statements

One of the most widely used types of impeachment consists of proving that a witness's testimony at trial doesn't square with a statement the witness previously made. The theory behind this type of impeachment is that accurate tales do not change in the telling. Not surprisingly, lawyers call this impeachment with a prior inconsistent statement.

Use of this cross-examination tool does not depend on whether the witness made the previous statement under oath during a deposition, in a letter to her Aunt Agnes or while playing tennis with a friend. If any statement previously made by a witness is inconsistent with the witness's in-court testimony, the previous statement is admissible for impeachment.

a.   Oral Statements

Our old but long-suffering friend Wilkins can provide us with an example of this type of impeachment. Assume that on direct examination, Wilkins testified that serious problems with your house's foundation necessitated the contractor's demand for an additional $20,000 to complete the remodeling job. You want to impeach Wilkins with a statement that he made to another construction worker, Alice Johnson. According to Ms. Johnson, after inspecting the foundation Wilkins told her, "There's no problem with the foundation. It's in great condition." Your cross-examination bringing out Wilkins' prior statement may go as follows:

1   You:

Mr. Wilkins, you testified that the reason for the demand of an additional $20,000 to complete the remodeling job was that you discovered a serious problem with the foundation, right?

2   Witness:

That's correct.

3   You:

Another person working on my job was named Alice Johnson, is that right?

4   Witness:

Yes, Alice was working on your job some of the time.

5   You:

And just after inspecting the foundation, you told Ms. Johnson that it was in great condition, didn't you?

6   Witness:

I did say something like that.

Transcript Analysis: This concludes your impeachment. You contrast Wilkins' testimony (No. 1) with his inconsistent prior statement (No. 5). You hope that the inconsistency will lead the judge or jury to conclude that Wilkins is untrustworthy.

What can you do if Wilkins denies making the statement to Alice Johnson? During the cross-examination of Wilkins, there is nothing you can do. However, after your adversary finishes presenting evidence (rests), you typically have a chance to pre–sent additional testimony impeaching your adversary's witnesses, even from witnesses who have previously testified for you. Here, if Wilkins denies making the statement to Alice Johnson, you could eventually call her as a witness to testify that Wilkins told her that the foundation was in great shape.

b.   Written Statements

Now let's look at how you can cross-examine Wilkins if, instead of an oral statement, you have written evidence of a prior inconsistent statement. For example, assume again that during direct examination Wilkins testifies that there were serious problems with the foundation of your house. But during his deposition, Wilkins admitted that his inspection revealed that your house's foundation was in very good condition.

To impeach Wilkins with his deposition statement, which is now in the form of a written transcript, mark the deposition as an exhibit, ask the judge for permission to approach Wilkins, and when permission is granted hand the exhibit to him. (See Chapter 12, Exhibits.) Open the deposition transcript to the signature page and ask Wilkins to verify his signature. Then tell the judge and your adversary what page of the deposition the inconsistent statement appears on and read the prior inconsistent statement into the record. You do not need to give the witness a chance to deny making the prior statement or to explain why he has changed his story. The impeachment will go as follows:

1 **You:**

Mr. Wilkins, you testified that the reason for the demand of an additional $20,000 to complete the remodeling job was that you discovered a serious problem with the foundation, right?

2 **Witness:**

That's correct.

You mark the deposition as an exhibit, ask the judge for permission to approach the witness, and once permission is granted you hand the deposition to Wilkins.

3 **You:**

All right, looking at your deposition, Exhibit 4, please examine it and tell us if this is the sworn deposition you gave in this case?

4 **Witness:**

Yes, it is.

5 **You:**

The signature on the last page, that's your signature?

6 **Witness:**

Yes.

7 **You:**

Your Honor, I'm reading page 23, lines 13-20 of Mr. Wilkins' deposition. "Question: What was your initial task in connection with my remodeling job? Answer: To inspect the foundation. Question: And what did that inspection reveal? Answer: That the foundation was in very good condition."

Transcript Analysis: Once you establish that the exhibit is the witness's deposition, you can read into the record any portion of the deposition that is inconsistent with the witness's testimony. And if the witness has given other direct testimony that is inconsistent with his deposition testimony, you can again impeach him without having to re-identify the deposition.

4.   Ability to Perceive

We have all seen movies in which the key eyewitness turns out to be legally blind, or someone who claims to overhear a crucial conversation is revealed to be almost deaf. In real life, chances are you will never be able to attack so decisively an adverse witness's ability to perceive.

But you may be able to cause a judge or juror to doubt a witness's ability to perceive what she claims to have seen or heard. Sometimes you will base your impeachment on adverse conditions in the outside world, such as when a witness claims to have overheard a whispered conversation while standing at a busy intersection. Other times, your best chance to impeach may be based on a witness's condition, such as when a nearsighted witness claims to have seen the color of a distant traffic light at dusk—or, if luck is really with you, ten minutes after leaving an optometrist's office where his eyes were dilated.

Let's go back to the negligence case involving your claim that you were crossing Main Street in a crosswalk when you were struck by a truck driven by Sarah Adams, a building contractor. Assume that Adams, the defendant, calls a witness named Kris Knaplund, who testifies that she was coming out of a nearby shop when the accident occurred. Knaplund further testifies that after you were struck by the truck you said, "Oh my God! Why didn't I use the crosswalk?" When you get a chance to testify later, you will deny making this statement. You will testify that what you really said was, "Oh my God! Why didn't you see me in the crosswalk?" But before that, during cross-examination of Knaplund you want to cast doubt on her ability to have overheard your statement accurately. Your cross-examination of Knaplund may go like this:

1   **You:**

Ms. Knaplund, you heard me say something after the accident?

2   **Witness:**

Yes.

3   **You:**

Isn't it true that what I really said was, "Oh my God! Why didn't you see me in the crosswalk?"

4   **Witness:**

No, that's not what I heard you say.

5   **You:**

You were just coming out of a shop when you heard me?

6   **Witness:**

That's right.

7   **You:**

The shop was a video game arcade?

8   **Witness:**

That's true.

9   **You:**

There were a number of noisy games being played at the time, right?

10   **Witness:**

Yes.

11   **You:**

Isn't it true that those machines and the people playing them are so loud that you have to talk extra loud to be heard inside the arcade?

12   **Witness:**

Well, they're noisy, that's true.

13   **You:**

And isn't the arcade about 75 feet away from where I was hit by the truck?

14   **Witness:**

I wouldn't know, I'm not too good at estimating distances.

Transcript Analysis: Here, you begin by asking Knaplund directly about your statement (No. 3). You do not expect her to suddenly admit that she made a mistake, but you have nothing to lose by having the judge or jury hear your side of things.

Then you mention some outside factors that may cast doubt on Knaplund's ability to accurately hear what you said: just coming out of a noisy video game arcade (Nos. 5-12) and being some distance away from the scene (No. 13). Your cross cannot prove that Knaplund was unable to hear your statement accurately. But together with your own testimony, your cross can lead the judge or jury to doubt Knaplund's credibility.

5.   Implausible Testimony

All of us carry around beliefs about how people usually behave and events usually occur. When we are told something that is at odds with these beliefs, we tend to doubt what we are told; we find it implausible. For example, if Jones tells you that he walked three blocks at 2 a.m. to return an overdue library book, probably you would doubt him. Your own life experience suggests that people do not go out in the middle of the night to return a library book when the library is closed and the book would have to go into a drop box.

In the same way you should examine an adverse witness's story for its overall plausibility. Even if you have no other basis on which to try to impeach a witness, perhaps you can show that the witness's story is in some way implausible. This is far from an ironclad method of impeachment. What you consider implausible may seem quite normal to a judge or jury. A judge who grew up in a family of librarians, for example, might think it quite admirable to return a library book at 2 a.m.

To see how to conduct this type of cross-examination, return again to Knaplund's testimony in the negligence case (Subsection 4 above). Assume that Knaplund gave a statement to the investigating police officer who came to the scene of the accident, but neglected to mention that just after being struck you said you should have been in the crosswalk. You consider this implausible; if she really had heard you say this, surely she would have reported it to prevent the truck driver from being unfairly held responsible for the accident. Your cross of Knaplund to emphasize the implausibility might go like this:

1   You:

Ms. Knaplund, you say that right after the accident I said "Oh my God! Why didn't I use the crosswalk?"

2   Witness:

Yes, that's what I heard.

3   You:

A few minutes later a police officer came to the scene, right?

4   Witness:

That's correct.

5   You:

The officer was in uniform, correct?

6   Witness:

Yes.

7   You:

You knew that he was there to investigate the accident, right?

8   Witness:

That's true.

9   You:

You wanted to make sure that the police officer got accurate information about what happened, right?

10   Witness:

I guess so.

11   You:

But you never told him that I said something about wishing I had been in the crosswalk?

12   Witness:

No, I didn't.

Transcript Analysis: In this excerpt, you use leading questions to suggest that Knaplund's failure to mention what she heard you say is implausible. You hope that the implausibility will lead the judge or jury to discredit Knaplund's testimony.

6.   Prior Convictions

In most court systems, you may impeach a witness by showing that the witness has been convicted of certain serious crimes. (For example, Federal Rule of Evidence 609 and California Evidence Code § 788 allow this.) However, in a civil case chances are that the witnesses you cross-examine will not have been convicted of a crime. Moreover, the rules are very strict and often confused as to what kinds of convictions are admissible. If you find out that an adverse witness has been convicted of a crime, consult your self-help law coach or do some legal research to determine whether the conviction is admissible in evidence.

When implying wrongdoing, be sure you are right. You cannot ask a witness about a criminal conviction or otherwise imply wrongdoing on the part of a witness unless you have what the law calls a "good faith basis" to believe that your charge is accurate. At the least, you need to be able to point to a reliable source of information that justifies your question.

For example, assume that you have no evidence that an eyewitness had been using drugs. Nevertheless you ask, "Had you been using any narcotic drugs just before you witnessed the accident?" If your adversary objects to the question, the judge may ask you to reveal your source. If you cannot identify a reliable source that the judge regards as a good faith basis for believing that the witness had used drugs, the judge will surely sustain the objection. And even allowing for your inexperience as a pro per litigant, a judge may restrict your right to ask further questions.

F.   BASE QUESTIONS ON EVIDENCE YOU CAN OFFER

One of the oldest cross-examination clichés is to "never ask a question that you don't know the answer to." This doesn't mean that you have to be 100% certain of how an adverse witness will answer your questions, because an adverse witness can always give an unexpected answer. What it does mean is that generally you should not ask a question unless you can offer evidence to contradict an unexpected answer. And this advice applies regardless of whether the information you seek on cross-examination supports your own fact or impeaches a witness.

Look back at some of the examples in this chapter. In one instance, you wanted to elicit helpful evidence from Linda that she has often asked you to take care of her children (Section D, above). Based on information you have from Dick, a friend of Linda's, you expect Linda to provide this evidence. But if Linda gives an unexpected answer, you can call Dick as a witness yourself to contradict her.

Similarly, in each of the impeachment illustrations you could contradict an unexpected answer because your cross-examination questions were based on evidence that you could produce in court. Thus, you could impeach Wilkins with his statement to Alice Johnson because if he gave an unexpected answer you could later call Johnson as a witness and ask her what Wilkins told her. In addition, you could impeach Wilkins with his deposition testimony because you could contradict an unexpected answer with the deposition transcript.

Without any way to contradict an unexpected answer, your cross-examination may amount to a foolish "fishing trip." Without your own source of evidence to fall back on, your firm belief that an adverse witness is either lying or mistaken does you no good. To see this, assume that you have solid information that Knaplund was just leaving a noisy video arcade when she supposedly heard your "crosswalk" statement. Unless you can produce the person who provided you with this information as a witness, cross-examining Knaplund about where she was when she heard the statement is risky. If she answers that, no, she wasn't leaving the arcade, but was standing outside the library, just ten feet from where you fell, you have no way to contradict her.

G. IF ONE OF YOUR WITNESSES IS IMPEACHED

If your adversary impeaches one of your witnesses, say with a prior inconsistent statement, talk to your witness during a recess (ask the judge for one, if necessary) or at lunch to see if she has a good explanation for the change of story. If your witness has an explanation that eliminates the negative impact of a prior inconsistent statement you can let her give it during redirect examination, which takes place immediately after cross-examination. (See Chapter 9, Direct Examination.)

For example, assume that in a case in which you are suing your employer for sexual harassment, Laura Rosas testifies for you on direct examination that she heard your employer tell you that you needed to date him if you expected a promotion. On cross-examination the employer's lawyer impeaches Rosas with a statement she previously made to an investigator from the Fair Employment Practices Department in which she said that she could not remember your employer ever asking you for a date. Talking to Rosas at the recess that immediately follows her cross-examination, you learn that the reason she made that statement was that your employer threatened to fire her if she gave any information to the investigator. By bringing out this explanation during your redirect examination of Rosas, you hope to convince the judge or jury that Rosas' testimony during direct examination is credible. Your redirect may go as follows:

1 **You:**

Ms. Rosas, did you tell the Fair Employment Department investigator something different than you told the court today?

2   **Witness:**

Yes, I did.

3   **You:**

And why is that?

4   **Witness:**

Because the day before the investigator came to the office, our employer said that he would fire me if I said that he had done anything wrong.

5   **You:**

Then why are you willing to testify against him today?

6   **Witness:**

I'm in court and I'm going to tell the truth. If he fires me, I guess he's going to have another lawsuit on his hands.

Transcript Analysis: Note how your questions on redirect (especially Nos. 3 and 5) are open questions. Just as during direct examination, during redirect you cannot ask leading questions of your own witnesses. (See Chapter 9, Direct Examination, for a discussion of the different types of questions.)

H. PREPARING FOR CROSS-EXAMINATION

Before trial, make an outline that briefly summarizes the testimony you expect an adverse witness to give on direct examination. Then in separate sections, list additional evidence a witness can provide that supports your version of events and evidence that impeaches the witness. You may even want to write down specific questions in each section, because on cross-examination you are likely to be limiting your questions to only a few pieces of information. Finally, you may list any exhibits you plan to refer to or introduce during cross-examination, though probably you will only offer exhibits during your own testimony or direct examination of your own witnesses.

 Make sure to update your trial notebook. Devote a separate section of your trial notebook to cross-examination, and make a separate Cross-examination Outline for each witness you will cross-examine. (See Chapter 15, Organizing a Trial Notebook)

Below is a form Cross-Examination Outline that you may want to use.

Cross-examination Outline

Witness:

Expected direct examination testimony:

Additional information that supports my
version of events (List specific questions):

Impeachment (List specific questions):

Exhibits that I will refer to or introduce:

ADDITIONAL RESOURCES
ON CROSS-EXAMINTAION

The Art of Cross-examination, by Francis Wellman (Macmillan & Co.). Many lawyers regard this 1906 book as the classic cross-examination work. While some of Wellman's language is dated, the book reviews the most common bases of cross-examination and is filled with colorful examples drawn from actual cases, including Abraham Lincoln's famous "almanac" cross-examination. (Lincoln impeached a witness who claimed to have seen an incident by moonlight by producing an almanac showing that there had been no moon that night.)

Winning Strategies and Techniques for Civil Litigators, by James Lyons (ed.) (Praotising Law Institute) is a briefer and more modern approach to cross-examination. One chapter of the book consists of the "10 rules of cross-examination" interestingly set forth by the late Irving Younger, a renowned speaker on trial techniques, in the form of a letter from the ancient Roman orator, Cicero; a second chapter consists of a modern lawyer's reply.

Trial Advocacy in a Nutshell, by Paul Bergman (West Publishing Co.) is an inexpensive review of trial techniques. Chapter 4 focuses on cross-examination and presents an approach for determining when you can contradict an unexpected answer.

Fundamentals of Trial Techniques, by Thomas Mauet (Little, Brown & Co.) reviews the common bases of cross-examination and provides numerous brief examples.

11

CLOSING ARGUMENT

Closing argument is your opportunity to tell the judge or jury why you should win. After repeatedly warning you not to argue when you deliver your opening statement, present evidence or cross-examine witnesses, we can finally say, "Go for it."

During the trial, your story is presented a piece at a time, through testimony and tangible evidence: You have some control over the evidence and the order in which it comes out, but no opportunity to tie it all together. Closing argument gives you the valuable chance to help the judge or jury fit the pieces together—and to convince them that the evidence presented at trial proves you should win.

Closing argument is also your chance to make a good last impression. But, contrary to *Perry Mason* films or scenes from *L.A. Law*, trials do not usually turn on dramatic closing arguments: Rather, most times, a case is won or lost because of the persuasiveness of the evidence presented. With that in mind, don't expect the judge or jurors to all nod their heads enthusiastically during your closing argument, and don't expect to (or feel you need to) give an award-winning performance. Just be yourself, and try to follow the guidelines below.

⚠️ **Don't be rude.** You are allowed to "argue" during closing argument, but not in the same sense as that word is often used in private. In the courtroom context, permissible argument is telling the judge or jury how the evidence proves you should win. There are limits; don't yell, pound the table or call your opponent names. You'll get a reprimand from the judge and alienate the jury, too.

A. WHEN YOU DELIVER CLOSING ARGUMENT

Closing arguments follow the presentation of all the evidence. That means they come after both you and your adversary have put all your witnesses on the stand and conducted direct and cross-examinations. Usually the plaintiff gives closing argument first, then the defendant. The plaintiff can ask the judge to reserve (save) a small amount of time—for example, five minutes—for rebuttal argument, after the defendant's closing argument. This gives the plaintiff one last chance to try to refute the defendant's argument.

During jury trials, judges instruct jurors as to their legal responsibilities in deciding a case before closing arguments, others after closing arguments. If yours is a jury trial, whether your closing argument comes before or after the jury instructions, you may use them to prepare your argument and you may refer explicitly to the language of the instructions during your closing argument. (For more on locating jury instructions, see Chapter 19, Legal Research.)

B. PREPARE AND REHEARSE YOUR CLOSING ARGUMENT BEFORE TRIAL

In order to decide what evidence to look for when you first investigate your and your adversary's legal claims and defenses, it helps to know what facts you will eventually have to prove or disprove in court. And, to win your case, you must show the judge or jury how the evidence presented has actually proved or disproved those same facts. For this reason, some experts actually suggest you start writing the outline for your closing argument when you are in the very first stages of investigating your lawsuit. The good news is that you have already learned how to connect evidence to the legal elements you need to prove or disprove (some call this "marshaling evidence"), in Chapters 5 and 6. And if you look back to those chapters, you will see that the outlines you learned to do then are really the first drafts of your closing argument.

It is also important to rehearse the closing argument you've prepared before your trial, because you may not be allowed much time to prepare during trial. If your case is fairly complex, the judge may give you an hour or more, after you and your adversary have rested your cases, to review your closing argument. But in many cases, for example those where less than $50,000 is at stake, your whole trial may last only a couple of hours. In these cases, especially if the court has lots of other cases on its calendar, you may be asked to go forward right after the close of evidence, and the judge may push you to finish up quickly. Even if the judge is pressed for time you can likely get a five- to ten-minute recess to use the restroom. That is better than nothing; it may allow you to gather your thoughts and regain your composure.

C. HOW TO PUT TOGETHER A CLOSING ARGUMENT

To convince the judge or jury to rule in your favor, the most important thing you can do is show how the evidence supports your case. While you cannot be untruthful, you can and should emphasize those facts that are favorable to you and explain away facts that hurt you. In addition, you can say why your witnesses were believable and your opponent's were not. And finally, you can review key pieces of evidence in an organized, persuasive way that is easy to follow and leads to the conclusion that your case is a winner. If you are the plaintiff, that review will emphasize the evidence that establishes that you have met your legal burden of proof; if you are the defendant, it will show that the plaintiff has failed to meet the requisite burden.

The main headings in the outline of your closing argument will be similar to the subheadings in this part of this chapter: introductory comment about your pro per status, the legal and factual issues to be decided, evidence marshaling, the burden of proof and the result you want. You will weave into the evidence marshaling section of your argument the points you want to make about the believability of witnesses and exhibits. The core of your closing argument outline will be your list of the facts satisfying the legal elements, with the key evidence that proves or disproves them underneath each element—the same core outline you did in Chapter 5 (if you are the plaintiff) or Chapter 6 (if you are the defendant).

Pointers for effective deliveries. Section E of Chapter 8, Opening Statement, includes a variety of suggestions for effective courtroom speaking. You may want to refer to that section when preparing to deliver your closing argument.

---

1. Make Introductory Comments

Some judges and jurors may respect and even be extra sympathetic towards you if you very briefly acknowledge that in representing yourself, you have tried your best and hope you have not made too many mistakes. But you probably don't want to make too big a deal about this. It could backfire if the judge or jury doesn't find you genuine or thinks you are deliberately playing on their sympathies. As an introductory remark to a judge, you may try saying something like:

Your Honor, you have heard all the evidence. You have heard about how my roof leaked so badly last winter that water fell onto the electric stove while I was cooking. As my friend, Jane Keith, testified, it was so bad that one time when she was making breakfast, a piece of the ceiling plaster fell into our omelet.

I know I am not as familiar with court procedures as my opponent, but I have tried my best. I hope I have shown you why I had to get out of that apartment and proven to you that my landlord breached his duty to keep the apartment habitable. Now, to review the key pieces of evidence.

In fact, in some simpler cases, where the whole trial lasts only an hour or two, the introductory remark may be almost enough for your entire argument, especially if you add a sentence stating how you want the judge to rule. For example:

Based on the evidence, I ask that you find that I did not breach my rental contract as the defendant contends, and that I do not owe the defendant any money for the rent since I left or any back rent for the money I withheld during those last months when the roof was leaking.

Make closing argument to a judge shorter than to a jury. If you are arguing to a judge alone, you should prepare and deliver a much shorter closing argument than if you have a jury trial, for these reasons:

- Judges know the meaning of legal terms; you don't need to explain them.

- Judges are used to hearing testimony from witnesses, applying the law to various factual situations and following along at trials.

- Judges can stop and ask you questions if they don't understand something; jurors cannot.

If you're addressing a jury, your introductory remarks may be:

Ladies and gentlemen, I have tried to present evidence to you today showing that the negligent driving of the defendant, Ms. Adams, caused the serious and painful leg injuries that I told you about. I know I made some errors during the trial. Frankly, as a non-lawyer I have felt somewhat like a fish out of water. Unfortunately the high cost of hiring a lawyer left me no choice but to go it alone. Nonetheless….

And, if your opponent's attorney was particularly stuffy or aggressive toward you, you may find it effective to add:

Probably it's clear that I don't have years of legal experience like my opponent's highly skilled lawyer, Anna Turney.

2. Identify the Issues to Be Resolved

You want to let the judge or jury know exactly which issues need to be determined—which questions of fact or law they must answer—in order to find for you. This is especially important in longer, more complex cases. To determine which factual and legal questions remain to be determined by the judge or jury, you have to look at three things:

- The elements of the plaintiff's claims. Remember, the plaintiff has to prove each element to win.

- Rulings the judge made during trial.

- Stipulations you made with your opponent. If you and your adversary agreed on an issue, the judge or jury doesn't need to rule on it.

Though you will want to keep it much shorter in a judge trial, narrowing the issues can be helpful to a judge or jury, since they may not remember exactly what has been cleared up. Saying what remains to be decided can help avoid confusion and prevent wasting time and energy on questions that have already been resolved.

The example below is based on the negligence case in which you are suing Sarah Adams, a building contractor, whose truck struck you as you crossed the street. In this version of the case, certain issues were resolved during trial, and you note that in your argument to the judge, as follows:

Your Honor, there are only two issues before you this afternoon: Whether Ms. Adams breached her duty to drive with due care, and whether her truck's hitting me caused my injuries. There is no question she owed me a duty; she stipulated that her truck struck me, so she owed a duty to me to use reasonable care. Also, there is no question about the amount of damages I suffered; the defendant stipulated that the doctor bills and employment records I introduced into evidence are accurate.

With a jury, you want to go into more detail:

Ladies and gentlemen, to prove the defendant was negligent and have you rule for me, I must establish all four of the legal elements of the negligence claim. Those are: one, that the defendant owed me, a pedestrian on a public street, the duty to drive carefully; two, that she breached that duty by driving carelessly; three, that her careless driving caused my injuries; and four, that I am out $100,000 because of money I had to pay for doctor bills, money I lost from being out of work, and money to compensate me for the pain I suffered from those injuries.

Element number 1 is not at issue. I was walking and she was driving on a public street, so she does not dispute that she has the duty that licensed drivers all have—to drive carefully. And element number 4, damages, has been resolved as well; the defendant stipulated that the doctor bills and work records I introduced into evidence were accurate, and that I in fact suffered a great deal of pain.

That leaves only two things for you to decide: element 2, whether or not Ms. Adams was driving carelessly and element 3, whether her truck's hitting me caused the injuries.

Starting with element number 2, did the defendant drive carelessly? Let's look at what the eyewitnesses who testified before you had to say about her driving. First, Cynthia White testified….

You can also use an exhibit to help show the judge or jury the issues to be decided. For example, if your case involves a dispute over a document like a contract, you may say:

We all admit the contract is valid, Your Honor. So this case really boils down to clause 2 [holding up the contract and pointing to the clause]. All it says is the defendant, Louis Coombs, agrees to repair my roof. You have to decide what that means. My position is that it means Mr. Coombs was required to use the quality of wood that experts, such as Ed Barr who testified in this case, say is used by other roofers in the community. But the defendant thinks he had every right to use cheap plywood, even though the roof fell in this past winter, just because this clause doesn't specify a certain type of wood….

3. Marshal the Evidence for Each Element You Must Prove

Marshaling evidence means connecting it up to the legal element it helps to prove or disprove. The outlines you prepared in Chapters 5 and 6, which help you do this, will form the backbone of your closing argument. (You may want to skim those chapters again before reading on.) In those outlines of your legal claims (or those of your adversary), you listed facts that would be used to try to prove each element, and items of evidence that would be used to prove these facts.

Using the negligence case discussed above, here's an outline of what the plaintiff must prove:

1. **Duty:** The defendant owed me the duty to drive carefully.

2. **Breach of duty:** She breached that duty by driving carelessly.

3. **Causation:** Her careless driving caused my injuries.

4. **Damages:** I am out $100,000 because of those injuries.

Element 1:

The defendant owed me a duty to drive carefully.

Fact to prove Element 1:

Defendant is a licensed driver, driving down a public street. That creates a duty to me, as a pedestrian in the vicinity, to drive carefully.

Element 2:

Defendant breached that duty by driving carelessly.

Facts to prove Element 2:

- Defendant was looking down at her car phone instead of at the road, and she was distracted by the call.

Evidence to prove this fact:

- Cynthia White's testimony that defendant was holding a car phone receiver to her ear and looking down, instead of paying attention to the road.
- Defendant's car phone records showing a call around the time of the accident.

Element 3:

Her careless driving caused my injuries.

Facts to prove Element 3:

- I was injured when her truck hit me.
- If she'd been paying attention, she wouldn't have hit me.

Evidence to prove these facts:

* Doctor's bills and my own testimony
* Cynthia White's testimony

Element 4:

I am out $100,000 because of those injuries.

Facts to prove Element 4:

* I paid $50,000 to doctors, lost $15,000 for four months of work, and suffered great pain.

Evidence to prove these facts:

* Doctor's bills
* Employment records
* My testimony about pain and suffering

When preparing your closing argument outline, select the key evidence that supports your claims and the key evidence that refutes your opponent's claims, and tell the judge or jury explicitly how the evidence proves or disproves those claims.

Updating your trial notebook: One section in your trial notebook (see Chapter 15) should be devoted to your closing argument. Here you should keep:

* an outline of your intended closing argument

* blank paper for notes, and

* exact quotes—for example, explicit language from jury instructions.

4. Discuss Credibility

When weighing evidence, the judge or jury evaluates its credibility. As you know, one thing you

tried to show in direct examination was why your witnesses were believable, and one of your main cross-examination goals was to attack the credibility of your adversary's witnesses. But in those earlier phases of trial, all you could do was bring out the evidence that supported or attacked the witnesses' credibility. You cannot, until closing argument, specifically tell the judge or jury why particular evidence should be discredited (because the witness was biased) or bolstered (because the witness was reliable). This type of information is an important ingredient to give the judge or jury as they move into final evaluations of evidence before making a decision.

One reason for a witness appearing less or more credible to the judge or jury is a personal connection, or lack of one, to the parties. (See Chapter 10, Cross-Examination.) For example, your not knowing the eyewitness to your car accident before it occurred may make the witness believable; why lie for you if the witness didn't even know you? But if your opponent's chief eyewitness is his mother, the judge or jury may be more skeptical and conclude that she is biased in your adversary's favor.

There can be more than one reason why testimony is not credible. You will want to bring out these facts explicitly in closing argument. For example:

Your Honor, the witness, Ms. Speevack, said there were never any roaches in the defendant's apartments and that the roof had never leaked in the 20 years Mr. Shelley (the defendant) owned the property. But, Your Honor, let's remember that Ms. Speevack is Mr. Shelley's mother, and she quite understandably may see things in his favor.

What's more, she doesn't live in the building. And while she may have come around often to visit her son, she admitted on cross-examination that she did not conduct regular inspections of the apartments or talk to the tenants. As I testified, I don't ever remember her coming into my apartment….

People also lose credibility when they make statements that are inconsistent. Once you have brought out the inconsistencies during trial, you can use them in closing argument. Here's an example:

Ladies and gentlemen, Cynthia White said this morning that she could see the defendant's truck perfectly clearly, that traffic was light and nothing was in front of her, and that she saw exactly what happened. But during a deposition that took place only three months after the accident, Ms. White said, under penalty of perjury, that there was a bus in front of her in the left turn lane at the time of the accident. Now this accident did occur some three years ago. Clearly, memories fade, and Ms. White seems to have forgotten about a bus that she herself had said was right in front of her at the time. How faded are the other details that she now claims to remember perfectly?

Notice, in the previous example, you didn't accuse White of lying but of simply forgetting. That is often a better tactic than accusing people of lying on the witness stand (which amounts to perjury, punishable as a crime). Judges and juries are reluctant to assume a witnesses is deliberately lying. By calling a witness a liar in your closing argument, you risk that the judge or jury will discount your version of what happened altogether rather than believe that an otherwise sympathetic person lied. But it isn't difficult to believe a witness forgot or made a mistake, especially if the events the witness described happened a long time before. Forgetting is not a crime.

Every day we use our perceptions, experiences and even prejudices to decide whether or not we find someone believable. Obviously our prejudices are as different as we are. Nevertheless, it makes sense to try to put yourself in the position of judge or jury and try to determine which witness may seem the most credible. For example, a person who wears a business suit and speaks in an articulate way may appear more believable to certain judges or jurors than someone wearing sweat pants and a T-shirt who mumbles. Or, for instance, since some people don't believe anything used car salesmen say, if your key witness sells used cars for a living, you might try to bolster his credibility in your closing argument by saying:

Ladies and gentlemen, you may have heard people say that no one is as untrustworthy as a used car salesman. But remember, that is a stereotype, and in the case of Mr. Reback, a totally false stereotype. As you heard, Mr. Reback is just working at the car dealer to put himself through school. He has finished three years and has only one to go to complete a degree in chemical engineering. He doesn't have a relationship with either myself or the plaintiff; he stands to gain nothing from this case. He, like Cynthia White, just happened to be at the corner of Elm and Main when the accident occurred. Mr. Reback told you he saw the plaintiff run out from between two parked cars, not in the crosswalk as Ms. White testified….

You want to integrate points about a witness's credibility into your closing argument outline. The easiest way to do this is to put the point in right where you talk about that person's testimony. For instance, if you are the defendant, part of your outline might look like the one shown below:

Element 2:

Breach of duty to drive carefully

Fact Plaintiff will try to prove:

I was careless.

Evidence to disprove this fact:

Testimony of Mr. Reback

- Eyewitness.
- Testified he saw me driving carefully and not speeding.
- Saw plaintiff run out between from parked cars; Noticed Plaintiff NOT in crosswalk.

Reback is credible:

- "Used car salesman" is bad stereotype.
- Reback is in college; car sales is just part-time job, not career.
- nothing to gain from lying….

My testimony

Under penalty of perjury I said:

- I was careful,
- not distracted,
- I'm used to car phone calls….

5.   Explain the Burden of Proof

Normally, the plaintiff has to prove each legal element of a claim by a measure lawyers call a "preponderance of the evidence." In other words, as the plaintiff you do not have to prove the evidence beyond a reasonable doubt (as does the prosecutor in a criminal trial), but just by something more than 50 percent.

Judges know these terms, so you don't need to explain them during a judge trial, though you may want to mention the burden of proof. For example, you might say simply:

Your Honor, I recognize that I have the burden of proof in this case. But given all the evidence I have put forward, as to each of the legal elements of negligence, it seems I have clearly met that burden….

To explain what this means to a jury or visualize it yourself, you may use the "scales of justice" metaphor. As the plaintiff, you can point out that if each side's evidence were piled on a scale, and the evidence tilts even a fraction of a feather weight toward you, then you have satisfied your burden. To make your explanation clear, you may want to hold your two hands in front of you as if each hand were one side of the scale and drop one hand ever so slightly lower.

Another way to explain the burden of proof to juries is to analogize it to a football field. If you are the plaintiff, you say:

Imagine I'm on a football field, ladies and gentlemen. Preponderance of the evidence does not mean I have to score a touchdown. I only have to make it past the 50-yard line.

You can never be certain if an explanation will go over well, but be cautious about images you think are universal. Some of your jurors may not know much about sports, for example, so if you use the football analogy, you may want to use the scale analogy, too. In one recent case, an attorney was reprimanded for using an analogy to batting averages while cross-examining a witness because the judge didn't know or like much about baseball.

If you are the defendant, emphasize that the plaintiff has the burden of proof—that it's not up to you to prove what did not happen, but up to the plaintiff to prove what did. Focus on the legal elements where the plaintiff was weakest, pointing out how he failed to prove them. Also, just as the plaintiff defines the legal term preponderance of the evidence for the jury, so too should you. But, in your comments, you will stress that if the jury does not believe there is more weight on the plaintiff's side of the scale—that is, if they feel the evidence weighs equally for both sides—they must find in your favor. For example:

Ladies and gentlemen, as the judge will instruct you, the plaintiff has to prove four things: one, that I owed a legal duty to him to drive with reasonable care; two, that I breached that duty by driving carelessly; three, that my careless driving caused his injuries; and finally four, that he was damaged because of those injuries. Number one, I admitted. That is an agreement we all make when we get our very first driver's licenses. And I do not dispute that the plaintiff's doctor bills show he was treated for injuries and spent the money he claims he spent.

But ladies and gentlemen, that is only two elements out of four. The plaintiff has failed to prove number two that I was driving carelessly, or number three that his injuries were caused by my truck hitting him. He has not proven them at all, let alone by a preponderance of the evidence, as he must in order for you to find for him.

The plaintiff told you that what the preponderance standard means. He said that meant if you weighed the evidence and the scale tipped in his favor, he would win. But if you believe that he has not proven any one of the elements—and I will point out the severe weaknesses in his evidence as to my driving and as to what actually caused his injury—then you must find in my favor. Also, the scales must tip. If after hearing all the evidence, you are not sure, you think that the evidence for both sides is more or less equal, then the plaintiff has failed to meet his legal burden of proof and you must find for me.

Now let's look at the evidence more closely….

After going through and showing why his evidence was weak and yours strong for each of the elements you dispute, you may conclude by saying:

At this point you may have some doubts. Part of you may think that the evidence shows I was careless, that Cynthia White is accurate when she says I was speeding. And part of you may believe I was driving fine and that the plaintiff caused the accident by running out in the middle of the street, as I and Mr. Reback testified. You also may not be sure what really caused plaintiff's injuries, the accident or a pre-existing condition.

It's human to have some doubts. We all do. Nevertheless, the law still makes your decision clear, ladies and gentlemen. As the judge will instruct you, the plaintiff must prove all these things to you by a preponderance of the evidence. That means you must be more than 50% sure. The plaintiff told you this means he doesn't have to score a touchdown. Well, he is right. But he does have to get past the 50-yard line—and he's already gotten tackled by a few big players. I mean there are a lot of holes in his evidence. The most important one is that he did not prove that I was careless. As the plaintiff, he bears the burden of proving each element of his case to you. And if you are not more than 50% sure that he's proven all four, you must find that I am not responsible for his $50,000 in doctor bills or other damages he has claimed.

6.   Use Exhibits and Other Visual Aids

Visualizing the facts you or your adversary have put into evidence can help make your version of the story clearer for the judge or jury. For example, assume that you're the plaintiff in the negligence case mentioned earlier. During your direct examination of Cynthia White, you had her make a diagram of the accident scene at Elm and Main, where Ms. Adams's truck hit you. She marked the places where you, the truck, the parked cars and the children playing on the street were located. You introduced the marked diagram into evidence. (See Chapter 12, Exhibits.) It may be very helpful and effective for you to hold White's drawing up for the judge or jury when you are reviewing her testimony. For example, you may say:

Ladies and gentlemen, you may recall that when Cynthia White testified, she marked on this map [holding it up] *where all the key players in the accident were located.* [Pointing as you talk] *Here I was, here's where the defendant was and here— where these children were playing. You can see how easily the defendant might have been distracted by watching these children instead of the road….*

Visual aids can help your argument, but there are some potential negatives in using them. You may feel clumsy carrying a bulky chart into court (you are already carrying a trial notebook); you may not be a great artist and might be concerned that your chart looks sloppy; you may not know where to set up your prop so that it can be clearly seen.

Judges may exclude visual aids they find misleading, if they were not admitted into evidence during trial. For example, a map of Elm and Main streets that your witness marked during trial is fine and likely helpful. But a judge may exclude a diagram, not introduced in evidence during the trial, that you drew up the night before your closing argument, especially if the judge feels your drawing misrepresents the evidence. Or the judge may view your diagram as an attempt on your part to introduce new evidence, which you cannot do in your closing argument. You can argue only from what is already in the record. (See Section D, below.)

To decide whether to use a visual aid, think about what aspects of your case it will help explain and whether you can adequately explain them in words. For instance, to explain the legal concept of "preponderance of the evidence," you may do better orally explaining the analogy rather than drawing a football field with the yard lines clearly marked. The cons (bulky, judge may not allow it) may outweigh the pros (clear image of how much evidence it takes to meet the burden). But if your visual aid relates to specific factual evidence in your case and will help the judge or jury clarify a key point, it may help make your argument more concrete and believable.

7. Tell the Judge or Jury What You Want

One good way to finish your closing argument is by asking for an explicit result in the case. Even though some people feel awkward asking for money, it is important to let the judge or jury know exactly what you want them to decide. Otherwise, they might not know what to do. Here's an example:

Your Honor, you have heard all the evidence showing how flimsy the wood was that the defendant used to repair my roof. My family and I were terrified the night the roof caved in. It cost $10,000 to repair the structural damage to my home that was caused by the collapse. And I spent $20,000 more than I bargained for in the original contract just to get a solid roof over our heads—not to mention the countless hours it took to clean up the mess. Your Honor, please find that the defendant breached the contract by using the cheap plywood and order that he pay me the $30,000 I lost.

D. WHAT NOT TO DO IN CLOSING ARGUMENT

Now that you know what to include in your closing argument, here are some things to avoid.

1. Do Not State Your Opinion

The basic principle is that you must argue from the evidence and show why it is or is not convincing. You must not interject what you believe unless you have presented some proof of the facts behind that belief to the judge or jury. For example, *do not* say:

Ms. Adams claims that the call she got on her car phone before she hit me was not important. But look at her, she is shifty-eyed, and I just know she's a liar.

You should use facts that came out in trial that bolster a witness's credibility, but it is not appropriate to add your opinion about that witness's honesty or other good qualities. It doesn't matter to the judge that you like and trust your witnesses. *Don't say* something like:

I trust Ira; I've know him for years. If he says he saw me cross the street in the crosswalk, then that's exactly what happened.

And don't put your own credibility on the line except as to particular facts you testified about during the trial. To illustrate, you can say:

As I testified, I have been a building contractor in this community for 25 years. I value my reputation, and if I thought I was responsible for the plaintiff's roof falling in, I would have repaired it immediately. But that is not what caused the damage to his roof. As you heard from the inspector, the plaintiff let the large oak tree grow too close to the power lines, and during the storm….

But avoid saying something like:

I'm an honest man; I wouldn't have brought this to trial if I didn't think I had a good case.

"…but I digress."

2. Don't Argue from Evidence Unless It Was Presented at Trial

A key rule in making your closing argument is: Don't talk about evidence, even if it will help you win, unless it is in the trial record —either testified to orally or in a document that was admitted into evidence. This is not the time to sneak in something you forgot to cover during the trial.

Take good notes during trial. It can be difficult to remember exactly what was said during your trial. So pay close attention and try these techniques.

- Keep your trial notebook open, and check off issues on your outline that your adversary stipulates to (admits).

- Note bits of testimony that strike you as particularly helpful or damaging to your case. You can use them to support your case or try to explain them away, as necessary, during closing argument.

- Have a friend or relative come with you and take notes too, in case you miss something. Although you could order a transcript of the trial record from the court reporter, it will be quite expensive and probably can't be done quickly enough for you to use in your closing argument.

While you must not misstate facts or argue what is not in the record, you can rely on logical inferences to show the judge or jury how particular evidence relates to the elements you must prove to support your legal claims. For example, assume you are the plaintiff in the car accident case and evidence was

introduced that Ms. Adams got a call moments before she hit you. You can properly argue:

Ms. Adams got a call on her car phone moments before she hit me. She was talking to someone in her office about the fact that her company messed up. They missed an important inspection. She said the job was an important one, potentially worth a lot of money. I ask you, is it possible that Ms. Adams's attention was not on the road, but on the call she got when she hit me? People who have just received important news, especially news that is likely to cost them a lot of money, are often distracted, even upset by such news. When someone is distracted, she has a harder time concentrating on traffic….

Notice that while no evidence was presented that Adams was distracted, you are able to ask the judge or jury to draw the inference, based on their common knowledge, that people who receive important phone calls are involved in their conversations and less attentive to the road. Making such inferences is perfectly acceptable during closing argument, and important to make to help the judge or jury interpret the evidence in a way that is favorable to you.

E. REBUTTAL ARGUMENT

If you are the plaintiff, and you decide to reserve a portion of your closing argument for rebuttal argument, your rebuttal should briefly state why particular things the defendant said in closing argument were wrong or misleading; you should not rehash things you already said or make brand new points. If you do, your opponent may object, and the judge may rule them outside the scope of rebuttal.

F.   OBJECTIONS DURING CLOSING

Either you or your adversary can object during the other's closing argument. If you do not follow the rules—for example, you argue facts that are not part of the record—your adversary may well object. Also, a more experienced opponent may try to use technical objections to throw you off balance. Even though it might look bad for a lawyer to bully a pro per, some do. If you get an objection to some point in your closing argument, think through what is being said, remain calm and stick up for yourself if you think the objection is wrong. (See Chapter 14, Making and Responding to Objections.) Or try rephrasing your statement. Here are two examples of how to handle an objection:

EXAMPLE 1

Plaintiff:

Therefore, Your Honor, since Ms. Adams admitted she got an important call on the car phone moments before she hit me….

Defendant:

Objection, Your Honor. There is no evidence in the record that the call was important.

Plaintiff:

Your Honor, may I rephrase my statement?

Judge:

You may.

Plaintiff:

Since Ms. Adams admitted that moments before she hit me she got a call on the car phone reporting a missed inspection….

EXAMPLE 2

Plaintiff:

Therefore, Your Honor, since Ms. Adams admitted she got an important call on the car phone moments before she hit me….

Defendant:

Objection, Your Honor. There is no evidence in the record that the call was important.

Judge:

Plaintiff?

Plaintiff:

There certainly is, Your Honor. The defendant made that statement in this courtroom last Tuesday when I was cross-examining her.

Judge:

Overruled. You may proceed.

Should you object to your opponent's argument? Object only if you really feel strongly that your adversary is misstating evidence or arguing about evidence that was not presented at trial, and that the argument is prejudicing your case. (See Chapter 14, Making and Responding to Objections.) It can be self-defeating to object at this stage, because judges often allow people a lot of leeway when making closing arguments.

G.   SAMPLE CLOSING ARGUMENT AND OUTLINE

Now that you've gotten a sense of the various key parts of closing argument, let's take one all the way through. Below is a sample argument in a jury trial of the traffic accident case in which you have sued Sarah Adams for negligence. You were hit by Adams' truck as you crossed the street. Following that is a short analysis and sample outline of the argument. You will likely want to write out your intended argument in full (to the extent you can) before trial so that you can practice it and perhaps show it your legal coach. Then, you can summarize it in outline form to use during your actual argument.

1 *Good afternoon. The evidence has come to a close and the task of deciding whose story you believe is in your hands, ladies and gentlemen. I have presented my evidence as well as I could —despite the fact that I am clearly not at home in the courtroom like my talented opponent.*

2 *You have heard lots of facts today, and you are very familiar now with what happened to me. As the judge instructed you, there are four legal elements I must show in order to prove that Ms. Adams was negligent. First, that she owed a duty to me as a pedestrian on a public street to drive attentively and follow the rules of the road. Second, that she breached her duty by driving carelessly. Third, that my injuries were caused by her truck hitting me. And last, that I lost $15,000 because of work I had to miss; I paid $50,000 in doctor bills; and it is fair to award me $35,000 to compensate me for the terrible pain I suffered as a result of her carelessness.*

3 *Let's take a look back to some of the key testimony that proves each of those four elements. First off, the judge instructed you that Ms. Adams had a duty to me to drive with due*

and reasonable care. She admits this, so the first element is proven.

4 *Second, I must show that the defendant breached her duty of care to me by driving carelessly. This has also been proven. The evidence shows that the defendant was not driving safely. She let her mind and eyes wander, ladies and gentlemen, because she was distracted. What distracted her? A business call on her car phone, which the telephone bills you saw show happened just moments before she slammed into me. A business call that, as she herself told you, reported a missed inspection on a big job. Now, the defendant told you this did not distract her at all, that inspections are missed all the time. But she may be forgetting exactly how much money was at stake in this job. Her own business records show it was a ten million dollar deal. She told you that the missed inspection could have caused delays both on this job and other ones. Ms. Adams is an entrepreneur who owns her own business. She is the one who is financially responsible if jobs are missed. And how many delays can occur before her reputation and business suffer? Isn't it likely that this phone call upset her and caused her to drive carelessly?*

5 *You also heard from Cynthia White. She told you she was waiting for a bus at the Elm Street stop. She saw the whole thing. Ms. White is a school teacher. She didn't know me or the defendant. She has no reason to be anything less than truthful with you. And she had a perfect view of the whole scene from the bus stop. Yes she told the defendant at her deposition that a bus was in front of her in the left turn lane, but she also told you she could see* *the crosswalk fine since it was off to the side of where she was. She told you that I was in the crosswalk when the defendant hit me, and that she watched the defendant sit in her truck and wait for the police. After hitting me, she didn't even check to see that I was all right. Ms. White's testimony proves that I was in the crosswalk, and that the defendant was negligent for not stopping for me.*

6   *I have also proven elements 3 and 4. The defendant's truck hitting me caused my injuries, and I have suffered a great deal—in physical pain, money, and lost wages. As I testified, when I saw her truck coming at me, I tried to get out of the way. But she hit me. I felt my leg snap as I fell to the ground. Dr. Duncan testified he treated me that day for a broken leg. It took four months to heal, though as Dr. Duncan testified, my limp may never go away. During those months, I was in constant and excruciating pain. I had difficulty sleeping, and as I testified, I couldn't do even the most basic of household chores like taking out the trash. I spent most of my time in bed and seeing doctors. I showed you the doctor bills.*

7   *Now, the judge has given you some important instructions on how you should weigh the evidence you've heard. She said I must prove my case to you by a preponderance of the evidence. Let me tell you what that means. It does not mean I must prove my case beyond a reasonable doubt. That is only in criminal trials, like what you may have seen in the movies. A preponderance of the evidence only means that if you imagine weighing the evidence on a scale and my side weighs a tiny bit more than the defendant's, then I have met my*

burden. That is all it takes. You don't have to be absolutely certain.

8   *It is up to you, now. Deliberate fairly and honestly. Make the right decision, and hold the defendant responsible for the accident she caused. Please have her pay me back for the $50,000 I had to pay in doctor bills, the $15,000 I lost being out of work, and the $35,000 I have requested to compensate me for the painful injuries she caused me to suffer. Thank you.*

Transcript Analysis: This closing argument begins with some simple introductory comments, then moves right into the legal elements (No. 2). Noting that the jury is familiar with the evidence, you appropriately suggest that this closing argument will not simply rehash the evidence. Next, you are up front that you have to prove all four legal elements, and begin immediately to show how you have done so. You first set out the elements (No. 2), then go back and connect the evidence to each one (Nos. 3, 4, 5 and 6).

If this argument had been to a judge alone, you would have done well to skip No. 2 and go right into the next sections. (You would also skip No. 7, of course.) Before a judge, make your arguments short, cut out as much as possible your explanations of the law, and hit only the key facts that prove each element.

Beginning in No. 3, you go element by element, emphasizing the key evidence that proves each.

In No. 4, you say that the defendant "let her mind and eyes wander." Evidence was presented that her eyes wandered (White saw her on the car phone, looking down), but you really don't know where her mind was; only the defendant knows that. But it is proper to ask the jury to make an inference that because she was engaged in an important phone call, she was thinking about business rather than the road. The jurors, after all, are free to disagree.

Next comes some rebuttal of the defendant's testimony. Without saying she is a liar, you suggest that she may simply not remember the amount of money involved, and how upset or distracted she really was.

Then, White's key testimony is summarized, along with some facts that bolster her credibility, such as her being a teacher and not knowing either party before the accident. You explain away the apparent contradiction in statements about her view being unobstructed, and add that the defendant did not even come to see how you were, perhaps to make her look cold or insensitive.

Next (No. 6), you hit the elements of causation (leg snapped when truck hit you) and damages (the doctor bills and pain and suffering). And last, you discuss the burden of proof, stressing that the jury doesn't need to be absolutely certain, and asks for a specific result.

Here is one possible way you would make an outline for the sample closing argument above. As you read it, note how much of it could have been done before trial. There of course will be evidence you first learn about during trial, points your adversary emphasized that you want to try to contradict or explain away, and other odds and ends you need to fill in during or just after the evidence has been presented. For that reason, it's a good idea to leave some room in your outline to add such items in.

I. Introduction

- Evidence finished. Decision in your hands
- I tried but I'm not at home in the courtroom
- You know what happened

II. Legal Elements

I must prove all 4
(Introduce 1st, then repeat w/evidence)

1. Defendant (D) has duty to follow rules of road, drive carefully
2. She breached duty by driving carelessly
3. My injuries were caused by her truck hitting me
4. I was damaged (money on doctors, lost wages, pain and suffering) as a result of her carelessness

(Evidence clearly proves each element)

1. Duty:
   - Public street. D has Driver's license. D has duty to be careful
2. Defendant was not driving safely: breached duty of care
   - mind and eyes wandered
   - she was distracted by call on her car phone
   - call moments before hit (telephone bills)
   - big job/ missed inspection (defendant admitted)
   - said missed inspections are common—not believable. This was big job, lots of money at stake
   - D owns business; she's responsible, might hurt her reputation and business

<u>Cynthia White testimony</u>

- White is credible—teacher, didn't know us
- White waiting for bus; saw whole thing
- Perfect view of scene—Yes, she said in depo that her view was blocked—but she meant her view of the street. Bus was in front, accident to side. So her view of the accident was clear
- She saw me in cross walk when defendant hit me
- She watched defendant sit in cab of truck, wait for police, didn't even check if I was okay

3. Causation

- Her truck hit me
- When I saw her truck, I tried to get out of way, but couldn't
- Leg broke on impact; I felt it

4. Damages

- Pain, suffering, 4 months to heal
- You saw doctor bills at trial
- Lost work wages

III. Jury Instructions/Burden of proof

Judge said I must prove case by "preponderance of the evidence"

- That does not mean beyond a reasonable doubt like criminal cases

- Scales—tiny bit more on my side, I meet burden
- "You don't have to be absolutely certain."

IV. Results

- Up to you, now

"Hold the defendant responsible for the accident she caused"

- Make her pay $ 50,000 (doctor bills and costs), $ 35,000 (pain and suffering), $ 15,000 (lost work)

V. Thank you

RESOURCES ON CLOSING ARGUMENT

Trial Advocacy in a Nutshell, by Paul Bergman (2nd Ed., West Publishing Co.), an easy-to-read, helpful and inexpensive paperback about effective and persuasive trial techniques. Chapter 5 covers both opening statements and closing argument.

The Trial Process: Law Tactics and Ethics, by J. Alexander Tanford (The Michie Co.), a textbook on trial practice which includes excerpts from many other leading books and dialogues of trial scenarios.

Art of Advocacy, by Lawrence J. Smith (Matthew Bender) includes an extensive separate volume filled with examples of actual closing arguments, titled *Summation.*

12

EXHIBITS

Exhibits are the tangible objects that you present to a judge or jury during trial to help establish your case. Typical exhibits include documents such as letters, contracts and receipts. Reports, such as those a child psychologist or a radiologist may prepare when testifying as an expert witness, are also exhibits. So too are photographs, X-rays and all other physical objects. For example, if you sue someone for injuries you received as a result of being struck by a badly-thrown boomerang, the boomerang can be an exhibit.

Under most circumstances you are under no legal obligation to offer exhibits into evidence. You can present your entire case through oral testimony from you and your witnesses. But you can dramatically add to the persuasiveness of your case in at least three ways by backing up testimony with exhibits:

- Just like the "show" part of "show and tell" in the first grade, tangible objects make your story more real and interesting.

- Exhibits have a longer shelf life than oral testimony. When it comes time to deliberate and arrive at a verdict, a judge or jury may forget oral testimony. But usually they have the opportunity to hold and examine an exhibit.

- A little like shy first graders, you and your witnesses may testify more confidently—and therefore more credibly—when holding and talking about tangible objects.

For an exhibit to officially become evidence that the judge or jury can consider when deciding your case, you must present it to the judge and demonstrate that it is authentic and trustworthy. You do this by offering (through your own testimony or that of your witnesses) what lawyers refer to as "foundational testimony." If the judge decides that your foundational testimony meets evidence rule requirements, the judge will formally admit the exhibit into evidence. This chapter describes and illustrates the process for handling exhibits during trial, and shows you how to elicit the necessary foundational testimony for many common types of exhibits.

A. ADMITTING EXHIBITS INTO EVIDENCE: AN OVERVIEW

The type of foundational evidence you need to offer to admit an exhibit into evidence varies greatly from one exhibit to another. Fortunately, the procedural steps are almost always the same. Here is an overview of those steps; you will read about each in more detail below.

Step 1:   Mark your exhibit for identification and allow opposing counsel (or your adversary, if neither of you is represented by counsel) to examine it. (See Section B below.)

Step 2:   Identify (authenticate) your exhibit by asking the judge for permission to approach the witness, handing the exhibit to the witness and asking the witness to state what the exhibit is. (In some courts your judge may ask you to hand the exhibit to the bailiff, who will then pass it along to the witness.) (See Section C below.)

Step 3:   Personally testify to or elicit from a witness any legally required foundational evidence. (See Section D below.)

Step 4: Ask the judge to admit the exhibit into evidence.

💡 **You can offer exhibits into evidence during cross-examination.** While you will probably offer exhibits into evidence through your own testimony or that of your witnesses during direct examination, you can also offer an exhibit during cross-examination of an adverse witness. Apart from perhaps receiving more grudging responses to your questions, the process is identical.

As an alternative to this four-step process for admitting exhibits into evidence, ask your adversary before trial to stipulate (agree) to the admissibility of your exhibits. Stipulations to the admissibility of exhibits are common. Especially when the admissibility of exhibits is clear, attorneys (and pro pers) often stipulate to the admissibility of each other's exhibits.

If you and your adversary do reach a stipulation, put it in writing and sign it to prevent your adversary from suddenly denying the stipulation at trial, leaving you with no way to produce foundational evidence. A sample stipulation is shown below.

SAMPLE STIPULATION

STIPULATION

Plaintiff Jean Nolo and Defendant Sherry Mason hereby stipulate that the lease agreement dated March 12 and signed by each of them, consisting of three pages, may be admitted into evidence in <u>Nolo v. Mason</u>, Superior Court No. 11359.

Jean Nolo   Date: March 1, 19XX

Jean Nolo, Plaintiff in Pro Per

Aaron Samuels   Date: March 1, 19XX

Aaron Samuels
Attorney for Defendant

💡 **It doesn't matter which side admits an exhibit into evidence.** If you are a defendant, you may find that by the time it is your turn to present evidence the plaintiff has already offered an exhibit into evidence that you planned to offer. For example, if you are the tenant in a landlord-tenant case, the landlord may offer the lease and some canceled checks into evidence, two exhibits that you planned to offer. This won't affect your planned testimony.

Whether you or an adversary offers an exhibit into evidence, you may testify about the exhibit yourself, hand it to your witnesses and ask them questions about it, and make the same arguments about it that you would have made had you offered the exhibit into evidence. Perhaps you can even thank your adversary for offering the exhibit into evidence: it saves you the trouble of offering foundational testimony.

Then, either in a brief pre-trial conference or when you or your witness is about to refer to the exhibit, inform the judge that you've reached a stipulation as to its admissibility. In the example above, you would say something like, "Your Honor, the defendant and I stipulate that the lease agreement of March 12, signed by me and Ms. Mason and consisting of three pages, may be admitted into evidence." The judge will almost certainly grant your request, because it saves court time.

B. STEP 1: MARK YOUR EXHIBITS AND SHOW THEM TO YOUR ADVERSARY

Marking an exhibit for identification consists of tagging an exhibit with a number or letter, to distinguish it from others. You do not have to be testifying under oath when you mark an exhibit, so you can mark an exhibit either while you are presenting evidence yourself or while you are questioning a witness.

Traditionally, plaintiffs' exhibits are numbered, and defendants' exhibits are lettered. But like the former practice of attaching only feminine names to hurricanes, this traditional system has been dropped by many courts. Read your local court rules or check with the court clerk in advance to find out what marking procedure your judge likes to follow.

In some courts, the court clerk does the actual marking of exhibits. Or the clerk may ask you to mark all your exhibits before trial starts. But usually, you'll mark an exhibit for identification and let your adversary examine it the very first time

you or a witness refer to it. For instance, assume that you are the plaintiff in a breach of contract case. You have testified to the oral discussions leading up to the contract, and you now want to offer the contract itself into evidence. Before you do, you must get it marked for identification like this:

"Your Honor, I have here a two-page document. It is headed 'Agreement,' and dated December 8 of last year. I am showing it to defense counsel. May it be marked Plaintiff's Exhibit No. 1 for identification?"

Keep calm as you move about the courtroom during the marking process. Going through the marking process while you are testifying personally can be something of a logistical challenge. You may have to move back and forth between the witness box, the clerk's desk, your adversary at counsel table and your file folder containing the exhibit. Do not panic; with the judge's guidance you will probably glide about the courtroom with the grace of Fred Astaire or Ginger Rogers.

When the judge gives you permission to mark the exhibit, you may write "Exh. 1" on the agreement itself with a pen. If an exhibit cannot be easily marked with a pen (for example, your exhibit is a boomerang or a hat), most court clerks provide small, gummed labels that you can attach to an exhibit and then mark. When you mark an exhibit, say no more than is necessary to identify it. For example, the statement above about the contract refers to objective characteristics of the exhibit: how many pages it consists of and its title and date.

Do not try to gild the lily by turning the marking process into an argument. Never say anything like, "Your Honor, I want to mark this contract that proves that the defendant owes me $25,000."

Once an exhibit has been marked for identification, keep the record clear by mentioning its assigned number or letter whenever you talk about it in court. For example, when testifying on direct examination you might say, "The first time I saw the lease, Exhibit 1, was when…."

💡 **Make extra copies of written exhibits.** When you mark an exhibit before showing it to a witness, hand extra copies that you have made before trial to opposing counsel and the judge. This speeds up the foundational process, because a single piece of paper does not have to pass through four different pairs of hands. More importantly, you may impress the judge with the care you have put into your case, and the judge may give you the benefit of the doubt if a ruling on the admissibility of an exhibit could legitimately go either way.

C. STEP 2: IDENTIFY (AUTHENTICATE) YOUR EXHIBITS

The next step is for you or a witness to identify (authenticate) an exhibit. Do this by offering brief testimony that tells the judge what the exhibit is and shows its connection to the case.

By way of illustration, assume again that you are the plaintiff in a breach of contract case and that you have just finished marking the contract for identification as "Exhibit 1." You are now testifying. Hold the exhibit and identify it as follows: "Exhibit 1 is the contract that the defendant and I signed on December 8 of last year." This testimony identifies the exhibit as the actual document that you and the defendant signed.

You can often add impact to authentication testimony by referring to the basis of your identification. With the contract, for example, you (or your witness, of course) could testify that, "I know that Exhibit 1 is the contract I signed because when I signed it I noticed that the upper right-hand corner of the top page was torn, as you can see here."

YOU DON'T ALWAYS NEED THE REAL THING

If you don't know the whereabouts of the actual physical object involved in your case, consider substituting a "look-alike." When (as is often true) the precise appearance of the actual object is not significant, you can use a substitute that is similar in appearance if you make sure that everyone understands it is a substitute. (If however, the exhibit is a document, you may be required to produce the original or explain why you can't. See Section F, below.)

For example, assume that you are suing a defendant for carelessly throwing a boomerang in a shopping mall and striking you with it. You do not have the actual boomerang that struck you, but want to use an exhibit to add impact to your testimony. You know what the boomerang looked like and have gotten another one that is in all important respects identical to the one that struck you. To offer the substitute into evidence, simply identify it as "a boomerang that looks just like the one that hit me."

D. STEP 3: LAY A FOUNDATION

Once an exhibit is marked and identified, the judge can consider whether to admit it into evidence. Often, however, simply identifying an exhibit is not sufficient to admit it into evidence. In addition, you have to elicit testimony called "foundational evidence" that demonstrates that an exhibit meets evidence rules requirements. Not surprisingly, the process of eliciting this evidence is called "laying a foundation."

To complicate this task, foundational requirements are different for different types of exhibits. For example, the foundation needed to admit a business receipt is very different from the foundation needed to admit a photograph. And the foundation needed to admit a hospital record is different from either of them.

We do not have space in this book to describe the necessary foundation for every possible type of exhibit you may want to offer into evidence. We do, however, illustrate how to lay a foundation for many common types of exhibits. If we do not cover the type of exhibit you want to offer, consult one of the books listed at the end of this section for help.

⚠ **Consider other rules of evidence before deciding that an exhibit is admissible.** Even if you lay a perfect foundation for an exhibit, other rules of evidence may bar the exhibit from being admitted into evidence. For example, you may provide foundational testimony for a letter, yet see the letter excluded because its contents are either irrelevant or inadmissible hearsay. Carefully study both this chapter and Chapter 13, Basic Rules of Evidence, before deciding that an exhibit is admissible.

1. When Identification Is Enough for Admissibility

Sometimes the testimony that identifies an exhibit also provides all the foundational evidence you need for the judge to admit it into evidence. Generally, identification evidence alone is a sufficient foundation when an exhibit is a physical object rather than a document, and you or a witness can identify it on the basis of your personal knowledge.

For example, assume again that you are testifying about how you came to be struck by the carelessly thrown boomerang. After you were hit, you picked up the boomerang and ran after the defendant. He got away, but his hat with his name in it fell off and you picked it up. To illustrate and add impact to your oral testimony, you want to offer the boomerang and the hat into evidence. One at a time, you go through the process of marking both the boomerang and the hat for identification and showing each to opposing counsel. Next, you identify each of them with this testimony: "Exhibit 2 is the boomerang that hit me on the back of my head. Exhibit 3 is the hat that fell off the defendant's head when I chased him. I know these are the actual objects because after I was hit I picked up the boomerang and the hat and took them home with me."

In this situation, you have personal knowledge of both exhibits, and your identification evidence is the only foundation necessary for the judge to admit the boomerang and the hat into evidence. After giving the identification testimony above you would ask the judge to admit both exhibits into evidence in this manner:

1 **You:**

Your Honor, now I'd like to offer the boomerang, Exhibit 2, and the hat, Exhibit 3, into evidence.

2 **Judge (To opposing counsel):**

Any objection?

3 **Opposing Counsel:**

None, Your Honor.

4 **Judge:**

Very well. Exhibits 2 and 3 are admitted into evidence.

Once the judge admits the exhibits into evidence, both you and your adversary can testify or ask questions concerning either of them.

⚠️ **Exhibits stay in court.** When an exhibit is admitted into evidence it becomes court property until it is released, usually after the verdict. Do not walk out of the court with "your" boomerang and hat at the end of the day, thinking you'll bring it back in the morning. Otherwise you, the boomerang and the hat may end up spending the night together in the courthouse, courtesy of the bailiff.

---

2. When an Exhibit May Have Been Tampered With

With most exhibits, such as a contract, a business record, a photograph or a boomerang, a witness with personal knowledge of the exhibit could likely readily detect any alterations in it. In such situa-tions, you do not have to account for an exhibit's whereabouts prior to trial. But with other kinds of exhibits, if your adversary objects, the judge may refuse to admit an exhibit into evidence until you show that you have kept it secure so that it has not been tampered with. Such a situation may arise if you offer a liquid, a food or drug or a similar perishable item into evidence.

For example, assume that you claim that your adversary was driving under the influence of alcohol. You want to admit into evidence the open bottle of liquid you found on the front seat of his car along with the testimony of a laboratory technician who tested the liquid and determined that it was vodka. In this situation, before you can get the bottle of vodka admitted into evidence you need to satisfy the judge that the liquid you had tested and are now offering into evidence is the same liquid you found in the car; lawyers call this "establishing a chain of custody."

To establish a chain of custody, both you and the laboratory technician must provide foundational testimony. You will need to testify to keeping the bottle and its contents in a secure place before and after it was tested, and then identify the bottle and its contents as the object that you delivered to the technician. The technician will have to identify the same bottle and contents as the one that she received from you, tested and then either returned to you or brought to court. The judge will not admit the exhibit into evidence until both of you have testified.

As you can see, establishing a chain of custody can be complex. If you seek to admit an important exhibit for which a chain of custody is necessary, refer to one of the evidence treatises listed at the end of this section or consult your self-help law coach if you are uncertain about how to do it.

3. Offering Foundations for Common Exhibits

This section examines the foundational requirements for the kinds of exhibits you are most likely to encounter as a pro per litigant.

a. Photographs

As suggested by the old expression that "a picture is worth a thousand words," photographs often make stories more convincing. But because a photograph is one step removed from whatever physical objects it depicts, you must lay a foundation beyond marking and identifying a photograph before you can offer it into evidence. When, as is usually the case, a photograph depicts an object that you or one of your witnesses can identify from personal knowledge, such as the interior of an apartment or a damaged car, the foundation for the photograph is quite simple. You offer testimony that the photograph is a "fair and accurate representation" of whatever it depicts. For example, assume that you want to introduce into evidence a photograph of your living room, showing a portion of the ceiling that collapsed due to water damage. The witness who is testifying is a friend who has just concluded describing what the damaged portion of the ceiling looked like. You now offer foundational testimony for the photograph:

1   **You:**

Your Honor, I'm holding a photograph that has been marked Plaintiff's Exhibit 3 for identification and have shown it to defense counsel. May I approach the witness to show her the photograph?

2   **Judge:**

You may.

3   **You:**

Ms. Tobias, please look at the photograph, Exhibit 3, and tell me if you recognize what it shows.

4   **Witness:**

Yes, this looks like a picture of your living room ceiling, showing the part that collapsed.

5   **You:**

Does the photograph fairly and accurately depict the way the room looks since the ceiling collapsed?

6   **Witness:**

Yes, it does.

7   **You:**

Your Honor, I ask that the photograph be received in evidence.

8   **Judge:**

Any objection? Hearing none, it is received.

Here, the key foundational testimony comes in Nos. 5 and 6. By testifying from personal knowledge that the photograph fairly and accurately depicts what she saw, the witness links the photograph to the damaged ceiling. Technical details such as the kind of camera, lens and film used to take the photograph are unnecessary. Note that a witness does not have to be absolutely certain of what a photograph depicts for the photo to be admissible in evidence. A qualified response like "I'm pretty sure that's your ceiling" or "I'd say that's your ceiling" normally demonstrates sufficient personal knowledge for admissibility (see No. 4, above). On the other hand, if a witness says something like, "I'm guessing that's a picture of your ceiling," the judge will probably rule that the witness has not shown sufficient personal knowledge to admit the photo into evidence. If you are going to show a photo (or other exhibit) to a witness during trial, first show it to the witness during a pre-trial rehearsal to make sure that the witness recognizes what it depicts.

More foundation is needed if a camera reveals what no witness saw. In very unusual circumstances, you may want to offer into evidence a photograph that depicts something that no witness actually saw. In one famous case, a photograph showed a stabbing taking place in the background; neither the photographer nor any other available witness had personally observed the stabbing. The photograph was admitted into evidence, but only after extensive foundational evidence about the camera, film type and other details. In the unlikely event that you want to offer a photo that depicts something that neither you nor one of your witnesses can identify from personal knowledge, consult an experienced trial lawyer.

Photographs don't have to be taken right away. As long as you or a witness can testify that a photograph fairly and accurately depicts a scene as it existed when relevant events took place, it does not matter how long after those events a photograph is taken. So if you suddenly realize days, weeks or even months after events took place that photographs will greatly help a judge or jury understand your version of events, don't worry. As long as the physical condition of whatever you want to photograph has remained largely unchanged, you can take a photograph of it and offer the photograph into evidence.

For instance, you might want to show a photograph to demonstrate that an accident occurred because the view of an intersection is obscured by a large leafy tree, or that in a car crash your vehicle was hit in the right rear, or that part of your living room ceiling collapsed after heavy rains. As long as you or your witness can testify that the photos fairly and accurately depict conditions as they existed when the events occurred, you can successfully offer into evidence a photo taken long after the incident in question took place.

b. Diagrams

A diagram is an excellent way to illustrate some types of testimony. You and your witnesses may testify with far more clarity and confidence when you can point at and make markings on a visual representation of an event. You can efficiently use a diagram to help you or a witness explain such things as the path of a car before a collision, the floor plan of an apartment or where on your child's body you saw bruises when he came home after a weekend visit with your ex-spouse. Be creative. A diagram is your chance to develop an exhibit on your own; you are not limited to tangible objects that existed when events giving rise to your dispute took place.

While you or a witness can draw a diagram directly on a courtroom blackboard (if there is one), a diagram becomes an exhibit that you can offer into evidence only if you or a witness draw it on a sheet of paper. To do this, obtain a large sheet of paper and vividly colored marking pens so the diagram you create will be clear to the judge or jury. You can prepare an entire diagram before trial and later testify to what it depicts. Or you can prepare a skeleton diagram before trial and complete it while you or a witness testify. Either way, a diagram does not have to be drawn to exact scale; it is enough for admissibility that a diagram fairly approximates whatever it depicts.

For example, assume that you are the plaintiff in a negligence case. You call Cynthia White to testify that a car driven by the defendant Sarah Adams made a left turn in an intersection and struck you in a crosswalk. During your pre-trial rehearsal, you and White can prepare a skeleton diagram of the intersection that may look like the one shown below.

As White testifies, have her refer to the diagram. Begin by laying a foundation showing that the diagram fairly approximates the intersection where the accident took place. Based on this diagram, the testimony might look like this:

1 **You:**

Your Honor, the bailiff has pinned a diagram to the easel. May it be marked Plaintiff's Exhibit 1 for identification?

2 **Judge:**

It will be so marked.

3 **You:**

Ms. White, looking at Exhibit 1, do you recognize what it depicts?

4 **Witness:**

Yes, it is the intersection of Elm and Main Streets.

5 **You:**

How do you know that?

6 **Witness:**

Well, I know that intersection and I drew this diagram of it when I met with you last night.

7 **You:**

Would you say it is a fair approximation of that intersection?

8   Witness:

Yes. Of course it's not exactly to scale.

9   You:

Can you explain the markings on the diagram?

10   Witness:

It shows that Elm is a north-south street; Main runs east-west. Each street has two lanes of traffic in each direction. There's a left-turn lane for traffic going east on Main to turn north on Elm. There are crosswalks between all the corners.

11   You:

The crosswalks are the parallel lines at all corners?

12   Witness:

Yes.

13   You:

I see you put an "X" on the northeast corner of the intersection. What does the "X" stand for?

14   Witness:

That's where you were standing when I first saw you.

15   You:

And what about these two boxes, one marked with a "V" and one with a "D?"

16   Witness:

The one with a "V" is my car; that's where I was waiting for the light to turn green so that

I could go south on Elm. The one with a "D" is the defendant's truck, at the place where I first saw it, going into the left-turn lane.

Transcript Analysis. This testimony lays the foundation to admit the diagram into evidence. Though it is not an exact depiction of the intersection, the diagram "fairly approximates" the scene of the accident (Nos. 7-8). Note that while No. 7 is a leading question asked on direct examination, judges generally allow leading questions to elicit foundational evidence. (See Chapter 9, Direct Examination, for a discussion of forms of questions and when each may be used.) The rest of the foundation simply explains the markings, giving you a chance to make White's testimony more vivid and real.

As a witness testifies, it is proper to ask the witness to make additional markings on the diagram. For example, assume that White testifies that the next time she saw you, you were in the crosswalk. To illustrate that testimony in a vivid way, ask her to walk over to the diagram and indicate your position:

23   You:

Where was I the next time you saw me?

24   Witness:

You were in the crosswalk.

25   You:

About how far from the curb?

26   Witness:

I'm not great at distances, I'd say about ten feet.

27   You:

Could you please mark "X-1" on the diagram to show where I was the next time you saw me?

28   Witness:

OK, right about here.

(The witness concludes her testimony about the diagram.)

55   You:

Your Honor, may the diagram be admitted into evidence?

56   Judge:

Any objection? All right, Exhibit 1 is admitted.

Transcript Analysis: You might have asked the judge to admit the diagram into evidence after No. 16, when the witness supplied foundational testimony for the skeleton diagram. But when you intend to ask a witness to make additional markings on a diagram (or when you personally will mark a diagram while testifying), it is proper to delay offering it into evidence until you are done.

Keep a diagram simple. When you use a diagram to illustrate a witness's story, include only major changes in location lest you have so many markings that the diagram becomes unintelligible. At all times a judge or juror should easily be able to follow what's going on. If you can, rehearse any drawing that you or a witness will make in court in front of an audience and ask for suggestions as to how you can improve your presentation.

c.   Letters and Faxes

To offer a letter or a fax transmission into evidence, you need to lay a foundation showing that the person or organization you claim wrote it actually did so. There are many ways to lay such a foundation. (See Federal Rule of Evidence 901.) For example, if you claim that Edelstein wrote a letter, here are some of the possibilities:

- Edelstein's own testimony that he wrote it

- the testimony of a witness who actually saw Edelstein write the letter

- if the letter is handwritten, the testimony of a witness who has personal knowledge of Edelstein's handwriting style

- if the letter is typed and signed, the testimony of a witness who is familiar with Edelstein's signature

- testimony that, based on the contents of the letter, it is unlikely that anyone other than Edelstein wrote it.

Here is a sample foundation for introducing a letter into evidence based on your personal familiarity with the writer's signature. Assume that you are involved in a breach of contract case, and you have testified that you talked to Edelstein about buying what he said was a valuable baseball card collection. You now want to offer into evidence a letter that you say was written by Edelstein and that contains what you claim are false statements about the collection. You are laying the foundation through your personal testimony:

1   You:

Two days later, I think it was on the 18th, I got this letter. May I mark it Exhibit 3?

2 **Judge:**

You may. What is the date?

3 **You:**

June 16.

4 **Judge:**

OK, a letter dated June 16 is marked Exhibit 3. Has defense counsel seen it?

5 **You:**

Yes, she has. This is the letter I received from Mr. Edelstein. I recognize the signature as Mr. Edelstein's because I've seen his signature on other letters that he sent me and we talked about. I'd like to offer Exhibit 3 into evidence.

6 **Judge:**

No objections? It is received.

By testifying from personal knowledge that you recognize the signature as Edelstein's, you lay an adequate foundation to admit the letter into evidence.

If the document you want to offer into evidence is a fax transmission, you may have no handwriting to identify. However, just as with an old-fashioned letter, you have to offer foundational testimony connecting the fax to the person or organization who you claim produced it. Again, you may do this in a variety of ways. For example, if you claim that the fax was sent by your adversary, before trial you may send a request for admission asking your adversary to admit that he sent it. (See Chapter 3, Starting and Investigating Your Case, for a discussion of requests for admission and other discovery devices.) In addition, you may testify that you had a conversation with or sent a fax of your own to the person whom you claim sent the fax, and that the exhibit in court was sent in response to the conversation or your fax. Even a letterhead or similar logo on a fax is likely to be sufficient for a judge to admit it into evidence.

d. Business Records

(See also Computerized Business Records, in Subsection e below.)

As all of us know only too well, most business activities generate paperwork. For example, if you are a manufacturer who shipped merchandise to a customer who has refused to pay for it, included in your paperwork will be the record of the unpaid bill and your delivery document (receipt). If you are a landlord, you probably have a rent book showing when the tenants paid and did not pay the rent. And if you are a parent seeking additional payments from your ex-spouse to cover your child's large medical expenses, you have medical bills.

At trial, exhibits such as these are generally referred to as "business records." The term is very broad; almost any document produced by any kind of organization, including nonprofit corporations and community groups, is considered a business record. To have business records admitted into evidence, you must lay a foundation proving that they are likely to be accurate. The requirements are nearly identical in every state. (See, for example, Federal Rule of Evidence 803 (6), New York Code of Evidence § 803 (c)(5), California Evidence Code § 1271, and Texas Civil Rule of Evidence 803 (6).) All provide that your foundation has to show three things:

- Your document was made in the normal course of business.

- It was prepared around the time of the event to which it pertains.

- The way the business makes and keeps records suggests that the document is trustworthy.

BUSINESS RECORDS AND THE HEARSAY RULE

Chapter 13, Basic Rules of Evidence, explains the hearsay rule, which excludes many out-of-court statements, and some of the important exceptions to the rule that make some types of hearsay statements admissible. A business record is hearsay when it is offered to prove that the transaction recorded by the record occurred. But if your case relies on a business record, you can relax: One of the most important hearsay exceptions is the one making business records admissible upon a proper foundational showing.

For example, assume that you are a manufacturer of car stereos and that you delivered 100 radios to the defendant, a retailer who has refused to pay for them. You want to offer your company's unpaid invoice into evidence to prove that the defendant owes your company $10,000. If you are offering the invoice through your own testimony, your foundational evidence would look like this:

I have this Invoice No. 229 that has been marked as Exhibit 1 and shown to the defendant. Exhibit 1 is one of my company's invoices. It was prepared by my assistant manager, Steve Von Till; I recognize his initials in the lower right hand corner of the invoice. Our company's business practice is to prepare an invoice for every order we receive the same day we receive it. Unpaid invoices are kept in a separate file folder by number. All payments received go to our bookkeeper, who stamps "paid" on these invoices and puts them into a folder labeled "paid invoices." I took this invoice from the folder holding the unpaid bills, and it has not been stamped as paid. I ask for Exhibit 1 to be admitted into evidence.

This foundational evidence qualifies the invoice as an admissible business record. You did not prepare the invoice personally, but that is not necessary. Its trustworthiness comes from the routine practice of preparing and keeping invoices. You identify the invoice as a record of your business, establish that invoices are prepared right after orders are received and explain your record-keeping system. This foundation suggests that the fact that the invoice has not been stamped "paid" is a reliable indication that it was not paid. Thus, the judge should admit the invoice into evidence.

💡 **Ask your adversary to stipulate to the admission of your business records.** Business records are often admitted into evidence by stipulation. Your adversary may well stipulate to the admissibility of business records, because there is often no doubt of their accuracy. (See Section C, above, for a form of stipulation you might use.)

Records from someone else's business. You will have to lay much the same kind of foundation for a business record that comes from someone else's business. Absent a stipulation, you may need someone familiar with the records of the other business to come to court and lay the proper foundation. For instance, assume that you are a parent seeking an award of additional money from your ex-spouse to pay for large medical expenses that your child recently incurred. You want to offer into evidence the sheaf of hospital bills you have received. The bills are business records of the hospital. If your ex-spouse will not stipulate to their admissibility, to admit them into evidence you will need to lay a foundation showing how and when the bills are prepared and maintained in the hospital's regular course of business.

To do this it is necessary to serve a document available for free from the court clerk, called a subpoena duces tecum, on the hospital's Custodian of Records. A subpoena duces tecum orders someone from the hospital's record-keeping staff to come to court on the date specified in the subpoena (that's the subpoena part) and bring along a copy of the hospital's bills (that's the duces tecum part). Then you will call the hospital employee as a witness and question the employee about the hospital's record-keeping procedures. (See Chapter 9, Direct Examination, for additional information about subpoenas.)

e. Computerized Business Records

Many businesses today store most of their records in computers. For example, if you are a manufacturer, employees probably regularly enter data into a computer reflecting merchandise delivered to and payments received from your customers. To prove at trial how much a customer owes, you will probably need to make a printout of the account and offer it as an exhibit.

Fortunately, evidence rules are flexible enough to permit admission of a business record consisting of a computer printout. As with any other business record, you will need to offer foundational evidence concerning how your business prepares and keeps records. Your foundation should include

Your court may have faster ways to admit business records. To save businesses the time and expense of employees going to court, many states have adopted a shortcut procedure for business records known as the Uniform Photographic Copies of Business and Public Records as Evidence Act. If your state has adopted this law, a business can comply with your subpoena duces tecum asking for a business record by mailing records to the court along with an affidavit signed under penalty of perjury as to how the records are prepared and kept. The records are then admissible in evidence without your having to offer any further foundation.

Look in your state's evidence statutes to see if it has adopted this uniform act. As of this book's publication date, the Uniform Act has been adopted by the following states:

Alabama	New Hampshire
Arkansas	New Jersey
California	New York
Colorado	North Carolina
Connecticut	North Dakota
Georgia	Pennsylvania
Idaho	South Carolina
Iowa	South Dakota
Kansas	Utah
Kentucky	Vermont
Maine	Virgin Islands
Maryland	Virginia
Massachusetts	Washington
Michigan	West Virginia
Minnesota	Wisconsin
Nebraska	

information about your business's computer system. Don't worry, you will not need to call an expert witness to explain the scientific theory behind and the reliability of computers. Simply have a computer-literate employee explain how your records are entered and retrieved, and that the computer from which the record was retrieved was in good working order. As long as your business has routine and reliable procedures for using and maintaining its computers, and the particular record was maintained according to those procedures, you should have no difficulty admitting the record into evidence.

f. Government Records

"Official records" is the legal system's label for reports and documents prepared by government officials and offices. For instance, if you are a tenant in a landlord-tenant case and you have your apartment inspected by a County Health Inspector, the inspector's report is an official record. Likewise, if a police officer investigates an accident, the police officer's report is an official record.

Because record-keeping by government offices is much like that of private businesses, the foundation you need to admit an official record into evidence is similar to that of business records. (See, for example, Federal Rule of Evidence 803(8), New York Evidence Code § 803(c)(7), California Evidence Code § 1280 and Texas Civil Rule of Evidence 803(8).) If anything, your judge will probably require less of a foundation for official records than for business records, based on a perception (reasonable or not) that official records are very likely to be accurate.

For example, assume that you are the defendant in an automobile accident case. To counter the plaintiff's claim that you drove on the wrong side of the road, you want to prove that your car left skid marks in your proper traffic lane. You know that soon after the accident, Officer Krupke arrived, examined the skid marks left by your car and later prepared a report as to the location and length of the skid marks. After calling the police department and inquiring how to subpoena an officer, you served a subpoena duces tecum on Officer Krupke by leaving it with the Watch Commander of Krupke's assigned police station. Krupke has come to court with the report, and you want the judge to admit this report into evidence as an official record. Your foundational evidence will look something like this:

1 You:

Officer Krupke, what is your occupation and assignment?

2 Krupke:

I'm a police officer for West Side City, assigned to routine traffic patrol.

3 You:

Did you investigate an accident in the 2100 block of Hillcrest Road on the afternoon of December 23?

4 Krupke:

Yes, I did.

5 You:

And what did you do?

6 Krupke:

After ascertaining that nobody was injured, I examined a set of skid marks that extended for approximately 50 feet behind the car you were in.

7 **You:**

Was there any reason you examined the skid marks?

8 **Krupke:**

It's routine investigation.

9 **You:**

Officer Krupke, did you prepare a report of your findings with regard to the skid marks following your investigation?

10 **Krupke:**

Yes, I did.

11 **You:**

When did you prepare it?

12 **Krupke:**

In line with department policy, I prepared the report before I went off duty, about three hours after I completed my investigation.

13 **You:**

How did you prepare that report?

14 **Krupke:**

From the notes about the skid marks that I made at the scene of the accident.

15 **You:**

Officer Krupke, the bailiff is handing you a document marked "Defendant's Exhibit C for Identification." Is this the report you prepared in this case?

16 **Krupke:**

Yes it is. This is my signature.

17 **You:**

Your Honor, I offer the report into evidence as an official record.

18 **Judge:**

Yes, I'll admit it.

Transcript Analysis: This excerpt demonstrates that Officer Krupke, a government official, prepared the skid mark report as part of his official, routine duties. It was prepared in timely fashion, just a few hours after his investigation. In Nos. 15-16, Krupke identifies the exhibit as the report that he prepared. Thus, you have met all requirements for admissibility.

RESEARCHING FOUNDATIONAL REQUIREMENTS

If you plan to offer an exhibit into evidence but are uncertain about the foundation you have to lay, you'll have to do some research. One book that you may find especially useful is *Evidentiary Foundations*, by Edward Imwinkelried (The Michie Co.). In a question-and-answer format, it illustrates foundational testimony for numerous kinds of exhibits.

Other books you may want to consult include:

McCormick on Evidence, by John Strong (ed.) (West Publishing Co.). This is a one-volume treatise widely referred to by lawyers and judges; Titles 8 and 9 review exhibits.

Evidence, by Ken Graham (Casenotes Publishing Co.). This is a paperback "outline," which is a quick, relatively inexpensive refresher aimed at law students. You will find this and other evidence outlines in most law book stores near law schools.

Researching evidence rules themselves is another way to find out about foundational requirements. The evidence rules governing trials in federal courts are found in the Federal Rules of Evidence. By way of example, Federal Rule 803 (6) lists the foundational requirements for business records, and Rule 901 lists foundations for authenticating documents. Many states have enacted the Federal Rules almost in their entirety and collected them in a separate volume of laws. In a few states, evidence rules may be harder to find because they are included in a more general collection of civil laws; in these states you may have to ask a law librarian to help you find evidence rules. (See Chapter 19, Legal Research.)

In addition to doing research, this is a good time to consult your self-help law coach, particularly if admission of an exhibit is crucial to your case. The brief time it should take an attorney to help you organize a sufficient foundation may be well worth the expense.

Finally, if you find yourself in the middle of trial uncertain about what you need to do to lay a foundation, do not be afraid to ask the judge for help. Ask to approach the bench, and say something like, "Your Honor, I've got this repair estimate that I want to introduce into evidence, but I'm not quite sure what to do." Some judges may even respond by asking questions themselves to develop the necessary foundation.

E. LETTING JURORS SEE YOUR EXHIBITS

If you review the mechanics for offering exhibits into evidence discussed above, you will realize that in a jury trial the jurors are frozen out of the process. An exhibit goes from your hand to the witness (sometimes via the bailiff) and then to the judge. Once an exhibit is admitted into evidence, the witness may give oral testimony concerning the exhibit, and then it is put in the custody of the court clerk.

Normally the judge allows the jurors to have all the exhibits with them when the case is complete and they deliberate. (See, for example, California Code of Civil Procedure § 612.) But that may be too late to influence them in your favor. If possible, you want to melt the jury freeze-out and allow the jurors to examine each exhibit as soon as the judge admits it into evidence.

Fortunately a procedure does exist for showing an exhibit to a jury at the time it is admitted into evidence. (In some courts, this is called "publishing an exhibit.") Immediately after an exhibit is admitted into evidence, ask the judge for permission to show the exhibit to the jurors. Say something like, "Your Honor, may I hand Exhibit C, the photograph [business record, letter, etc.] to the jurors?" The judge, who probably wants to keep the trial moving, may respond by asking you to justify your request. If so, you can do two things to encourage the judge to rule in your favor:

- Explain why seeing the exhibit during the testimony will help the jury understand your evidence. For example, you may point out, "I'm going to be testifying about the damage to my car, and seeing the photo now will help the jury follow my testimony."

- If feasible, make enough copies of an exhibit to give to each juror. That will save time that otherwise will be wasted if testimony has to

halt while a single page or photo wends its way amongst the jurors.

F. WHEN EXHIBITS ARE REQUIRED: THE "BEST EVIDENCE" RULE

In most situations, you are not required to offer an exhibit into evidence. That is, though it may lack the storytelling impact of an exhibit, oral testimony describing an object is often admissible without the need of a physical back-up. For example, when you testify that you were struck by a boomerang, you are not legally required to offer the boomerang into evidence. Similarly, you or a police officer may orally testify to the skid marks left after a car accident without offering the officer's police report into evidence.

"Your Honor, after the trial will it be possible to purchase items from the exhibit table?"

But when you want to offer testimony about the contents of documents such as letters, business records and photographs, a legal doctrine known as the "best evidence rule" restricts your right to rely on oral testimony. This rule is also known as the "original writing rule." (See Federal Rule of Evidence 1002, New York Evidence Code § 1002, California Evidence Code § 1500, Texas Civil Rule of Evidence 1002 and similar statutes in almost every state.) The rule states that you (or a witness) cannot orally testify to the contents of a document unless you produce the document in court or prove to the judge that you have a valid reason for being unable to do so.

Offer at least a copy whenever possible.
Though you or a witness may be allowed to testify orally to the contents of a document, if you cannot produce an original try your best to locate and introduce into evidence a copy. To offer a copy of a document into evidence, follow the same foundational procedure as for any other exhibit, but make sure that you tell the judge that your document is a copy, not an original.

To see how the rule works, assume that you want to prove that Ihori wrote you a threatening note. Because of the best evidence rule, you cannot simply testify that, "I got a note from Ihori and this is what it said…." You have to produce the note itself in court. If you cannot do so, you should offer a copy of the note if you made one. If you do not have a copy, you can testify orally to what the note said if you lay a foundation showing the judge you have a valid excuse for not having the document. For example, you may testify that Ihori stole the note from you, or that it was accidentally thrown

out by your six-year-old child. (This descending order of preferences for originals, then copies, then oral testimony might remind you of the old folk song: "If you haven't got a penny then a hay-penny will do; if you haven't got a hay-penny, then God bless you.")

G. OBJECTING TO YOUR ADVERSARY'S EXHIBITS

In addition to offering your own exhibits into evidence, you have the right to object to those your adversary tries to offer. (Of course, your adversary has the same right with respect to your exhibits.) An objection asks a judge to exclude (refuse to admit) an exhibit, which means that the judge or jury cannot consider the exhibit in reaching a verdict. (See Chapter 14, Making and Responding to Objections.)

If the admissibility of an exhibit is challenged, the judge may have to halt the trial and conduct a short "mini-trial" on the spot to decide whether an exhibit is admissible. During the mini-trial, you and your adversary can present whatever evidence you have pertaining to the adequacy of the foundation. After listening to the evidence, the judge decides whether or not to admit the disputed exhibit into evidence. The main trial then continues.

For example, assume you offer foundational evidence that a letter was written by Edelstein, your adversary. But Edelstein objects to admission of the letter into evidence and asks to offer foundational evidence of his own that he did not write it. The judge holds a short mini-trial, during which you offer your evidence supporting your contention that Edelstein wrote the letter, and Edelstein offers evidence that he did not. The judge's decision about admissibility of the letter concludes the mini-trial, and the main trial resumes at once with or without the letter in evidence.

> **You can ask the judge to exclude the jury during the mini-trial.** The judge can exclude or permit a jury to remain during a mini-trial. If you do not want the jurors listening to evidence about an exhibit that you hope the judge will exclude, ask the judge to exclude the jury during the mini-trial. However, do not ask to exclude a jury unless the danger of prejudice is very high; jurors resent being left out of things, and excluding them delays the trial.

Here are the most common reasons for objecting to the admissibility of an exhibit.

1.   Insufficient Foundation

You can object to an adversary's exhibit on the ground that the adversary has not laid a sufficient foundation. For example, suppose that you are the tenant, Marjorie, in a landlord-tenant case. The owner calls the apartment manager as a witness and asks the manager to identify a photograph allegedly showing you throwing a rock through the manager's window. (You deny throwing the rock.) In response, the manager testifies, "That looks like Marjorie, but I really can't be sure." If the landlord attempts to offer the photo into evidence based on this foundation, ask the judge to exclude it on the ground that the manager lacks personal knowledge or that the foundation is insufficient.

You can also object by offering conflicting foundational evidence. For instance, assume that your adversary offers a computerized printout of a business record showing that you owe your adversary a lot of money. Your adversary offers evidence about her business's careful record-keeping procedures. However, your position is that the printout is wrong, and you have information from a former employee of your adversary's business who is willing to testify on your behalf about the business's sloppy record-keeping procedures that regularly get accounts mixed up.

You may object when the adversary offers the computer printout into evidence and ask the judge to listen to your evidence before making a decision about whether to admit the print-out. Saying something like, "Objection, Your Honor. Lack of foundation. I'd like to call a witness to show that the printout is not trustworthy." Your objection may require the judge to conduct a mini-trial in which the issue is the admissibility of the computer printout. If the testimony from the former employee convinces the judge that the adversary's printout is not trustworthy, the judge will exclude it from evidence. And because your adversary's whole case may be based on the contents of the printout, by excluding the printout you may win the whole trial!

> **You can attack the reliability of an exhibit after it is admitted into evidence.** If your judge admits your adversary's exhibit into evidence over your objection, it means only that the exhibit is admissible in evidence, not that it is necessarily accurate. You can still offer your own evidence attacking the exhibit's reliability and argue (as part of your closing argument) that the exhibit is so untrustworthy that the judge or jury should not pay any attention to it when arriving at its decision.

2. Violations of Other Rules of Evidence

Even if an exhibit offered by your adversary satisfies all foundational requirements, you may still ask the judge to exclude it on the ground that it violates another rule of evidence, such as the hearsay rule or the rule of relevance. (See Chapter 13, Basic Rules of Evidence.) If you are uncertain about whether or not one of these other rules may bar an exhibit offered by your adversary, research the issue in a law library or talk to your self-help law coach. (See Chapter 19, Legal Research, and Chapter 18, Getting Help from Attorneys: Hiring a Legal Coach.)

The following examples may help you understand how to use evidence rules to object to your adversary's offered exhibits:

Example 1: Hearsay. To prove that your carelessness caused an accident, your adversary offers into evidence a letter written by a person named Julie Even saying that you ran a red light. Object and ask the judge to exclude the letter as hearsay. The letter is made inadmissible by the hearsay rule even though your adversary properly marks, identifies and lays a foundation showing that it was written by Even.

Example 2: Unfair prejudice. A judge can exclude relevant evidence as "unfairly prejudicial" if its legitimate impact is outweighed by the likelihood that it will inflame the emotions of the judge [or jury against] you. For example, assume that your [adversary claims that you c]arelessly ran a red light [and injured him. H]e wants to offer into [evidence photos of your c]ar, one of which promi[nently shows a bumper st]icker with the name of a [rock group that many people claim pro-

motes violent antisocial behavior. You may object that the photograph showing the bumper sticker is unfairly prejudicial. On the one hand it has minimal relevance; your adversary has offered into evidence other photos of your car. On the other hand, it is likely to prejudice you in the eyes of the judge or jury as a fan of an outlaw rock group. The judge may decide to exclude the photo even though your adversary properly marks, identifies and lays a foundation for the photo as a fair and accurate representation of your car.

⚠ **Only part of an exhibit may be admissible.** Whether you or your adversary offers an exhibit into evidence, be aware that only part of it may be admissible. For example, an admissible medical report may contain irrelevant material, or a police officer's report may contain the inadmissible hearsay statement of a bystander. In such situations, the improper matter must be "severed" from the exhibit. Depending on the type of exhibit and the extensiveness of the improper matter, severing may be accomplished by crossing it out, cutting it out with a scissors or preparing a new document without the improper matter.

H. ORGANIZING EXHIBITS FOR TRIAL

To be thorough, refer to your exhibits in at least two different portions of your trial notebook. (See Chapter 15, Organizing a Trial Notebook.)

First, remember that Chapter 9, Direct Examination, advised making outlines of your planned testimony and the direct examinations of your witnesses. Include in each outline of a witness's testimony a reference to any exhibit you plan to offer during the direct examination of that witness. For instance, assume that you want to offer a photograph of the intersection of Main and Elm Streets into evidence during your direct examination of Cynthia White. In your outline of her testimony, write down a simple reminder such as, "photo of intersection." Also, you may want to briefly note key foundational requirements: "Ask if the photo is 'fair and accurate representation' of the intersection." (Normally you offer exhibits when you and your witnesses testify. But if you plan to offer an exhibit during cross-examination of an adverse witness, note that fact in your cross-examination outline for that witness.)

It's also wise to keep a separate list of all of your exhibits in a separate section of your trial notebook. You can then check off the exhibits as each is admitted into evidence.

What about the exhibits themselves? Generally, keep all your exhibits together in the order in which you plan to introduce them into evidence so that you can easily lay your hands on them during trial. But usually it is unwise to keep them in your trial notebook because you should not make notebook holes in original documents. And some of your exhibits may be too bulky for a notebook—for example, a boomerang and a hat are not well suited to storage in a trial notebook. It is usually best to keep your exhibits in a folder or box, separate from your trial notebook.

13

BASIC RULES OF EVIDENCE

The preceding chapters have explained many important evidence rules that apply to specific parts of the trial process. For example, you know that:

- During your opening statement, you cannot argue. (Chapter 8, Opening Statements.)

- During direct examination you are generally limited to asking open and closed questions. During cross-examination, you may (and indeed should) ask leading questions. (Chapter 9, Direct Examination, and Chapter 10, Cross-Examination.)

- Exhibits are not admissible in evidence until you lay a proper foundation. For example, a photograph is not admissible unless a witness testifies that it is a fair and accurate representation of whatever it depicts. (Chapter 12, Exhibits.)

- You may use any kind of document to refresh a forgetful witness's recollection. But you must show the document to your adversary, who may offer it into evidence. (Chapter 9, Direct Examination.)

By contrast, the evidence rules described in this chapter apply to every aspect of trial. They regulate information regardless of whether you are testifying personally, asking questions of your witnesses or those of your adversary, offering an exhibit into _____ or making your opening statement or

_____ ules run counter
_____ s prevent you from
_____ that you probably
_____ nore important that
_____ ly when you prepare
_____ you are still not sure

about whether important evidence that you or your adversary plans to offer is admissible, consult one of the books listed at the end of the chapter or talk to your self-help law coach.

THE ROLE OF OBJECTIONS IN ENFORCING EVIDENCE RULES

Evidence rules are not self-enforcing. If one side offers legally improper evidence at trial, the evidence will normally be admitted, and can be considered by the judge or jury in arriving at a verdict, unless the other side objects. To keep out improper evidence, you must ask the judge to rule that the evidence is improper by making an objection and the judge must uphold (sustain) the objection and exclude the evidence. On occasion, if evidence is blatantly inadmissible, a judge will exclude evidence without waiting for an objection. Chapter 14, Making and Responding to Objections, explains the objections process.)

A. RELEVANCE

The most fundamental rule of evidence requires a logical connection between a piece of evidence you offer and the legal claim you are trying to prove or disprove. It's called the relevance rule. (See for example, Federal Rules of Evidence 401-402, California Evidence Code §§ 140 and 351; New York Code of Evidence §§ 401-402, and Texas Civil Rules of Evidence 401-402.)

To be relevant, evidence does not have to prove a certain point conclusively. Evidence is relevant if it makes a fact that a party is trying to prove a little more probable, or a party is trying to disprove a little less probable. For example, say you are attempting to prove that Melinda was speeding, and you offer evidence that at the time of the accident she was late for an important meeting. Your evidence is relevant. Melinda's being late by no means conclusively proves that she was speeding. But common sense tells you that sometimes people do speed when they are late for meetings. The evidence of lateness adds to the probability that Melinda was speeding.

Let's turn this example around, and assume that you are Melinda and you are attempting to prove that you were not speeding. You offer evidence that at the time your were driving you had a valuable crystal vase on the back seat of your car. This evidence too is relevant. Again, common sense sug-gests that people sometimes drive more slowly when they are carrying expensive, breakable objects.

Judges have broad discretion to decide what evidence is relevant. Whether your judge deems particular evidence relevant or not is often a close call that depends on considerations such as the facts of a case, the importance of the issue to which the evidence pertains, other evidence already in the record and the need to keep a trial moving efficiently. On the theory that, like snowflakes, no two trials are ever the same, legal precedent (prior court decisions about relevance) has almost nothing to do with the determination of whether evidence is relevant.

"I don't give a damn what Judge Wapner said!"

! **Not all relevant evidence is admissible.**
Evidence must be relevant to be admissible. But the converse is not true; relevant evidence is not always admissible. The rules you will read about in this chapter often exclude evidence even though it is relevant. For example, relevant evidence may be excluded because it is unfairly inflammatory, or hearsay.

Perhaps the best way to demonstrate the meaning of relevance is with a few more examples, some of which are favorites of law professors:

• Lipkis is on trial for murder. The prosecution offers the murder weapon into evidence. Lipkis objects that the gun is irrelevant, because a police officer found it precisely halfway between Lipkis and a person standing next to Lipkis at the murder scene. *Ruling:* The gun is relevant. True, the gun evidence does not distinguish between Lipkis and the other person as the possible murderer. Nevertheless, evidence that the gun was found somewhere near Lipkis adds to the probability that he committed the murder. Again, evidence does not have to be conclusive to be relevant.

• In a divorce case, you are seeking custody of your young child. You testify that you recently ~~spouse verbally abusing your~~ ~~pick up your child.~~ ~~testify that the~~ ~~ged in a short~~ ~~e's request. She~~ ~~t the same spot~~ ~~when you testified~~ ~~e, and that she was~~ ~~ven though your ex-~~ spouse claims to have been yelling loudly. *Ruling:* Shelley's evidence is irrelevant. There is no logical connection between what two people can hear on two different occasions. Not only do people vary in their hearing ability, but also the external circumstances are likely to have been different. For example, it is unlikely that your ex-spouse used exactly the same tone of voice on both occasions or that background noise from cars and other people was the same.

• You have sued Jones, a co-worker, for assaulting you. You offer evidence that about a week before the assault, Jones told a third co-worker, I'm "going to get Nolo [you] the next chance I get." The defendant objects that the evidence is irrelevant, because people often make threats that they do not carry out. *Ruling:* Your evidence is relevant. Evidence that the defendant made a threat against you increases the probability that the defendant later assaulted you.

• The plaintiff has sued you for negligence, claiming that your speeding was the cause of an accident on 3rd Street. You deny that you were speeding or otherwise negligent. To help prove that you were going too fast, the plaintiff offers testimony that about a week earlier, you were seen speeding on 9th Street. *Ruling:* The plaintiff's evidence is irrelevant. There is no logical connection between how you drove at one time and location and how you drove at another time and location.

• You sue Universal Metals for fraud and breach of contract. You claim that Universal's personnel director, Dottie Geary, induced you to leave another job by promising to hire you at an increase in salary, and that she later reneged. Universal denies that any employment offer was made to you. To show that Geary did violate an agreement with you, you offer evidence that a week after you filed the suit against Universal, Universal fired Geary. *Ruling*: The evidence that Universal fired Geary is irrelevant. Because Universal's decision to fire Geary could have been based on so many different factors, there is no logical connection between your claim and her firing.

How to object to irrelevant evidence. To ask the judge to keep out irrelevant evidence offered by your adversary, simply say, "Objection, Your Honor. Irrelevant." Do this as soon as you realize that your adversary's question seeks, or the adverse witness's answer refers to, irrelevant evidence. Do not make an argument as to why the evidence is irrelevant unless the judge asks you to do so. (See Chapter 14, Making and Responding to Objections.)

B. EXCLUDING RELEVANT BUT UNFAIRLY PREJUDICIAL EVIDENCE

If a judge believes that evidence offered has minimal relevance, which is outweighed by the risk that admitting the evidence will unfairly prejudice the other side, the judge can exclude the evidence. (See, for example, Federal Rule of Evidence 403, California Evidence Code § 352, New York Code of Evidence § 403, and Texas Civil Rule of Evidence 403.)

Evidence may be excluded as unfairly prejudicial when it is so likely to inflame the emotions of the judge or jury that the judge or jury will attach too much importance to it. For example, assume that you have been sued for fraud for supposedly intentionally concealing a dangerous condition in a house that you sold to the plaintiff, as a result of which the plaintiff suffered head injuries. Your defense is that no dangerous condition existed at the time of the sale. After testifying to her injuries, the plaintiff offers into evidence a series of photographs depicting her bloody head injuries before and during medical treatment. The photographs are of some relevance, because they support the plaintiff's testimony about the extent of her injuries. But their relevance is slight since they do nothing to answer the question of whether the dangerous condition existed at the time of sale. And there is a risk that the photographs will inflame the passions of the jury against you and cause the jury to rule in favor of the plaintiff no matter what the condition of the house. So if you object, the judge may conclude that the risk that the photographs will be unfairly prejudicial outweighs their relevance and exclude them from evidence.

As is true with many rules of evidence, your judge is more likely to exclude evidence as unfairly prejudicial when your case is being heard by a jury rather than by the judge sitting without a jury. Judges tend to think that while jurors are likely to be unduly influenced by prejudicial evidence, judges are able to sort the relevant wheat from the prejudicial chaff. Nevertheless, even in a judge trial you should make the objection if you think the situation warrants it. Even if the judge overrules (denies) your objection may remind the judge that your adversary's evidence carries a risk of unfair

💡 **How to object to unfairly prejudicial evidence.** To ask a judge to exclude unfairly prejudicial evidence offered by your adversary, say, "Objection, Your Honor. The evidence is unfairly prejudicial." Object as soon as you realize that your adversary's question seeks, or the adverse witness's answer refers to, unfairly prejudicial evidence. Do not make an argument as to why the evidence is unfairly prejudicial unless the judge asks you to do so. (See Chapter 14, Making and Responding to Objections.)

If yours is a jury trial, also consider making a "motion in limine" to exclude unfairly prejudicial evidence before trial gets underway. (See Chapter 14, Section B.) The fact that you are a pro per litigant may work in your favor, because the judge should realize that you may be unable to prevent a jury from hearing unfairly prejudicial evidence if you have to wait to object until the evidence is offered at trial.

C. THE RULE AGAINST OPINIONS

If you are old enough to remember the character of Sgt. Joe Friday in the television show *Dragnet*, you remember that he always asked witnesses for Sgt. Friday's warning sums up the witnesses are supposed to not to opinions to decide what observations. (See lifornia Evidence vidence § 701, and 01.)

Like the relevance rule, the opinion rule is impossible to define with precision. Your judge necessarily has wide discretion to decide what constitutes an improper opinion. To see why, let's take what may seem like a silly example. Ruth testifies, "I saw a car." Fact or opinion? It seems like a factual observation that would satisfy even Sgt. Friday. But if you stop to think about it, you will see that Ruth is giving an opinion. After all, she could have testified to greater factual detail: "I saw a large metal object with four round metallic objects covered with a black, rubbery material…" and left it to the judge or jury to conclude that what she saw was a car. But if a judge were to ban this kind of opinion, most types of information that people rely on every day to make sensible judgments would be forbidden, and a simple trial might last for weeks.

In practice, what the opinion rule really means is that witnesses can testify to opinions if these three things are true:

1. The witness has personal knowledge of the facts on which the opinion is based.

2. The opinion is of a common-sense type that people make every day.

3. The opinion does not consist of an unnecessary legal judgment that the judge or jury is supposed to make.

To illustrate, let's return to Ruth and the car. Ruth would probably not be allowed to testify that, "In my opinion, the blue car caused the accident." Even if she saw the events leading up to the accident, Ruth would be attempting to perform the job of the judge or jury. Also, a judgment of legal fault is not a common-sense, everyday opinion. It is reasonable to ask Ruth to testify to what she saw, and leave to the judge or jury the job of deciding who caused the accident.

Again, perhaps the best way to get a feel for the opinion rule is with concrete examples. A judge will normally allow a witness to give opinions such as the following:

- "When I saw him, Kebo was happy (or angry or sad)."

- "I watched Johnson for a half hour, and he seemed drunk."

- "Especially considering it was a rainy day, the car was going too fast."

- "In the couple of years that our families have been friends, Becky has always seemed more comfortable around her father than around her mother."

In each example, the opinions are likely to be admissible because they meet the three-part test set out above.

At the other extreme are a variety of opinions that witnesses cannot give because they combine observations with unnecessary legal judgments. A judge will probably not allow a witness to state opinions such as:

- "Philippe was driving carelessly."

- "It will be in Becky's best interests to live with her father."

- "Her former attorney committed legal malpractice."

- "I think the plaintiff should get a million dollars in damages."

In each example, it is reasonable to expect a witness to describe the behavior underlying the opinion, and leave the legal judgment to the judge or jury.

⚠️ **Expert witnesses march to a different drummer.** Expert witnesses are allowed to state opinions even if those opinions make legal judgments and are not based on personal knowledge. For example, a trained family counselor can testify to an opinion that a father should be granted custody of a minor child. (See Chapter 16, Expert Witnesses.)

💡 **How to object to improper opinions.** To ask your judge to exclude an improper opinion offered by your adversary, say, "Objection Your Honor. The question calls for an improper opinion." Object as soon as you realize that your adversary's question seeks, or the adverse witness's answer refers to, an improper opinion. Do not make an argument as to why an opinion is improper unless the judge asks you to do so. (See Chapter 14, Making and Responding to Objections.)

Don't worry if the judge rules that the opinion you are testifying to or seeking from a witness is improper. You can almost always bring out the information you are after. You just need to testify, or elicit from a witness, the details on which the opinion was based. Consider this example in which you are questioning a woodsman:

1   You:

And what happened next?

2 **Witness:**

The wolf intended you to think that he was your grandma.

3 **Adversary:**

Object and move to strike the testimony as to the wolf's intent as an improper opinion.

4 **Judge:**

Yes, the witness lacks personal knowledge as to the wolf's actual intent. Objection sustained.

Transcript Analysis: Here your witness's opinion (No. 2) is ruled inadmissible. But the ruling does not prevent you from offering evidence about the wolf's intent. You can continue by asking the witness to describe the behavior leading him to form this opinion:

5 **You:**

Please tell us exactly what you saw.

6 **Witness:**

Okay. When I arrived outside the cottage I saw the wolf in bed dressed in a ladies' nightgown and cap, with the covers pulled all the way up to his chin.

7 **You:**

And what was the wolf doing?

8 **Witness:**

He was talking in a very soft voice, saying over and over how nice you were for coming to visit your dear sweet grandma.

9 **You:**

And then what happened?

10 **Witness:**

You said something about what big eyes your grandma had, and the wolf said in the same soft tone of voice that he had just gotten new contact lenses that made his eyes look a little funny.

11 **You:**

Yes, go on.

12 **Witness:**

….

Transcript Analysis: This brief series of questions seeks the factual information underlying the witness's improper opinion about the wolf's intent. In fact, compare the improper opinion (No. 2) with the factual information; doesn't the latter have more persuasive impact? Evidence rules aside, you are probably better off eliciting the details underlying the improper opinion.

D. THE RULE AGAINST CHARACTER EVIDENCE

Character evidence is evidence of past behavior that suggests that a person has a propensity (a "trait of character") to behave in a certain way. In daily life, we commonly use what we know of people's past behavior to make judgments about their characters. For instance, we may think of a person as being careful, violent, honest or nasty. And once we form an opinion about a person's character, we are likely to project it onto their specific conduct. For example, once we conclude that a person has a propensity to drive carefully, we may reason that the person was probably driving carefully on a particular occasion.

But for a variety of reasons, evidence rules contain a strong policy forbidding character evidence in civil trials. (See Federal Rule of Evidence 404, California Evidence Code § 1101, New York Code of Evidence § 404, and Texas Civil Rule of Evidence 404.) One reason is simply to save time. Trials would be much too long if parties were allowed to fight not only about how specific events took place, but also about each other's character traits. Another reason is that character evidence is thought by our legal system to be of dubious value: people simply do not always behave in accordance with their character traits. And a third reason is that evidence of character itself may be untrustworthy: witnesses are not omniscient, and they may easily misjudge the character of you or your adversary.

Some examples may help you understand the type of information forbidden by the rule against character evidence:

- To prove that you were driving carefully before a traffic accident, you cannot ask a witness who has carpooled with you for 20 years to testify that in her opinion you are a safe driver. Similarly, you cannot offer evidence that you've never gotten a traffic ticket for a moving viola-

tion or that you've never before been involved in an accident. In each situation, you improperly ask the judge or jury to infer that because you have a propensity (a character trait) to drive safely, you were driving safely at the time of the accident involved in your trial.

- Although by way of introduction you are allowed to briefly question your witnesses about their personal backgrounds when conducting their direct examination (see Chapter 9, Direct Examination), generally you cannot ask about a witness's good deeds, community activities, awards and the like. As a judge is likely to view it, such evidence amounts to an improper attempt to prove that a witness is of upstanding moral character.

- To prove that a defendant assaulted you, you cannot offer evidence that the defendant has been involved in other fights. And you cannot call a witness, who knows the defendant well, to give an opinion that the defendant is violent. Again, such evidence improperly asks the judge or jury to infer that because the defendant has a propensity (a character trait) to be violent, the defendant assaulted you.

- Similarly, to prove that you struck the defendant only in self-defense, you cannot offer evidence that you have never instigated a fight or that in the opinion of a friend who knows you well, you are a peaceful person. This evidence, too, improperly asks the judge or jury to infer from evidence of your peaceful character that you were not the aggressor in the fight with the defendant.

- To prove that your landlord falsely promised to install a new central heating system in your apartment, you cannot offer evidence of a witness's opinion that your landlord is dishonest or that she has made false promises to others.

💡 **How to object to improper character evidence.** To object if your adversary tries to introduce favorable character evidence about himself or one of his witnesses, or unfavorable character evidence about you or one of your witnesses, say, "Objection, Your Honor. That's improper character evidence." Object as soon as you realize that your adversary's question seeks, or the adverse witness's answer refers to, improper character evidence, but do not make an argument as to why the evidence constitutes character evidence unless the judge asks you to do so. (See Chapter 14, Making and Responding to Objections.)

E. HEARSAY

This section explains the hearsay rule, which potentially comes into play whenever parties offer evidence of out-of-court statements, which are simply statements made outside the courtroom. Because the rule does not apply to many kinds of out-of-court statements, and because it is riddled with exceptions, out-of-court statements are often admissible in evidence. If an out-of-court statement is important evidence either for you or your adversary, study this section very carefully. If you are still not sure about the admissibility of an out-of-court statement, refer to the Resources listed at the end of the chapter or consult your self-help law coach.

⚠️ **The hearsay rule applies to both oral and written out-of-court statements.** Don't be fooled by the word hearsay. The rule potentially applies to all out-of-court statements, whether they are made orally or written down in a letter, business record or other document.

1. The Rule Against Hearsay

In our trial system, we do not think it fair to admit into evidence statements from witnesses who are not in court where they can be seen and cross-examined. Hence we have adopted the hearsay rule, which under certain circumstances forbids a witness from testifying, "He said...." or "She said...." (For example, see Federal Rule of Evidence 802, California Evidence Code § 1200, New York Code of Evidence § 802, and Texas Civil Rule of Evidence 802.)

For example, assume that you are defending yourself against a claim that you were speeding. The plaintiff calls Andrea as a witness against you. Andrea testifies, "A couple of days after the accident I talked to Mark, who saw the whole thing. He said that he saw Nolo [you] going at a speed of at least 75 m.p.h." The plaintiff offers Andrea's testimony about what Mark said to her to prove that you were speeding.

An objection to Andrea's testimony as hearsay should be quickly sustained by any judge. Our system of justice does not consider it fair for the plaintiff to use what Mark said as evidence against you. The reason is simple: Since Mark is not in court to testify personally, you cannot cross-examine him, and the judge or jury cannot observe his demeanor and credibility. Of course the judge or jury can observe Andrea, and you can cross-examine her. But that will do you little good. She is not claiming to have seen the accident; all she can do is repeat what Mark said.

The hearsay rule can also prevent witnesses from testifying to their own out-of-court statements. For example, assume that you are testifying on your own behalf in a case in which you are seeking to limit visitation with your child, Summer, by your ex-spouse. To prove that your ex-spouse has been neglecting Summer during weekend visits, you testify that, "Last weekend I said to my neighbor Mr. Binder that my ex-spouse always returns Summer to me with torn and dirty clothes." Your testimony as to what you said to your neighbor is inadmissible hearsay. To avoid the hearsay problem, testify to the incident itself (that Summer always arrives home with torn and dirty clothes), and do not testify to your out-of-court statement to your neighbor.

2.   When Out-of-Court Statements Aren't Hearsay

Despite the hearsay rule, witnesses can often properly testify to out-of-court statements, because they are not always hearsay. Confused? Don't worry, so are many lawyers. The hearsay rule makes out-of-court statements improper only if they are offered for their truth. If an out-of-court statement is relevant regardless of whether or not it is true, the statement is "non-hearsay" and admissible.

When would you want to admit an out-of-court statement if no one cares if it's true? Let's look at some examples. First, assume that you are trying to prove that Bob was alive on March 5. As

evidence of this, you call Marisa as a witness to testify, "On March 6, I heard Bob say that all sports car drivers drive too fast." Here, you are not offering Marisa's testimony for the truth of Bob's statement, so there is no need to cross-examine Bob about the statement. Regardless of whether Bob's statement about sports car drivers is true or false, we know that people who say things on March 6 were alive on March 5. Thus, you are not offering Bob's statement for its truth, and it is fair to admit Marisa's testimony as non-hearsay.

Consider a more subtle example of a non-hearsay use of an out-of-court statement. Remember the negligence case involving the building contractor, Sarah Adams, who made a careless left turn and struck a pedestrian in a crosswalk. Assume that you're the pedestrian, and you have evidence that moments before she hit you, Adams got a call on her car phone from Holden, her assistant manager. In this phone call Holden told Adams, "There's a major problem on the Jennifer Drive job. It looks like it'll set us back a few weeks. You'd better get right over there." You can offer Holden's statement to Adams into evidence as non-hearsay to prove that Adams was not paying attention to the road. Apart from the truth of whether there was really a major problem on the Jennifer Drive job, Holden's making this statement to Adams is likely to have distracted and upset her and made it more likely that she would drive carelessly. Lawyers refer to this type of non-hearsay use as "effect on the hearer." Holden's statement is admissible as non-hearsay because of its possible effect on Adams, the hearer of the statement.

Here's another example of non-hearsay. You are involved in a child custody dispute with your ex-spouse. A neighbor of your ex-spouse tells you that when your child, 11-year-old Margaret, recently had an overnight visit with your ex-spouse, your ex-spouse screamed at her and said, "You are the worst little brat in the whole world. You deserve to be locked in your room for a week." You can properly call the neighbor as a witness to testify to your ex-spouse's statement. You are not offering the statement because you think it's true—that Margaret is the worst brat in the world who deserves to be locked in her room for a week. Instead, what your ex-spouse said is itself some evidence that your ex-spouse is a poor parent who should not have custody of Margaret. Thus, the neighbor's testimony is non-hearsay.

Consider a final example. Assume that Tobias sues you for assaulting him. You admit exchanging blows with Tobias, but claim that you acted in self-defense. To help prove that you did not assault Tobias, you will testify that about a week before your fight with Tobias, you got a letter from Pat in which Pat wrote, "Tobias beat up a friend of mine yesterday." You want to testify that this letter made you afraid of Tobias, and that therefore you would not have tried to assault him. Pat's letter is admissible as non-hearsay. You are not offering it as proof that Tobias in fact hit Pat's friend, but for its effect on the hearer (you). Since the person (you) whose demeanor the judge or jury needs to observe and who Tobias needs the opportunity to cross-examine is in court, it is fair for you to testify to the content of Pat's letter. Of course, Tobias can argue that Pat's letter made you want to get in the first blow. But this possibility affects how much credence (weight) the judge or jury attaches to Pat's letter, not the question of whether the letter has a valid non-hearsay use.

At this point, the difference between hearsay and non-hearsay may seem like a semantic distinction dreamed up by a gaggle of bored judges for the sole purpose of confusing you. But if you look back at the examples of non-hearsay, you will see that it really is fair to admit out-of-court statements when they are not offered for their truth. Only when an out-of-court statement is offered because the party offering it wants the judge or jury to believe it's true does the judge or jury need an opportunity to cross-examine the maker of the statement.

As you can see, you cannot tell merely by looking at an out-of-court statement whether or not it is hearsay. You have to know what the statement is offered to prove. If it is offered for its truth, it is hearsay and inadmissible in evidence—unless a hearsay exception applies. (See Section 3 below.) If it is offered for a relevant purpose other than its truth, it is non-hearsay and likely to be admissible. So whenever you want to offer evidence of what someone said out of court (whether the out-of-court statement is oral or written), always consider whether you can offer it for some purpose other than its truth.

> 💡 **How to object to hearsay.** To object to a hearsay statement offered by your adversary, say something like, "Objection, Your Honor; hearsay." Make your objection as soon as you realize that your adversary's question seeks or the adverse witness's answer refers to hearsay evidence, but do not make an argument as to why the evidence constitutes hearsay unless the judge asks you to do so. (See Chapter 14, Making and Responding to Objections.)

3. Exceptions to the Hearsay Rule

Finding a relevant non-hearsay use for an out-of-court statement is one way of making it admissible. (See Section 2, above.) You can also successfully offer a hearsay statement into evidence (that is, you can offer it for its truth) if it qualifies under one of the many exceptions to the general rule barring hearsay. Usually, exceptions apply when statements have been made under conditions making them likely to be accurate.

This section briefly reviews the most commonly used of the at least 30-40 hearsay exceptions that are recognized by statutes and court opinions. (Some are so obscure that you could probably try cases for 25 years and not run up against them.) For the full panoply of common hearsay exceptions, see Federal Rules of Evidence 803-804, California Evidence Code §§ 1220-1350, New York Code of Evidence §§ 802-803, and Texas Civil Rules of Evidence 802-803, or the comparable rules in your state.

a. Admissions

An admission is legal jargon for any out-of-court statement made by your adversary that you offer into evidence. The key word here is "adversary"; you can't offer your own statements or those of others as admissions. Despite the label of admission, your adversary's statement does not have to amount to a confession of wrongdoing for you to admit it into evidence. As long as your adversary made a statement—orally, in writing, during a deposition or pulled behind a blimp during the Super Bowl—that is relevant to the dispute, you can offer it as an admission if you think it helps your case.

For example, assume that you are suing Citron, the previous owner of your house, for fraudulently concealing the fact that the house had a leaky roof. In a conversation before the sale, Citron told Abby, a real estate broker he had previously employed, "I've never done a thing about the leaky roof, so I'd better sell the house during the summer." You can offer Citron's out-of-court statement to Abby as an admission. For instance, you may conduct the following direct examination of Abby:

1 **You:**

Did you speak with Mr. Citron on February 22?

2 **Witness:**

Yes, I did.

3 **You:**

Was anyone else present at this conversation?

4 **Witness:**

No, just the two of us.

5 **You:**

Do you remember where the conversation took place?

6 **Witness:**

I remember it was in the backyard, because we were talking about how warm it was for April.

7 **You:**

What was the purpose of the conversation?

8 **Witness:**

The house had been on the market for some time, and my exclusive contract period to sell it had just expired. Mr. Citron asked me to

*come over and he told me that he was going to
try to sell the house himself.*

9   You:

*Do you remember Mr. Citron saying anything
about the condition of the house?*

10   Witness:

I do.

11   You:

And what did he say?

12   Witness:

*He said that he had never taken care of the
leaky roof, so that he wanted to sell the house
during the coming summer months.*

13   You:

How did you respond?

14   Witness:

*I told him that he had never told me about the
leaky roof, and that what he was talking about
was illegal. He just said that I should take care
of my business and he'd take care of his.*

Transcript Analysis: Abby's testimony in Nos.
12 and 14 about what Citron told her is hearsay, but
admissible in evidence as Citron's admission. Because Citron is your adversary and you are offering
into evidence a statement he made, the hearsay rule
does not exclude it. Also, if you look back at No. 14,
you will see that Abby testifies not only to what
Citron told her, but also to what she told Citron.
This is in line with the general rule of "complete-
ness" that if statements made by one party to a
conversation are admissible, then so are statements
made by the other party.

 **How to respond to your adversary's
objection that an admission is improper
hearsay.** When you testify or ask a witness to testify
to a hearsay statement that qualifies as an admission, your adversary may object that it is hearsay.
(Your adversary may be attempting to harass you or
may not realize that the statement is an admission.)

To respond, say something like, "Your Honor,
I am offering the statement as Citron's admission."
Or wait a moment before responding; the judge
may recognize that the statement is an admission
and overrule the objection immediately. (See Chapter 14, Making and Responding to Objections.)

ADMISSIONS BY CORPORATIONS AND OTHER ORGANIZATIONS

If your adversary is a corporation or similar organization, you can probably offer into evidence a
statement made by an employee or other representative of the organization as an admission. For
a judge to admit such a statement, you typically
have to show either that the organization specifically authorized the employee to make the statement or, more simply, that the employee's statement relates to her job duties with the organization.

For example, assume that you suffer injuries as a
result of slipping on a banana peel in a supermarket, and sue the supermarket. To prove that the
supermarket carelessly allowed the dangerous
condition (the banana peel on the floor) to exist,
you seek to offer into evidence a statement by the
store manager, who came up to you right after you
slipped and said, "I'm really sorry. I asked someone to clean up this peel hours ago." The manager's
statement is admissible as an admission of the
defendant supermarket because the statement
relates to the manager's job duties.

b.   Present Sense Impressions

A "present sense impression" is a statement that a person makes about an event while it is going on or right after it has taken place. The exception to the hearsay rule for present sense impressions is based on the theory that statements made about ongoing events are likely to be reliable. Offering present sense impressions into evidence is often a useful way of explaining to a judge or jury the meaning of conduct that may otherwise be ambiguous.

For example, assume that you are involved in a dispute with your landlord, Patrick, about substandard and illegal conditions in your apartment house. One day you ask Alison, who is doing some work in the apartment hallways, what she is doing. She replies, "Oh, Patrick asked me to remove the fire detection devices now that the inspection has taken place." Alison's statement explains what she is doing and is admissible as a present sense impression. Without the statement, you may have difficulty proving the significance of Alison's actions to the judge or jury.

The key to showing that hearsay statements qualify as present sense impressions is to show that they were made during or very shortly after an event. For instance, assume that you spoke with Alison three days after you saw her working in the hallway of your apartment house. You asked, "What were you doing the other day?" Alison replied, "I was removing the fire detection devices because we had already been inspected." Now Alison's statement probably does not qualify as a present sense impression because it was made three days after the event, not during or right afterwards.

Some states allow present sense impressions to be admitted into evidence as exceptions to the hearsay rule only if the event described by the statement was startling or exciting. (These statements are sometimes called "excited utterances.") The evidence rule drafters in these states believe that only when people are excited are they likely to blurt out the truth, and that otherwise a present sense impression may not be sufficiently reliable. For example, assume that you have evidence that Kevin opened a door and said, "Hi, Hilary. Nice to see you. Watch your step." Kevin's statement will probably not be admissible to prove that Hilary was at the door in states that require the events described by present sense impressions to be exciting, unless of course Hilary is a long-lost relative who owes Kevin $30,000.

💡 **How to respond to an objection that a present sense impression is hearsay.** When you testify or ask a witness to testify to a hearsay statement that qualifies for admission into evidence as a present sense impression, your adversary may object that it is hearsay. (Your adversary may be attempting to harass you, or may not realize that the statement qualifies as a present sense impression.)

To respond, say, "Your Honor, I am offering the statement as the witness's present sense impression." Or you may wait a moment before responding; the judge may recognize that the statement is admissible and overrule the objection immediately. (See Chapter 14, Making and Responding to Objections.)

---

c.   Declarations of State of Mind

Statements in which people describe their then-existing emotions, physical sensations, intents, plans and the like are admissible as exceptions to the hearsay rule. Called declarations of state of mind, evidence rule drafters believe that such statements are likely to be reliable.

In the colorful 19th century United States Supreme Court case that created this rule of evidence, there was a question of the identity of a corpse found at Cripple Creek, Colorado. One party to the lawsuit, trying to prove the body was that of a man named Walters, offered into evidence Walters' statement that, "Next week I'm going to go meet my friend Hillmon at Cripple Creek." The Court ruled that the statement was admissible as non-hearsay, reasoning that people's declarations about their future plans (their intentions) are generally reliable and should not be barred by the hearsay rule.

The state of mind exception has many applications. Here are some examples of statements that describe present thoughts or feelings and so qualify as declarations of state of mind:

- You are trying to prove that Joe's arm was broken. The fact that Joe said "Ouch! That really hurts!" when someone touched his arm is admissible. (Note that this statement would also qualify for admission as a present sense impression.)

- You are trying to prove that a salesperson made a false statement to induce you to buy a product. The fact that the salesperson told a friend, "I'll do anything to make a sale; I really need the money" is admissible.

- You are trying to prove that you didn't start a fight with Lenny. The fact that two days before the fight you wrote to a friend, "I'm scared to death of Lenny" is admissible.

How to respond to an objection that a declaration of state of mind is hearsay. When you testify or ask a witness to testify to a hearsay statement that qualifies for admission into evidence as a declaration of state of mind, your adversary may object that it is hearsay. (Your adversary may be attempting to harass you, or may not realize that the statement qualifies under the state of mind exception.)

To respond, say, "Your Honor, I am offering the statement as a declaration of the witness's state of mind." Or you may wait a moment before responding; the judge may recognize that the statement is admissible and overrule the objection immediately. (See Chapter 14, Making and Responding to Objections.)

---

d.   Statements Made to a Medical Practitioner

Statements made to a medical practitioner for purposes of treatment or diagnosis are admissible as an exception to the hearsay rule. Again, the drafters of evidence rules think such statements are likely to be reliable. After all, most patients don't want the doctor taking out their gallbladder when it's their right knee that hurts!

Here are some examples:

- Some months after an automobile accident, you go to a doctor for treatment. You tell the doctor or doctor's assistant, "My back has been hurting for the last six months." Your statement is admissible under this hearsay exception. You, the doctor, the doctor's assistant or whoever else heard you say it can testify to your statement.

- You go to see a doctor not for treatment, but just so the doctor can diagnose your condition and testify as an expert witness on your behalf at trial. The statements you make to the doctor are still admissible under this exception, because it covers statements made for purposes of treatment or diagnosis.

This exception may not cover everything said to a medical practitioner. A judge might admit into evidence some of what you've said and exclude the rest. For instance, assume you tell a doctor, "My back has been hurting ever since that idiot the defendant ran a red light and hit me." Your statement about your back pain is admissible. But the doctor really does not have to know what you think of the defendant and the color of the light in order to treat or diagnose you, so that part of your statement will not be admitted into evidence; it is inadmissible hearsay.

> 💡 **How to respond to an objection that a medical declaration is hearsay.** When you testify or ask a witness to testify to a hearsay statement that qualifies for admission into evidence as a declaration of a medical condition, your adversary may object that it is hearsay. (Your adversary may be attempting to harass you, or may not realize that the statement qualifies under the medical declarations exception.)
>
> To respond, say, "Your Honor, I am offering the statement as a declaration made to a medical practitioner for the purpose of treatment (or diagnosis)." Or may wait a moment before responding; the judge may recognize that the statement is admissible and overrule the objection immediately. (See Chapter 14, Making and Responding to Objections.)

e. Business and Government Records

Written records reflecting regular business and government activities are admissible as hearsay exceptions. You must, however, lay foundations showing that the records are reliable. (See Chapter 12, Exhibits.)

f. Other Hearsay Exceptions

We have discussed only a few of the numerous hearsay exceptions. Some others carry colorful titles such as "dying declarations" and "ancient documents." Others carry no title at all; in some court systems, judges simply have discretion to admit into evidence hearsay statements that they consider trustworthy. Again, if either you or your opponent has important evidence that consists of an out-of-court statement, and you are uncertain about whether or not it is admissible, you should probably seek legal advice as to its admissibility.

4. Having Trouble? You're Not Alone

If you are feeling a bit perplexed, take heart from the fact that the sometimes subtle distinctions between inadmissible hearsay statements, admissible non-hearsay statements and statements that are admissible under an exception to the hearsay rule are often as much a mystery to lawyers as they may be to you. Do not automatically assume that if a lawyer for your adversary makes what you think is an improper hearsay objection, or offers what you think is improper hearsay evidence, that the lawyer understands the hearsay rule better than you do.

Remember that the touchstone of the hearsay rule is fairness. If you think it is fair for you to offer an out-of-court statement into evidence against your adversary, or unfair for your adversary to offer an out-of-court statement into evidence against you, consider offering or objecting to the statement even if you are not sure of the correct legal analysis. Whatever a state's specific evidence rules, an overall policy of modern evidence law is to depend on a judge's discretion to ensure a fair trial for both sides in which truth emerges. Especially in a judge trial, a judge may discount technical concerns and make a ruling based on the trustworthiness of an out-of-court statement.

RESOURCES ON EVIDENCE

Wigmore on Evidence, by John Wigmore (Little Brown & Co.). This multi-volume treatise, which has been revised by other authors since Wigmore's death in 1943, has been termed the greatest treatise ever written on any legal subject. It masterfully explores the history of and policies behind most modern rules of evidence, and its updates have case citations from every state. You should probably refer to the treatise only if you already have a basic understanding of evidence principles.

McCormick on Evidence, by John Strong, ed. (West Publishing Co.). A one-volume evidence text widely referred to by lawyers and judges.

Weinstein's Evidence Manual, by Judge Jack Weinstein and Margaret Berger (Matthew Bender). A single-volume treatise based on the Federal Rules of Evidence. It sets forth and explains the text of each rule.

Evidence, by Ken Graham (Casenotes Publishing Co.); *Evidence,* by Steven Emanuel (Emanuel Law Outlines). These books are single-volume evidence outlines designed as quick refreshers for law students. They are usually available in law bookstores near law schools.

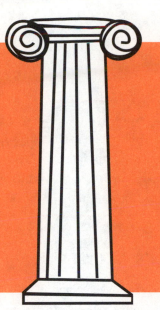

14

MAKING AND RESPONDING TO OBJECTIONS

An objection is a request to a judge to rule that an adversary's statement or offer of evidence is improper under the rules of evidence. If the judge grants the request (sustains the objection), the improper evidence or statement will be excluded. Neither the judge nor a jury may then consider it when arriving at its verdict. This chapter shows you how to make and respond to objections. It also includes a list of common objections, which you can take with you into the courtroom and refer to.

You can make an objection at any point during a trial. For example, you can object to a statement made by your adversary during his opening statement or closing argument, to a question asked by your adversary during direct or cross-examination, or to an adverse witness's answer.

Nonetheless, in general you will be wise to follow a practice of many experienced attorneys: Do not object just because you believe that a technical evidence rule violation has occurred. One reason is that even if a judge sustains your objection, often your adversary can get the evidence admitted anyway simply by rephrasing an improper question or answer. Also, as a pro per litigant you are likely to come off second best if you turn your trial into a war of objections against your adversary's lawyer. So unless you think that the evidence your adversary is attempting to offer is both important and should be excluded from evidence altogether, an objection may serve only to slow down your trial and incur the wrath of the judge or jury. Hollywood images notwithstanding, attorneys often manage to try entire cases with few or no objections.

Evidence rules are covered in other chapters. This chapter focuses on the procedures for making and responding to objections. Please refer to other chapters for discussions of the evidence rules on which objections are based.

A. OBJECTIONS: AN OVERVIEW

Many people believe that a judge plays a role similar to that of a football referee—that is, making sure that the "game" of trial is played according to the rules, in this case rules of evidence. If so, it may seem strange to you that you have to object at all. After all, referees call penalties on their own whenever a rule is violated; they do not wait for one team to object to something the other team has done.

But at trial, it's your responsibility to object to important impermissible evidence or statements. If you fail to object, you give up (waive) the objection, and the judge or jury may consider the impermissible information along with the rest of the evidence in arriving at its verdict.

Unfortunately, this system really works well only when both sides are represented by skilled trial lawyers. It may be less satisfactory when one side is a pro per litigant who doesn't (and can't reasonably be expected to) have in-depth knowledge of evidence rules. Fortunately, many judges understand this unfairness and will exclude obviously improper evidence on their own. But others will not, perhaps believing that being at a disadvantage serves you right for not hiring a lawyer. (Of course, many lawyers aren't exactly experts on the rules of evidence, either.)

Typically, objections are made orally and refer to the rule of evidence that a party believes has been violated. For example, if your adversary asks a witness to testify to an out-of-court statement, you might say, "Objection, Your Honor. Hearsay."

Normally, a judge makes an immediate ruling in response to an objection. If the judge thinks that the objection is erroneous—that is, that the offered evidence or statement is proper—the judge will deny (overrule) the objection. If the judge thinks that the objection is correct, the judge will uphold (sustain) it.

B. OBJECTIONS MADE BEFORE TRIAL: MOTIONS IN LIMINE

A "motion in limine" (rhymes with "Jiminy") is Latin legal jargon for any objection you make before trial starts. You may choose to make a motion in limine when you believe that important evidence your adversary plans to offer during trial is not admissible. However, you needn't make a motion in limine; you always have the option of waiting until your adversary offers the evidence at trial and making your objection at that time.

Why bother to make a motion in limine if you can object during trial? Two good reasons. First, you can plan more effectively if you know before your trial starts whether a judge will allow your adversary to offer a particular item of important evidence.

Second, if you wait to object until your adversary offers evidence, the jury may well hear some or all of it before you can object. Even if the judge sustains your objection, excludes the evidence and instructs the jury to disregard it, some jurors may still be influenced by it. Far better to exclude evidence in advance. This explains why motions in limine are primarily made only in jury trials. In judge-tried cases, the judge will hear about the disputed evidence anyway in order to rule on its admissibility.

To make a motion in limine, typically all you have to do is notify your adversary and the court clerk, or the judge during a pre-trial conference, that you want to make a motion in limine. If the judge agrees to hear the motion (the judge might refuse and ask you to raise the point during trial), the judge will conduct a short hearing on your objection before trial starts. During the hearing, orally tell the judge what evidence the adversary plans to offer and why you think it's improper. Your adversary will, of course, have a chance to respond to your argument.

⚠️ **Check your local court rules.** Carefully read your local court rules for procedures that you must follow to make a motion in limine. For example, you may have to give your adversary ten days' notice (perhaps in writing) of your intention to make a motion. (For general information on pre-trial motions, see Chapter 4, Pre-Trial Hearings and Motions.)

The judge may rule on your motion in limine on the spot, or may postpone a decision by asking you to renew your objection when the evidence is actually offered. By delaying a ruling, the judge has a chance to evaluate how important or prejudicial the evidence is. Nevertheless, even if the judge postpones a ruling your motion will not be wasted effort. The fact that you have brought the judge's attention to the problematic evidence early and in an organized way is likely to encourage the judge to think more seriously about excluding the evidence than if you first raise the point during trial.

Motions in limine made by attorneys are sometimes submitted in the form of written arguments that lawyers call briefs (though their long-winded complexity often makes them just the opposite). Like an oral motion, a brief identifies the evidence that the lawyer seeks to have excluded and the grounds for objection. In addition, a written brief may include references (citations) to supporting legal authorities such as statutes and cases.

You, too, may find it sensible to do a little research and to present a written brief in support of your motion in limine. The sample below illustrates what a simple written brief in support of a motion in limine may consist of. (As with other sample documents in this book, this one is for illustration only. The motion you might file could well look very different, depending on your state's law and rules of procedure.)

USING A MOTION IN LIMINE AFFIRMATIVELY

In theory, you can also use a motion in limine to ask a judge for an advance ruling that evidence you plan to offer is admissible. But generally you should not do this. The motion may act as a red flag that admissibility of the evidence is in doubt. Put the burden on your adversary to object if the adversary thinks it's warranted.

C. HOW TO MAKE OBJECTIONS DURING TRIAL

As with so many things in life, success at making objections depends not only on what you say but how and when you say it. Or in the words attributed to Albert Einstein, "God is in the details." Follow these procedures:

1. Stand Up

When you make or respond to objections, stand up as a sign of respect to the court. You can begin speaking as you rise.

2. Speak Only to the Judge

Always state your objection directly to the judge rather than to opposing counsel or your adversary. If you want to talk directly to your adversary, ask the judge for permission to go "off the record."

3. State Your Objection Succinctly

To object, it is normally sufficient to refer briefly to the reason (legal basis) for the objection. For example, you might say, "Objection, Your Honor. Hearsay," or "Objection, Your Honor, Irrelevant."

When you object to only a portion of a statement, a question or an answer, specify the portion

SAMPLE MOTION IN LIMINE

```
1    Fred Nolo
     [Street Address]
2    [City, State, Zip Code]
     [Phone Number]
3    Plaintiff in Pro Per

4            THE _____ COURT OF _____ COUNTY

5                       STATE OF _____

6    Fred Nolo                              )
                                            )  CASE NO. 11359
7                          Plaintiff,       )
         v.                                 )
8                                           )  PLAINTIFF'S MOTION
     Amy Binder,                            )  IN LIMINE
9                                           )
                           Defendant,       )
10   _____   )

11

12       Plaintiff Nolo submits this Motion in Limine for an order excluding from evidence Plaintiff's three-

13   year-old conviction for reckless driving.

14                          STATEMENT OF THE CASE

15       Plaintiff Nolo has filed suit against Defendant Binder for careless driving resulting in both personal

16   injuries to Plaintiff and property damage to Plaintiff's car. Defendant claims that Plaintiff's careless

17   driving caused the accident. As part of the Defendant's proof that Plaintiff drove carelessly, Defendant

18   has indicated that she intends to offer into evidence a record of Plaintiff's three-year-old conviction for

19   reckless driving.

20                              ARGUMENT

21       Plaintiff's conviction can not properly be admitted into evidence. This is a civil case governed by

22   the laws of the State of California, and California Evidence Code § 1101 provides that character

23   evidence is not admissible in a civil case to prove conduct. Plaintiff's prior conviction would be

24   character evidence, as its only purpose is to prove that Plaintiff has a propensity to drive carelessly

25   and therefore was driving carelessly when Plaintiff collided with Defendant Binder. Therefore, the

26   conviction should not be admitted into evidence.

27   Respectfully submitted,

         Fred Nolo
28   _____
     Fred Nolo, Plaintiff in Pro Per
```

to which you object. For example, if your adversary asks a proper question and the witness refers to an improper hearsay statement while answering, you may say something like, "Objection to the portion of the answer in which the witness referred to what Mr. Moore said as hearsay." (If the judge sustains your objection, you should also ask the judge to delete (strike) the improper testimony from the record. See Subsection 6, below.)

4. Object Promptly

If your adversary's question calls for improper evidence, object immediately after the question—before the answer if you can. If you wait until after the witness answers to object, the judge or jury may hear improper information. More importantly, the judge may refuse to sustain your objection because it is untimely, or because by waiting you are deemed to have waived the objection. Similarly, if a question is proper but an adverse witness throws improper evidence into the answer, object immediately after (or even during) the answer and before another question is asked.

Don't be overly polite—interrupt to object when necessary. If an adverse witness's improper answer is longer than a sentence or two, you do not have to wait until the witness is done talking but can interrupt the answer to object to improper evidence. Try not to "talk over" the witness; the judge and especially the court reporter are likely to become quite testy if you and a witness are both talking at once. Instead, say "Excuse me" and perhaps hold up your hand to stop the witness in mid-answer, then make your objection.

Consider this example of a late objection during your adversary's direct examination of a witness:

1   **Adversary:**

What's the next thing that happened?

2   **Witness:**

Well, just like she had done many times before, Ms. Nolo [you] *began drinking a bottle of beer.*

3   **Adversary:**

How much beer did Ms. Nolo drink this time?

4   **You:**

Objection to the testimony that I had done this many times before. That's irrelevant.

This ground for objection is discussed in Chapter 13, Basic Rules of Evidence.

5   **Judge:**

I agree with your objection, Ms. Nolo. But you should have made that objection before counsel asked the next question. I'll overrule the objection as untimely.

Transcript Analysis: In this example, opposing counsel's question (No. 1) is proper, but the answer that introduces prior drinking (No. 2) refers to evidence that you think is improper. Your objection should have come immediately after the answer, before your adversary asked another question.

A judge has discretion about how rigidly to enforce the rule that you must object as soon as the ground for objection appears, and a more sympathetic judge may treat you more leniently. Consider this example:

1 **Adversary:**

What did the person standing next to you say?

2 **Witness:**

He said that the blue car ran the red light.

3 **You:**

Objection, hearsay.

This ground of objection is discussed in Chapter 13, Basic Rules of Evidence.

4 **Judge:**

Mr. Nolo, you really should have objected before the witness answered, as it was apparent that the question called for hearsay. But I'll overlook that this time and sustain the objection. The answer is stricken and I instruct the jury to disregard it.

5. Don't Argue the Merits of Your Objection

Do not include in your objection an argument about why the judge should sustain it. Here's an example of how *not* to object to a witness's answer:

Your Honor, I object to that entire answer as irrelevant. This is a case about what happened on April 24. The witness is talking about things that took place three months earlier, and that has nothing to do with what we're talking about now.

This is called arguing an objection, and it is improper. State an objection concisely: "Objec-

tion, irrelevant." A judge who wants an explanation will ask for one. In that case, an explanation like the one above would be proper.

6. Ask to Strike Improper Evidence

Ask the judge to strike any improper testimony given or statements made before your objection was made and sustained. By striking (removing) improper evidence or statements from the official record, the judge indicates that the evidence can't be considered by the judge or jury when arriving at a decision.

Requests to strike improper testimony are necessary because, as you've seen, it's not always possible to object before objectionable testimony is given. For example, if the opposing attorney asks a proper question, but the witness gives improper testimony while answering, you cannot possibly object until the improper testimony has already been given.

A judge who sustains your objection to testimony that has already been given may strike the answer without being asked (as in the second example in Subsection 3, above). However, if the judge neglects to do this, it's up to you to request that the improper testimony be stricken by saying something like, "Your Honor, I also move to strike the answer."

If there is a jury, you should also ask the judge to instruct the jury to disregard the stricken testimony. Unless the judge instructs the jury to disregard it, the jury can properly consider even stricken testimony when arriving at a decision.

You can't unring a bell. Whenever possible, try to keep a jury from hearing improper evidence in the first place rather than rely on a jury's ability to follow a judge's instruction to disregard it. Just like telling someone not to think about pink elephants may cause him to think of nothing but, so a judge's instruction to disregard stricken evidence is easier said than done. Or as lawyers are fond of saying, you can't unring a bell. This human weakness is a primary reason to consider making a motion in limine before trial. (See Section B above.)

Here is an example of how to follow up an objection with a motion to strike:

1 **Adversary:**

After the blue car completed making the left turn, what happened?

2 **Witness:**

It started swerving back and forth, like the driver had had too much to drink.

3 **You:**

Objection to "too much to drink," Your Honor. Lack of personal knowledge and an improper opinion.

The first ground of objection is discussed in Chapter 9, Direct Examination and the second in Chapter 13, Basic Rules of Evidence.

4 **Judge:**

Objection sustained.

5 **You:**

I move to strike the testimony, and ask that you instruct the jury to disregard it.

6 **Judge:**

The motion to strike is granted. Jurors, the witness's remark about drinking was improper, and I instruct you to disregard it.

Transcript Analysis: Here, you properly specify the portion of the answer to which you object. (No. 3) At your request, the judge strikes that portion and instructs the jury to disregard it.

Don't thank a judge for sustaining your objection. Like a baseball umpire calling a strike, a judge is doing her job, not doing you a favor, by sustaining your objection. Many toadying lawyers ignore this advice and thank the judge early and often; most judges hate it.

7. Object Only When Absolutely Necessary

As mentioned at the beginning of this chapter, if evidence to which you object is unimportant, or if your adversary can get around your objection by simply rephrasing a question or an answer, your repeated objections may succeed only in depriving you of whatever empathy the judge or jury may feel towards you. Use this chapter to learn the mechanics of objecting, but remember that your goal is to object as infrequently as possible, especially in a judge trial.

D. HOW TO RESPOND TO YOUR ADVERSARY'S OBJECTIONS

Of course you are not the only one playing the game called trial. The opposing attorney (or your pro per adversary) can object to a statement you make, a question you ask or testimony you or one of your witnesses gives. That means you also need to understand how to respond to objections.

HARASSMENT BY YOUR ADVERSARY'S LAWYER

As radio therapists remind us regularly, you can control only your own behavior. Your sensible reluctance to make objections may not be reciprocated by your adversary. Particularly in a jury trial, the adversary's attorney may try to take advantage of your "new kid in court" status by sending a barrage of objections your way, no doubt trying to intimidate you. If this happens, your best bet is to ask the judge for permission to approach the bench or to have a conference in chambers (the judge's office). Ask the judge for the court reporter to be present and to take down what's said so that the official record will show that you sought the judge's help. Tell the judge that the attorney is using the rules of evidence improperly to try to harass and intimidate you and to prevent your having a fair trial. Ask the judge to warn the attorney that repeatedly trying to invoke technicalities to thwart the larger purpose of achieving a fair trial won't be tolerated.

In addition, during your final argument, you may use your adversary's unfair tactics to try to gain the judge's or jury's understanding. Point out that while you are not familiar with all the technical rules of evidence, you have done your best to present your case fairly and honestly and, unlike your adversary, did not try to hide behind a smoke screen of objections.

Abusive lawyering is less likely to occur during a judge trial. Compared to a jury trial, where judges tend to enforce evidence rules more strictly, in a judge trial a judge is less likely to put up with numerous technical objections. She even may regard repeated objections as interfering with her power to decide what evidence she will listen to. It's another reason why as a pro per litigant you are usually better off with a judge than a jury trial. (See Chapter 7, Selecting the Decision-Maker.)

1. Making a Counter-Argument

Rule No. 1 is: Don't immediately follow an adversary's objection by arguing why the judge should overrule it. Instead, wait for the judge to either make a ruling or ask you to respond. In most cases, a judge will rule without asking for your position. Here's an example of the procedure you should follow:

1 You:

And after you saw the two cars collide, what happened?

2 Witness:

I remember this person standing right next to me said, "My God, that red car went right through the stoplight."

3 Adversary:

Objection, hearsay.

4 Judge:

Ms. Nolo, any response?

5 **You:**

Yes, Your Honor. I think that what the witness heard this person say is admissible as a present sense impression made in response to a startling event. The person saw two cars collide, so that's an exciting event, and he made a statement about what he saw right away.

See Chapter 13, Basic Rules of Evidence, for a discussion of this evidence rule.

6 **Judge:**

All right, I'll overrule the objection and allow the testimony.

7 **You:**

Thank you, Your Honor.

8 **Judge:**

What's that, Ms. Nolo? Didn't you read the earlier section telling you not to thank the judge after a favorable ruling?

9 **You:**

Oh, right, sorry. I'll move on. Now, after….

Transcript Analysis: In this excerpt, you properly wait for the judge to ask you to respond (No. 4) before telling the judge why you think the evidence should be admitted (No. 5).

If you believe that a judge's ruling is clearly wrong, ask the judge to reconsider. When a judge follows the typical practice of making a ruling without giving you a chance to respond to your adversary's objection, you may ask for an opportunity to change the judge's mind if you are confident that you have a sound legal reason for thinking that the judge wrongly sustained the adversary's objection. Since the judge has already made a ruling, you first have to ask the judge for permission to talk about it.

For example, if the judge has sustained your adversary's objection that your evidence is irrelevant, you may say something like, "Your Honor, might I speak briefly as to why I think the evidence is relevant?" If the judge denies permission, that ends the matter. You have no right to argue evidence rulings. If the judge grants permission, you may then try to persuade the judge to change the ruling. And unlike baseball umpires, judges sometimes do reverse their rulings when an argument sheds additional light on the purpose of evidence. Nevertheless, it's just plain dumb to repeatedly challenge a judge's rulings. Save your fire for when it really counts.

---

2. Laying a Better Foundation

When your adversary objects, it will probably often be on the ground that you have failed to lay a sufficient foundation for evidence to be admissible. (See Chapter 9, Direct Examination, and Chapter 12, Exhibits, for additional discussions of laying a foundation.) If the judge is uncertain about whether a foundation is sufficient or simply wants to hear more foundational testimony to see what you are driving at, the judge may delay a ruling on the objection and let you lay a further foundation.

For example, assume that after your adversary objects to the out-of-court statement about the red car going through the stoplight (No. 5 in Subsection 1, above), the following dialogue takes place:

6 **Judge:**

Well, you may be right that the statement qualifies as a present sense impression, Ms. Nolo. But before I make that ruling, I'd like to hear additional foundational testimony.

See Chapter 13, Basic Rules of Evidence, for more information about this hearsay exception.

7 **You:**

What would that be, Your Honor?

8 **Judge:**

Well, it's really not my job to tell you the rules. But as you're representing yourself I'll tell you that before I rule I want to be satisfied that the person's statement really was blurted out in the excitement of the moment, which this state requires for a present sense impression to be admissible. Can you ask some questions that might satisfy me about that?

9 **You:**

I'll try. Mr. Grady, how far away from you was this person standing?

10 **Witness:**

Oh, not more than a few feet. He was as close to the collision as I was.

11 **You:**

How long had he been standing there, if you know?

12 **Witness:**

Well, we both came out of the store the same time, so he'd been there the same amount of time as me, about 30 seconds.

13 **You:**

And how long after the cars collided did you hear him say that the red car ran the stoplight?

14 **Adversary:**

Objection, Your Honor, leading.

15 **Judge:**

Overruled. The witness has already testified to what the person said [see No. 2 in the previous section]; Ms. Nolo is simply seeking to establish the time framework. Please refrain from meaningless objections.

16 **Witness:**

I'd say just a second or two. It was right away.

17 **You:**

That's all the questions I can think of, Your Honor.

18 **Judge:**

Let me ask one or two. What tone of voice did this person use?

19 **Witness:**

He really shouted. He made my ears hurt.

20   Judge:

And where did he go after he said this?

21   Witness:

I'm not really sure. I ran over to see if the drivers were OK, and I didn't see him again.

22   Judge:

Well, the issue is a close one, but on balance I think that there's enough of a foundation to admit this as an exception to the hearsay rule on the ground that it qualifies as a present sense impression. The objection is overruled. Ms. Nolo, you may resume questioning.

💡 **There's no harm in asking.** As we have emphasized throughout this book, a judge is a human being who, within the limits set by the adversary system, may be willing to help you cope with the nuances of technical evidentiary rules. So if you are not sure of what foundation the judge has in mind, do not be too embarrassed to ask. The judge, you hope, wants to have the benefit of considering all proper evidence before making a decision, and may suggest the kind of foundational testimony you need to elicit.

E.   CHECKLIST OF COMMON OBJECTIONS

Making objections is obviously a demanding task. In about the same tiny interval that it takes the average cab driver to honk a horn when a light changes from red to green, you have to decide not only whether to object, but also what objection to make. The following checklist of common objec-tions should help, especially if yours is a jury trial where it often makes sense to object to inadmissible evidence.

1.   Objections to the Form of Questions

An objection to the form of a question—for example, on the ground that it is leading—asserts that a question is improper. However, an objection to form does not challenge the admissibility of the information the questioner is trying to elicit. So even if the judge sustains the objection, the questioner can ordinarily elicit the information simply by rephrasing the question.

Object with caution when it comes to form of question objections: do not make them unless a question is so poorly phrased that you are not sure of what the witness will say in response, or your adversary is attempting to browbeat a reluctant witness into giving your adversary's desired testimony.

Here are common objections to the form of a question:

a.   "Objection; the question is vague [or ambiguous or unintelligible]."

You may object on this ground when you are unsure of what a question means. Questions should be clear enough so that you can reasonably determine in advance what information a witness is being asked to give.

If the judge sustains your adversary's objection that your question is vague or unintelligible, think about the specific information you are after and rephrase your question.

b. "Objection; the question is compound."

You can object on this ground when opposing counsel combines two questions into one, leaving you unsure about which part the witness will answer. For example, say your adversary asks a witness, "What time did he arrive and what did he do when he got there?" But again, especially if there is no jury and the question is not otherwise improper, you are probably better off not making this kind of technical objection.

If the judge sustains your adversary's objection that your question is compound, break up the single question into two different questions.

c. "Objection; the question calls for a narrative response."

You can object on this ground when opposing counsel's direct examination question asks a witness to narrate a series of events. (See Chapter 9, Direct Examination, for a discussion of narrative questions.) Also, if an adverse witness starts into a lengthy narrative response to a proper narrow question, stop the witness in mid-answer and state, "Objection. The witness is narrating."

If the judge sustains your adversary's objection that your question calls for a narrative response, ask a question with a more limited scope.

"I object, Your Honor! This line of questioning is really weird."

d. "Objection; the question is repetitive [has been asked and answered]."

An opposing attorney may try to take advantage of you by trying to hit the judge or jury over the head repeatedly with the same information. This is improper because it wastes time and artificially boosts the importance of evidence. You may object on this ground when opposing counsel persists in asking questions about information a witness has already given.

If the judge sustains your adversary's objection that your question has been asked and answered, move on to a new topic.

e. "Objection; counsel is misquoting the witness."

You may object on this ground when opposing counsel misstates testimony that has already been given. This problem typically arises during cross-examination, when the proper use of leading questions allows your adversary to refer to evidence in a question. (See Chapter 10, Cross-Examination.) For example, assume that a witness who testified for you stated that "the red car was going at least 60 m.p.h." On cross-examination, adverse counsel asks, "Now, you said that the red car was going pretty fast, right?" This question misquotes the witness's actual testimony.

If the judge sustains your adversary's objection that your question misquotes a witness, rephrase your question if you are able to recall the witness's actual testimony. If you cannot recall the actual testimony and want to refer to it, you may ask the judge to ask the court reporter to read back the previous testimony. However, the judge may not grant your request, especially if considerable time has elapsed since the answer was given. A third possibility is not to refer to the previous testimony in your question, but to ask the witness to repeat what was said earlier.

f. "Objection; the question is leading."

Consider objecting on this ground when opposing counsel asks an improper leading question during direct examination, especially if the witness seems reluctant to give your adversary's desired answer unless verbally bullied into doing so. This can be an important objection, because under some circumstances your judge may not allow your adversary to rephrase so as to elicit the evidence with a proper question. If the judge believes that your adversary is overtly trying to put words in the witness's mouth, the judge may not only sustain your objection but also forbid any testimony on the same subject from that witness.

If the judge sustains your adversary's objection that your question is leading, rephrase it in a way that does not suggest your desired answer. Or if the judge allows you to respond to the objection, perhaps point out that your leading question is proper because the information you seek to elicit is background or preliminary. (See Chapter 9, Direct Examination, for a discussion of when leading questions are proper during direct examination.)

g. "Objection; the question is argumentative."

You can object on this ground when opposing counsel cross-examines your witness in a hostile or angry way, or asks a question before you or your witness have completed the answer to a previous question. (In movies and TV shows, this practice is often referred to as "badgering the witness.")

For example, assume that opposing counsel asks you or your witness, "So you're willing to perjure yourself," or "You couldn't possibly have done what you've said you did, could you?" These questions do not ask a witness to provide evidence. Instead, they amount to your adversary making an argument in question form.

If the judge sustains your adversary's objection that your question is argumentative, rephrase the question so as to elicit evidence rather than to state your point of view.

h. "Objection; the question assumes facts not in evidence."

You can object on this ground when opposing counsel surreptitiously inserts new evidence into the record while asking for other information.

For example, assume that you are a tenant in an eviction case, and that there has been no evidence admitted about complaints from other tenants concerning your supposedly loud stereo. The landlord's attorney asks you this question: "Ms. Nolo, even after numerous other tenants complained to you about your loud stereo, didn't you say to the landlord that she had no right to tell you how to live your life?" Here, the question asks only about a statement you may have made to the landlord. The material about other tenants' alleged complaints is improperly inserted into the trial without giving you a chance to deny that there were complaints. As you may guess, this ground of objection is more important in a jury than a judge trial since you can expect a judge to disregard this sort of unsubstantiated remark.

If the judge sustains your adversary's objection that your question assumes facts not in evidence,

make the portion of the question that assumes facts into a separate question. If you were the landlord in the cross-examination sample above, for instance, you could properly have asked, "Didn't you receive complaints from other tenants about playing your stereo too loudly?"

2. Objections to the Content of Testimony

Unlike form objections, content objections assert your belief that the information opposing counsel seeks is inadmissible no matter what type of question is asked. Because most of these grounds for objection have already been discussed in earlier chapters we make only brief references to them here.

a. "Objection; lack of personal knowledge."

You may object on this ground when an adverse witness has not personally seen, heard or otherwise acquired first-hand information about what he is testifying about. Clues that a witness lacks personal knowledge are in introductory phrases like, "It later came to my attention that…," "I later found out that…," "I'd guess that what happened is…," and "My best estimate is…"

If the judge sustains your adversary's objection that your witness lacks personal knowledge, ask the judge for permission to ask additional questions to lay a foundation showing that the witness is testifying from personal knowledge. (See Chapter 9, Direct Examination, for a discussion of the requirement of personal knowledge.)

b. "Objection; speculation [or improper opinion]."

You can object on this ground when an adverse witness testifies to matters that are hypothetical, beyond her powers of observation or impermissible legal judgments. Often, a lack of personal knowledge objection is equally correct in these situations.

Here are some examples of improper speculative testimony:

- A witness testifies that "Nelson intended to mislead me into buying the defective car." Instead, the witness must testify to Nelson's words and deeds, leaving it to the judge or jury to determine what Nelson intended.

- A witness gives an improper opinion, such as, "If there had been any truth to the rumor, I would have known about it." In most circumstances, a witness can testify only to what did happen and what she does know.

- A witness testifies to a legal judgment such as, "Bryant was negligent." Again, a witness has to describe factual circumstances and leave it to the judge or jury to determine their legal consequences.

If the judge sustains your adversary's objection that your question is speculative or calls for an improper opinion, ask questions that elicit factual details about which the witness has personal knowledge. (For more examples and an explanation of the opinion rule, see Chapter 13, Basic Rules of Evidence.)

c. "Objection; hearsay."

Object on this ground when an adverse witness testifies to hearsay, which is an out-of-court statement offered for its truth.

If the judge sustains your adversary's objection that your question calls for hearsay, consider whether you can respond that the statement is admissible as an exception to the hearsay rule or as non-hearsay. (See Chapter 13, Basic Rules of Evidence, for a discussion of the hearsay rule, the exceptions to it and non-hearsay.)

d. "Objection; irrelevant."

Object on this ground when you believe that the adversary's evidence has no logical connection to the claims that either party is trying to prove or disprove.

If the judge sustains your adversary's objection that the information you seek is irrelevant, move on to a new topic. (See Chapter 13, Basic Rules of Evidence, for a discussion of the relevance rule.)

e. "Objection; the value (probative value) of this evidence is outweighed by the unfair prejudice it will cause."

Object on this ground when you recognize that the adversary's evidence is relevant, but think that its slight relevance is outweighed by the likelihood of unfair prejudice to you.

For example, assume that an adverse witness is describing your car as the one involved in an automobile accident. The witness is about to mention that among a number of things she remembers about your car, it had a bumper sticker identifying you as a fan of a rock group that many people believe promotes antisocial behavior. You may object on this ground to prevent the witness from mentioning the bumper sticker. It has slight relevance to prove the identity of your car, and is likely to cause you to suffer unfair prejudice.

Make a motion in limine. Unfairly prejudicial evidence typically consists of gruesome photographs, improper character evidence and the like. Often you will know or strongly suspect that your adversary plans to offer such evidence before trial, so in a jury trial you should strongly consider making a motion in limine. (See Section B, above.)

If the judge sustains your adversary's objection that the probative value of your evidence is outweighed by its likely prejudicial effect, move on to a new topic. (See Chapter 13, Basic Rules of Evidence, for a discussion of the unfair prejudice rule.)

f.   "Objection; lack of foundation."

Object on this ground when adverse counsel has failed to elicit a proper foundation for evidence. This is a catch-all objection, because all evidence, whether it is oral or written, must be supported by some type of foundation. For instance, if a witness lacks personal knowledge, or there is insufficient evidence to show that a business record is reliable or that a photograph fairly and accurately represents what a witness actually saw, you may object based on lack of foundation. This can also be an important objection, as your adversary may be unable to supply the missing foundational evi-

dence. (See Chapter 9, Direct Examination, and Chapter 12, Exhibits, for a further discussion of foundational requirements.)

Because it is a catch-all, you may be uncertain about what's missing if the judge sustains your adversary's lack of foundation objection. If so, you may need to ask the judge for help. Say something like, "Your Honor, I'm not really sure what foundational evidence is missing. Might you or opposing counsel tell me what evidence I need to introduce to lay a proper foundation?" If the judge sympathetically accedes to your request, ask additional foundational questions. (Note that, as suggested above, you ask the judge to ask opposing counsel to tell you what foundation is missing; don't ask opposing counsel directly.)

g.   "Objection; cumulative."

Object on this ground when your adversary calls a number of witnesses to testify to the same point. For example, you may object if your adversary is a home buyer who bought a house from you, claims that you concealed the fact that it had a leaky roof, and attempts to call five witnesses to testify that on one particular day, the roof leaked.

If the judge sustains your adversary's objection that your evidence is cumulative, move on to a new topic. Alternatively, you might ask the adversary to stipulate (agree) that if your additional witness were called and sworn, they would all testify that, for example, "On September 22, the roof leaked."

h. "Objection: improper character evidence."

Object on this ground when your adversary offers character evidence. Character evidence suggests that you have a propensity to engage in conduct associated with a particular character trait, and it is almost never admissible in civil cases. (See Chapter 13, Basic Rules of Evidence, for a discussion of character evidence.)

If the judge sustains your adversary's objection that your question seeks improper character evidence, move on to a new topic.

 Make a copy of the list of common objections. Place it in your trial notebook, so you can refer to it throughout trial. (See Chapter 15, Organizing a Trial Notebook.)

COMMON OBJECTIONS

Objections to the Form of Questions

a. "Objection; the question is vague (or ambiguous or unintelligible)."

b. "Objection; the question is compound."

c. "Objection; the question calls for a narrative response."

d. "Objection; the question is repetitive (has been asked and answered)."

e. "Objection; counsel is misquoting the witness."

f. "Objection; the question is leading."

g. "Objection; the question is argumentative."

Objections to the Content of Testimony

a. "Objection; lack of personal knowledge."

b. "Objection; speculation (or improper opinion)."

c. "Objection; hearsay."

d. "Objection; irrelevant."

e. "Objection; the value (probative value) of this evidence is outweighed by the unfair prejudice it will cause."

f. "Objection; lack of foundation."

g. "Objection; cumulative."

RESOURCES ON OBJECTIONS

Transcript Exercises for Learning Evidence, by Paul Bergman (West Publishing Co.). This book consists of brief explanations of many of the rules of evidence and 19 sample transcripts in a variety of civil and criminal case examples. Various questions, answers and judicial rulings within the transcripts are numbered; your task is to decide the legal propriety of each numbered transcript portion. An appendix gives the correct responses.

Trial Advocacy in a Nutshell, by Paul Bergman (West Publishing Co.)

Fundamentals of Trial Techniques, by Thomas Mauet (Little, Brown & Co.)

Trial, by Roger Haydock and John Sonsteng (West Publishing Co.).

These books discuss trial advocacy generally, but have specific explanations and examples of the objections process.

15

ORGANIZING A TRIAL NOTEBOOK

Organizing key documents and trial prepar–ation outlines into a trial notebook can help you present your case effectively and persuasively. At trial, you want to make sure that you introduce all your planned evidence and ex-hibits and that you tie them to the facts you are trying to prove or disprove. By making a trial notebook, you will have the documents that can help you do this close at hand throughout trial. For example, you can refer to a Direct Examination Outline when you question a witness and to your Closing Argument Outline when you present your final argument.

This chapter reviews the documents that you are likely to need in your trial notebook and sug-gests how to organize them efficiently.

A. SETTING UP YOUR NOTEBOOK

A typical trial notebook is an ordinary three-ring binder in which documents are grouped and sepa-rated by index tabs. Be sure to buy a set of index tabs that are easy to write on or otherwise customize, and lay in a good supply of blank three-hole paper. You may also want to have a three-hole punch handy in case you need to punch holes in docu-ments you want to have in the notebook.

! Never punch holes in materials you will offer as evidence. Never alter originals of documents that you plan to offer into evidence, and keep them in a manila envelope or accordion file separate from your trial notebook. (You may have to keep larger exhibits, such as a piece of defective machinery or an article of clothing, in a bag or a box.) However, you may place copies of each original in the notebook to give to the judge, opposing counsel and the jury.

Now let's look at what you should place into your trial notebook.

B. INDEX TAB 1: LEGAL PLEADINGS

The pleadings (the complaint and answer) should be in your notebook because they form the legal backdrop of the trial. Unless a judge allows you or your adversary to slightly change the theory set forth in a complaint or answer to match the evi-dence presented at trial (this is called "conform–ing a pleading according to proof"), the pleadings control such matters as what facts each party can prove or disprove and the relevance of evidence. You can punch holes in your copies of the pleadings because the originals will already be in the court's file.

Your judge may issue a Pre-Trial Order (which you, your adversary or the judge herself will prepare) following a conference with you and your adversary. (See Chapter 4, Pre-Trial Hearings and Motions.) A Pre-Trial Order is essentially a plan of trial that supersedes the pleadings and identifies the facts each party may prove or disprove as well as each party's witnesses and exhibits. (See Federal Rule of Civil Procedure 16.) If your judge does issue a Pre-Trial Order, include it in this section of your notebook.

> **You probably don't need to include pre-trial motion documents in your notebook**. Usually, issues that give rise to pre-trial motions are (other than motions in limine, see Chapter 14) disposed of before the start of trial. You will probably not have to refer to the pre-trial motion papers during trial, and so needn't include them in the notebook.

C. INDEX TAB 2: DISCOVERY MATERIALS

Discovery is the formal process parties use to uncover evidence before trial. As a pro per litigant, the discovery devices you are most likely to encounter are depositions, interrogatories and requests for admission. (See Chapter 3, Starting and Investigating Your Case.)

If you use formal discovery procedures, you might want to punch the information you get and insert it as is into your notebook. In most cases, however, even a short deposition or a single set of answers to interrogatories is likely to be too unwieldy for you to refer to quickly in the middle of trial. Instead, make summaries of the important information in your adversary's responses and put the summaries in your notebook. Include in the summary a reference to the specific page or interrogatory number where the important information appears in the original.

For example, a portion of your summary of a deposition you took of a witness named Prager might look like the one shown below.

> ### Summary of Prager Deposition
> ....
> 9. Jack fell down and broke his crown and Jill came tumbling after. (P. 24, lines 11-22)
> 10. Jack waited two days before going to see a dentist to repair his broken crown. (P. 25, lines 25-28)

A portion of your summary of answers you received in response to the written interrogatories you sent out might look like this:

> ### Summary of Berkowitz Co. Answers to Interrogatories
> ....
> 5. The person at Berkowitz Co. who inspected the car stereos before they were shipped is Stella Ong. (Answer to Interrog. 4)
> 6. Ong's inspection consists of testing the AM/FM switch on each radio. (Answer to Interrog. 5)

If you prepare summaries, you can keep the original discovery documents in your case file. Then, if you need information from a discovery document during trial (perhaps to impeach a witness with a prior inconsistent statement; see Chapter 10, Cross-Examination), refer to the summary in your notebook to find the exact whereabouts of the information.

D. INDEX TAB 3: LEGAL CLAIM OUTLINE

Whether you are a plaintiff or a defendant, you should prepare a legal claim outline. (See Chapter 5, What You Need to Prove at Trial: The Plaintiff's Perspective, and Chapter 6, What You Need to Prove at Trial: The Defendant's Perspective.) This outline is not tied to the testimony of any single witness, but rather lists the elements of the claim you are seeking to prove or disprove, identifies the fact satisfying each element, and lists the important evidence from all your witnesses tending to prove or disprove each fact. As the outline organizes important evidence according to facts, you want it near at hand to serve as a roadmap to the testimony you bring out and the arguments you make.

E. INDEX TAB 4: OPENING STATEMENT OUTLINE

An opening statement outline summarizes the information you will present to the judge or jury during opening statement. (See Chapter 8, Opening Statements.) You do not want to read your opening statement to the judge or jury, but you can use the outline as a reminder when you speak.

F. INDEX TAB 5: DIRECT EXAMINATION OUTLINES

Direct examination outlines identify, by witness, the important evidence you plan to elicit, selected specific questions you plan to ask, and any exhibits you plan to offer. (See Chapter 9, Direct Examination.) While you don't want to script a witness's direct examination, you can refer to an outline during questioning to make sure you elicit the witness's story in chronological sequence and do not overlook evidence or exhibits.

For example, let's say you own a small shopping center and that you have brought suit to evict a tenant, The Broccoli Shop, owned by Elvin Goodman, for non-payment of rent. One witness you plan to call is your on-site property manager, Brice Catlin. A direct examination outline for Catlin is shown below.

Direct Examination Outline
Witness: Brice Catlin
Background Information:
Married with three children; has been manager of the shopping center for six years; responsible all matters related to leases, maintenance and security for the center.
Important Evidence:
• Broccoli Shop became a tenant about 15 months ago.
• Terms of lease: Rent due on 1st of each month; $1,500 per month.
• Six months ago—Broccoli Shop started paying rent two weeks late.

- April 14—last rent payment received from Goodman.
- May 1: No rent paid.
- May 3: Brice talks to Goodman and Goodman says he's busy opening another store but will pay rent within three days.
- May 8: Brice again talks to Goodman. He says bookkeeper was supposed to send check, he'll see to it immediately.
- No further contact with Goodman.
- May 23: Brice serves eviction notice on Goodman.

Important Questions:

- When I bring out the foundation for the lease, remember to ask Brice to ask him how he knows it's Goodman's signature on the lease (Brice saw him sign it.)
- Show that Rent Book is admissible as a business record.
  Be sure to ask what the rent book is, and about our business practice of what the bookkeeper uses the rent book for. Then ask, "Does the rent book indicate any payments from Mr. Goodman after April 14?" (No)

Exhibits:

- Lease Agreement will be Exhibit 1.
- Rent Book will be Exhibit 2.
- Eviction Notice will be Exhibit 3.

⚠ Make a more detailed outline for an expert witness. Your outline for an expert's direct examination can follow this format, but it should be far more detailed. For example, you should list the background information that qualifies the witness as an expert and identify not only the expert's opinion but also the reasons for it. (See Chapter 16, Expert Witnesses.)

G. INDEX TAB 6: CROSS-EXAMINATION OUTLINES

Cross-examination outlines identify, for each adverse witness, the witness's expected direct examination testimony, evidence you plan to elicit to support your version of events, evidence you plan to elicit that impeaches the witness and (occasionally) exhibits you plan to offer. (See Chapter 10, Cross-Examination.) Because you may want to be sure you ask leading questions that seek to elicit very specific information, you may write down your questions and read them to an adverse witness during cross-examination.

For example, let's say that you're a plaintiff in a negligence case. You claim that due to defendant Sarah Adams's careless driving, you were struck by her truck while you were in a crosswalk. Adams claims that she was driving carefully, and that she unavoidably struck you when you suddenly ran out from between two parked cars some distance away from the crosswalk. You are planning to cross-examine Kris Knaplund, who will testify for Adams that after the accident you said that you should have been in the crosswalk. Based on information you gathered before trial, the cross-examination outline you put in your trial notebook and use as the basis of your questioning of Knaplund might look like the one shown below.

> ### Cross-Examination Outline
>
> Witness: Kris Knaplund
>
> Summary of expected testimony:
>
> Knaplund will testify that she heard me say that I should have been in the crosswalk.
>
> Additional information that supports my version of events: none
>
> Questions I have for impeaching her:
>
> - "Ms. Knaplund, isn't it true that you were coming out of a video game arcade when you heard me say something after the accident?"
> - "The arcade was noisy, wasn't it?"
> - "Several arcade games were being played near you?"
> - "Those games are so loud that you have to talk extra loud to be heard inside the arcade, right?"
> - "And where you were standing is about 75 feet away from where I was hit by the truck, right?"

H.   INDEX TAB 7: CLOSING ARGUMENT OUTLINE

A closing argument outline summarizes the introductory remarks you plan to make, lists the elements and facts you seek to prove or disprove and important items of evidence, the burden of proof, the exact language of important jury instructions (in a jury trial) and the results you want the judge or jury to reach. (A sample outline is in Chapter 11,

Closing Argument.) As in opening statement, you do not want to read your argument to the judge or jury. However, referring to the outline from time to time as you speak will ensure that you do not overlook important evidence or arguments. You can also ask the judge for a few moments to review your outline before you make your argument.

I.   INDEX TAB 8: JURY TRIAL DOCUMENTS

In a jury trial, you'll need a blank Jury Chart on which to write down information about prospective jurors as it emerges during voir dire questioning. You can review this information when deciding whether you will challenge any jurors. For use during the questioning process, you may also want a make a list of topics or, if your judge asks all the questions but allows you to submit questions you want asked, a list of specific questions. (See Chapter 7, Selecting the Decision-Maker.)

J.   INDEX TAB 9: MISCELLANEOUS DOCUMENTS

Depending on the complexity of your case and your judgment concerning what documents may prove important, you may want to have a "Miscellaneous" section of your trial notebook where you put documents such as the following:

- A list of all the exhibits that you plan to introduce. Keep this list at the top of this section so that you can easily check off the items as the judge admits them into evidence. If you have made extra copies of exhibits to hand to opposing counsel, the judge or the jury, place them immediately beneath the list. If you have copies of numerous exhibits, you may want to have a separate section of your notebook tabbed something like, "Exhibit List and Copies of Exhibits."

- A copy of any rules of evidence that may be important if you or your adversary is likely to object to the admissibility of important evidence during trial, having the text of the controlling rule of evidence in front of you will strengthen your argument.

For example, assume that your trial is in federal court and you want to offer an important business record into evidence. Your adversary has indicated an intention to object to the exhibit as hearsay. (See Chapters 12, Exhibits, and 13, Basic Rules of Evidence.) You may want to make a copy of Federal Rule of Evidence 803 (6), which specifies the foundational requirements for business records, and put it in this section of your notebook.

Have all evidence rules with you during trial. Your court system's rules of evidence should be available in a book which you can buy. If the rules are part of a larger collection of rules that is too expensive for you to buy, perhaps you can photocopy the section on evidence. Either way, you should have the evidence rules with you during trial. You should also make a copy of a rule that is likely to be the focus of argument and put it in your trial notebook.

- If you or your adversary submits a written "motion in limine" (a pre-trial request to the judge to exclude evidence), insert the motion and any written response into this section. (See Chapter 14, Making and Responding to Objections.) Especially if the judge has "reserved" (postponed) a ruling on the motion until the evidence is actually offered, having the written motion in front of you during trial can help you present a stronger argument.

- A copy of any written stipulations.

- A list of the names, addresses and phone and fax numbers of your self-help law coach (if you have one who has agreed to be on standby to help you during trial) and your witnesses. If your witnesses are late to court, you or the judge may want to contact them immediately, sometimes with the sheriff's help!

- A copy of the list of common objections. (See Chapter 14, Making and Responding to Objections.)

- The names and addresses of a few good restaurants within easy walking distance of the courthouse.

16

EXPERT WITNESSES

Experts are witnesses who have acquired specialized knowledge through education, training or other experience. Experts testify to opinions about the legal significance of evidence that is beyond the everyday understanding of the average judge or jury, and give the reasons underlying those opinions. Experts commonly appear in trials; as daily affairs have become more complex, parties have increasingly had to turn to expert testimony to prove their claims.

If proving your claim or disproving your opponent's claim requires making a judge or jury understand the significance of scientific, specialized or technical information, you may have to hire an expert witness. However, an expert witness is likely to be very expensive. This chapter helps you recognize when you really need an expert witness, tells you how to find the right expert and explains how to work efficiently with and elicit testimony from an expert.

⚠️ **The final decision rests with the judge or jury.** A judge or juror is free to disregard an expert's opinion. Evidence rules make experts' opinions admissible in evidence; the rules do not make the opinions binding on judges and jurors. It's up to you to find an expert who is well-qualified and likely to be convincing.

A. WHO ARE EXPERT WITNESSES?

As you might expect, given the variety of situations that end up in court, a wide spectrum of professional people offer their services as expert witnesses. One recent legal journal contained expert witness advertisements not only by doctors, lawyers and accountants, but also by experts in alarm system failures, architectural engineering, tree growth problems, accident reconstruction, escalator maintenance, corporate histories, ladders and other household devices, railroad accidents, bicycles, skydiving and many other subjects.

A person does not need an advanced professional or scientific degree to qualify as an expert. As long as a subject is beyond the understanding of the average judge or juror, any person who has special knowledge, experience or skill in that subject can qualify as an expert. (See Federal Rule of Evidence 702.) For example, if your case involves the cause of rutabaga crop failure, a farmer who has grown rutabagas for many years would likely qualify as an expert. Or if your case involves defective house paint, an experienced painter may qualify as an expert. (See Section E below for a discussion of how to qualify a witness as an expert.)

B. DO YOU NEED AN EXPERT WITNESS?

One of the first things you must determine is whether the subject matter of the claim you are trying to prove (or, if you are a defendant, disprove) requires expert testimony. The test is this: If understanding the subject matter of a claim requires specialized knowledge that is beyond the everyday experience of the average judge or jury, you will need an expert.

For example, assume that you have sued an accountant for negligently (carelessly) preparing an analysis of a financial statement for you. To prevail, you must prove that the accountant's preparation fell below the professional standards to which accountants are held. The average judge or jury doesn't know what those standards are. So you'll need another accountant, in the role of an expert witness, to describe the professional standards governing accountants and to explain how the accountant you sued negligently deviated from those standards. The defendant is likely to counter with another accounting expert in an effort to show that professional standards were complied with.

Here are some other types of claims that would probably require expert testimony:

- To prove your claim that a new home you purchased was built on improperly compacted landfill, you need an expert in soil engineering.

- To prove your claim that injuries you suffered as the result of an accident are likely to be permanent, you need a medical expert.

- To prove your claim that a piece of jewelry sold to you as a valuable "flawless" diamond is actually an inexpensive imitation, you probably need an expert in gemology.

- To prove your claim that you were injured because a lawn mower you purchased was defectively manufactured, you probably need an expert in lawn mower design and safety.

- To prove your claim that a series of psychological tests administered to your child demonstrates that your ex-spouse is not taking proper care of the child, you probably need an expert in child psychology.

What each of these examples has in common is that the average judge or jury cannot evaluate the truth of the claim without an expert's help. You would have to hire an expert with the proper qualifications prior to trial, demonstrate to the judge that your witness is sufficiently qualified to give expert testimony and then elicit the expert's testimony so as to convince the judge or jury that your claim is true.

By contrast, let's look at a few examples where expert testimony is *not* necessary:

- You claim that your opponent drove negligently by driving 50 m.p.h. in a residential area.

- You claim that a landlord's failure to fix problems in your apartment rendered it uninhabitable and so excused your obligation to pay rent.

- You claim that a witness who testified against you should not be believed because he is biased and has made inconsistent statements.

- You claim that a developer intentionally made false statements about the number of home sites in a tract of land to induce you to purchase one of the sites.

In these types of situations, a judge would not permit you to use an expert witness because the subjects are within the understanding of the average judge or jury. The legal system expects and trusts judges and juries to decide the truth of such claims based on their common sense and everyday experiences.

If you are uncertain about whether the subject matter of the claim you are making requires expert testimony, consult one of the reference works listed at the end of the chapter. Also, you may want to seek the advice of a self-help law coach well before trial. If you need an expert, it will take time to find and hire the right one and for the expert to familiarize herself with your case so that she can testify clearly and persuasively.

> ⚠️ **You must notify your adversary and the court well before trial that you will call an expert witness.** Check your local court rules for deadlines for advising your adversary and the court that you intend to call an expert and disclosing the expert's identity. If you fail to meet the deadline, the judge may not permit your expert to testify. For example, in federal court your expert must be named before the judge makes the final pre-trial order. (See Federal Rule of Civil Procedure 16.)

JUDGES ARE NOT EXPERTS

A savvy or sympathetic judge cannot take the place of an expert witness, even if the judge is very knowledgeable about a subject ordinarily thought of as reserved for experts.

For example, assume that you will offer evidence of your medical condition. Based on the fact that your judge was a doctor before becoming a judge, you may think that you do not need a medical expert to testify about how your medical condition will affect your future activities. Or, you may be suing your former lawyer for legal malpractice for omitting an important clause from a contract. Based on the fact that your judge was recently a practicing lawyer in the same field, you may think it unnecessary to call a legal expert to testify that omission of the clause was legal malpractice.

Think again—the rule is that a judge's personal knowledge is no substitute for expert testimony. The law regards all judges as having no more than everyday knowledge regardless of their actual personal backgrounds. If the subject matter of your claim is beyond the understanding of the average judge or jury, you must produce a qualified expert witness no matter what your judge's background.

C. SPECIAL RULES FOR EXPERT WITNESSES

The rules of evidence reward experts—who, after all, have pleased their parents by developing special skills and knowledge—by bestowing on them three general advantages not shared by lay (non-expert) witnesses.

1. Personal Knowledge Is Unnecessary for Experts

Unlike lay witnesses, experts are not required to testify from personal knowledge. (See Federal Rule of Evidence 703.) Evidence rules allow an expert to gain information second-hand and then give the judge or jury an opinion about the significance of that information. An expert's review of documents and discussions with you and other people can substitute for the expert's lack of personal knowledge about what actually happened. For example, even though a medical expert does not know how you got hurt and never treated you, evidence rules allow the expert to examine your medical records and testify that your injuries are permanent. Similarly, even though a legal expert has no first-hand knowledge about what took place between you and a lawyer who once represented you, evidence rules allow the expert to testify that you were the victim of legal malpractice based on the expert's analysis of the lawyer's actions.

2. Experts Can Give Opinions Forbidden to Non-Experts

Unlike ordinary witnesses, experts can provide opinions about the meaning of scientific, technical or specialized evidence, even if that opinion refers directly to the legal issue the judge or jury has to decide. (See Federal Rule of Evidence 704.)

For example, a lawyer who qualifies as an expert witness can testify that it is his opinion that the attorney you have sued for legal malpractice deviated from professional standards, even though this is exactly the issue the judge or jury has to decide. Similarly, a child psychologist expert can give an opinion that it would be in the best interests of your children for them to remain with you rather than go to live with your former spouse, and a medical expert can give an opinion that an injury will cause lifetime discomfort. In each instance, the expert can render an opinion based on specialized knowledge that an ordinary witness would be unable to give.

3. Experts Can Testify to Otherwise Inadmissible Evidence

Because experts do not have to testify from personal knowledge, to form their opinions they often rely on information in reports and on statements made to them by the party who hired them and others. As long as the information is of a type that other experts in the same field reasonably rely on, the expert can testify to that information even if it would not otherwise be admissible under the rules of evidence. (See Federal Rule of Evidence 703.)

SCIENTIFIC EVIDENCE

For many years, judges have admitted scientific evidence if the evidence was based on principles that were "generally accepted" by the scientific community.

In federal court, however, it is now up to judges to make sure that scientific evidence admitted at trial is not only relevant, but reliable. Under a 1993 U.S. Supreme Court ruling, judges cannot admit scientific evidence just because it is based on generally accepted scientific principles. Judges must make their own decisions about the scientific validity of evidence. *Daubert v. Merrell Dow Pharmaceuticals Inc.,* 113 S. Ct. 2786 (1993).

For example, assume that in a lawsuit against your ex-spouse, you have hired a child psychologist as an expert to testify that in the expert's opinion, you should have sole custody of your minor children. In arriving at this opinion, the expert may have spoken to the children's teachers, read evaluations prepared by school personnel and consulted books written by other child psychologists. Much of this information would not itself be admissible under the rules of evidence. For instance, the hearsay rule would normally bar the expert from testifying to the teacher's out-of-court statements and to statements in a book. (See Chapter 13, Basic Rules of Evidence.) But if experts in the field of child psychology reasonably rely on such information, your expert can refer to it while testifying.

In formulating this rule, the drafters of modern rules of evidence have shown uncharacteristic humility. They have reasoned that if courts need expert testimony to dispense justice, there is no sense telling experts what information they may or may not use to arrive at an opinion.

Your own expert can tell the judge what experts in the same field rely on. How does a judge, who after all is not an expert, know whether information is "of a type reasonably relied upon by experts in the particular field?" From your expert, of course. So when your child psychologist expert testifies to the information on which his opinion is based, ask, "Mr. Expert, do child psychologists commonly rely on information from teachers and from books written by other child psychologists in forming their opinions?"

The rule that lets experts themselves determine what information they can rely on has common sense limits. A judge may rule that the expert's reliance on certain information is unreasonable no matter what the expert says, and forbid the expert from testifying to the information or relying on it in forming an opinion. For instance, assume that your child psychologist expert testifies that "in forming my opinion I consulted the children's astrological chart, and we child psychologists commonly rely on astrological readings." A judge would undoubtedly forbid the expert from testifying to or relying on such information.

D.   FINDING AND HIRING AN EXPERT WITNESS

The expert you hire should have good credentials that your adversary cannot easily impugn, be knowledgeable about the specific subject matter of your case, be able to communicate what she knows in language that a judge or jury will understand, and employ a credible manner of testifying in response both to your friendly direct examination and your adversary's challenging cross-examination. This section describes how to find and hire such a person.

1.   When to Look for an Expert

If you need an expert witness, the best time to hire one is well before trial, when you are still looking for evidence to prove your claim or disprove your opponent's claim. Your expert can help coach you as to what evidence to gather, and the expert will have time to conduct whatever tests or research are necessary to formulate a reliable opinion.

USING AN EXPERT TO ENHANCE YOUR SETTLEMENT POSITION

Another reason to hire an expert as soon as possible is that the overwhelming percentage of cases do not go to trial; most are settled. Before you hire an expert, an adversary's attorney may try to take advantage of your limited trial skills by making you a "lowball" offer. But having a credible expert in your corner well before trial strengthens your case no matter how rough your trial skills and is likely to induce your adversary to eventually make you a better settlement offer.

2. Paying an Expert

Expert witnesses can be and almost always are compensated for their testimony. In most states, statutes prohibit ordinary witnesses from being paid to testify, allowing them only a small fee as reimbursement for the expense of traveling to and from the courthouse. But the legal system regards an expert's specialized knowledge and training as a personal asset for which the expert can charge whatever the market will bear.

Most experts charge an hourly fee—often hundreds of dollars per hour—for time spent in reviewing a file, conducting necessary tests, preparing a written report, preparing for trial and testifying. The expert may also charge you for out-of-pocket expenses incurred for materials and travel. Win or lose, you have to pay the expert—usually up front.

The potential for profit has spawned an army of experts who peddle their services for substantial sums. Like buying the services of a roofer or a piano teacher, if you need to hire an expert witness you'll need to be a wise shopper. Make sure your fee arrangement is in writing. And if one expert quotes you a fee that you think is too high, look for one with good credentials who will provide the help you need for less.

COURT-APPOINTED EXPERT WITNESSES

If you need the services of an expert but can't afford to hire one, consider making a written pre-trial motion to request a judge to appoint the court's own expert. (See Chapter 4, Pre-Trial Hearings and Motions.) In most court systems, a judge has the power to appoint experts and pay them out of an expert witness fund. (See Federal Rule of Evidence 706.) A judge may even order your opponent (especially if it is a large corporation or the government) to pay all or most of the court-appointed expert's fees.

However, judges rarely use their power to appoint experts. If you do make a request, stress the public's interest in the issue involved in your case. For example, in one case in which a pro per litigant challenged a government swine flu vaccination program, a trial court appointed (at government expense) a panel of three experts to investigate and testify because of the importance to the public and the complexity of the medical issues. *(Gates v. United States,* 707 F.2d 1141 (10th Cir. 1983).) Another court appointed an expert on behalf of a pro per prisoner who claimed that forced exposure to second-hand smoke inside prison constituted cruel and unusual punishment, because the prisoner was indigent and could not find an expert who would testify without being paid. *(McKinney v. Anderson,* 924 F.2d 1500 (9th Cir. 1991).) (See Chapter 19, Legal Research, for information on how to find and use cases such as these.)

THE LOSER'S OBLIGATION TO PAY EXPERT WITNESS FEES

The judge normally awards the winner of a lawsuit "costs of suit" in addition to any other relief to which the winning party is entitled. One of the costs that the judge may award is the fee paid to an expert witness. So keep written records of your expert's charges and, if you win the case, ask the judge to order your opponent to pay you those charges.

Of course, a judge's ability to order payment of expert witness fees is a double-edged sword. If your opponent uses an expert witness and you lose, your opponent will surely ask the judge to order you to pay. Be ready to give the judge reasons for denying your adversary's request or limiting how much you have to pay. These reasons might include:

- **Lack of necessity:** Argue that your adversary's claim could have been proved without an expert. You may also be able to argue that your adversary, knowing you were not represented by a lawyer, needlessly hired an expert just to run up costs and try to force you to give up your right to a trial.

- **Too many experts:** If your adversary called two or three experts who gave similar testimony, ask the court to award your adversary costs only for one expert. Most judges resent cumulative testimony, so you may prevail on this argument.

- **Excessive fees:** If your adversary's expert's fee is based on what you think is an excessive hourly rate, or if the expert put in an excessive number of hours (especially compared to the amount of money at stake in the lawsuit), ask the court to order payment of only a portion of the fee. One way you can demonstrate that a fee is excessive is to point out to the judge that the expert who testified (or offered to testify) for you charged a much lower fee.

3. Where to Look

If you need an expert, you can start by checking the listings and advertisements in magazines aimed at trial lawyers. For example, the magazine *Trial*, published monthly by the American Trial Lawyers Association and available in most law libraries, lists experts according to subject matter. Many state and county bar associations (lawyers' organizations) also publish magazines or newsletters in which local experts advertise their services. Universities and local branches of professional associations (for example, the American Medical Association) are also possible sources of expert witnesses.

Many experts list their services by specialty in national "expert witness registries."

 WHERE TO GET EXPERT WITNESS REGISTRIES

Expert Resources Inc.; 4700 N. Prospect Road, Peoria Heights, IL 61614, 309-688-4857; also local branches in many cities.

Legal Resource Network; 800-969-1441

National Forensic Center; 800-526-5177. It annually publishes the *Forensic Services Directory*, a book of approximately 1400 pages listing experts by specialty all across the country. It costs about $100. The Center also publishes an annual *Guide to Expert Witness Fees*, which lists experts across the country according to their area of expertise and then divides them according to whether their fees are in the low, median or high range. This year's *Guide* costs about $30.

4. How to Choose the Right Expert

The expert you hire must be able to render an opinion that backs your claim, and must be able to give convincing reasons in support of the opinion. When you do find an expert you are interested in hiring, here are some of the steps you can take to make sure you spend your money wisely.

When you contact a potential expert, ask for a "Curriculum Vitae" (VY-TAY) that includes the expert's personal background, education, job history, publications and honors. If you contact more than one expert, compare their CVs before deciding who to hire. Try to gauge whether a judge or jury will be impressed with your expert's credentials.

Ask for a list of cases (the more recent the better) in which the person has been hired as an expert and the names and phone numbers of the attorneys involved. Then check references to make sure the expert gets a good recommendation from cooperative attorneys and parties who hired the expert. If, however, a person has excellent credentials, do not automatically dismiss the person just because she or he has never before been hired as an expert. Everyone has to start somewhere.

Try to get as close a fit as possible between an expert's area of expertise and the facts of your case. For example, say you're involved in a legal malpractice case against the lawyer who failed to advise your stepmother that she had to change her will to accomplish her stated wish to disinherit a child born after the will was signed. You need a legal expert who will give an opinion that the estate planning lawyer's failure to give the advice constituted legal malpractice. Look for a lawyer who specializes in estate planning (will drafting and related matters) and is knowledgeable about the ethical rules of that aspect of legal practice. Do not hire as your expert a lawyer who has only general legal expertise.

Before you agree to hire an expert, make sure that the expert takes the time to analyze your legal position thoroughly before forming an opinion. (You may have to pay for the expert's time to conduct this analysis.) Give the expert whatever information the expert requests in order to formulate an opinion. You don't want to hire an expert who will jump at the chance to deliver whatever opinion you are willing to pay for. Nor do you want to invest time and money in an expert who is unwilling to render a favorable opinion.

Tell your expert the truth. Reveal all relevant information—good or bad— to your expert. Never try to hide bad information in order to get a favorable opinion from an expert. If you do and later at trial your adversary reveals the negative information to your expert, the embarrassed expert may change her opinion and do irreparable harm to your case.

If time, finances and number of potential experts permit, talk to more than one expert before hiring one. If the first expert you contact is unwilling to render a favorable opinion, of course you'll need to seek another opinion. Many areas of expertise involve judgment. Even if one expert disagrees with your position, a second expert may honestly make a favorable assessment.

But even if the first expert you talk to renders a favorable opinion, you may want to talk to others before deciding whom to hire. You want an expert who not only has a favorable opinion, but who is also knowledgeable, convincing and easy to work with. Remember that you will pay well for the expert's help, so there is absolutely no reason to be intimidated by the "expert" label. No matter how good an expert looks on paper, or no matter how solid the recommendations, your expert has to testify in a way that gives a judge or jury confidence in the correctness of the expert's opinions. If the expert cannot explain an opinion clearly and credibly to you, probably the expert will also be unconvincing in front of a judge or jury. It is your case, and you should hire only a person who is both well qualified and who can explain the meaning of evidence in clear, everyday terms.

Find out whether your expert has in the past represented more than one point of view. Generally you want to avoid experts whose opinion is the same in every case—for example, that doctors are negligent or that custody of children should be awarded to fathers. Your adversary is likely to bring this fact out at trial, leading a judge or jury to disbelieve your expert on the grounds of bias. Far better for your expert to testify that she testifies for different litigants and that her opinions reflect the unique circumstances of each case.

E. QUESTIONING YOUR EXPERT WITNESS AT TRIAL

There are two major phases of your expert's direct examination. First, you must elicit foundational testimony qualifying the witness as an expert. Then it's time to elicit testimony about the expert's opinion and the reasons justifying it.

1. Laying a Foundation

Before a witness can give expert testimony, you have to offer foundational evidence showing that the witness is qualified as an expert in the field to which the testimony relates. (For a refresher on the concept of evidentiary foundations, see Chapter 9, Direct Examination, and Chapter 12, Exhibits.) That means that you must begin the direct examination with questions about the expert witness's background. The idea is to demonstrate that the witness really does have specialized "knowledge, skill, experience, training or education" in the field of claimed expertise. Only after the judge rules that your witness qualifies as an expert can you go on to bring out the testimony that helps to prove your case.

Make your expert seem as knowledgeable as possible. Though the purpose of foundational questions is to show that your witness possesses the necessary qualifications to give expert testimony, your questions have a secondary purpose. This is to show a judge or juror what an outstanding, credible expert your witness is. The more your expert comes across as a star, the more convincing the expert's testimony is likely to be.

So even if the judge tries to hurry you along, or your opponent offers to save time by stipulating (agreeing) that your witness is an expert, you should politely resist, especially if you are in a jury trial and your expert has a very distinguished background. For example, you might reply to the judge by saying something like, "I appreciate the offer to stipulate. I promise that I will not waste the court's time. But I need to bring out a few more facts about my expert's background to show the jury how well qualified he is."

Obviously the specific foundational questions you ask will depend on your witness's field of expertise. If your expert has testified previously, he should be able to tell you what topics to cover to bring out his qualifications to give expert testimony. Your foundational questions of an expert are likely to cover the following general topics:

- Education. This is particularly important for experts like doctors, lawyers and others who need advanced degrees to enter their profession. Ask about college and any graduate school degrees. It's also a good approach to ask about special courses the expert might have taken after completing formal training. For example, a tax attorney may just have completed a two-week course in "Tax Planning for Estate Planners," and a police officer expert may have taken a special Police Academy course in "Accident Reconstruction."

- Professional experience. For example, what is your expert lawyer's specialty, what does your expert doctor's practice consist of, or what is your expert farmer's experience with the growing of rutabagas? Your questions should allow your expert to describe whatever it is that constitutes her professional life or specialized knowledge, and the length of time she has been at it. Also elicit evidence about any licenses your expert holds, such as a doctor's license to practice Internal Medicine.

- Professional organizations of which the expert is a member. For example, a doctor may be a member of the American Medical Association and the College of Orthopedic Surgeons. If your expert is an elected officer of such an organization, or if she needed special qualifications to qualify for admittance to the organization, be sure to bring that out and have the expert explain what it means.

- Any courses taught by your expert, either in colleges or in special training courses.

- Any books or articles that your expert has written.

- How many times your expert has been previously qualified to give expert testimony.

To see how these factors combine into foundational testimony, let's go back to one of the sample cases used throughout this book: a legal malpractice claim against an attorney. You're suing the lawyer for failing to advise your stepmother that she needed to change her will in order to accomplish her stated wish to disinherit her child who was born after the will was signed. To prove that the defendant attorney committed malpractice, you may need to call another attorney as an expert witness to explain how the defendant's conduct violated professional standards. The foundational testimony that qualifies your witness to give expert testimony might go as follows:

1 **You:**

What is your name and occupation?

2 **Expert:**

My name is Anna Turney, and I am a lawyer and a part-time law teacher.

3 **You:**

How long have you been doing these things?

4 **Expert:**

I've been a lawyer for ten years, and a part-time law teacher for the last four years.

5 **You:**

What is your educational background?

6   Expert:

I graduated with a Bachelor of Arts degree from the University of Chicago 13 years ago, then went to law school at UCLA. I graduated with a law degree, known as a Doctor of Jurisprudence, ten years ago, passed the California Bar Exam and entered the practice of law.

7   You:

Are you licensed to practice law?

8   Expert:

Yes, I'm licensed by our State Bar. I'm also admitted to practice before the federal courts of our state.

9   You:

Can you briefly describe your practice experience?

10   Expert:

Yes, I began practice with Hoffman, Upham and Downey, a local law firm that specializes in estate planning. Five years ago I left the private practice of law to go to work for the Enforcement Division of the State Bar, which disciplines lawyers who violate the rules of the profession. I've been there ever since. I also teach a course in Professional Ethics every other semester at the Milwaukee Law School.

11   You:

Have you ever written about legal ethics?

12   Expert:

Yes, I've written three articles on ethical duties of lawyers. Two of these have been published in our state magazine for lawyers, the Bar Journal, and the other in a local county bar journal.

13   You:

How much of your work deals with professional standards for estate planning lawyers?

14   Expert:

Well, one of the articles that was published in the state Bar Journal dealt specifically with that topic, and because that was my practice specialty I regularly discuss the ethical responsibilities of estate planners in my Professional Ethics course. Working with the State Bar, I'd estimate that about 20% of the discipline cases that I investigate and prosecute involve estate planning lawyers.

15   You:

Can you give me any idea how many of these cases you handle in an average month?

16   Expert:

Well, if you mean estate planning discipline cases, I'd say about ten per month. This is about how many I investigate; of course I don't necessarily prosecute that many.

17   You:

Have you ever previously testified as an expert witness involving legal malpractice by an estate planning attorney?

18   Expert:

Yes, on two occasions within the last three years. In addition I was hired in connection with two other cases, but the cases settled before I testified.

19   You:

Your Honor, I request that Ms. Turney be accepted as an expert witness.

20   Judge:

Defense counsel, do you have any foundational questions you would like to ask the witness?

21   Adversary:

None, Your Honor.

22   Judge:

Very well, I rule that the witness is qualified to give expert testimony. Mr. Nolo, you may proceed with your questioning.

Transcript Analysis: This testimony establishes that the witness is qualified to give expert testimony in your legal malpractice case. Your witness has five years of experience enforcing professional rules of conduct, teaches a course on Professional Ethics, and has written articles about lawyers' eth-

ical duties (Nos. 10 and 12). Moreover, throughout her career she has been concerned with estate planning matters. In private practice she was an estate planning attorney (No. 10); both her articles and her teaching have focused on ethical rules in the estate planning contest (No. 14); and she regularly investigates and prosecutes disciplinary cases involving estate planners (No. 16). Finally, she has twice qualified as an expert witness in similar matters (No. 18).

Note that many of your foundational questions, especially Nos. 5, 9 and 13, ask the expert to provide a narrative of her background. These questions encourage the expert to describe her background fully in her own words, letting her display her expertise and bolster her credibility in the eyes of the judge or jury. As you may remember from Chapter 9, judges usually do not allow you to ask narrative questions during direct examination. But they often make an exception for experts because they trust experts to keep their answers within legal bounds.

⚠️ **The adversary may be saving an attack for cross-examination.** Your adversary's response in No. 21 indicates only that the adversary has no questions pertaining to Turney's qualifications as an expert. During cross-examination, your adversary may nevertheless attack Turney's credibility—for example, by showing that Turney always testifies on the side of plaintiffs who are suing their former attorneys.

2. Eliciting the Expert's Testimony

Once your witness has qualified as an expert, you may elicit testimony in whatever way you decide. Unlike with ordinary witnesses, who usually describe events in chronological order, there is no standard format for expert testimony. Your main task is to bring out the expert's opinion and the reasons supporting that opinion in whatever way seems most credible. Remember, when testifying to the reasons for an opinion, the expert can refer to information that is not itself admissible in evidence.

Elicit the reasons for your expert's opinion. You aren't required to ask your expert the reasons for her opinion. (Rule 705 of the Federal Rules of Evidence and similar rules in most states.) But it is almost always far more convincing to elicit your expert's opinion and then ask for the reasons for that opinion.

When planning the direct examination, get help from your expert. Ask the expert to tell you all the reasons that support the expert's opinion. Then ask for the expert's advice as to how much of this information you should be sure to bring out during the expert's direct examination.

Here is an example of a format you may want to follow to elicit an expert's opinion and the reasons for it. Assume that you have already finished foundational questioning, and that the judge has ruled that your witness is qualified to give expert testimony. In the case of the legal expert in the legal malpractice case, your questioning would go as follows:

1 **You:**

Ms. Turney, do you have an opinion as to whether the defendant committed legal malpractice?

2 **Expert:**

Yes, Ms. Nolo, I do.

3 **You:**

And what is that opinion?

4 **Expert:**

My opinion is that the defendant breached the professional standard of care and committed legal malpractice.

5 **You:**

Can you please tell the judge how you arrived at this opinion?

Transcript Analysis: It is generally a good idea to ask the expert whether she has been able to arrive at an opinion (No. 1) before eliciting the opinion (No. 3). You can then go on to elicit the reasons underlying the opinion with a broad, narrative-type question (No. 5). Again, judges typically allow such questions of experts because they trust experts to stay on point.

The reasons supporting an expert's opinion will, of course, depend on the kind of expert a person is. An engineering expert may rely primarily on a stress test of a piece of metal, a medical expert on a physical examination of you and your medical history, an accident reconstruction expert on an inspection of the accident site and the condition of the cars, and a child psychology expert on the results of psychological testing and conversations with the child's parents, teachers and other counselors.

The following suggestions should help you maximize the credibility of your expert's testimony.

- Ask the expert to explain her field of expertise. If the expert's field of expertise is likely to be unfamiliar to a judge or jury, ask the expert to briefly explain it. For instance, since many people know that a "radiologist" takes and interprets X-rays, you may not have to ask your expert radiologist a question like, "What is it that radiologists do?" But a judge or jury may not be familiar with more unusual fields of expertise such as "linguistics" or "ceramic coatings." Therefore, you might ask your linguistics expert questions such as, "What is linguistics?" and "What kinds of things do linguists do?"

- Ask the expert to explain any tests that were performed. Have the expert explain what the tests were, why they were administered, how they work and what the results mean. Any working models, charts, photographs, slides or other materials your expert can bring to court to illustrate how the tests were performed will almost certainly bolster the expert's credibility.

- Have the expert read from a treatise. If your expert consulted an authoritative textbook or treatise that supports the expert's opinion, consider asking the expert to read a clear, brief portion to the judge or jury. (See Federal Rule of Evidence 803 (18), which is a hearsay exception that allows an expert to read information from a reliable treatise to a judge or jury.) Before the expert does so, ask him why he consulted it and what makes it authoritative. Then, mark the book as an exhibit, have the expert testify that it is authoritative, and ask the expert to read the supportive portion to the judge or jury.

- Have the expert explain reports. If your expert prepared a written report before trial, have the expert explain how and when she prepared it. Then mark the report as an exhibit, have the witness authenticate it and offer it into evidence. (See Chapter 12, Exhibits.) This is especially important when an expert is a professional with an advanced degree, because the judge or jury will probably expect such an expert to document an opinion in writing.

- Have the expert describe discussions with others. If your expert based his opinion in part on statements from other people, ask him to describe who he talked to, why he consulted them, what they said and how their statements influenced his opinion. Ordinarily, testimony about the out-of-court statements of other people constitute inadmissible hearsay. (See Chapter 13, Basic Rules of Evidence.) But experts are allowed to refer to hearsay and other inadmissible evidence as long as it is of a type that experts in the particular field reasonably rely on.

- Have the expert use everyday language. Ask the expert to translate technical jargon into plain English. Almost every field of expertise has its own jargon, and experts tend to use it automatically without realizing that an ordinary judge or jury might not have the faintest idea what the expert is talking about. Up to a point this can sound like impressive "insider talk," but its impact will be lost if the judge or jury has no idea what it means. A good general rule is that if your expert had to explain a term to you, you should ask the expert to explain it to the judge or jury.

For example, a stock market expert might refer to "convertible subordinated debentures," a term that would baffle most judges or juries. Here's how you could ask your expert to explain this term:

1 You:

> *Ms. Expert, you used the term "convertible subordinated debenture." What exactly is a convertible subordinated debenture?*

2 Expert:

> *A convertible subordinated debenture is a bond that a corporation issues to a person from whom it borrows money. The bond is paid back with interest or, if the lender chooses, is convertible into stock in the corporation, usually at a price set out in the bond. Obviously, the lender will take advantage of the convertible feature only if the price of the stock on the open market is higher than the price set out in the bond, so that the lender stands to make a profit by acquiring the stock.*

3 You:

> *Thank you. Now let me ask you….*

• Let the expert testify in her own words. You want the expert to impress the judge or jury with her expertise, so ask narrative and open

questions frequently. Broad questions allow experts to testify convincingly in their own words.

Make a direct examination outline. Make an outline of the expert's testimony just as you do any other witness's testimony and include it in the Direct Examination section of your trial notebook. Include the important personal background information that qualifies the person as an expert, the expert's opinion, and the reasons supporting it. You might also want to include any specialized jargon that you want your expert to explain, as well as exhibits you plan to offer while the expert is testifying. (See Chapter 15, Organizing a Trial Notebook.)

---

3. Hypothetical Questions

Until evidence rules changed 20 years or so ago, experts almost always testified in response to hypothetical questions. Lawyers asked experts to assume that certain facts were true and then asked them to state what their opinion would be given those facts. Today, there is no need to use hypothetical questions to question experts, and we generally recommend against it. You can get trapped in a "Twilight Zone" between not putting enough information into a hypothetical to support your expert's opinion, and putting in so much information that the judge rules that you have improperly launched into your closing argument.

However, many attorneys (especially those whose legal education predated modern evidence rules) still use hypothetical questions, and they are still permitted. If your adversary uses a hypothetical question, make sure that the "assumed" facts in it accurately reflect testimony. If the facts are not accurate, you should object to the question. For example, if your adversary's hypothetical question misstates a witness's actual testimony, state your objection by saying that "The question is misleading because it does not accurately reflect the evidence before the court." (See Chapter 14, Making and Responding to Objections.)

F. CROSS-EXAMINING YOUR OPPONENT'S EXPERT WITNESS

If cross-examination of an expert were a pack of cigarettes, it would carry a warning label, "Caution. Cross-examining an expert witness may be hazardous to your health." The problem is that unless you have as much expertise in the subject area as the expert you are questioning, cross-examination is likely to give the opposing expert the chance to restate and even elaborate on her opinions.

In many cases, the smartest choice is to decline the invitation to cross-examine an expert witness. You can instead rely on your own expert as well as your other evidence to convince a judge or jury that your claims are accurate.

But if you cannot pay for your own expert testimony, and the judge refuses to appoint an expert, you may have no choice other than to try to undermine the adversary's expert's conclusions. In that situation, you may want to at least hire an expert for some pre-trial consultation. Tell your expert consultant what you expect the opponent's expert to say, and ask what areas of weakness you might probe during cross-examination. Even if you come up with no more than four or five good questions, you may give the judge or jury some reason to question the expert's testimony.

Seek your consulting expert's help in wording your questions, and write down the questions exactly as you expect to ask them in your cross-examination outline. When you cross-examine an expert, the exact words you use are often more important than when you cross-examine ordinary witnesses.

If you do want to cross-examine your adversary's expert, here are some possible approaches. You may be able to use them during cross-examination without giving an adverse expert the opportunity to rehash all of his opinions.

- Demonstrate weaknesses in the expert's qualifications. Perhaps the expert testified impressively that he is a member of numerous professional organizations. If you show that any attorney, electrical engineer, accountant or other expert can join those organizations merely by paying a membership fee, the impressiveness may evaporate. For example, any lawyer willing to pay the required fee can join the American Bar Association—no special qualifications are required.

- Show that the expert lacks certain qualifications that she might be expected to have. For instance, medical experts are often "Board Certified" in particular medical specialties such as surgery or radiology, meaning that they have passed tests conducted by a national board of experts in their field. If you ask your adversary's medical expert if she is Board certified and the answer is no, you may undercut her credibility.

You may attack a qualified expert's background. You may attack an opposing expert's qualifications on cross-examination even though the judge has ruled that the witness is qualified to give expert testimony. Your questions are relevant to the credibility of the expert's opinions.

- Ask the witness about his fee. If you know from pre-trial discussions or answers to your formal discovery requests that your opponent's expert is receiving what the average judge or juror will think is a large fee, ask how much the expert is being paid. The judge or jury may conclude that the expert is slanting his testimony in favor of the hand that is feeding him.

- Show that the witness is biased. If you know that the expert always testifies on behalf of one position, ask the expert how often she testifies, and then how often she testifies for the same position. For example, assume that your opponent has called an expert legal witness to testify that your former lawyer, whom you have sued for legal malpractice, was not negligent. You may learn through discovery that this expert has testified in 20 other legal malpractice cases, and has always testified that there was no legal malpractice. When you bring out this background, you suggest that the expert is slanting her testimony (is biased) to favor an ideological position she favors rather than providing the truth.

- Contradict the expert with a reliable published opinion. If you know that the expert's opinion is at odds with a passage in a treatise or textbook that the expert regards as reliable, show the book to the expert, ask him to admit that experts in the same field generally regard that treatise or textbook as "authoritative," and then read into the record the conflicting opinion.

Cross-examining an expert based on a passage in a treatise that is at odds with an expert's opinion is a cheap way for you to introduce expert evidence favorable to your side. Although it requires you to find an authoritative book that takes a position at odds with that of an expert, this may not be so difficult if you have hired an expert to help you prepare for trial.

For example, assume that the adversary's expert, an economist, testifies that he can predict with reasonable accuracy the future rate of inflation by tracking the Consumer Price Index for the last five years. You have located a book that you are told is generally regarded as authoritative that says that "anyone who says that he can predict the rate of inflation is an idiot." On cross-examination, mark the book as an exhibit, show it to the expert and ask him to authenticate it as one that experts in the field regard as "generally authoritative," and then read the quoted language into the record.

You may also use widely respected books and articles to demonstrate that the information on which the expert's opinion is based is less than complete. For example, assume that an expert testifies that an important factor in his conclusion is "the results of test A," which he conducted. You have an authoritative treatise which states that "the best test is test B." By reading this conflicting passage into the record, you may lead the judge or jury to question the expert's methodology and by extension his opinion.

You can use formal discovery to prepare for the testimony of your adversary's expert witness. Federal Rule of Civil Procedure 26 (b)(4) is typical of rules that provide for pre-trial discovery of the identity of your adversary's expert and the expert's qualifications and opinions. Under this rule, you can send a written interrogatory (question) to your adversary asking if your adversary intends to call an expert witness and, if so, the expert's name and address. In a separate interrogatory, you can also ask your adversary to summarize the expert's likely testimony. Finally, if you need additional information you can take the expert's deposition. Doing so is likely to be costly, however. (For more information on depositions and interrogatories, see Chapter 3, Starting and Investigating Your Case.)

Make a cross-examination outline. Include an outline of the evidence you expect to elicit from your adversary's expert in the Cross-Examination section of your trial notebook. This outline may be quite short. For example, you might limit it to the fee your adversary is paying for the expert's testimony and to reminders to probe for one or two weaknesses in the expert's qualifications. (See Chapter 15, Organizing a Trial Notebook.)

REFERENCES ON EXPERT WITNESSES

Federal Rules of Evidence in a Nutshell, by Michael Graham (West Publishing Co.). A review of evidence principles organized according to the Federal Rules of Evidence, with an emphasis on their practical application.

Evidentiary Foundations, by Ed Imwinkelreid (Michie Co.). This book contains numerous sample foundational transcripts, including how to qualify an expert.

McCormick on Evidence, by John Strong, ed. (West Publishing Co.). A basic treatise on evidence, frequently used by judges and attorneys.

Weinstein's Evidence Manual, Student Edition, by Jack Weinstein and Margaret Berger (Matthew Bender). Also a well-regarded work organized according to the Federal Rules of Evidence.

Expert Witnesses and the Federal Rules of Evidence, by James McElhaney, 28 Mercer Law Review 463 (1977). This article was written shortly after the Federal Rules of Evidence were enacted, and it explains the provisions concerning expert witnesses.

17

WHEN YOUR TRIAL ENDS:
JUDGMENTS AND APPEALS

After both you and your adversary rest (have finished presenting) your cases and the trial ends, the judge or jury will render a verdict—make a final decision stating who wins and who loses. If your case is tried before a jury, the verdict will be read at the close of the case. But if your trial is before a judge alone, the judge may take the case "under submission" or "under advisement." That means the judge will think the matter over for anywhere from a day or two to several months and then let you know the final decision in writing.

Even when you find out the decision in your case, that may not be the last word. This chapter looks at three things that can happen after a verdict is rendered:

• The judge can overturn the jury verdict, in some circumstances.

• The decision can be appealed and reconsidered by a higher court at the request of a party).

• If you win the trial and your adversary doesn't appeal, you still have the sometimes time-consuming task of collecting your judgment—getting your adversary to pay you the money the judge or jury awarded you.

As you know, this book's primary focus is conducting your trial. It may be helpful for you to have an idea of what can face you after trial, however, as you make certain decisions along the way. This chapter is an overview, aimed at giving you a general picture of what you may encounter at and after the close of your trial; it is not a guide on how to actually make post-trial motions or appeal your case. Where possible, we have tried to refer you to other resources for further guidance on post-trial proceedings.

"After careful deliberation, Your Honor, we'd rather not get involved."

A. HOW FINAL DECISIONS ARE MADE AT THE END OF TRIAL

In many jury trials, the jury is just instructed to decide who wins and how much money that person is entitled to; the jury doesn't state the reasons for the decision. Some juries, however, are requested to return what is called a "special verdict." This means the jury makes a statement about particular facts it has found to be true, often in response to specific questions in the jury instructions. For example, in some states, each party to a personal injury action can be found partly responsible for the injury under a theory called "comparative negligence." In such states, a jury may be asked to make a special verdict in which it decides which party was responsible for what percentage of the harm.

Remember that jury verdicts in civil trials do not have to be unanimous. In most states, only three-fourths of the jurors have to agree in order to render a verdict. This means that if a jury panel consists of 12 jurors, 9 jurors must agree in order for there to be a verdict.

At the end of a judge trial, the judge may rule from the bench and orally declare a winner. Or a judge may rule later, in a document stating who won and how much the winner was awarded. Sometimes when a judge writes a decision, it is a one-liner, called a "Judgement," "Order" or "Final Order." A sample is shown below.

Other times, judges write longer opinions, which include the legal and factual reasons for their decisions. These documents are sometimes called "Opinions" or "Findings of Fact and Conclusions of Law." A judge can also state findings (legal and factual reasons for the decision) orally, from the bench.

The final decision or judgment in a case is often written up by the court's clerk. But sometimes, especially if the judge rules from the bench at the close of trial, the judge may ask you or your adversary to write up the findings and the judgment (who wins and what the loser is ordered to pay). The process is similar to the one sometimes followed with a court order on a pre-trial motion. (See Chapter 4, Pre-Trial Hearings and Motions.)

If the judge requests that you write up the decision or findings, ask the court clerk for a sample or form from another case. Ask also for an explanation of what document you should prepare and how you should prepare it, who must get copies and any other advice about the process. For example, in some courts, a party who prepares an order is expected to send a draft (sometimes called a proposed order) to the judge and the other party. Then, if the draft correctly reflects the judge's decision and there are no objections, the judge will sign the document.

Lawyers often jump at the opportunity to write the findings at the end of a case. Even though it takes work, the writer can sometimes interpret what the judge said in a way that is favorable to her client. Because appellate courts don't hear evidence themselves, if your case is appealed to a higher court, that court will rely on these findings to determine the facts the trial judge found to be true. And once a decision becomes part of the written record of the trial court, it is likely to take on a life of its own and be difficult to change.

For all these reasons, if you are asked to draft the judge's decision or specific findings, or if you are reviewing a document drafted by your adversary, pay attention to detail. And, if possible, have

SAMPLE JUDGMENT

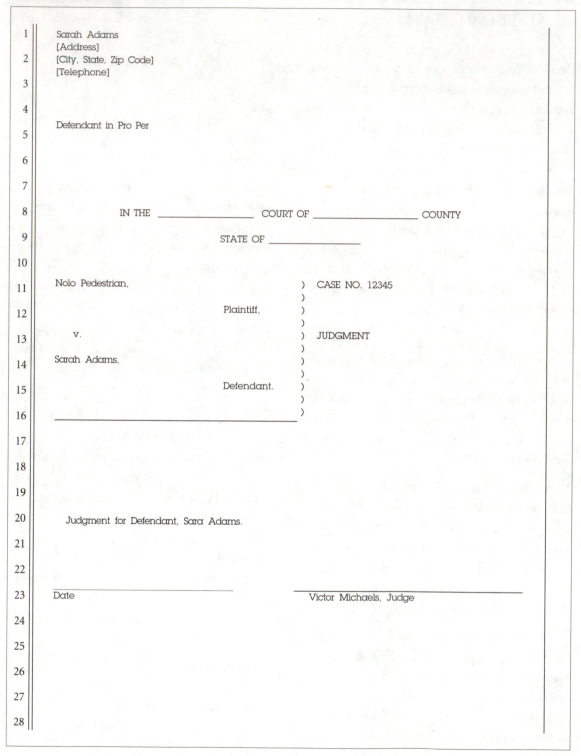

```
1    Sarah Adams
     [Address]
2    [City, State, Zip Code]
     [Telephone]
3

4
     Defendant in Pro Per
5

6

7

8              IN THE _____ COURT OF _____ COUNTY

9                         STATE OF _____

10

11   Nolo Pedestrian,              )   CASE NO. 12345
                                   )
12              Plaintiff,         )
                                   )
13        v.                       )   JUDGMENT
                                   )
14   Sarah Adams,                  )
                                   )
15              Defendant.         )
                                   )
16   _____   )

17

18

19

20   Judgment for Defendant, Sara Adams.

21

22

23   _____        _____
     Date                          Victor Michaels, Judge
24

25

26

27

28
```

your self-help law coach or someone else whose legal savvy you trust read the document to see if it is open to interpretations you have not seen.

After the judgment is signed by the judge, it will be "entered"—which means it becomes part of the final, permanent court record. Only when a judgment is entered into the court records is it considered final. Understanding this is important because it is only when a judgment is final that you are able to appeal. Also, if you want to appeal, you may have to file a Notice of Appeal within a certain number of days after the judgment is entered. (See Section C2 below).

Make sure you are notified of the judgment. To be sure that you are properly notified when the judgment is entered in your case, ask the clerk whether you will receive a Notice of Entry of Judgment. You may want to also give the clerk a stamped self-addressed envelope in order to be sure you get a copy.

B. REQUESTING A NEW TRIAL OR CHANGE IN THE VERDICT

After a judge trial, the loser, be it you or your adversary, can ask the trial court judge to modify the judgment or vacate it (withdraw it altogether and order a new trial). Because you are asking the very judge who made a decision to change it, such a request is often unsuccessful—unless it asks merely to correct a typographical or mathematical error. But if you have a good reason to be unsatisfied with the judgment, such a motion may be worth a try, if only because it is generally simpler and less expensive to prepare, file and argue than an appeal.

1. Mathematical Errors in Judgments

One request that is usually successful is to modify the judgment if a party has found a mathematical error in the computation of the judgment amount. If you review the judgment and find such an error, ask if the clerk can fix it without any formal proceedings. If not, you may have to make a motion asking the court to change the judgment to reflect the correct amount. (For reference, see Federal Rule of Civil Procedure 60(a) on correcting clerical errors in federal court.)

If you do have to bring a motion, the judge will likely make a decision without a hearing, based on your and your adversary's prepared written papers. (See Chapter 4, Pre-Trial Hearings and Motions, for more on making motions.)

2. Other Reasons to Modify or Vacate Judgments

You can also ask the court to modify or vacate its judgment if you can show that the judge made errors of law or there was serious misconduct on the part of your adversary or the judge. (See Federal Rule of Civil Procedure 59, on requesting new trials and amendment of judgments in federal court, for reference.) Although unlikely, your written request (motion) could convince the judge to reconsider a decision, especially if you persuasively explain your reasons and clearly support them with citations to relevant, binding legal authorities. (See Chapter 19, Legal Research.)

Examples of the types of errors for which a court may change a judgment are:

- The judge excluded highly important, relevant and admissible evidence—for example, keeping out the computer records that were essential to your case as hearsay when they clearly fell within the business records exception as you argued at trial. (See Chapter 13, Basic Rules of Evidence.)

- The judge allowed your adversary to introduce highly prejudicial, irrelevant evidence despite your objections.

- Your adversary engaged in serious misconduct by making one-sided contact (ex parte) with the judge during trial, which prejudiced your case.

You can also request a new trial if after the judgment is entered you discover new and extremely helpful evidence which, for some very good reason, was not available at the time of trial. Not preparing because you were on vacation is not a good reason, but finding out your adversary lied about critical evidence during discovery would be. Another good reason is if something happens after the trial that you certainly would have wanted to introduce evidence about. For example, say you sue your roofer, Monica Doherty, for using inferior quality wood when repairing your roof. Two weeks after trial, five other houses on your block, also repaired by Doherty, collapse due to the same problem of inferior quality wood. You may be able to get a new trial to introduce this new evidence.

3. Overturning or Changing Jury Decisions

Judges have the power to overturn or modify a jury's verdict, but they rarely exercise it. You may, however, try to convince the judge to overturn the jury's verdict or change the amount of damages that the jury awarded. To do this, you make a written request (motion) for something called a judgment notwithstanding the verdict, often called by the abbreviation "JNOV." (See Federal Rule of Civil Procedure 50(b), for reference.)

A motion for JNOV in effect says to the judge: No reasonable jury could reasonably have concluded what the jury in this case did. And because the jury verdict was so preposterous, you, as a judge of reason, should overturn their outrageous verdict—or at least change the ridiculously unfair amount of damages they awarded.

Here's an example of a situation where a judge might lower the amount of a jury's verdict. Assume that you are Sarah Adams, a building contractor who was sued by a pedestrian. The plaintiff alleged that you negligently struck him as he crossed the street. You defended yourself, but the plaintiff was represented by a lawyer.

The plaintiff, a fire fighter, was a community hero. Because of the injuries, he was confined to a desk job, unable to work on the front lines, and the jury clearly sympathized. Even though the jury found that you were only partly responsible for the injuries (the jury found that the plaintiff's own carelessness was a significant cause of the injuries), the jury still awarded the plaintiff a million dollars in damages.

You may be successful in arguing to the judge that the damages should be reduced because, however unfortunate his injuries are, the plaintiff is partly responsible for injuring himself.

Judges very rarely order new trials. A judge might order one if a juror admits some wrongdoing—for example, if one or more jurors say they did not follow the judge's instructions, were coerced to vote in a certain way and do not in their hearts and good consciences support the verdict or had one-sided contacts with your adversary outside of the courtroom during the trial, which prejudiced your case. Judges also order new trials in the event of a mistrial (a trial which ends before the full proceeding is completed because of some prejudicial conduct or error.)

If you decide to try making a post-trial motion to change the judgment or request a new trial, remember that it is not common to win. In all likelihood, you will have to appeal if you are not satisfied with the trial court judgment.

RESEARCHING POST-TRIAL MOTIONS

To find information at a law library (see Chapter 19, Legal Research), ask the librarian to point you to reference books on "civil practice" in your state. Look for a section on post-trial motions or in the index under the following or a similar entry:

- Motion for a New Trial

- New Trial

- Judgment—Amendments to

- Judgment—Vacating.

C. APPEALS

If you lose your trial, you may have grounds for an appeal. Appeals, however, are often complex; you may be wise to have an attorney represent you even if you successfully conducted the trial.

While explaining the appeals process in detail is far beyond the scope of this book, here is a brief overview.

1. What Appellate Courts Do

An appeal is a request to a higher court to review and overturn the decision of a lower court. If it's

appealed, your trial court verdict will be reviewed by an appeals (appellate) court. Appeals of federal trial court (district court) decisions are heard by the U.S. Court of Appeals; in state court systems, appellate courts go by various names.

If either party is dissatisfied after the first appeal, that party can appeal to the highest court in the state or federal system, sometimes known as the court of last resort. For the federal courts, this is the United States Supreme Court; most states also call their highest court the state supreme court. These courts accept only a few of the appeals submitted to them. If they don't accept your appeal, you are stuck with the decision of the lower appeals court.

Appeals courts generally resist overruling trial judges on appeal. Normally, a higher court can overturn the decision of a lower court only if the lower court made a significant error of law.

The appellate court will not conduct a new trial or look at new evidence. Instead of putting witnesses on the stand and conducting a new trial for the appellate court, you will need to present a "brief"—a written argument setting out what mistakes the trial court made and the laws that support your positions. To write a brief, you will almost certainly have to look at how other courts have decided similar legal problems and apply their reasoning to your case. (More on researching case law in Chapter 19, Legal Research.)

The appellate court will review the official record (a transcript of the testimony plus exhibits) of the trial court, focusing on the legal errors you claim were made. It's up to you and your adversary to bring important portions of the trial transcript and exhibits to the appellate court's attention. Appellate courts will not scour the record of the trial court looking for injustices or mistakes that you neglect to identify.

2. Filing a Notice of Appeal

There are strict time limits for filing appeals. You will probably have to file a paper called a "Notice of Appeal" very soon after you receive Notice of Entry of Final Judgment—often between 10 to 30 days. The Notice of Appeal notifies your adversary and the court of your intention to bring an appeal. Later, if you change your mind, you can withdraw your Notice of Appeal without penalty. But if you don't file it by the deadline, your right to appeal will likely be forever lost (waived).

You may have very little time to appeal. Even before your case is decided, find out the deadline for filing a Notice of Appeal. If you think you may possibly consider appealing, do not wait until the case is over; start work immediately. Usually a court clerk, your legal coach or a law librarian can show you the procedural rules on appeals in your court system. Also, check to be sure of when the court clerk will be sending the Notice of Entry of Judgment in case it gets delayed in the mail.

3. The Appeals Process

Appealing a case involves preparing documents and making an oral argument before an appellate court. Appellate courts have their own sets of rules that differ from the rules in trial courts. This section outlines the basic process of an appeal. For further details, consult a book on appellate procedure for your court.

a. Making and Preserving a Record

Because appellate courts do not hear evidence—they review the written record from the trial court—the trial record is all-important. The official trial record consists of:

- what is said and taken down by the court reporter during court proceedings
- exhibits that get admitted into evidence
- documents that are filed with the court.

Make a good record at trial. To make a complete record during trial, you must articulate clearly and make sure all the witnesses do as well. Also, if someone gestures or makes remarks that are not clear, clarify them "for the record."

For example, assume your witness in the faulty roof case, your neighbor Marla Kristy, testifies that her roof (repaired by Doherty Roofers, the same roofing company as the one that repaired your roof) also caved in during the heavy storms. As she is testifying, Ms. Kristy holds up a photograph of her collapsed roof (that you had previously marked as Exhibit A and asked the judge to accept into evidence). You ask, "Now, Ms. Kristy, how did you know that Doherty Roofers used inferior grade wood?" She replies, "I could see that the wood was a lighter color there [pointing to the left bottom corner of the photo where the roof fell in] than the rest of the roof." Unless you stop and say aloud, "Let the record reflect the witness is pointing to the left-bottom corner of the photograph of her house, Exhibit A," an appellate court will not necessarily know from reading the record that the witness was pointing to a photo.

b. Getting Necessary Documents

If you appeal, you will have to order a trial court transcript from the court reporter. (See Chapter 2, for more on court reporters). Transcripts are usually quite costly. But the court of appeal must have the official record from the lower court in order to review what happened at the trial court, and you must prepare and assemble that record for them. To do that, you may need to attach other documents to your appellate brief, such as:

- all or relevant parts of the trial court transcript, especially anything you refer to in your written papers

- copies of exhibits

- a copy of your Notice of Appeal (and Proof of Service of that Notice)

- a copy of the trial court's judgment.

c. Writing a Brief

Once you decide to appeal a case and file a Notice of Appeal, you will get a briefing schedule and hearing dates from the appellate court. To make sure you don't miss any deadlines, you may want to make a list of important dates, like the one shown below.

SAMPLE SCHEDULE

IMPORTANT DEADLINES

Event	Date
Judgment entered	_____
Deadline for filing Notice of Appeal	_____
Deadline for filing Appellant's Opening Brief	_____
Deadline for filing Respondent's Brief	_____
Deadline for filing Appellant's Reply Brief	_____
Oral Argument	_____

The person who brings an appeal (the "appellant" or "petitioner") usually files an opening brief, the other side (the "appellee" or "respondent") files a response, and then the appellant can file a response to that.

Appellate courts have extensive and often picky requirements for most every aspect of appellate practice; written briefs are no exception. The appellate rules often limit the number of pages, and specify the type of paper and binding, color of binding cover and size of print type. For that reason and because the law can be complex, drafting an appellate brief can be difficult even for an experienced attorney. You may have to do extensive legal research to effectively understand and make appropriate references to necessary statutes, court cases, administrative regulations and sometimes even your state or the federal constitution. (See Chapter 19, Legal Research.) It may be wise to hire a lawyer for your appeal.

RESOURCES ON APPEALS

For more information on appeals, an easy-to read inexpensive source is *Appellate Advocacy in a Nutshell*, by Alan D. Hornstein (West Publishing Co.). This book reviews the appellate process, appellate courts, and discusses the content of oral appellate arguments and written appellate briefs.

If you decide to write your own brief, ask a librarian for some references to appellate brief-writing resource books. One helpful resource is the *Handbook of Appellate Advocacy*, prepared by UCLA Moot Court Honors Program (West Publishing Co.). Though geared for law students writing briefs for hypothetical arguments (called moot court), this will give you an idea of what you must do.

d.   Making an Oral Argument

After the briefs are all in, you and your adversary may have the opportunity to appear before the appellate court to argue the appeal. It is common practice, however, for courts to decide many appeals on the papers alone. If you do appear in person you will normally have a limited amount of time—from two to five minutes in some state appellate courts, to 30 minutes in some federal courts, to make arguments about why you should be granted the appeal or your adversary denied the appeal. Because you and your adversary will have submitted your arguments in writing ahead of time, the appeals court will know what the issues are, and they may have specific questions for you or your adversary.

Watch appellate court arguments before it's your turn. If you are going to argue before an appellate court, make an effort to observe that court in action before the date of your hearing. That is one of the best ways to find out what you are facing. Also, reference books you consulted for assistance writing your appellate brief may have helpful suggestions for oral argument.

4.   Should You Appeal?

In deciding whether to appeal your case, consider:

- The monetary costs—for filing fees, transcripts, and other fees, consulting a lawyer and missing work.

- The costs in time—doing legal research, writing a brief and preparing for oral argument.

- The emotional stress on you and your family.

- Your chances of succeeding.

You may also consider your desire for justice if you feel it was unfairly denied at trial. You may benefit psychologically by taking the case as far as you can because it's important to you to get fair treatment and respect. This may be especially true, for example, in lawsuits involving unlawful discrimination or similar civil rights claims. But before you appeal for these reasons, consider that you may feel far worse if you again lose after spending more time, money and energy to appeal.

Before committing yourself to taking an appeal, carefully review the procedural rules you'll need to follow and the paperwork you'll have to prepare. Next, draft a realistic timeline, estimating how long it will take, and a budget outlining how much it will cost. Then consult your legal coach to get an assessment of your chances for success. Armed with this information, you will be much better able to make a satisfying decision.

Find an attorney who specializes in appeals. Ask the lawyer who serves as your coach about experience with appellate practice. An attorney who handles nothing but appeals may be better suited than a trial lawyer to evaluate your appeal prospects, and advise you or handle the appeal for you if you decide to proceed. Your present legal coach may be able to refer you to an appellate lawyer, or you can use the process outlined in Chapter 18, Getting Help from Attorneys: Hiring a Legal Coach, to find an appellate specialist.

5. If Your Adversary Appeals

Even if you win, remember that your adversary may appeal or may threaten to appeal. Don't party too hard quite yet, and whatever you do, don't throw out any of your files, papers or notes; you will need them if you do face an appeal.

Don't be intimidated if your adversary threatens to appeal. First off, if your adversary appeals but does not have valid grounds to bring an appeal, you may be able to request reimbursement for the attorneys' fees you incur defending yourself. Be aware that this also cuts the other way; if you file a frivolous appeal (one without validity), you may have to pay your adversary's fees. Second, an experienced attorney may cynically threaten to appeal to get you to settle for less money than the full amount of the judgment. And, third, it is common practice to file a notice of appeal to preserve the right to appeal even though no appeal may actually be filed.

If you receive a notice of appeal from your adversary, consult your legal coach, assess the pros and cons of continuing the process, and stand your ground unless there is a good reason to give in now. Remember, you won at trial, so the odds are strongly in your favor now.

D. COLLECTING AND PAYING JUDGMENTS

After the trial ends and you are notified of the court's decision, you will have to take specific actions in order to collect your judgment if you won, and to pay the judgment if you lost.

1. If You Won

Just because you win your trial, and the judge tells your adversary to pay you $50,000, doesn't mean the check will appear in your mailbox the next week. Unfortunately, enforcing or collecting a judgment (getting the dollars in your hands) can sometimes be as difficult, if not more difficult, than winning at trial. This is especially true if you won by default (your adversary did not appear in court and the judge ruled in your favor after you showed enough evidence to prove your claim).

⚠️ **Your opponent can still stall.** Appeals and post-trial motions usually have the effect of putting a judgment on hold, sometimes called "staying" the judgment. If your opponent appeals or makes a post-trial motion, you will have to wait until it is resolved to collect your judgment.

It's important to understand that, generally, neither the judge nor the court clerk will help you collect a judgment. In some cases, however, you can ask the court to intervene. If your adversary intentionally disobeys the court's order—for example, by refusing to pay a judgment even though you have evidence that he clearly has sufficient funds to pay—you can bring a motion requesting the court to compel your adversary to come to court and explain why he or she is not complying with the court's order.

If the court concludes that the person deliberately disregarded the court's order, it is likely that the judge will find such a person in contempt of court (in violation of the court order) and impose sanctions, usually a monetary fine on top of the judgment. This often happens, for example, in family matters where a parent refuses to pay alimony or child support.

ENFORCING NON-MONETARY JUDGMENTS

If the court judgment ordered the losing party to do something other than pay you money, special rules apply when you try to enforce (get the loser to comply with) the judgment. For example, a judgment may require a losing party to fix your roof, reinstate your employment, not come near you (a restraining order) or not to build the second story that will block your view. These are all examples of what lawyers call "injunctive relief" as opposed to "monetary relief." Your best bet is to consult reference books on injunctive relief in your court system.

For some basic information on injunctive relief, see *Injunctions in a Nutshell*, by John F. Dobbyn (West Publishing Co.), an inexpensive paperback which describes the different types of injunctions and the elements courts look at to grant and enforce them.

Common sense usually suggests you wait until the appeal period has ended before you push your adversary to pay the judgment. If you have still not been paid by a reasonable time after the deadline for filing a Notice of Appeal, you may begin the process of collecting your judgment.

First try writing a demand letter to your adversary. Sending a copy ("cc") to your self-help law coach and noting that at the bottom of your demand letter may provoke your adversary into responding. A sample is shown below.

SAMPLE DEMAND LETTER

[address]

[city-state]

November 16, 19__

Re: *Nolo v. Adams*, Case No. _____

Dear Ms. Adams:

As you know, the court entered a judgment against you on May 27 in the sum of $80,000. It is November 16, and I still have not received payment from you. If you do not send the full payment to me within 2 weeks, I will have no choice but to begin enforcement proceedings against you.

Sincerely,

William Nolo

William Nolo

cc: Victor Rosenberg, Esq.

As with every document you send or receive in connection with your lawsuit, save a copy, mark the date and time you sent it and keep it organized along with other important papers relating to your case. If one demand letter doesn't work, you may want to follow it up with another sent registered mail, return receipt requested.

If you do not succeed by simply asking for your judgment, you will have to take steps to enforce it. If it's a money judgment, you will want to research and use one of the powerful legal remedies available to enforce judgments, such as attaching bank accounts, garnishing wages or requesting that the sheriff (or federal marshal, in federal cases) seize your adversary's assets.

RESOURCES ON ENFORCING JUDGMENTS

Telling you how to follow through on specific enforcement proceedings in your state is beyond the scope of this book, but information may be available from:

- The sheriff's or marshal's office where your opponent lives, does business or owns property.

- Your law library. (See Chapter 19, Legal Research.) It will have continuing education and practice books for lawyers that explain the steps necessary to collect judgments in your state. (Ask a librarian or look in the index under "collection of judgments," "judgments," "enforcement of judgments" or "debt collection.")

- Your legal coach or your coach's secretary or paralegal who may be able to put advice you and your hands on specific forms needed for enforcement proceedings.

- *Collect Your Court Judgment*, by Scott, Elias and Goldoftas (Nolo Press), an easy-to-use guide designed specifically for pro pers in California.

2.   If You Lost

Even at this stage of the game, you still have some options. One, you can pay immediately and be finished with the whole matter. If you feel you did your best, had your day in court and lost after a relatively fair fight, it may be time to put the matter behind you.

Two, you can try to negotiate with your adversary. If you do not have the money to pay the judgment, for example, you might suggest that your opponent accept a lesser amount in exchange for a cashier's check payment in full now of that lesser amount. Your adversary may decide that it's more costly and time-consuming to fight with you and deal with a lengthy collections process than to accept less money now and be done with it all.

You could ask your adversary to accept a monthly payment plan, something workable within your budget. You may want to remind your adversary that he will not collect anything on the judgment if you are forced into filing for bankruptcy. An honest offer of a realistic payment plan will be appreciated much more, in the long run, than promising the full sum and not delivering.

If you and your adversary agree to settle the matter now for an amount or arrangement other than what was decided in court, be sure to get everything in writing. Your settlement agreement is in effect a new contract which, if breached, can give rise to another lawsuit for its breach.

Also, check your local rules to see if you are required to file any new agreements with the court. Since these settlements can change the terms of the judge's order (for example, less money for cash up front or a payment plan over time), they are sometimes called substituted judgments, because they substitute your agreement with the adversary for the court's judgment.

The court may order time payments. In some courts, if your adversary will not agree voluntarily to accept a payment plan from you, you have the right to go to court and ask the judge to order the other side to accept such payments.

Finally, you may not own any collectible assets; you may be what is called "judgment-proof." Generally, property that is necessary for basic living, such as food, clothing, and limited allowances for things like medical care, transportation and housing cannot be seized by creditors. It is said to be "exempt." This means your adversary cannot collect the shirt off your back to satisfy a judgment.

18

GETTING HELP FROM ATTORNEYS:

HIRING A LEGAL COACH

Even though you are determined to prepare and try your own case, consulting a lawyer along the way can be a big help. When a lawyer advises you on how to conduct your own case but does not actually represent you, the lawyer is serving as what we call a "legal coach." Instead of turning your case over to the lawyer, you pay—by the hour, usually—for limited help and advice. This arrangement can be an affordable way to get the help you need.

This chapter reviews some of the situations where a legal coach can help out and explains how to find and get the most out of your coach.

A.   WHY CONSULT A LAWYER?

Even though you are representing yourself, a legal coach can help you in several important ways.

1.   To Confirm That You Have a Good Claim or Defense

Not every wrong amounts to a valid legal claim that is worth pursuing in court. For instance, if a home appliance breaks, explodes and burns your hand, causing injuries that are painful and require a doctor's treatment, you likely have a good case against the product's manufacturer, the store where you purchased the product and possibly other defendants. If, however, the home appliance breaks after its warranty has expired and doesn't do any damage to anyone or anything, you may be inconvenienced but not have grounds to bring a lawsuit.

The process of preparing, filing and serving a complaint takes time and money. (Chapter 3, Starting and Investigating Your Case.) And if you file a frivolous lawsuit (one without valid grounds), you may be penalized by having to pay the other side's costs. For these reasons, you may want to consult a lawyer before you go to the trouble.

For example, say you want to sue a lawyer who drafted your stepmother's will because the lawyer failed to advise her to change her will to reflect her stated desire to disinherit a child born after the will was signed. Your stepmother told you, before she died, that she wanted all her money and property to go to you; because of the lawyer's bad advice, you will have to split it. You began investigating by talking to your stepmother's friends and other relatives to see if they ever heard her say what she really wanted. You assembled letters she wrote you saying that she wanted you to have everything. And you read the will. But you are not sure you understand the language in the will, what responsibilities the lawyer had to your stepmother or whether you could actually prove the lawyer did anything wrong. You may want a legal coach to help you determine whether you have a good case.

2.   To Find Out the Law That Applies in Your Case

To determine what evidence to look for and eventually present in court, you must know what substantive law applies to your case. It may be relatively easy to determine what law applies to your case, especially after you have read this whole book.

For example, say you are suing the driver of a truck who hit you because she was driving carelessly. You know from Chapter 5, What You Need to Prove at Trial, and Chapter 19, Legal Research, that the general area of the law that governs your case is called "tort law" (personal injuries), and the particular legal theory that likely governs your case is called negligence. You even know (from Chapter 5) what the standard elements of a claim for negligence are.

But it is still likely to be more difficult for you, the non-expert, than for an experienced attorney to identify applicable law.

Ask to use your legal coach's law library. Your legal coach may be able to tell you fairly easily about the laws that govern your case. If your coach doesn't know right off, a law clerk or paralegal who works with your coach may be able to do the research (at a lower rate than the lawyer) or show you what books to look in. If you need a place to do research, you may want to use your coach's library. That way you can verify that you are finding and correctly applying relevant laws.

3.   To Assist with Preparing Documents

Your legal coach may be able to help you make sure any legal document you prepare is correct, logical and persuasive. A legal coach can help you draft or respond to the initial pleadings (the complaint or answer) or proofread pleadings you have prepared. If these documents are not properly prepared, you may unintentionally waive (give up) important legal rights. For example, if you are the defendant and fail to state some types of "affirmative defenses" (reasons why you are not legally responsible for the wrongs the plaintiff alleged in the complaint) in your answer, you may not be able to raise them later at the trial. (See Chapter 3, Starting and Investigating Your Case.)

A coach won't sign or be responsible for your documents. A lawyer acting as your legal coach, not your attorney, will not sign your legal documents but simply help you prepare them. You will sign all papers you file with the court in your own name. The caption (heading) on your legal documents will state your name, address and phone number, and that you are representing yourself. (See sample pleadings in Chapter 3, Starting and Investigating Your Case.)

You may also wish to ask your coach to go over any pre-trial motions or discovery documents, such as interrogatories (written questions), which you want to send to your adversary. (See Chapter 3 for information on discovery.) Or you may want assistance responding to your adversary's motion for summary judgment. (See Chapter 4, Pre-Trial Hearings and Motions.)

Your coach may also be a big help if the judge asks you to write some legal document—for example, if she asks you to "brief" a question (write a

persuasive argument about a legal issue) or draft a court order or factual or legal findings.

Ask your coach for sample forms. If you have to prepare a pleading or other legal document, ask your coach to see a sample of a pleading she filed in a similar case so that you can see what it's supposed to look like. Once a document has been filed in court, it is almost always public record and therefore no longer confidential. You can also consult a form book. (See Chapter 19, Legal Research.) Reviewing a sample before preparing your own draft will give you a good place to start, and your coach can edit what you did instead of starting from scratch.

---

4. To File and Serve Your Legal Documents

In addition to helping you draft documents, your coach, or assistants in her office such as paralegals or legal secretaries, may be able to help you put those documents together in the right format. Legal documents often have to be written up in certain ways—sometimes even on a specific kind of paper—and filed and served according to detailed rules. (See Chapter 3, Starting and Investigating Your Case.) Your legal coach may be able to assist you a great deal by typing court documents into final form and filing and serving them on your opponent for you.

5. To Answer Questions Along the Way

Ultimately, what to say and do at trial will be your judgment call. But preparing and trying a case necessarily involves maneuvering within a complex and impersonal system. You not only need to understand legal rules, but also to plug them into a winning strategy—a strategy you'll typically have to fine-tune as your adversary reacts to your actions. It can help you a lot to run your general plans by an experienced lawyer. You may also come to particular points of confusion where some expert legal advice can save you much time and frustration. For example, you may want assistance planning a deposition (see Chapter 3, Starting and Investigating Your Case), subpoenaing documents (see Chapter 9, Direct Examination) or deciding whether to accept a settlement proposal from your opponent.

It may be especially helpful to have your coach review your outlines of what you expect to testify to and what you plan to ask witnesses on direct and cross-examination. (See Chapters 9 and 10, Direct Examination and Cross-Examination.) Your coach may spot areas where you reveal information you are better off keeping to yourself or questions that are likely to get you into trouble. For example, your proposed questions might give a hostile witness too much of a chance to expand upon testimony that might damage your case. And asking your adversary's expert witness certain questions would allow the expert to repeat harmful information.

Legal Help Lines. A fairly new type of legal service now provides answers to some legal questions by phone. Two such services are Telelawyer at 800-835-3529 or 900-370-7000 (which is charged to your phone bill) and the California Divorce Help Line at 800-359-7004.

---

6. To Be "On Call" During Trial

It may help to have a knowledgeable attorney who is familiar with your case available for last-minute consulting in case something happens at trial that throws you for a loop. If your coach agrees to be available by phone, you can ask the judge for a five-minute recess, even during the middle of trial if necessary, and make a quick call for advice. For example, say at trial, your adversary, Marie Driscoll, calls all the witnesses you expected her to. Then, unexpectedly, she calls Dr. Dean Duncan to the stand. Since she never told you that she was going to call the doctor as a witness, you have not had time to investigate him, conduct appropriate discovery or prepare cross-examination. A quick phone call to your coach may calm you down and give you some options. Your coach may remind you that Ms. Driscoll violated court rules by failing to mention, during the pre-trial conference, that she planned to call Dr. Duncan. (Federal Rule of Civil Procedure 16 (c)(5) and similar state court rules.)

Your coach may recommend that you go back into the courtroom and request that the judge either refuse to allow Dr. Duncan to testify altogether, or grant a continuance and have the doctor testify later so that you have time to prepare a cross-examination. Your request would be based on Ms. Driscoll's failure to reveal her intention to call the doctor at your pre-trial conference. Your coach may also tell you if the judge allows Dr. Duncan to testify despite the surprise, you should state your objections clearly for the record to preserve your right to appeal in case his testimony seriously damages your case.

7. To Take Over If Things Get Out of Control

You may know right now that there is no way you can afford to hire a lawyer and that you will try your whole case from start to finish no matter what. But, although you want to save as much as possible on legal fees by handling the case yourself, don't rule out hiring a lawyer to take over if you really need help and can afford it. If you have consulted a legal coach from time to time in preparing for trial, that lawyer may be in a good position to step in for you if feel you are unable to continue representing yourself.

8. To Handle an Appeal

Even if you represent yourself at the trial, you may want to hire an attorney if you or your adversary appeals the case. Appeals can be complicated, and you want to be sure that the legal principles you rely on and the procedures you follow are correct. (See Chapter 17, When Your Trial Ends: Judgments and Appeals.)

B. WILL LAWYERS AGREE TO BE COACHES?

Some will and others won't. Lots of lawyers agree that the legal system has become overly costly and complicated, and they are opening up to new approaches. They understand and are sympathetic to the fact that the average person can no longer afford to pay for full service representation in many lawsuits, especially since lawyers' fees can run upwards of $25,000 in even fairly uncomplicated trials.

Many lawyers also need work. Some may view legal coaching as a good way to develop future business. By providing helpful consultations on cases that are routine or involve small dollar amounts, a lawyer can generate referrals for full-service representation on bigger, more complex matters that you (or your friends or family) face in the future. Some lawyers may even view helping pro pers as combining the concept of pro bono work (free services provided for the public good or public assistance) with earning a modest fee.

But many lawyers won't go for the legal coach arrangement. Some simply don't want to get involved in what they see as the messy world of self-representation. Others will claim that their malpractice insurance won't allow them to or that they don't want to risk being legally liable if you make a mistake.

The bottom line, however, is that lawyers can and do sell advice by the hour without being responsible for every use to which their counsel is put. And with close to one million lawyers in the United States, you are likely to find more receptivity to the self-help law coach approach than you would think—especially if you help by educating a lawyer about what the relationship entails.

C. HOW TO FIND AND SELECT A QUALIFIED LEGAL COACH

Finding a good legal coach isn't impossible, but it is likely to require some searching. You want a lawyer with trial experience and familiarity with the legal issues involved in your case. You also want someone you are comfortable with—someone who understands, respects and agrees to perform the role

of legal coach. Use the techniques suggested below to select several qualified people, and then interview the possible choices before making your final selection.

1. Obtain Referrals

To develop a pool of potential legal coaches to interview, try the following sources of lawyer referrals.

a. Your Friends and Family

Many people find lawyers—especially those who handle routine matters such as small business contracts disputes or family law—by asking friends or relatives about lawyers they have been happy with. Law practice is increasingly specialized, though, so a fine attorney who handled your friend's divorce may not be able to help coach you through a lawsuit against your former employer for wrongful termination. But, since lawyers tend to know lots of other lawyers and know of their reputations, even if the lawyer you are referred to can't help, she may be able to recommend someone else who can. Tell the first lawyer the name of the friend who referred you, that your friend felt the lawyer did a superb job and that you would appreciate a referral to a lawyer who specializes in your type of case.

b. Small Businesses

Business people almost always know and work with lawyers. And, a small business person savvy enough to run a good business is likely to work with a trustworthy lawyer. So one good strategy for finding a legal coach is simply to call a company whose work relates to the type of problem you have or a local business with similar operations to your own (if you are a business person), and ask for the names of the lawyers they use.

c.   Legal and Other Community Organizations

Try writing or calling a local legal aid center (non-profit law office that usually handles cases for lower income people), the local chapter of a national legal organization such as the ACLU, or a community organization focusing on the issues in your case, like a tenants' rights group (for landlord-tenant disputes) or a women's organization (for sex discrimination cases). Ask to speak with an attorney or paralegal and ask for a referral. Explain that you intend to represent yourself but that you need assistance from a lawyer.

People who work in these organizations may know of lawyers in the community who have good reputations. And chances are that lawyers who are involved in or supportive of such organizations will be sympathetic to your situation.

You may qualify for free legal help. Some organizations represent clients who either meet certain financial hardship requirements or whose cases focus on large policy issues. If either is your situation, you may be able to get direct representation, free of charge. (Chapter 1, Going It Alone, Section B, discusses sources of free legal help.)

d.   Paralegals

Independent paralegals, non-lawyers who help people complete and file court papers but do not give legal advice, frequently refer clients to lawyers and get feedback on the lawyers' work. They are typically listed in the Yellow Pages under "Paralegals" or "Typing Services." You can also call the National Association of Independent Paralegals at 800-542-0034 for lawyer referrals.

e.   Bar Association Referral Services

Many local bar associations have lawyer referral services. For a few dollars or sometimes without charge, you will be referred to a lawyer, who will give you an initial consultation for a reduced fee or free of charge. Unfortunately, bar associations usually provide minimal screening for lawyers they list. In many areas, any local lawyer who has joined the association (paid the required dues) will be listed.

Despite the obvious weakness of an uncritical referral system, it can be a starting point. And you can check the names you get with referrals from friends, family and local businesses, look up the referred lawyers' qualifications in a legal directory such as the *Martindale-Hubbell Law Directory* (discussed below), or phone a legal organization to see if an attorney or paralegal can confirm the referral.

2.   Investigate Qualifications

Lawyers aren't hard to find—but you're not looking for just any lawyer. You want someone who is philosophically amenable to the legal coach role, and you want someone who has actual litigation experience, as well as work experience in areas similar to your case. Just because someone is a lawyer does not mean she has experience with your type of case or can adequately help coach you to try your case in court. Beginning lawyers and even law students may be able to research the law, but many

FINDING A LAWYER: AN EXAMPLE

You are a homeowner who bought a house from Colleen Larky, who told you that the roof was in very good condition. You have just discovered that she lied. The roof, patched in several hard-to-see places, must be replaced before the winter. And your neighbor, Craig Jamner, just told you that he is planning to build a guest house on part of your garden near his house, which he claims belongs to him. Craig said that he had allowed Colleen to plant rosebushes there while he wasn't using the land, but that she knew he would eventually want it back. You want a lawyer to tell you whether you would have a good lawsuit against Colleen for misrepresenting these important facts, and to serve as a legal coach to help you prepare and try the case if you decide to.

To find some initial referrals, you ask friends and family. All you come up with is that your uncle Pat was very happy with a lawyer who recently wrote his will. You call the lawyer and say you were referred by Pat. You explain (briefly) what your case involves and that you understand that this area is not the lawyer's specialty. And you politely ask for the name of one or more good lawyers in your community who regularly handle property disputes. You get two names.

Then, you phone several businesses in your area: a title insurance company, a real estate brokerage firm and a lumber yard, and ask who they use. The title insurance company says "None of your business," but the other two supply you with names of lawyers they recommend.

Then you look in *Martindale-Hubbell*, a nationwide directory of lawyers, under your city's listing. You find one attorney who has written an article on property law and belongs to the local real estate lawyers' groups, and two more who are part of the real estate group.

One lawyer on your list was referred by two of your sources. It is sensible to start your interviews with that lawyer.

of them have no more experience trying a case in court than you do. Even among very experienced attorneys, many rarely handle trials. Some, such as those who advise on tax and other business matters, may never have set foot in a courtroom even after practicing law for decades.

Law is rapidly becoming a field dominated by specialists. Wrongful job terminations, medical malpractice and sexual harassment are just a few of the areas that usually require a specialist. Sometimes you can tell if an attorney has special expertise in a particular substantive area of law by checking the attorney's professional background, the associations to which he belongs or the articles he has written. To find out such information, consult a set of reference volumes called the *Martindale-Hubbell Law Directory*, which is available in most law libraries. It lists law firms by state and city. Each firm lists and gives a brief biological sketch of its lawyers.

In addition, you can call ahead and ask for an attorney's professional resume (curriculum vitae or "cv") and articles the attorney has written, if any. The law firm may also have a brochure describing its practice. Many lawyers will give you names of clients—after, of course, getting permission from those clients—so that you can talk to people who have used the lawyer's services. Naturally, you'll get the names of satisfied customers. But you can still learn a lot by asking them about how the attorney handled their cases.

Perhaps the most important qualities you should look for are matters of personality—those you can find out only by interviewing someone yourself. A lawyer who is patient and caring may be more helpful to you than the most experienced trial lawyer in the country.

3. Interview Prospective Legal Coaches

When you've narrowed your list to a few possibilities, call the recommended lawyers' offices. Briefly explain the facts of your case, say why you think it is a good case and state your reasons for representing yourself. If the lawyer isn't open to coaching or doesn't handle your type of case, you needn't waste your time even scheduling an appointment.

If after your interview you find the lawyer to be a promising candidate, you will probably want to discuss further what exactly you expect of the coach relationship and assure the lawyer that you are sincere and hard-working.

Don't expect something for nothing. When calling for an appointment, be sure to ask how much the initial interview will cost. Nothing starts a relationship off worse than being slapped with a bill you did not expect. Many lawyers do give initial consultations for free or for minimal fees. But don't expect this. Since you are asking for an unconventional relationship, one where you will be paying for isolated services rather than full representation, the lawyer is not likely to do as much work (or earn as big a fee) in your case. It may be fair to have you pay for all consultations, even the first interview.

a. Ask About Fees

You'll want to ask about cost—from the initial interview forward. It obviously defeats your purpose if you have to spend more to consult a legal coach than to hire a lawyer to handle your entire case.

Typically, lawyers use hourly, fixed or contingency fee arrangements. Most likely, someone serving as your legal coach will charge you by the hour.

Hourly rates for lawyers who do personal legal services work typically run from $100 to $250 per hour. Certain experts and big firm lawyers charge even more. It is important to find out exactly how the lawyer will calculate the bill. For example, some lawyers who charge by the hour bill in minimum increments of 15 minutes (quarter hour), and others bill in increments of six minutes (tenth of an hour). That means that a five-minute phone conversation, for which you are billed the minimum amount, could cost you different amounts, depending on how the lawyer figures the bill.

Although getting good value for your money is key, this doesn't mean always looking for the lowest hourly fee. You can often benefit by hiring a more experienced attorney, even if her hourly rates are high, since she may take less time to review and advise you on particulars of your case.

Many lawyers routinely ask clients to pay a "retainer"—a deposit or advance fee—which is kept in a trust account and used as services are provided. Your legal coach may ask for a retainer in order to see that you are serious and have the money to pay. However, you shouldn't be expected to come up with a large amount of money, since you do not plan on running up high legal bills. A fee of more than $500 is excessive, especially before you know whether the legal coach relationship is really working out.

Choose a coach you are comfortable with. Offering piecemeal (sometimes called "unbundled") legal services as a self-help legal coach is a fairly new approach for lawyers. It may not be clear from the first consultation how much you can do on your own and how much help you will need as your case proceeds. You and the lawyer you choose may have to decide together what the fairest approach is for you to pay for the lawyer's services. For this reason and many of the others stated above, be sure to choose a lawyer whom you feel comfortable enough with to frankly discuss fee arrangements and other thorny issues.

OTHER KINDS OF FEE ARRANGEMENTS

Contingency Fees. When representing people in a personal injury cases, lawyers often take a percentage of the final judgment—often one-third, but varying depending on factors such as whether a case settles before trial—as their fees. Since you will try your own case, you will probably not use a contingency fee arrangement. If your coach suggests one, do not agree to give too high a percentage, since you will really be doing all the work.

Fixed Fees. A fixed fee is a set fee for a particular project. For example, a lawyer may charge $500 to write your will. It is unlikely that an attorney will suggest a fixed fee to coach you through your whole case, because the lawyer will have little idea of the amount of work involved. But the lawyer may suggest fixed fees for particular services along the way. For example, you may find a lawyer willing to charge you no more than a specific sum of money to review and edit your complaint or help you respond to your opponent's interrogatories.

b.   Ask About Accessibility

The self-help legal coach arrangement likely won't work for you unless the lawyer promptly answers your questions by returning phone calls and responding to letters. Because this is something many busy lawyers are notoriously weak at, it may be helpful at the outset to sketch a time frame, noting when your case was filed and the likely trial date (if you know it). That way, you and the lawyer can assess with more accuracy the kind of time your case will need, and the lawyer can determine whether or not she has enough time to devote to coaching you.

If you talk to other clients, among your first questions should be whether the lawyer returns phone calls promptly and is generally easy to reach.

Ask when and how to contact the lawyer. The lawyer you choose as a legal coach is probably busy with many other cases. You are likely to have a much more effective working relationship and save yourself time and aggravation if you are sensitive to the lawyer's time constraints. For instance, some attorneys may find it helpful if, as much as possible, you call before 9 a.m. or after 5 p.m. when they are not likely to be in the middle of other cases.

c.   Say What You Want

Let the attorney know that you intend to work hard to put together your case, but that you want help to keep you on the right track. Be as specific as you can. Explain, for instance, that you want the attorney's help with locating the law that governs your case, consulting with you as to your trial plans and strategies and, if possible, being available by phone or fax during your trial in case you need help pulling yourself out of a legal hole.

You may even show the lawyer this book and particularly this chapter, or at least let the lawyer know you have a book to consult for guidance.

4. Put Your Agreement in Writing

The lawyer may reasonably request that you sign an agreement that makes it clear that the lawyer is merely advising you, that you are making your own decisions and are responsible for the results in the case. It may also be to your benefit to have an agreement so that the terms don't change in the middle of the relationship. And in some states, certain fee agreements are required by law to be in writing. For example, California requires a written agreement whenever a lawyer and client expect legal fees to exceed $1,000, or if the client agrees to a contingency fee.

A sample agreement, which you and your legal coach may adapt to your own circumstances, is shown below.

> **Pay your bills on time.** However your legal coach charges, be sure to pay your bills on time. You will likely get much more prompt and polite service in return if you do.

D. KEEPING LAWYER BILLS DOWN

A legal coach relationship with a competent, supportive lawyer will likely be well worth the expense. But there are certain approaches you can use to keep the bills down and get the most for your money.

1. Prepare Before You Talk to Your Coach

Prepare for all sessions, including the initial interview and phone calls, by sending or bringing the attorney copies of all key background documents, such as the contract if you have a contract dispute. Preparation will make you speak more concisely— and remember, time really is money when you're paying by the hour. Preparation will also help ensure that you don't forget to mention important details.

2. List Your Questions Before You Meet

Whenever possible, put your questions in writing and mail, fax or deliver them to your coach before meetings, even if they are phone meetings. That way the lawyer can find answers if he doesn't know them off the top of his head without having to call you back and charge for a separate phone conference. This also helps focus the meeting so there is less of a chance of digressing into (and having to pay to discuss) unrelated topics.

3. Consolidate Your Questions

Because hourly charges are divided up into parts of an hour, you may be charged for more time than you actually spend. For example, if your legal coach bills in 15-minute intervals and you only talk for five minutes, you may still be charged for the whole 15. If that is your coach's practice, it pays

SAMPLE LEGAL COACH AGREEMENT

LEGAL COACH AGREEMENT

William Nolo, a pro per litigant ("Nolo"), and Anna Turney, an attorney in the state of

_____ ("Lawyer"), agree as follows:

Lawyer will serve as Nolo's legal coach to advise Nolo on the negligence action he has filed against Sarah Adams.

1. Nolo is representing himself in the Nolo v. Adams case. Lawyer is not representing Nolo, but merely advising Nolo on an as-needed basis if and when Nolo seeks Lawyer's advice.

2. Nolo takes all responsibility for decisions made in litigating the case and for all results that stem from the case.

3. Lawyer will keep all communications made by Nolo to Lawyer in connection with this case confidential.

4. Nolo will pay for Lawyer's advice at the rate of $_____ per hour. This advice may include but is not limited to matters such as helping Nolo research the legal issues involved in his case, reviewing pleadings that Nolo has prepared or received in connection with the case and assisting Nolo in developing and implementing a litigation strategy.

5. Nolo may also arrange, through Lawyer, for assistance from Lawyer's office personnel, such as a paralegal at the rates of $ ___ per hour and a legal secretary at the rate of $ ___ per hour.

6. Nolo will pay Lawyer a $300 retainer. Lawyer will bill Nolo monthly.

7. Nolo will have reasonable access to Lawyer's office services, as needed, including the conference room and library.

William Nolo
William Nolo

March 24, 19XX
Date

Anna Turney
Anna Turney

March 24, 19xx
Date

to gather your questions and ask them all at once, rather than calling every time you have a question.

4.   Beware of Other Costs

Whatever the formal fee arrangement, always verify if there will be any incidental fees, such as photocopy and fax charges. If there are, you may be able to find ways to cut them down. For example, if you learn the law office charges $3 or more for each page it faxes, and you live nearby, pick up a document instead of having it faxed to you. And request generally that unless papers are urgent, your legal coach use regular mail, not fax. Make extra copies of documents so the lawyer doesn't have to do it. Often lawyers charge more than the local copy shop since they charge for the time it takes to make copies.

Carefully review lawyer bills. Read your bill. Lawyers make mistakes, and your charges may be wrong. For example, a ".1" (six minutes) may be transposed into a "1." (one hour) when the data is entered into the billing system. That's $200 instead of $20 if your lawyer charges $200 per hour.

5.   Try to Answer Questions on Your Own

Remember that you are hiring a legal coach, not a full-service lawyer. That means doing as much as you can by yourself and only turning to the coach when you are really stuck. By reading this book all the way through and consulting a nearby law library, you can answer many of your questions on your own. And those you cannot answer completely you can often narrow down.

19

LEGAL RESEARCH

In law, as in life, there is always more information to be had, and for a variety of reasons you may want to do some legal research into matters not covered by this book. But if your case is relatively straightforward, you may not need to conduct extensive legal research in order to effectively represent yourself in trial.

The purpose of this chapter is to introduce you to some basic legal research tools and give you practical suggestions for getting information from commonly available resources. The chapter is not a comprehensive guide to conducting legal research. If you want a thorough explanation of the legal system, legal authorities and how to use a law library, consult two excellent Nolo Press resources, both of which are relatively inexpensive and also usually available in most law libraries:

- *Legal Research: How to Find and Understand the Law,* by Stephen Elias and Susan Levinkind, an easy-to-read book that provides step-by-step instruction on how to find legal information.

- *Legal Research Made Easy,* a 2½ hour video tape, hosted by Robert Berring, an experienced law librarian and legal research professor, that clearly explains what resources to use and how to go about efficiently researching a legal problem.

A. WHAT YOU MAY WANT TO RESEARCH

Normally, the information you may want to research in order to try your own case in court will fall into three areas:

- substantive law, governing your and your opponent's legal claims and defenses.

- rules of evidence, and

- rules of civil procedure.

1. The Substantive Law of Your Case

"Substantive" law is the term for rules that govern the heart of your dispute, like particular laws about a contract or tort (civil wrong or personal injury) lawsuit. The term "substantive" law is used in contrast to "procedural" law, which deals with the rules that govern how your case moves through the court system and is tried.

Substantive law can be classified into certain discrete subjects—for example, contracts, torts, wills, property, tax, immigration and bankruptcy. But keep in mind that your case may involve more than one subject.

For example, if you are involved in a divorce and child custody battle, naturally you'll need to deal with "family laws" covering divorce, alimony, child custody, child support and division of marital property. But in dividing your property, you may also deal with federal and state tax laws and state property laws.

The same is true if your case deals with a car accident. You claim that your adversary was negligent in that he made an unsafe lane change and sideswiped your car. To find laws relating to what lane a car must be in when making a turn, you will look at your state's traffic laws (perhaps grouped together in a section, title, chapter or code under "Vehicle" or "Traffic"). Laws relating to the standard elements of a negligence claim may be in state laws under a general "Civil" category, perhaps grouped under the heading "negligence" or "torts"and supplemented by the decisions of judges (case law).

State or Federal Law. Both state and the federal governments enact laws that may affect your case. Some areas of law are unique to the federal system, such as bankruptcy, copyright and patent. Other areas of law are typically state court subjects—for example torts (personal injury), contracts, family law (divorce, child custody, guardianship) and wills. Your case may involve both federal and state laws. For instance, divorce cases may involve state family law and federal income tax law, and claims of civil rights violations may be made under federal and state civil rights laws.

a.   Elements of the Claims in Your Case

Probably your most important substantive research task is to learn the legal elements of each of the legal claims (sometimes called "causes of action") or defenses in your case. (See Chapter 5, What You Need to Prove at Trial: The Plaintiff's Perspective, and Chapter 6, What You Need to Prove at Trial: The Defendant's Perspective.) You need to know these elements to prepare for trial, present relevant evidence during trial and make persuasive legal arguments to the judge or jury at the close of trial.

One good place to look for lists of elements is standard jury instructions (instructions the judge reads to the jury at the close of trial). These instructions identify the elements that a jury has to find in order for a plaintiff to win a particular legal claim. Judges use the same elements in deciding cases without a jury.

 RESOURCES ON JURY INSTRUCTIONS

Many states have books that set out complete jury instructions for common kinds of lawsuits. For example, federal jury instructions are published in a book called *Modern Federal Jury Instructions,* by Leonard Sand (Matthew Bender). Michigan has a book called *Michigan Standard Jury Instructions,* Civil Committee on Standard Jury Instruction (Institute of Continuing Legal Education). New York has *New York Pattern Jury Instructions, Civil*, Committee on Pattern Jury Instructions (Lawyers Co-Operative Publishing Co.). And in California, there's the *California Jury Instructions, Civil: Book of Approved Jury Instructions (BAJI)*, Committee on Standard Jury Instructions (West Publishing Co.). Ask a law librarian where to find the published jury instructions in your state.

b.   Understanding the Elements

Once you've found the elements of each of the claims in your case, you've got to figure out what they mean. So you may need to do some more research to find out more about particular elements of your legal claim. For example, assume that you bring a breach of contract action against a painter who agreed to paint your roof, then stopped midway through the job. You want to recover both the deposit you gave the painter originally and the difference between the amount of money you were going to pay this painter and the sum you ended up having to pay another painter to complete the job. You know (from Chapter 5) that a claim for breach of contract usually consists of four elements:

1. **Formation:** You and the defendant had a legally binding contract.

2. **Performance:** You performed as required under the contract.

3. **Breach:** The defendant failed to perform as required under the contract.

4. **Damages:** The defendant's failure to perform caused you economic loss.

But you may need to do some legal research to find out what the abstract legal jargon of the elements means in English. For instance, what constitutes a legally binding contract, the first element? What if you had only spoken with the painter, and neither of you had anything in writing? When he walked off the job, he was angry and said something like "I'm outta here. Just try to sue me; we don't even have a contract. You'll never be able to prove anything."

One question you may ask is, "Can an oral contract be valid?" For the answer, you may first try asking a reliable resource person, such as your legal coach, or you can go to a law library and look up the answer. Ask a law librarian to direct you to some resources about oral contracts. You may consult a treatise (reference book) about contract law, such as *Contracts Law in a Nutshell*, by Gordon Schaber and Claude Rohwer (2d Ed., West Publishing Co.), or a legal encyclopedia. (See Section B, below, for more on reference books.) You will find that you do not need a written contract or other document to form a valid contract for painting a house; an oral contract is sufficient as long as it can be proved. (Of course, you may have more trouble proving the terms of an oral contract than a written contract.)

2. Evidence Rules

After you understand the substantive law affecting your case, you will want to be sure you are up to speed on evidence rules. These rules govern how you and your adversary present your own testimony and that of witnesses, the exhibits you and your adversary refer to and what you both attempt to introduce into evidence.

Chapter 13, Basic Rules of Evidence, explains the most frequently encountered rules of evidence and refers to particular Federal Rules of Evidence. The Federal Rules are good starting places for research because they have been adopted or used as a guideline in over half the states. But you may want to read a particular rule of evidence in your state or find out how courts in your state have interpreted some aspect of a particular rule of evidence. Ask a law librarian to show you where to find the evidence rules for your state, or where the library keeps the Federal Rules of Evidence if your case is in federal court.

3. Procedural Rules

Procedural rules govern the process of conducting litigation before, during and after trial. Rules of civil procedure control such things as how many days you have to answer your adversary's complaint, the deadline for requesting a jury trial, how many interrogatories you can ask the other side during discovery and dozens more details of litigation.

Procedural rules for civil cases may be grouped together in a particular chapter, title or section of general state laws under the heading called "Civil Procedure." Some states have conveniently separated books of rules called "codes." In those, you will find a separate "code of civil procedure." In other states, you will likely have to use the general index to the statutes to find the rules you need. In the federal court system, they are in the Federal Rules of Civil Procedure. Before you begin looking around, you may want to ask a law librarian how to find the rules of civil procedure that apply to your case.

Local court rules also affect procedure, and they can be critical to effectively trying your case. Local rules can govern many details—for instance, how many copies of legal documents you must submit or the type of paper you must use. These sound like picky little details, and they are. But they are details that you must follow. Even different counties within the same state can have different rules—for example, one area's local rules may allow ten days to reply to a motion, another's two weeks. So as early on as possible in the process, go to the court clerk or law clerk where your case is pending (or the courthouse law library), and ask for a copy of all local rules of court.

B. SOURCES OF INFORMATION

Many people faced with a legal research task are tempted to begin by poring over stacks of books. For the novice, this too frequently results in floundering for hours through material that doesn't relate to your case. Fortunately, there are better ways to get the information you need. One, simply enough, is to just ask someone; another is to consult a book that explains and organizes the substantive law. Finally, you may want to look up the law itself—a piece of legislation or the written decision of a court. This section discusses all these sources of information.

1. People

You may not always get a right answer or even an answer at all, but you can often get quick and helpful information by asking someone who regularly deals with legal documents. The most likely candidates for help with your case are court clerks, law librarians and your legal coach.

a. Court Clerks

Clerks at the court where your case is pending can sometimes be very helpful, especially when it comes to procedural details. For example, court clerks can help you greatly by locating for you or telling you where to obtain copies of documents such as:

- local court rules

- state or federal court rules

- legal forms (pleadings, motions or court orders), or

- jury instructions.

You may, however, encounter resistance or even outright hostility from court clerks, some of whom view pro pers as people who will waste their and the court's time. For example, a clerk may refuse to answer your questions, saying something like, "I'm not allowed to give legal advice." But asking how to get forms and copies of court rules is not seeking legal advice. Being polite and expressing how much you appreciate the help may make the difference between getting assistance from clerks and not. You have nothing to lose by asking.

b. Law Librarians

All sorts of legal information, including legal forms, reference books explaining particular areas of law, rules of evidence and procedure, court cases, statutes and more are available at law libraries. Law librarians, who usually have extensive legal training, can be most helpful in pointing you to these and other resources.

Do not ask or expect a law librarian to do your research for you, and don't ask for legal advice. They can't and won't provide these services. But they will help you find what you need and, often, how to use the research tools you've found.

FINDING A LAW LIBRARY

In some states, finding a well-stocked law library that is open to the public is no problem; at least one library will be at a principal courthouse in every metropolitan area. But in other states, courthouse libraries are nonexistent or inadequate, and the only decent law libraries open to the public are located at a publicly funded law school. Some private law schools also open their law libraries to the public, at least for limited hours.

For simple legal research tasks, a public library can be a fine place to start. The main branch of your public library may have a small but helpful legal section where you can find your state's statutes as well as county and local ordinances. Another possibility is to ask for permission to use your legal coach's law office library.

---

c. Your Self-Help Legal Coach

Consulting a lawyer doesn't mean you have to hire the lawyer to handle the whole case for you. As discussed in Chapter 18, you can hire a lawyer to be your advisor or "coach," to help you prepare and try your case, on an as-needed basis. And one of the first and most important areas a legal coach can help you with is advising you where to locate laws, legal forms, court cases and other information that is relevant to your case.

2. Books and Other Publications About the Law

Books that summarize and explain court cases, statutes and other rules of law can be your most important legal research tools. They are a good place to start your research because they can help you get a picture of where you are going, maybe give you an answer or at least point you to a resource where you will find an answer. By streamlining your research, they can cut down on time and frustration.

⚠️ **Publications about the law are not the last word.** If you find a useful explanation in an encyclopedia, treatise or article, keep in mind that the conclusions expressed are not the law itself but the analysis of the authors, and a judge does not have to follow what they say. Also, the author may be mistaken or information in the article may be outdated. If you want to use the laws that the author cites to support your position, look them up yourself.

a. Legal Dictionaries

Law, just like any other specialized aspect of our society, has its own jargon. When you are representing yourself it is very important for you to become fluent (or at least comfortable) with a lot of new terms. You probably have already increased your legal vocabulary a great deal by reading and consulting the Glossary in this book, but a good legal dictionary will be most helpful.

Obviously, you need to look up words you don't know. But it can even pay to look up words you think you know, since they may have different connotations in a legal context. Take "discovery." To non-lawyers, a discovery is a "find," as in "Columbus discovered America." But in law, discovery is the pre-trial process of gathering information, usually from your opponent. Another example is "hearsay," an important word you need to understand. Non-lawyers typically define hearsay as unsubstantiated talk or rumors. For example, someone said, "Loretta told me there were going to be mass layoffs next month, but I don't believe her; it's just hearsay." In legal language, hearsay means, "an out-of-court statement offered in court for the truth of that statement." It's similar to the non-legal meaning, but not identical. (Chapter 13, Basic Rules of Evidence, explains the hearsay rule.)

 READABLE DICTIONARIES

Traditionally, many lawyers refer to *Black's Law Dictionary*, but several published more recently are easier to understand:

Law Dictionary, by Stephen Gifis (Barrons).

Dictionary of Legal Terms: A Simplified Guide to the Language of Law, by Stephen Gifis (Barrons).

Law Dictionary for Non-Lawyers, by Daniel Oran (West Publishing Co.).

Legal Thesaurus-Dictionary, by William Statsky (West Publishing Co.).

Dictionary of American Legal Usage, by David Melinkoff (West Publishing Co.)

Family Law Dictionary, by Stephen Elias and Robin Leonard (Nolo Press). Explains family law terms in plain English.

b. Treatises on Particular Subjects

Treatises have been written on almost every conceivable legal subject. They summarize whole areas of law, and can be one of the most useful research tools. But since the great majority are written for lawyers or law students, you may have to wade through a lot of legal jargon to get valuable information. Ask your law librarian or legal coach to recommend a treatise about the area your case involves—for example, torts or contracts.

"Nutshells," published by the West Publishing Company, are paperback treatises written in more down-to-earth language. Nutshells cover a wide range of legal subjects including trial advocacy, civil rights, community property, constitutional law, environmental law, worker's compensation and employee protection laws and lots more. To find out if there is a Nutshell for the subject you are interested in, check the first few pages in any Nutshell book for a list, in alphabetical order, of all the other Nutshell books. Also listed are West Publishing's major law textbooks and "hornbooks" (longer, usually hardbound treatises).

Only a few publishers, such as Nolo Press, gear their books especially toward non-lawyers. Nolo Press publishes books on a very wide variety of subjects including landlord-tenant law, wills, divorce, bankruptcy, tax, buying and selling property, sexual harassment and many more. Look at the back pages of any Nolo book for a list of all Nolo Press books and software.

Also, Southern Illinois University Press publishes a series of books edited by the American Civil Liberties Union (ACLU). These explain many civil rights—for example, the rights of crime victims, employees, gay people, Native Americans and women, and the right to government information.

c. Form Books

Form books are collections of model legal documents. Most include fill-in-the-blank documents, which you can copy and complete. Form books can help you enormously when you have to prepare any legal paperwork such as initial pleadings (complaint and answer) and discovery tools such as interrogatories, pre-trial motions and stipulations. With a form in front of you, you don't have to reinvent the wheel, although you'll probably have to change the model forms a bit to fit the circumstances of your case.

Form books also usually explain the procedural background for each form. They can provide helpful explanations of the laws you will have to follow and instructions for completing the forms, and they refer you to other resources should you need further information.

Some states provide their own fill-in-the-blank forms that you must use for specific purposes. These are available for small sums of money at local courts. Ask the court clerk, a law librarian or your legal coach to assist you in locating either a book of forms or court approved forms.

A list of form books can be found in *Legal Research: How to Find and Understand the Law,* by Stephen Elias and Susan Levinkind (Nolo Press).

d. Legal Encyclopedias

Legal encyclopedias, like regular encyclopedias, contain detailed explanations of various topics, organized alphabetically by topic. There is a detailed index at the end of the last volume, which you can look at to find the topic you want. Encyclopedias can give you a great deal of general background information about a particular subject and often refer you to state and federal statutes and cases. That makes them a good place to start if you just want to get a general understanding of the legal principles that govern your dispute.

![icon] **NATIONAL AND STATE-SPECIFIC ENCYCLOPEDIAS**

The two main national law encyclopedias are *American Jurisprudence* (Am. Jur.) and *Corpus Juris.* They include broadly based discussions on the laws of all 50 states. Both are now in their second series, so you'll find cites to "Am. Jur. 2d." and "C.J.S." (Corpus Juris Secundum). Many of the larger states have their own encyclopedias as well. Here are a few examples:

- *Pennsylvania Law Encyclopedia*
- *New York Jurisprudence 2d*
- *Encyclopedia of Georgia Law*
- *Florida Jurisprudence*
- *California Jurisprudence 3d .*

Check a law library to find an legal encyclopedia for your state.

e. Journals and Law Reviews

Many legal organizations publish journals (magazines) that contain articles covering current legal issues. For example, in a journal published by a state bar association, you may find a review of recent changes in your court's local rules or an analysis of a recent court opinion.

Law schools also produce journals, called "law reviews," which consist of scholarly articles written by law students, law professors and practicing at-torneys. While law reviews are notorious for their complex and confusing language, they sometimes cover timely topics and can provide leads on where to find relevant state or federal laws.

To locate relevant articles, you can use the *Index to Legal Periodicals,* the *Current Law Index,* or a computerized index called LEGALTRAC, found in many law libraries.

f. Lawyers' Practice Guides

Books written for practicing lawyers can be helpful resources for finding instructions, practical suggestions and forms for specific areas of state and federal law practice.

These publications, sometimes called continuing legal education (CLE), cover a huge variety of subjects, such as negligence, copyright, bankruptcy, mechanic's liens, tax law and many more. There are also specific guides on pre-trial, trial and post-trial tactics, such as practice guides on pre-trial motions, discovery, direct and cross-examination, opening statement, closing argument, appeals and more. They are available in many states, and some publishers gear their materials specifically toward lawyers in particular states. For example, the Practising Law Institute (PLI) gears some materials toward New York lawyers, and the Rutter Group and Continuing Education of the Bar (CEB) toward California lawyers. Check a law library near you.

3. The Law Itself

The law itself consists of constitutional provisions, statutes, court cases, ordinances and administrative regulations.

COMPUTERIZED RESEARCH

Most legal sources that you can look up in law books are also now available "on-line" on computers. But generally speaking, if you are new to legal research, it's better to research with books.

Two major systems, Lexis and Westlaw, maintain on-line databases of court cases, statutes, legal articles and a host of other resources (nationwide and even some worldwide). Users are usually charged for the amount of time spent on-line, which can get quite expensive, especially if you are not familiar with the system. There are some computerized systems that are free to users in public law libraries, such as the LEGALTRAC and INFOTRAC guides to legal periodicals. For more information on computerized research, ask a law librarian or consult *Legal Research: How to Find and Understand the Law,* by Stephen Elias and Susan Levinkind (Nolo Press).

a.   State and Federal Legislation

Legislation is rules enacted by federal and state legislatures. These rules are sometimes called statutes, acts or, simply, laws. State statutes are grouped by subject matter. Most sets of statutes take up many volumes, but they are divided into "codes," "chapters" or "titles," which are in turn divided in sections and subsections. Federal laws are published in the "United States Code."

As are some other statute books, the U.S. Code is divided into titles and sections. Each statute has a particular number, called a citation or cite. Once you've found a citation to a statute, for example, from a treatise or article, you can easily find the statute. For example, an encyclopedia mentions a statute called the Civil Rights Act of 1964 and gives the citation, 42 U.S.C.A. sections 2000 a-h. To find this statute, look in Title 42 in the United States Code Annotated (U.S.C.A.) and then find the volume of that title containing section 2000, subsections a through h.

Statute books typically include a subject index in the last volume, where you can look for references to relevant laws. When using an index, try to think of several possible headings for the subject you are looking for. To do this, review headings in a treatise or encyclopedia or ask a librarian. If you don't find anything under the first logical heading, keep searching, or look in a legal dictionary to find related words or phrases. For example, if you don't know the name or citation to the federal law that forbids racial discrimination, you might first look in the index under "Civil Rights." If that doesn't work, you might try "Discrimination" or "Racial discrimination."

Legal subjects overlap, so you may find what you need under more than one heading. For example, a law regarding an exception to the hearsay rule may be listed under "evidence," "hearsay," "hearsay rule, exceptions to" and under the specific name of the exception itself—for instance, "business records."

When you look up statutes, try to use an "annotated" version of the statute books. Annotated versions contain the actual language of an official statute, along with short summaries of the significant court cases (including their legal citation for easy reference; see below) that have discussed each statute, and references to other resource books and articles.

Once you have found a relevant statute, here are some suggestions for reading and making sense of it:

- Make sure you understand all the terms. Refer to a legal dictionary to look up words in the statute. In longer statutes, the first parts often define terms used in other parts of the law.

- Always check to see if the law is current. Laws are often revised and sometimes repealed (removed from the books). So, after you find a statute in the main section of your state's hardbound statute book, be sure to look in the paper-bound supplement or update, called a "pocket part" usually located inside the back cover of the book. Pocket parts contain the changes that have been made to a law or its wording since the publication of the hardbound volume. Some pocket parts are also annotated with references—for example, citations to recent cases discussing a statute.

b.   Local Ordinances

Cities and counties pass a wide variety of ordinances—rules which, subject to state and federal laws, have the force and effect of law. They can have a great impact on your daily life and business. Among other things, they can affect:

- parking and driving

- health and safety standards in rental properties

- new building requirements, and

- zoning (restrictions on how land can be used).

Local governments vary as to how they organize and publish their ordinances, so you may have to check with a law librarian to find what you need. Public libraries often have local ordinances, too. Sometimes you can obtain copies of local ordinances from a city office, such as a police or motor vehicles departments for traffic concerns or a planning department for zoning and building rules. If you know the specific subject of the ordinance you are looking for, you can probably get a copy by just calling the City or County Clerk's Office, or the City or County Attorney. They will usually send you a copy, free or for a small photocopying fee.

c.   Court Cases

In cases that come before appellate courts, appellate judges review the record and decisions of trial courts. They interpret the meaning of statutes, constitutional provisions and other court cases, making what's known as "common law" (judge-made law). Sometimes, appellate courts write decisions (called opinions, case law or cases), in which they summarize the facts that the trial judge or jury found to be true and set forth the appellate court judges' legal reasoning and "holding" (decision).

Appellate court cases are collected and published in hardbound volumes called "reporters," "reports" or "case reports." There are many separate reporters for different courts and geographical areas. For example, a case from the New York Court of Appeals may be published in a series of state reporters called *New York Appeals* and also in a regional reporter series called the *Northeastern Reporter,* which includes cases from several states. Federal cases are published according to the court that decided them. For example, decisions by the U.S. Courts of Appeal are collected in the *Federal Reporter.* At present in its second series, this is called the *Federal Reporter, Second Series* (F.2d).

Recent cases, not yet included in a hardbound reporter, are located in softbound supplements. And cases decided in the last few days or weeks may often only be available from the appellate court itself or a computer reporting service. If you want to look up a new case you just read about in the newspaper, for example, ask the librarian to assist you; it won't yet be in the hardbound books.

Cases, like statutes, have citations that let you look them up easily. Let's say you want to read the famous school desegregation case *Brown v. Board of Education.* Consulting an encyclopedia or legal dictionary, you learn its citation is 347 U.S. 483 (1954). The first number means the case is located in volume 347. The letters in the middle (U.S.) are the abbreviation for *United States Reports,* the case reporter series where the *Brown* case is published. The last number tells you the case begins at page 483. The names reflect the parties to the lawsuit, and the date at the end is when the United States Supreme Court decided the case.

d. State Constitutions and the U.S. Constitution

The U.S. Constitution is the supreme law of the land, which means all local, state and federal laws must comply with it. State constitutions have the same authority over state laws, but state constitutions must also comply with the U.S. Constitution. Courts decide whether or not laws comply with constitutional provisions. Courts also interpret what constitutional provisions mean, just like they interpret statutes.

The research you do is not likely to involve constitutional law. Most of what you need will be found in reference materials, statutes and court cases. Because constitutional law is often complex, if your case involves a constitutional issue—for example, if you want to challenge a law that you feel is unconstitutional—you probably should consult a lawyer for assistance.

THE NUMBERING SYSTEM FOR REPORTERS

Case reporters are published in numbered volumes. After a series accumulates years of numbered volumes, the publisher starts over with another series. So, you may find a cite to 2d or 3d series. For example, *York v. Story,* 324 F.2d 450 (1963) is at volume 324 of the Federal Reporter, second series, beginning on page 450.

In addition to the full text of the court's opinions, reporters include "headnotes," short summaries of the legal issues in a case. Headnotes are numbered in the order in which the issues are discussed in a case. They can be quite useful, both for a quick look at what a case is about and as a table of contents to help you locate issues that interest you.

Headnotes are not written by the judge who wrote the opinion, but by the editors of the reporter. They can be inaccurate and are not "law," so don't quote them to support for your position when making an argument to a judge. You must rely on the decision of the court itself.

Once court cases are published, they are usually not removed from the books even if later courts conclude that the decision is no longer correct. Thus, you always need to check that a case you rely on is still "good law," meaning that it has not been "overruled" by a later case. A series of case histories called *Shepard's Citations for Cases* reports the status of published cases. Ask a law librarian how to use *Shepard's* to verify that any case you intend to rely on is still good law. *Shepard's* can also help you find more recent cases that discuss (but don't overrule) the case you're interested in.

WHAT RULES JUDGES MUST FOLLOW

Sometimes it can be confusing to know which of the rules you may find in your research the judge will have to follow. Primary authorities (statutes, cases, administrative regulations and local rules and ordinances) can be "mandatory," which means that a court has to follow them. But they can also be just "persuasive," which means a court can consider them but does not have to follow them. For example, a state court in New York may find it helpful and convincing that a California court recently decided the same legal question now before the New York court. But the New York court does not have to follow the California court's decision.

A judge must, however, follow the decisions of higher courts in the same state. For example, a Los Angeles trial judge must follow a decision of the California Supreme Court (the highest state court in California), but a trial judge in Alabama doesn't have to.

When researching cases, it is best to find an appellate court case from your own state (or from your Circuit in the federal court system); that way the case is binding on your trial judge. But if all you can find is an out-of-state case that is nonetheless right on point and very helpful to your case, you may try to convince your judge that it's reasoning is persuasive.

Similar rules apply to statutes. Statutes are mandatory if they were enacted by the legislature in the state where your case will be tried.

e. Administrative Regulations

Administrative regulations ("regs") are enacted by federal, state and local agencies. For example, the federal Equal Employment Opportunity Commission, a state Veterans' Board, and a local school board probably all make their own rules. Administrative laws govern agencies' policies and procedures, such as how they conduct hearings and why they grant or withhold benefits.

You'll need to research agency regulations if you are presenting your case at a hearing before an administrative agency. Although the hearing may resemble a trial, in reality it is quite different. For example, most agencies do not follow the rules of evidence, and you have no right to a jury. Lawyers may be excluded, and you may not be able to subpoena witnesses or documents or even have witnesses testify. Some hearings are not open to the public.

C. RESOLVING LEGAL RESEARCH PROBLEMS

Now that you have a general sense of the types of legal research tools available to you, keep this three-step process in mind as you look for the answer to a legal question:

1. Try to find a resource person who can give you an answer or direct you to the place where you can find it.

2. Look for reference materials that explain and summarize the area of law your question involves. These may be able to guide you to the law itself.

3. When looking at the law itself, try to find pertinent statutes first. Then look for court decisions that clarify and interpret the statutes.

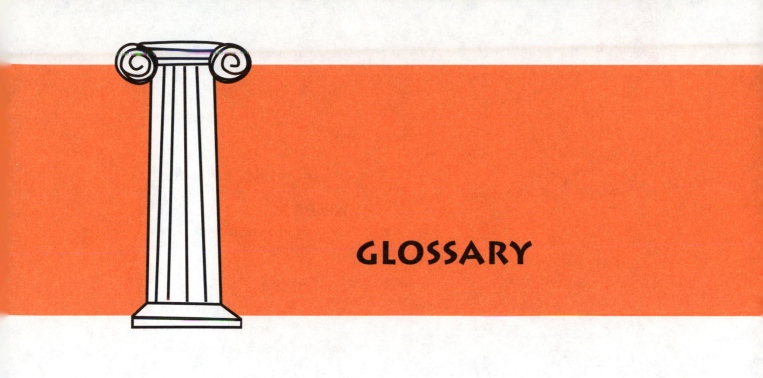

GLOSSARY

This glossary, which defines many of the terms that appear in this book, is intended for quick reference. A list of recommended legal dictionaries is in Chapter 19, Legal Research, Section B.

Action

Another word for a lawsuit. ("I began this negligence action last fall after the defendant, Ms. Adams, struck me while I was crossing the street at Elm and Main.")

Admission

An out-of-court statement by your adversary which you offer into evidence as an exception to the hearsay rule.

Affidavit

A written statement of facts made under oath. (See also, "Declaration.")

Affirmative defense

A claim made by a defendant in an answer that acts as a bar to a claim in a complaint. One common affirmative defense is that the plaintiff should not win because the "statute of limitations" (time limit within which to sue) has passed.

Allegation

A statement by a party in a pleading saying what that party's position is and what that party intends to prove.

Answer

A defendant's response to a plaintiff's complaint. It often both denies allegations made by the plaintiff and asserts affirmative defenses.

Appeal

A request to a higher court to review the legal decisions made by a lower court.

Appellant

The party who brings an appeal to an appellate court.

Appellate court

A higher court that reviews the decision of a lower court. ("The appellate court reviewed and overturned the decision of the trial court.")

Appellee

The party who responds to an appeal brought by an appellant.

Arbitration

A procedure for resolving disputes by an impartial third party (the "arbitrator") without a formal, court trial.

Argument

A persuasive presentation of the law and facts of a case or particular issue within a case to the judge or jury.

At issue memorandum

A document that states that all parties have been served, that the parties disagree (or are "at issue") over one or more points to be resolved at trial, and how much time the parties estimate will be required for trial.

Authenticate

Identify. You "authenticate" an exhibit by offering testimony that tells the judge what the exhibit is and its connection to the case.

Bailiff

A court official, classified as a peace officer and often dressed in uniform. The bailiff performs a wide variety of duties, such as maintaining order in the courtroom, escorting witnesses in and out of court and handing exhibits to witnesses who are testifying.

Battery

A legal claim of an uninvited touching. If someone hits you, you may have a claim of battery against that person.

Bench

The seat where a judge sits in the courtroom during a trial or hearing. Sometimes the word "bench" is used in place of the word "judge"—for example, someone might say she wants a "bench trial," meaning a trial by a judge without a jury.

Best evidence rule

A rule that restricts a witness from orally testifying to the contents of a document unless the document is produced in court, or it is proved to the judge that there is a valid reason why it can't be produced.

Breach

A failure or violation of a legal obligation.

Breach of contract

A legal claim that one party failed to perform as required under a valid agreement with the other party. ("The roofer breached our contract by using substandard supplies when he repaired my roof.")

Brief

A legal document written by a party to convince a judge of the correctness of the party's position on one or more issues in the case.

Burden of proof

The requirement that a party convince the judge or jury that his or her claim is correct. In most civil cases, the burden is a "preponderance of the evidence," which means something more that 50%.

Business records exception

An exception to the hearsay rule, which allows a business document to be admitted into evidence if a proper foundation is laid to show it is reliable.

Caption

A heading on all pleadings submitted to the court. It states basic information such as the parties' names, court and case number.

Case

Lawsuit. "Case" also refers to a written decision by a judge, found in books called case reporters or reporters. A party's case or "case-in-chief" also refers to the evidence that party submits in support of her position.

Cause of action

See "Legal claim."

Challenge for cause

A way to get a juror dismissed from your case in which you state a reason why the juror is objectionable.

Chambers (also called "judge's chambers")

A judge's private office, often located adjacent to the judge's courtroom.

Circumstantial evidence

Evidence that proves a fact by means of an inference. For example, from the evidence that a person was seen running away from the scene of a crime, a judge or jury may infer that the person committed the crime.

Civil

Noncriminal. Civil lawsuits are generally between two private parties; criminal actions involve government enforcement of the criminal laws.

Claim

See "Legal claim."

Claim for relief

See "Legal claim."

Clear and convincing evidence

The burden of proof in a few types of civil cases, such as cases involving fraud. "Clear and convincing" is a higher standard than "preponderance of the evidence," the standard typical in most civil cases, but not as high as "beyond a reasonable doubt," the standard in criminal cases.

Clerk's Office

The administrative office in a courthouse where legal documents are filed, stored and made available to the public.

Closing Argument (final argument)

A persuasive presentation of your side of the case to the judge or jury at the conclusion of the evidence.

Complaint

The initial pleading, setting out the plaintiff's legal claims, which starts a lawsuit. Sometimes called a petition.

Common law

Judge-made law, resulting from appellate court decisions. Common law is often contrasted with "statutory law," which is enacted by legislatures.

Compensatory damages

Money that is meant to compensate or make up for the losses the plaintiff suffered.

Consideration

Something of value which is given in exchange for a promise in order to form a legally binding contract.

Contempt of court

Behavior, in or outside of court, that obstructs court administration, violates or resists a court order or otherwise disrupts or shows disregard for the administration of justice. It is punishable by fine or imprisonment.

Contingent fee

A method of compensating a lawyer for legal services in which the lawyer receives a percentage of the money a client is awarded at the close of a trial or by a settlement.

Continuance

A delay. A party who wants the court to postpone a deadline requests a continuance.

Contract

A legally valid agreement to do or not to do something, such as an employment contract or contract of sale for real estate.

Counsel

Attorneys or lawyers (also called counselors). To counsel means to advise.

Counterclaim

A legal claim by a defendant against a plaintiff.

Court clerk

A court employee who assists a judge with the many administrative tasks of moving cases through the court system. For example, the court clerk may prepare and maintain the judge's calendar, retrieve case files from the main Clerk's Office, administer oaths to witnesses during trial and prepare orders and judgments.

Court reporter

A person who records every word that is said during official court proceedings and depositions, and sometimes prepares a written transcript of those proceedings.

Costs (also, "costs of suit" or "court costs")

Expenses of trial other than attorneys' fees, such as fees and costs for filing legal documents, witness travel, court reporters and expert witnesses. Sometimes, the party who wins a lawsuit can recover costs from the opposing party.

Cross-examination

A party's opportunity to ask questions of her adversary's witnesses, including the adversary if he or she testified on direct examination.

Damages

Money sought by a party who has suffered some legal wrong.

Declaration

A signed statement of facts personally known to the "declarant," the person signing the statement.

Default

A party's failure to do what is required—for example, a defendant's failure to respond to the complaint.

Default judgment

A court order for judgment against the defendant to pay the amount requested by the plaintiff, because the defendant failed to answer and defend against a properly filed lawsuit.

Defendant

A party who is being sued. Sometimes called a respondent.

Demurrer

Another name, used in some court systems, for a motion to dismiss a complaint for failure to state a legally valid claim.

Deponent

A person whose deposition is being taken.

Deposition

A discovery (formal pre-trial investigation) tool in which a party (or her lawyer) asks a series of oral questions of another party or witness. The questions are answered under oath and taken down by a court reporter.

Direct examination

The initial questioning of a witness by the party who called that witness.

Directed verdict

A ruling by a judge, typically at the close of the plaintiff's evidence in a jury trial, which awards judgment to the defendant.

Discovery

Formal investigation that parties conduct before trial in order to obtain information from each other about the case to prepare for settlement or trial. The primary discovery tools in most cases are depositions and interrogatories.

Docket

The term is used in two ways:

1. A formal record of all the legal documents that have been filed and court proceedings and orders in a particular case.
2. A calendar or list of all the proceedings on a court's agenda.

Elements ("legal elements")

Component parts of legal claims. To win, a plaintiff must prove all elements of a claim.

Equitable relief

A court order that a party perform an act (such as cut down a tree), rather than (or in addition to) pay money damages.

Evidence

Information presented to a judge or jury, including testimony of witnesses and documents.

Excited utterance

An out-of-court statement made about a startling event while the speaker is experiencing that event. Such statements are admissible in evidence under an exception to the hearsay rule.

Exhibit

A tangible object that a party presents to the judge or jury during trial to help establish his or her case.

Ex parte

One-sided. A contact with the judge by one party outside the presence of the other party is considered an "ex parte contact" and is generally forbidden.

Expert witness

A person who testifies based on his or her special knowledge or training.

Fast track

A system certain courts have adopted to help streamline the administration and litigation of lawsuits.

Foundation

A basis for the admission of testimony or exhibits into evidence.

Frivolous motion

A motion that is made without legally valid grounds, such as a motion that is designed to harass an opponent or delay proceedings.

Hearsay

An out-of-court statement offered in court to prove the truth of what that statement asserts.

Hostile witness ("adverse witness")

A witness so hostile to the party who called him that the party can ask the witness leading questions.

Impanel ("empanel")

The act of assembling a panel of prospective jurors for jury selection.

Impeach

Discredit. To impeach a witness' credibility is to cast doubt on that person's believability.

Inadmissible

When evidence offered by a party is ruled inadmissible by the judge, it is not allowed to become a part of the court record.

Injunction or injunctive relief

A form of equitable relief, such as an order that the defendant stay away from the plaintiff.

Interrogatories

A set of written questions submitted by one party to another party to answer under oath as part of the pre-trial investigation of a lawsuit.

Irrelevant

Not related to. Evidence that is irrelevant to the claims at issue in a lawsuit is not admissible in trial.

Judge

A public officer who presides over court hearings and trials.

Judge pro tem

A temporary or substitute judge, often a lawyer, who temporarily fills in for a regular judge. Parties can refuse to have their case heard by a judge pro tem.

Judgment

A final court ruling resolving the claims at issue in a lawsuit and determining the rights and obligations of the parties.

Judgment notwithstanding the verdict (JNOV)

A decision by the judge to overturn a jury's verdict because, as a matter of law, the jury's decision was unreasonable. This procedure is like a directed verdict but comes at the end of the case.

Jurisdiction

The scope of a court's authority. Often the term refers to the geographic area where a court has power.

Juror

A person selected to serve on a jury.

Jury

A group of people selected to apply the law, as given by the judge, to the facts jurors find true, to decide the outcome of a case.

Jury instructions

Legal rules given by the judge to the jury.

Jury selection

See "Voir dire."

Lawsuit

A legal case initiated in court.

Law clerk

An assistant to a judge, typically a recent law school graduate, who helps the judge with things like researching the issues and drafting court opinions or decisions.

Leading question

A question asked of a witness at trial that suggests the answer. It's really just a statement phrased as a question.

Legal claim (also called "claim for relief" or "cause of action")

A statement of the legal wrong (such as negligence or breach of contract) for which the plaintiff seeks legal relief.

Litigant

A party to a lawsuit.

Litigation

The process of resolving a dispute by a lawsuit in court.

Litigator

An attorney whose practice involves handling lawsuits.

Local rules

Rules adopted by specific courts or specific regions regulating case administration and litigation. Local rules sometimes modify state and federal rules, and it is critical to understand them to effectively present a case in court.

Magistrate

A court official who acts as a judge in certain (often lower level) court proceedings.

Malpractice

Professional negligence; the failure to use the type of care a professional should reasonably use in a given situation.

Marshal

A law officer who is empowered to enforce certain court rulings and orders. The federal government has U.S. Marshals, and some states have marshals, similar to sheriffs.

Mediation

An out-of-court dispute resolution procedure where parties use a neutral, third party (a mediator) to help them come to an agreement or settlement.

Memorandum of Points and Authorities

A document that cites (refers to) legal authorities such as statutes and court cases, and explains how those authorities support the position advocated by the party who wrote the memorandum.

Mistrial

A trial that the judge ends before the full proceeding has been completed because a prejudicial error or wrong has occurred.

Motion

A request to the court for an order or ruling. Some motions are made orally, others in writing. Depending on the ruling sought, a motion can be made before, during or after trial.

Motion for Summary Judgment

See "Summary Judgment."

Motion for a Continuance

See "Continuance."

Motion in limine

A request for a court order excluding irrelevant or prejudicial evidence, typically made before a jury trial.

Movant

The party making or bringing a motion.

Moving Party

See "Movant."

Negligence

A legal claim that alleges a failure to use "ordinary and reasonable care" in a given situation.

Nonsuit (sometimes called "dismissal")

The court's dismissal of a lawsuit that a plaintiff began but did not follow through with.

Notice

Notification. To give someone notice of a hearing date is to let them know when and where it will take place and other basic information they need.

Notice of Motion

A document that notifies an adversary about when and where a hearing on a motion will be held, what the reason for the motion is and what supporting documentation will be relied on in making the motion.

Objection

A party's request, made during trial, asking the court to prevent certain testimony or exhibits submitted by the other side from being admitted into evidence.

Opening Statement

A statement made by an attorney or pro per at the beginning of a trial (before the evidence is introduced) to preview the evidence and set the stage for the trial.

Order

A ruling or decision by a court. A court order can be made orally or in writing.

Overrule

Deny. When the judge overrules an objection the judge denies the objection, and the evidence objected to is allowed.

Pain and suffering

Inconvenience and discomfort resulting from injuries for which damages can be sought in a lawsuit.

Party

A person or entity who has brought a lawsuit, or one who is defending against or responding to a lawsuit.

Percipient witness

A witness who perceived the facts she testifies about. A percipient witness is an ordinary witness. (Compare an expert witness who, because of special knowledge or training, may testify about things she did not actually observe.)

Peremptory challenge

An opportunity for a party to challenge (dismiss or excuse) a potential juror during jury selection without having to give a reason. Each party gets a limited number of peremptory challenges.

Perjury

The crime of lying while under oath—while testifying during trial, in a sworn affidavit or in a deposition or interrogatories.

Personal property

All property that isn't real estate ("real property").

Petitioner

A person who brings a petition (in some court systems, another word for complaint) before the court.

Plaintiff

The person who initiates a lawsuit. Sometimes called a "petitioner."

Pleadings

Legal documents filed in court that set forth the legal claims and defenses of the parties to a lawsuit

Points and Authorities

See "Memorandum of Points and Authorities."

Prayer for relief

The concluding portion of a complaint, where the plaintiff specifies what she wants from the court.

Prejudice

Bias or discrimination.

Prejudicial error

A wrong that occurs during trial that seriously impairs a party's ability to have a fair trial.

Preponderance of the evidence

The burden of proof in most civil actions (amounting to something more that 50%).

Present sense impression

A statement made about an event while, or just after, the event occurs. Such statements are admissible in evidence under an exception to the hearsay rule.

Pre-trial conference

A meeting of the parties, before trial, in order to resolve and narrow the disputed issues, identify undisputed facts and sometimes try to settle the case. Pre-trial conferences may be conducted by a judge in court or the parties themselves out of court.

Pre-trial motion

A request to the court made before trial for an order or ruling. Typical pre-trial motions include a motion for continuance, motion to dismiss for failure to state a claim, motion for default judgment and motion for summary judgment.

Pre-trial memorandum

A document prepared before a pre-trial conference in which a party identifies undisputed and disputed facts, legal issues, witnesses expected to testify and other basic information to facilitate the pre-trial conference. Some courts require parties to meet and prepare this document together (then called a "joint pre-trial memorandum").

Pre-trial order

A document prepared after a pre-trial conference and signed by the judge. It sets out the agreed upon facts and those remaining factual and legal issues to be resolved at trial, the anticipated witness list, exhibits the parties will introduce and other decisions made during the pre-trial conference.

Privileges

Legal rules and principles that keep certain information confidential and out of court or discovery. Some common privileges include communications made to a spouse, doctor, lawyer, psychotherapist or member of the clergy.

Privileged

Confidential. Information that is confidential because of a particular legal rule, such as information revealed during a private doctor-patient examination or lawyer-client meeting, is said to be privileged.

Probative

Tending to prove or disprove some contested issue. This term is usually used to describe evidence.

Pro bono

Legal services performed pro bono are done for free or a reduced fee. (Comes from the Latin meaning "for the good.")

Pro per

Someone who represents him or herself in court without a lawyer.

Pro se

Same as "Pro per."

Procedural law

Laws or rules that govern how a case is administered and tried in court. (Contrast rules of "substantive law," which define the rights and duties of parties.)

Process server

A person who is legally authorized to serve (deliver) legal papers to a party in the case, such as a sheriff.

Proof of service

A document, often attached to a pleading, motion or brief, that states who the document was served on and how and when the service was made. A proof of service must often be filed with the court.

Protective order

A ruling by the court that limits or disallows a party's discovery requests. A party might seek a protective order, for example, if the other side's interrogatories ask for confidential, privileged information. The protective order would allow the party not to answer the objectionable questions.

Punitive damages

Damages meant to punish the person who committed a wrong, not simply to compensate the person who was wronged. Punitive damages are allowed only in certain circumstances—for example, when the defendant's conduct is shown to have been malicious.

Real property

Land or real estate (house, condo), as opposed to "personal property" such as money, cars and stereos.

Rebuttal evidence

Evidence offered to contradict evidence presented by the adversary.

Recess

A break in a hearing or trial.

Record

The official written transcript of court proceedings and depositions. When something goes "on the record," it appears in the official transcript. If some aspect of the case is "off the record," such as a brief procedural question at the judge's bench, it will not appear in the official transcript.

Recross examination

Additional cross-examination of witnesses called by an adversary on redirect examination.

Redact

To delete or cover up part of a document because it refers to inadmissible evidence.

Redirect examination

Additional direct examination of a witness by the party who called that witness. It takes place just after that witness has been cross-examined by the adversary.

Release

The abandonment of a claim against a party, often in exchange for a promise or offer by the other party.

Relevancy

A connection or applicability to the issues in the case. Relevant evidence is evidence that helps to prove or disprove some fact in connection with the case.

Remedy

The relief a party seeks in a case. Remedies for a typical tort (personal injury) claim, for example, are compensatory damages and monetary relief for pain and suffering.

Relief

The benefit, compensation or redress sought in connection with a legal claim.

Request for Admission (Request to Admit)

A discovery tool in which a party asks an adversary to admit that certain facts are true. If the adversary admits the facts or fails to respond in a timely manner, they will be deemed true for the purposes of trial.

Request for Production of Documents (Request to Produce)

A discovery tool in which a party asks an adversary to produce (deliver or make available) specific documents.

Reply

A plaintiff's answer or responsive pleading to a defendant's counterclaim.

Response (or responsive pleading)

A general term for a legal document in which a party responds to an adversary's pleading, motion or brief.

Respondent

The name for the defendant (responding party) in cases where the plaintiff is called a "petitioner." Also, the party who responds to an appeal (the appellee) is often called a respondent.

Sanctions

Penalties, often fines, imposed by a judge for improper conduct during litigation.

Service of process

The delivery of legal documents, such as initial pleadings, to an opposing party.

Settlement conference

A meeting of the parties, with or without the judge present, to discuss settlement of a lawsuit. Many courts require the parties to have at least one settlement conference, called a mandatory settlement conference (MSC), before trial.

Statutes

Laws enacted by legislatures.

Statute of frauds

A law requiring certain contracts to be in writing—for example, contracts to buy or sell real property. Most other contracts can be oral.

Statute of limitations

The legal time limit in which a lawsuit can be filed for a particular legal claim.

Stipulation

An agreement between parties. For example, you and your adversary may stipulate (agree) to the admissibility of certain testimony or an exhibit.

Strike

Delete testimony from the official court record.

Subpoena (subpena)

A court order compelling someone to appear in court.

Subpoena duces tecum

A court order compelling someone to appear in court and bring along with them certain tangible objects or documents.

Substantive law

Rules defining the rights and duties of parties (as opposed to procedural laws, which govern the litigation process).

Summary judgment

A final decision by the judge resolving the claims in a lawsuit before trial, based on affidavits and written evidence. A summary judgment is issued when the parties have no issues of fact to litigate, only legal questions.

Summons

A notice, typically served along with a complaint, informing the defendant that a lawsuit has been initiated and notifying the defendant of where and when he or she must respond.

Sustain

Uphold. When a judge sustains an objection, it is upheld, and the evidence objected to is not allowed in.

Tentative ruling

A preliminary decision of a judge in a hearing or trial, based on the papers submitted and typically issued sometime before the scheduled court proceeding.

Transcript

A written record of a court proceeding or deposition.

Testify

To give testimony under oath.

Testimony

Evidence given by a witness under oath, in court or in a deposition.

Tort

A legal claim of civil wrong (other than a breach of contract), often referred to as a personal injury.

Trial

The in-court examination and resolution of issues between litigants.

Trial notebook

A notebook or binder set up to help you organize your case.

Treatise

A legal reference book, usually covering an entire legal subject.

Venue

The geographic area in which a court has authority to hear a case.

Verdict

The jury's final decision in a lawsuit.

Voir dire

The process of questioning and selecting a jury.

Witness

A person who testifies in court.

INDEX

S

ILLUSTRATION CREDITS

CARTOONS

All cartoons in this book were drawn by Mike Twohy. The following cartoons are being reprinted with permission from the artist:

Pages 2/8, 12/17, 13/8, 16/13, © 1987 Mike Twohy, originally appearing in *The National Law Journal*.

Page 4/3, © 1987 Mike Twohy, originally appearing in *The Wall Street Journal*.

Page 7/10, © 1991 Mike Twohy, originally appearing in *The National Law Journal*.

Page 8/4, © 1979 Mike Twohy.

Page 4/25, 10/13, 14/4, © 1981 Mike Twohy, originally appearing in *Criminal Defense*.

Page 11/12, © 1991 Mike Twohy, originally appearing in *Trial Diplomacy Journal*.

Page 12/19, © 1980 Mike Twohy, originally appearing in *Saturday Review*.

Page 2/12, 13/17, 16/6 © 1981 Mike Twohy.

Page 13/3, © 1984 Mike Twohy, originally appearing in *The National Law Journal*.

Page 14/13, © 1986 *The New Yorker Magazine, Inc.*

Page 17/2, © 1981 Mike Twohy, originally appearing in *Medical Economics*.

COMPUTER DRAWN ILLUSTRATIONS

All computer drawn illustrations were done by Terri Hearsh.

CATALOG

...more books from Nolo Press

 = DISK INCLUDED

TO ORDER CALL 800-992-6656

BUSINESS & WORKPLACE

Employers Legal Handbook, Steingold .... 1st $29.95 EMPL

The Legal Guide for Starting & Running a Small Business, Steingold .... 1st $22.95 RUNS

The Legal Guide for Starting & Running a Small Business
on Disk—Windows 1st $24.95 RUNSW1

Your Rights in the Workplace, Repa .... 2nd $15.95 YRW

How to Write a Business Plan, McKeever .... 4th $21.95 SBS

Software Development: A Legal Guide, Fishman—DOS .... 1st $44.95 SFT

Marketing Without Advertising, Phillips & Rasberry .... 1st $14.00 MWAD

Sexual Harassment on the Job, Petrocelli & Repa .... 2nd $18.95 HARS

The Partnership Book, Clifford & Warner .... 4th $24.95 PART

The California Nonprofit Corporation Handbook, Mancuso .... 6th $29.95 NON

How to Form a California Nonprofit Corporation With Corporate
Records Binder and Disk, Mancuso—DOS & Macintosh .... 1st $49.95 CNP

How to Form a Nonprofit Corporation (National), Mancuso—DOS .... 2nd $39.95 NNP

How to Form Your Own California Corporation, Mancuso .... 8th $29.95 CCOR

How to Form Your Own California Corporation
With Corporate Records Binder and Disk, Mancuso—DOS .... 1st $39.95 CACI

The California Professional Corporation Handbook, Mancuso .... 5th $34.95 PROF

How to Form Your Own Florida Corporation, Mancuso—DOS .... 3rd $39.95 FLCO

How to Form Your Own New York Corporation, Mancuso .... 3rd $39.95 NYCO

How to Form Your Own Texas Corporation, Mancuso—DOS .... 4th $39.95 TCI

Taking Care of Your Corporation, Vol. 1:
Director and ShareholderMeetings Made Easy, Mancuso .... 1st $26.95 CORK

How to Start Your Own Business: Small Business Law,
Warner & Greene (audio cassette) .... 1st $14.95 TBUS

The Independent Paralegal's Handbook, Warner .... 3rd $29.95 PARA

 = DISK INCLUDED

Getting Started as an Independent Paralegal, Warner (audio cassette) .... 2nd $44.95 GSIP

Business Plans to Game Plans, Merritt Publishing .... 1st $26.95 GAME

Rightful Termination, Merritt Publishing .... 1st $29.95 RITE

Workers' Comp for Employers, Merritt Publishing .... 2nd $29.95 CNTRL

MONEY MATTERS

Money Troubles: Legal Strategies to Cope With Your Debts, Leonard .... 3rd $18.95 MT

How to File for Bankruptcy, Elias, Renauer & Leonard .... 5th $25.95 HFB

Stand Up to the IRS, Daily .... 2nd $21.95 SIRS

Simple Contracts for Personal Use, Elias & Stewart .... 2nd $16.95 CONT

Nolo's Law Form Kit: Power of Attorney, Clifford, Randolph & Goldoftas .... 1st $14.95 KPA

Nolo's Law Form Kit: Personal Bankruptcy, Elias, Renauer, Leonard & Goldoftas ... 1st $14.95 KBNK

Nolo's Law Form Kit: Rebuild Your Credit, Leonard & Goldoftas .... 1st $14.95 KCRD

Nolo's Law Form Kit: Loan Agreements, Stewart & Goldoftas .... 1st $14.95 KLOAN

Nolo's Law Form Kit: Buy & Sell Contracts, Elias, Stewart & Goldoftas .... 1st $9.95 KCONT

GOING TO COURT

Represent Yourself in Court, Bergman & Berman-Barrett .... 1st $29.95 RYC

Everybody's Guide to Municipal Court (California), Duncan .... 1st $29.95 MUNI

Everybody's Guide to Small Claims Court (National), Warner .... 5th $18.95 NSCC

Everybody's Guide to Small Claims Court (California), Warner .... 11th $18.95 CSCC

Collect Your Court Judgment (California), Scott, Elias & Goldoftas .... 2nd $19.95 JUDG

Fight Your Ticket (California), Brown .... 5th $18.95 FYT

How to Change Your Name (California), Loeb & Brown .... 6th $24.95 NAME

The Criminal Records Book (California), Siegel .... 3rd $19.95 CRIM

Winning in Small Claims Court, Warner & Greene (audio cassette) .... 1st $14.95 TWIN

TO ORDER CALL 800-992-6656

CONSUMER

Title	Edition	Price	Code
How to Win Your Personal Injury Claim, Matthews	1st	$24.95	PICL
Nolo's Pocket Guide to California Law, Guerin & Nolo Press Editors	2nd	$10.95	CLAW
Nolo's Pocket Guide to California Law on Disk	Windows	$24.95	CLWIN
	Macintosh	$24.95	CLM
Nolo's Law Form Kit: Hiring Child Care & Household Help, Repa & Goldoftas	1st	$14.95	KCHLD
Nolo's Pocket Guide to Consumer Rights, Kaufman	2nd	$12.95	CAG
The Over 50 Insurance Survival Guide, Merritt Publishing	1st	$16.95	OVER50
What Do You Mean It's Not Covered?, Merritt Publishing	1st	$19.95	COVER
Glossary of Insurance Terms, Merritt Publishing	5th	$14.95	GLINT

FAMILY MATTERS

Title	Edition	Price	Code
The Living Together Kit, Ihara & Warner	7th	$24.95	LTK
A Legal Guide for Lesbian and Gay Couples, Curry & Clifford	8th	$24.95	LG
Divorce & Money, Woodhouse & Collins with Blakeman	2nd	$21.95	DIMO
Smart Ways to Save Money During and After Divorce, Collins and Wall	1st	$14.95	SAVMO
How to Raise or Lower Child Support In California, Duncan & Siegel	2nd	$17.95	CHLD
Nolo's Pocket Guide to Family Law, Leonard & Elias	3rd	$14.95	FLD
How to Adopt Your Stepchild in California, Zagone & Randolph	4th	$22.95	ADOP
The Guardianship Book (California), Goldoftas & Brown	1st	$19.95	GB
How to Do Your Own Divorce in California, Sherman	19th	$21.95	CDIV
How to Do Your Own Divorce in Texas, Sherman & Simons	5th	$17.95	TDIV
Practical Divorce Solutions, Sherman	1st	$14.95	PDS

 = DISK INCLUDED

TO ORDER CALL 800-992-6656

THE NEIGHBORHOOD

Neighbor Law: Fences, Trees, Boundaries & Noise, Jordan .... 2nd $16.95 NEI

Safe Home, Safe Neighborhoods:
  Stopping Crime Where You Live, Mann & Blakeman .... 1st $14.95 SAFE

Dog Law, Randolph .... 2nd $12.95 DOG

LANDLORDS & TENANTS

The Landlord's Law Book, Vol. 1: Rights & Responsibilities (California),
  Brown & Warner .... 4th $32.95 LBRT

The Landlord's Law Book, Vol. 2: Evictions (California), Brown .... 5th $34.95 LBEV

Tenants' Rights (California), Moskovitz & Warner .... 12th $18.95 CTEN

Nolo's Law Form Kit: Leases & Rental Agreements (California),
  Warner & Stewart .... 1st $14.95 KLEAS

HOMEOWNERS

How to Buy a House in California, Warner, Serkes & Devine .... 3rd $24.95 BHCA

For Sale By Owner, Devine .... 2nd $24.95 FSBO

Homestead Your House, Warner, Sherman & Ihara .... 8th $9.95 HOME

The Deeds Book, Randolph .... 3rd $16.95 DEED

OLDER AMERICANS

Beat the Nursing Home Trap: A Consumer's Guide to Choosing
  & Financing Long Term Care, Matthews .... 2nd $18.95 ELD

Social Security, Medicare & Pensions, Matthews with Berman .... 5th $18.95 SOA

TO ORDER CALL 800-992-6656

LEGAL REFORM

Fed Up With the Legal System, Nolo Press .... 2nd $9.95   LEG

JUST FOR FUN

29 Reasons Not to Go to Law School, Warner & Ihara 4th $9.95   29R

Devil's Advocates, Roth & Roth .... 1st $12.95   DA

Poetic Justice, Roth & Roth .... 1st $9.95   PJ

 **Nolo's Favorite Lawyer Jokes on Disk** .... DOS $9.95   JODI

  Macintosh $9.95   JODM

  Windows $9.95   JODWI

RESEARCH/REFERENCE

Legal Research, Elias & Levinkind .... 3rd $19.95   LRES

Legal Research Made Easy: A Roadmap Through the Law Library Maze
(2 1/2 hr videotape & manual), Nolo & Legal Star .... 1st $89.95   LRME

IMMIGRATION

How to Get a Green Card: Legal Ways to Stay in the U.S.A.,
Lewis With Madlanscay .... 1st $22.95   GRN

Como Obtener La Tarjeta Verde, Lewis With Madlanscay .... 1st $24.95   VERDE

 = DISK INCLUDED

TO ORDER CALL 800-992-6656

SOFTWARE

			RETAIL PRICE	YOUR PRICE	CODE
WillMaker 5.0		Windows	$69.95	$48.96	WI5
		DOS	$69.95	$48.96	WI5
		Macintosh	$69.95	$48.96	WM5
Nolo's Personal RecordKeeper 3.0		DOS	$49.95	$34.96	FRI3
		Macintosh	$49.95	$34.96	FRM3
Living Trust Maker 2.0		Windows	$79.95	$55.96	LTWI2
		Macintosh	$79.95	$55.96	LTM2
Patent It Yourself 1.0		Windows	$229.95	$160.96	PYW1
Nolo's Partnership Maker 1.0		DOS	$129.95	$90.96	PAGI1
California Incorporator 1.0		DOS	$129.00	$90.30	INCI

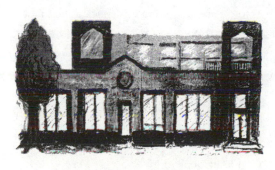

VISIT OUR STORE

If you live in the Bay Area, be sure to visit the Nolo Press Bookstore on the corner of 9th & Parker Streets in west Berkeley. You'll find our complete line of books and software—all at a discount.

CALL 1 (510) 704-2248 for hours.

TO ORDER CALL 800-992-6656

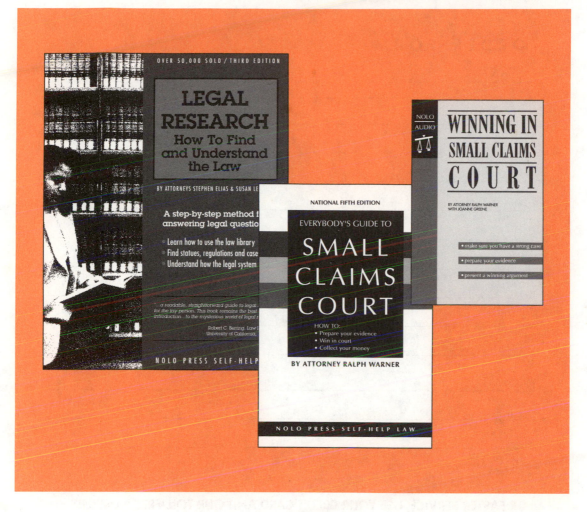

Legal Research: How to Find & Understand the Law

$19.95 / LRES • Attorneys Stephen Elias & Susan Levinkind

Excellent for paralegals, law students, legal secretaries and journalists, this book gives step-by-step instructions on how to find legal information. Shows you how to find and research a case, and read statutes and regulations. Also takes you step-by-step through the process of solving eight hypothetical research problems.

Everybody's Guide to Small Claims Court

$18.95 / NSCC • Attorney Ralph Warner with Joanne Greene

So, the dry cleaner ruined your good flannel suit. Your roof leaks every time it rains and the contractor won't call you back. This book will help you decide if you should sue in small claims court, show you how to file and serve papers, tell you what to take to court and how to collect a judgment.

Winning in Small Claims Court

$14.95 / TWIN • 60 minute audio tape • Attorney Ralph Warner with Joanne Greene

This tape guides you through all the major issues involved in preparing and winning a small claims case—deciding if there is a good case, assessing whether you can collect if you win, preparing your evidence, and arguing before the judge.

ORDER FORM

Code	Quantity	Title	Unit price	Total
			Subtotal	
		California residents add Sales Tax		
	Shipping & Handling ($4 for 1st item; $1 each additional)			
	2nd day UPS (additional $5; $8 in Alaska and Hawaii)			
			TOTAL	

Name

Address

(UPS to street address, Priority Mail to P.O. boxes)

FOR FASTER SERVICE, USE YOUR CREDIT CARD AND OUR TOLL-FREE NUMBERS

Monday–Friday, 7 a.m. to 6 p.m. Pacific Time

Order Line	1 (800) 992-6656 (in the 510 area code, call 549-1976)
General Information	1 (510) 549-1976
Fax your order	1 (800) 645-0895 (in the 510 area code, call 548-5902)

METHOD OF PAYMENT

☐ Check enclosed

☐ VISA ☐ Mastercard ☐ Discover Card ☐ American Express

Account #   Expiration Date

Authorizing Signature

Daytime Phone

Allow 2-3 weeks for delivery. Prices subject to change.   RYC1.2

NOLO PRESS, 950 PARKER ST., BERKELEY, CA 94710

FREE NOLO NEWS SUBSCRIPTION

When you register, we'll send you our quarterly newspaper, the *Nolo News*, free for two years. (U.S. addresses only.) Here's what you'll get in every issue:

■ INFORMATIVE ARTICLES

Written by Nolo editors, articles provide practical legal information on issues you encounter in everyday life: family law, wills, debts, consumer rights, and much more.

■ UPDATE SERVICE

The *Nolo News* keeps you informed of legal changes that affect any Nolo book and software program.

■ BOOK AND SOFTWARE REVIEWS

We're always looking for good legal and consumer books and software from other publishers. When we find them, we review them and offer them in our mail order catalog.

■ ANSWERS TO YOUR LEGAL QUESTIONS

Our readers are always challenging us with good questions on a variety of legal issues. So in each issue, "Auntie Nolo" gives sage advice and sound information.

■ COMPLETE NOLO PRESS CATALOG

The *Nolo News* contains an up-to-the-minute catalog of all Nolo books and software, which you can order using our "800" toll-free order line. And you can see at a glance if you're using an out-of-date version of a Nolo product.

■ LAWYER JOKES

Nolo's famous lawyer joke column continually gets the goat of the legal establishment. If we print a joke you send in, you'll get a $20 Nolo gift certificate.

We promise *never* to give your name and address to any other organization.

COMPLETE AND MAIL TODAY

REPRESENT YOURSELF IN COURT   Registration Card

We'd like to know what you think! Please take a moment to fill out and return this postage paid card for a free two year subscription to the *Nolo News*. If you already receive the *Nolo News*, we'll extend your subscription.

Name _____ Ph.(   ) _____

Address _____

City _____ State _____ Zip _____

Where did you hear about this book? _____

For what purpose did you use this book? _____

Did you consult a lawyer?	Yes	No		Not Applicable			
Was it easy for you to use this book?	(very easy)	5	4	3	2	1	(very difficult)
Did you find this book helpful?	(very)	5	4	3	2	1	(not at all)

Comments _____

_____

_____

_____

_____

THANK YOU   RYC 1.2

[Nolo books are]..."written in plain language, free of legal mumbo jumbo, and spiced with witty personal observations."

—ASSOCIATED PRESS

"Well-produced and slickly written, the [Nolo] books are designed to take the mystery out of seemingly involved procedures, carefully avoiding legalese and leading the reader step-by-step through such everyday legal problems as filling out forms, making up contracts, and even how to behave in court."

—SAN FRANCISCO EXAMINER

"...Nolo publications...guide people simply through the how, when, where and why of law."

—WASHINGTON POST

"Increasingly, people who are not lawyers are performing tasks usually regarded as legal work... And consumers, using books like Nolo's, do routine legal work themselves."

—NEW YORK TIMES

"...All of [Nolo's] books are easy-to-understand, are updated regularly, provide pull-out forms...and are often quite moving in their sense of compassion for the struggles of the lay reader."

—SAN FRANCISCO CHRONICLE

NO POSTAGE
NECESSARY
IF MAILED
IN THE
UNITED STATES

BUSINESS REPLY MAIL

FIRST-CLASS MAIL PERMIT NO 3283 BERKELEY CA

POSTAGE WILL BE PAID BY ADDRESSEE

NOLO PRESS
950 Parker Street
Berkeley Ca 94710-9867